1998

A GUIDE TO EDITING MIDDLE ENGLISH

A GUIDE TO EDITING MIDDLE ENGLISH

Vincent P. McCarren and Douglas Moffat

Editors

Ann Arbor

THE UNIVERSITY OF MICHIGAN PRESS

Copyright © by the University of Michigan 1998
All rights reserved
Published in the United States of America by
The University of Michigan Press
Manufactured in the United States of America
⊗ Printed on acid-free paper

2001   2000   1999   1998   4   3   2   1

A CIP catalog record for this book is available from the British Library.

Library of Congress Cataloging-in-Publication Data

A guide to editing Middle English / Vincent P. McCarren and Douglas
  Moffat, editors.
    p.   cm.
  Includes bibliographical references (p.   ) and index.
  ISBN 0-472-10604-X (alk. paper)
    1. English literature—Middle English, 1100–1500—Criticism,
Textual. 2. Manuscripts, Medieval—England—Editing.
3. Manuscripts, English (Middle)—Editing. 4. Transmission of
texts.   I. McCarren, Vincent P. II. Moffat, Douglas.
PR275.T45G85   1997
820.9′001—dc21   97-36540
                                        CIP

Preface

The purpose of this volume is to raise the standard of scholarly editing for Middle English texts. Years of working on the *Middle English Dictionary* with the widest variety of editions has convinced us that this standard must be set higher for the good of the field at large. There will always be some unevenness between particular editions, because of the varying talents and experience of their makers and the nature of the material they work on, but our perception is that many who have undertaken the editing of Middle English texts in the past have been unable or unwilling to shoulder all of the many burdens that fell to them. Some would seem to have even been unaware that such tasks were their responsibility. At the very least we hope this volume will provide prospective editors with an indication of the magnitude of the work they would undertake.

But we also hope to provide especially the new editor with a great deal of practical advice about how to get this job done expediently and well. To this end we have called upon a number of leading figures in the field to write essays addressing particular aspects of editing in which they are distinguished practitioners. We instructed our contributors to write their essays for someone contemplating editing for the first time. The book is not, therefore, necessarily designed for the seasoned veteran of manuscript study and archival work who has already produced scholarly editions. However, we hope that even such experienced editors will find something of use here.

The first section, "Author, Scribe, and Editor," emphasizes directly what we think is the central task of the editor: the struggle with variant readings within a manuscript tradition and the application of judgment to this evidence. Nicolas Jacobs and Jennifer Fellows argue for quite different approaches to editing romance texts, but perhaps the key point of agreement that emerges between them is that the editor must judge what the evidence will allow in the way of method rather than impose a method on the evidence. This section concludes with an essay by the editors that provides bibliographical background for the important questions raised by Jacobs and Fellows.

The second section, "Perspectives on the Editing of Literary Texts," contains essays that are primarily concerned with examining the strengths and weaknesses in editorial treatments of some central literary texts in the Middle English corpus. Norman Blake focuses on editions of *Sir Gawain and the Green Knight, The Owl and the Nightingale,* and *Piers Plowman;* Helen Cooper examines editions of Chaucer's works; A. S. G. Edwards surveys editions of various alliterative works. All three essays investigate the presuppositions and goals of past editors; future editors of literary texts are bound to benefit from their insights. As well, each of the essays, particularly that of Edwards, pays attention to the place of the edition in the classroom where it must function both as a teaching and a scholarly tool.

The third section, "Editing Works of a Technical Nature," deals with the editing of less well known texts that are often as intriguing as they are difficult. We think that space must be devoted to the editing of these kinds of works for two reasons. First of all, so much of unedited Middle English falls within this realm of "technical" or "practical" subject matter. Secondly, unlike the popular literary texts, these technical works, once they are edited, are rarely re-edited, regardless of whether the first edition is good, indifferent, or bad. Each of the papers by George Keiser, Linne Mooney, Constance Hieatt, and Vincent Mc-Carren focuses on specific kinds of texts, offering advice to the editor who would work in these areas. However, we believe that the editor of a technical text in a field not exactly covered by one of these papers would still find much pertinent information in them.

The fourth section, "Elements of an Edition," is a series of essays on what we feel should be the essential components of most editions. The essays concentrate on offering practical advice that will take the editor from the initial steps of research through to submission to the publisher. The topics covered are description of manuscripts (A. S. G. Edwards), treatment of language (Peter Lucas), use of the *Linguistic Atlas of Late Mediaeval English* (Maldwyn Mills), treatment of sources (Mary Hamel), annotation (A. S. G. Edwards and Douglas Moffat), and making a glossary (Douglas Moffat).

The fifth section, "Editing and the Computer," consists of two essays. Peter Robinson focuses on how the computer can be used to help the editor carry out various tasks, while Peter Baker focuses on the use of the computer in presenting the edition to the reader. Both essays are very detailed, but given the rapid pace of development in this area, both Robinson and Baker have taken care to write forward-looking pieces that will remain relevant as the details themselves change.

For the final essay, we have asked David Greetham to write a "Postduction" to the volume. While he mentions the individual essays in the collection, his primary concern is to consider the ideas that inform the volume as a whole and to situate this guide within the larger contexts of textual and literary scholarship.

The volume concludes with three appendices: a basic guide to manuscript work designed for the beginner; a bibliography of facsimile editions of Middle English manuscripts compiled by Richard Beadle; and a list of dictionaries most useful to an editor of Middle English.

We would like to thank a number of people who have helped bring this work to its conclusion. First of all we must acknowledge all of our contributors for their efforts, cooperation, and patience. A number of people read essays for us and made helpful comments: Hoyt N. Duggan, David Greetham, George Keiser, Frances McSparran, as well as the readers for the Press. Ellen Bauerle, our editor at the University of Michigan Press, was a cheerful and reassuring presence from the volume's early days right up to its publication. The Middle English Dictionary at the University of Michigan provided us with support by way of supplies and other necessaries. In particular we want to acknowledge the assistance of Louise Palazzola.

However, we must make special mention of A. S. G. Edwards. Tony did more than contribute exceptional essays and insightful comments on a number of other contributions. He was a constant source of advice and encouragement for us. We owe him a great debt of gratitude.

Contents

Author, Scribe, and Editor

Kindly Light or Foxfire? The Authorial Text Reconsidered

Nicolas Jacobs

"Mycel yfel déþ se unwrítere, gif hé nele hys wóh gerihtan." So wrote Ælfric more than once: "The inaccurate scribe does great harm, if he is not willing to correct his error."[1] Editors have until recently agreed with him. It is common ground that copyists are apt to alter their copy; the mere existence of variant readings demonstrates as much. From the point of view of an author who is concerned to compose a definitive text, as classical authors evidently were, or of a church that regards its Scriptures as the word of God, such alterations will be viewed as corruptions, and, given that the techniques of modern textual criticism were originally devised in order to edit biblical and classical texts, it is not surprising that the concepts of manuscript corruption and scribal error have gone unquestioned. The circumstances of the composition and transmission of medieval vernacular texts, where authorship is in some ways problematic and the concept of a definitive text not universal, have lately given rise to some doubts regarding the applicability of such concepts as corruption and error to these traditions.[2] Is it appropriate here to speak of correctness, and is there any legitimate appeal to an authorial text against which it can be measured?

The idea that some readings, and thus some versions, are corrupt is, though

---

I am grateful to Dr. John Gray for reading and commenting on this chapter, a shortened version of which was read at the 28th International Congress on Medieval Studies at Western Michigan University, Kalamazoo, on 7 May 1993.

1. "Ælfrics Vorrede zur Genesis," ed. C. M. W. Grein in *Bibliothek der angelsächsischen Prosa*, vol. 1 (Cassel and Göttingen, 1872), 24, 33–34 (v.1. *gewrit* for *woh*, see EETS 160 [1922], 80); *Ælfrics Grammatik und Glossar*, ed. J. Zupitza (Berlin, 1880), 3.24–25; cf. *The Homilies of the Anglo-Saxon Church*, ed. Benjamin Thorpe (London, 1844), 1:8, *Micel yfel déð séðe léas writ, búton hé hit gerihte, swylce hé gebringe þá sóðan láre tó léasum gedwylde.*

2. For a concise statement of the rationale of this and related positions, see Jerome J. McGann, *A Critique of Modern Textual Criticism* (Chicago, 1983).

unfashionable, not wholly arbitrary. In particular, misreading, misunderstanding, and misdirected attempts to make sense are always possible; given a combination of these processes, especially at more than one stage, the original may eventually become unrecognizable and the copy partly unintelligible, at a time when, unlike today, unintelligibility had no rhetorical function. In the case of Middle English the simplicity of the language and meter, the brief period across which the texts are transmitted, and the consequent lack of opportunity for serious incomprehension make such a lapse into unintelligibility unlikely, but the same is not true in all languages. The early Welsh poem *Y Gododdin,* at least in its B version, together with some of its related texts, is a case in point. It would be perverse to attribute to the existing versions of these texts, some passages in which can hardly have been ever understood by anyone, even by those who copied them, any standing other than as damaged witnesses to a more coherent original. The same may be true, though this is disputed, of the early Irish law-text *Bretha Nemed.*[3]

But in the case of the most commonly studied medieval English texts it is generally not intelligibility but literary quality that is in question, and here judgment becomes subjective. Whereas, for instance, anyone who has followed the text of any Middle English romance through the protracted sequence of French whispers that constitutes the textual tradition of most of them may be tempted to think in terms of textual degeneration,[4] it remains true that any variant reading that is not simply an error of transcription represents a decision on the part of a copyist that is evidence for the reception of the text if not of a creative impulse. For this or similar reasons, editorial interest has tended to shift from the reconstruction of a critical text to an examination of scribal variants as readings in their own right and of the versions defined by them as legitimate realizations of the texts they represent.

Differing degrees of this tendency are evident. What may be called weak relativism is well exemplified by the remarks of Barry Windeatt in the introduction to his edition of *Troilus and Criseyde,*[5] where he characterizes the

---

3. For *Bretha Nemed* see *Corpus Iuris Hibernici* 2211–32; I am grateful to Prof. Liam Breatnach for bringing this text to my attention, though he is not responsible for my comments on it. On the texts of the *Gododdin,* see *Canu Aneirin,* ed. Ifor Williams (Cardiff, 1938), xii–xiv; for the problems faced by scribes and editors, see especially XLV A–C, LI A–C.

4. I document these processes in *The Later Versions of Sir Degarre: A Study in Textual Degeneration,* Medium Aevum Monographs, n.s. 18 (Oxford, 1995).

5. Geoffrey Chaucer, *Troilus and Criseyde,* ed. Barry Windeatt (London, 1984), 26b. The terminology of weak and strong relativism was suggested by Nicholas G. Round, *On Reasoning and Realism: Three Easy Pieces,* Manchester Spanish and Portuguese Studies, 2 (Manchester, 1981), 7–9.

scribes' reaction to their copy as "their equivalent of literary analysis, in that they can reveal to us exactly what the scribes found difficult or unusual in Chaucer's work. . . . The scribal rewriting may reflect a sense of what is out of the ordinary and needs to be 'made normal.'" Windeatt thus acknowledges the authority, at least for practical purposes, of the authorial text but directs attention to scribal variants as evidence—our only evidence, in most cases—of contemporary response to it. This is certainly a historical conclusion of a kind, and might in some cases provide valuable information regarding the ways in which texts were read and the developing tastes of those who read them, though nearly thirty years of editing texts have left at least the author of this paper with the impression that such contemporary response amounts for the most part to little but dim-wittedness, literal-mindedness, and triviality.

What may be called strong relativism consists in the view that there is no good reason, at least with a medieval work, to privilege the authorial over the scribal text, such distinctions being anachronistic. In a recent paper by Tim William Machan this proposition serves as the basis of an exhortation to turn from the traditional object of textual criticism—the reconstruction of an archetypal and the conjectural restoration of an authorial text—to the study of texts in their wider context as social constructs in whose constitution readers as well as authors, and scribes in both functions, play a part.[6] In the terms of such a study all manuscript versions are of equal interest, and textual authority comes into question only to the extent that readers and scribes themselves impute it to a particular version or regard it as appropriate to a particular poet. What for weak relativism is a subsidiary focus of interest incidental to editing the text becomes for strong relativism the sole object of study, and the authorial text a matter of only incidental concern.

The practical implications of strong relativism for an editor are that he or she should in effect cease to edit, and should merely reproduce (perhaps with the minimum of interference necessary to render them readable to those unversed in paleography) as many versions of the chosen text as are to hand, and draw from each of them the appropriate conclusions regarding the contexts within which they were produced. Whether or not such an editor will allow himself or herself to consider—as a weak relativist can—the implications of the processes by which one version is derived from another will presumably

---

6. Tim William Machan, "Middle English Text Production and Modern Textual Criticism," in *Crux and Controversy in Middle English Textual Criticism,* ed. A. J. Minnis and Charlotte Brewer (Cambridge, 1992), 1–18. On literature as social product, see also McGann, *Critique,* 44; for further comments on some strong relativist beliefs, see Ralph Hanna III, "Producing Manuscripts and Editions," in *Crux and Controversy,* 120–21.

depend on the extent to which the concept of priority as between different readings is regarded as ideologically acceptable. If strong relativism were carried to its logical conclusion, such evidence would appear to be excluded.

Rather than pursue logical conclusions of this kind, I would argue that the deprivileging of the authorial text is in principle unsatisfactory, both methodologically and philosophically. The methodological objection is that to consider a group of versions synchronically as a self-contained system irrespective of the processes that gave rise to it misrepresents the historical and social realities that are proposed as an object of study, while in any consideration of process the starting point of that process inevitably privileges itself as a focus of attention. The philosophical objection derives from nothing less than the proposition that the whole approach rests on false premises.

The rejection of the authorial text as a valid concept in medieval vernacular culture depends on our supposing that in that context authorship itself is an anachronism and the definitive text an illusion. The second point is not generally in dispute, though I will argue that its implications are not quite as either sort of relativist supposes. The first assumption, however, is at least an oversimplification, and in all probability simply wrong. But before we consider its validity, three distractions need to be cleared out of the way: the etymological argument concerning the word *auctor,* the much-quoted analysis by St. Bonaventura of the processes of textual production, and the matter of authorial originality.

It is not disputed that the term *auctor* is used, at least down to the later Middle Ages, only of Latin authors of standing: that in effect it carries the modern senses of both *author* and *authority.* Alastair Minnis has suggested that both Gower and Chaucer, if in rather different ways, reflect the development by the end of the fourteenth century of the idea of the vernacular *auctor:* "if Gower was a compiler who tried to present himself as an author, Chaucer was an author who hid behind the 'shield and defence' of a compiler." This is presented as a late and, in the terms of the argument, eccentric development, though Dante might be cited as a precedent.[7] But, whereas it is certainly true that most of those who composed in the vernacular in the Middle Ages lacked the status, dignity, and authority to be considered as *auctores* in the medieval sense, that does not mean that they were not authors in any sense, and specifically in the sense that they were aware of generating a composition, which is

---

7. A. J. Minnis, *Medieval Theory of Authorship: Scholastic Literary Attitudes in the Later Middle Ages* (London, 1984), 168–210; on Dante, 161, 165, 214–16. Machan states ("Middle English Text Production," 7) in an apparently circular argument, that "it is important to remember that this concern is non-medieval by nature."

what is really in question here. The etymological argument proves to be an etymological fallacy.

Nor is the applicability of Bonaventura's fourfold classification of the participants in the production of texts self-evident.[8] Such formulations are at best not a reliable guide even to how things are commonly conceived to be, still less to how they actually are. This example, even if we take it at its face value, is clearly designed to account for a particular kind of scholarly compilation. It is no argument to claim that vernacular authorship must have been inconceivable for most of the Middle Ages simply because the concept does not fit into a theoretical scheme never designed to accommodate it. It may be observed in addition that Bonaventura's formulation, which has tended to be cited as a general statement about authorship, is in context a refutation of, among other things, the objection that God, not Peter Lombard, is the true author of the *Sentences;* this may raise further doubts as to its evidential value regarding attitudes to or on the part of vernacular authors.

Finally, it can be argued that authorship, in the sense with which we are concerned, does not depend on originality of material or even of treatment so much as on an intention to communicate on a wider scale than that of immediate personal interaction. Subsequent readers may find little of interest in an author who reproduces commonplaces in an altogether unimaginative way; some might even dismiss him as an inferior writer, but that does not mean that he ceases to be an author at all. Again, whereas most vernacular authors would undoubtedly have been surprised and baffled to be told that they were composing literature, that does not mean that they did not suppose that they were composing anything.

It has been argued that the anonymity of the great bulk of compositions in Middle English is evidence of the lack of a sense of authorship in the period.[9] This situation is, however, anomalous in Western Europe and cannot be explained in terms of general cultural development. The greater portion of *trobador* lyric is attributed to named authors, and the fact that many of these were provided with biographies, however fictitious those may be, suggests that authorship was a matter of some interest among their audience; attributions occur also in the case of their French, Italian, Catalan, and, especially, German and Portuguese followers. The same is of course true of the authors of French and German romances; one of the former, Hue de Rotelande, was actually resident in England, while one of the most eminent of the latter, Gottfried von

---

8. *In primum librum sententiarum,* Prooemium, q. iv, conclusion, in *Opera,* (Quaracchi, 1882), 1:14–15. Quoted in Hamel in this volume.

9. Machan, "Middle English Text Production," 3 and citations.

Strassburg, provides in his celebrated critical digression further evidence that the attachment of names to vernacular texts was no mere formality, at least by the beginning of the thirteenth century.[10] The compositions of the poets of the Welsh princes and their successors, active from the beginning of the twelfth century on, are assiduously attributed to their authors in the manuscripts in which they are preserved; the earlier poetry preserved in manuscripts of roughly the same date is similarly attributed, though less reliably and in some cases certainly wrongly.[11] Such attributions, true or false, demonstrate plainly that the concept of vernacular authorship was taken for granted in medieval Wales as it was on the continent of Europe.[12]

In face of this evidence we are assured that what was a commonplace on the other side of the English Channel and beyond the Welsh border was largely unknown to the English until the time of Chaucer, or else that, while aware of it for writings in French, they never thought to extend it to compositions in their own language. This is unbelievable. The anonymity of most Middle English literature is a phenomenon whose causes must be sought elsewhere. The natural explanation is that the low status of English in the earlier Middle Ages made it a special case: it was little used for compositions important enough for authors to acknowledge, and conversely a work composed in English might not seem of sufficient account to justify attribution. This would leave room for such early exceptions as Orm or Layamon, whose work may be considered unusually ambitious, though some other attributions, like those to Laurence Minot, seem merely anomalous. By the late fourteenth century, the growing status of English may explain the attribution even of such trivial works as

---

10. Gottfried von Strassburg, *Tristan*, 4587–4819. On Hue de Rotelande, see *Ipomedon, poème de Hue de Rotelande*, ed. A. J. Holden (Paris, 1979), 8, and note also the jocular pseudo-biographical details at the very end of the poem.

11. On the genuine and spurious poems attributed to Taliesin in the manuscript that goes by his name, see John Morris-Jones, "Taliesin," *Y Cymmrodor* 28 (1918), 1–290; *The Poems of Taliesin*, ed. Ifor Williams, English version by J. E. Caerwyn Williams (Dublin, 1975), xiv–xxiii. The implication may be that Taliesin was viewed as an *auctor* in medieval Wales.

12. For lists, not exhaustive, of the Romance and German lyric poets, see Peter Dronke, *The Medieval Lyric* (London, 1968), 247–55; for the *vidas* of the *trobadors*, Jean Boutière and A. H. Schutz, *Biographies des troubadours: Textes provençaux des xiii et xiv siècles*, new ed. (Paris, 1964); for the Welsh court poets, D. Simon Evans, *A Grammar of Middle Welsh* (Dublin, 1964), xxv–xxix. On the related topic of poetic individuality in vernacular texts, see Dronke, *Poetic Individuality in the Middle Ages* (Oxford, 1970), chap. 1; Linda M. Paterson, *Troubadours and Eloquence* (Oxford, 1975), 1–7. The inadequacy of an insular view of medieval English literature is impressively demonstrated in Elizabeth Salter's unfinished work provisionally entitled *An Obsession with the Continent;* see her *English and International: Studies in the Literature, Art, and Patronage of Medieval England,* ed. Derek Pearsall and Nicolette Zeeman, (Cambridge, 1988), 1–100.

Chestre's *Sir Launfal.* Authorial humility may be a countervailing factor: the visions of Julian of Norwich, for instance, are said to have been "shown" to her, so that the credit for authorship is in a way disclaimed while the fact of it is implicitly acknowledged.[13]

The late development of English as a language of high status may also go some way to explain the rarity before the very end of the fourteenth century of *makere* in the sense of author or poet. Since the corresponding verb *make* is comparatively well attested, together with the somewhat rarer *dihte,* it cannot be argued that the activity of composing verse was conceptually alien to medieval speakers of English; and an activity without an agent is hard to imagine. On the other hand, if in consequence of the supposed rusticity of the medium the activity was one of low status, one need not expect much reference to it in written sources, especially as its practitioners would have in many cases performed as well as composed and might well have been publicly perceived in the former function. By comparison the high status attributed to poets in Welsh society and the abundance of reference to them in written sources, which include, by the end of the fourteenth century, treatises on the art of poetry, evidently go together.[14]

---

13. On Julian, see the title to the short version of her text: Edmund Colledge and James Walsh, *A Book of Showings to the Anchoress Julian of Norwich,* Studies and Texts, 36 (Toronto, 1978), 1:201. We are left in no doubt of Orm's grandiose ideas about his project; see his dedication, *The Ormulum,* ed. R. M. White, revised by R. Holt (Oxford, 1878), 1–78; see also *Early Middle English Texts,* ed. Bruce Dickins and R. M. Wilson (London, 1951), 83–85. On the exceptional nature of Layamon's enterprise, see Françoise H. M. Le Saux, *Laȝamon's Brut: The Poem and Its Sources,* Arthurian Studies, 19 (Cambridge, 1989), especially 184–227. Robert Mannyng may also be mentioned here, on the strength of his *Chronicle* as well as *Handlyng Synne.*

14. Poets are listed among the court officials in the Welsh laws; see Dafydd Jenkins, *Hywel Dda: The Law* (Llandysul, 1986), pp. 20, 38–39; these references go back to the Latin text, which was in writing by the end of the twelfth century: see *The Latin Texts of the Welsh Laws,* ed. Hywel D. Emanuel (Cardiff, 1967), 118, etc. For the treatises on poetry, see *Gramadegau'r Penceirdd-iaid,* ed. G. J. Williams and E. J. Jones (Cardiff, 1934), in which three types of composition *(klerwriaeth, teulwryaeth,* and *prydydyaeth)* are defined in ascending order of dignity, each associated with its own grade of poet (6–8). These formulations may be no more than an idealizing reconstruction of a presumed order, which may never have existed in precisely that form, in response to the collapse of poetic organization following the fall of the princes, on which see Ceri W. Lewis, "The Context of Poetry and the Crisis in the Bardic Tradition," in A. O. H. Jarman and G. O. Hughes, *A Guide to Welsh Literature* (Llandybïe, 1979), 2: at 97–103; but this concession leaves the concepts intact, and the generic term *bardd* is in any case widespread. See also A. T. E. Matonis, "The Concept of Poetry in the Middle Ages: The Welsh Evidence from the Bardic Grammars," *Bulletin of the Board of Celtic Studies* 36 (1989): 1–12, especially at 5. References are even more copious in Irish law-tracts: see Fergus Kelly, *A Guide to Early Irish Law* (Dublin, 1988), 43–51, and, especially, *Uraicecht na Ríar: The Poetic Grades in Early Irish Law,* ed. Liam Breatnach (Dublin, 1987).

But even if the concept of vernacular authorship in medieval England is, contrary to current doctrine, valid, the same is not necessarily true of the idea of the definitive text. That is a concept that may well have become relevant at different stages for different kinds of writing and indeed for different authors; and, though it appears to have been a consideration for both Chaucer and Gower, the evidence of textual variation suggests that it was considered as being of little importance before their time and not always much regarded afterward. The freedom with which romance scribes in particular habitually altered the texts they were copying suggests that few of them saw any reason not to do so; it would not be altogether fair to claim that authors on the whole acquiesced in this activity, since there was little they could have done about it even if they had disapproved, but the lack of a widespread topos on the subject, at least before Chaucer, may be significant. The comparative metrical laxity in Middle English, as against for instance Welsh, where a rigid syllabic count and an elaborate system of alliteration and rhyme make it much easier to identify certain readings as objectively wrong, may have contributed to a sense that scribal variation did not much matter, but, as I have suggested, the residual memory of a tradition of oral recomposition, where the text was effectively defined by the current performance, is probably the fundamental cause.[15]

Thus, to Machan's question "is there *a priori* historical cultural justification for privileging the texts of 'poets' over those of 'scribes'?" the answer is that, so long as both shared the habits of mind characteristic of an oral culture, there might be none, or little, but that such justification develops pari passu with the habits of mind characteristic of literacy, and it is hard to argue in the case of any given text that the latter are not relevant. The scribes themselves may indeed not have become uniformly conscious of such a development until somewhat

---

15. See my remarks in "Regression to the Commonplace in Some Vernacular Traditions," in Minnis and Brewer, *Crux and Controversy,* 65–66. The classic discussions of orality are those of Milman Parry, "Studies in the Epic Technique of Oral Verse-Making," *Harvard Studies in Classical Philology* 41 (1930): 73–147, 43 (1932): 1–50, and A. B. Lord, *The Singer of Tales* (Cambridge, Mass., 1960); the theory was rather uncritically applied to Old English by F. P. Magoun, Jr., "The Oral-Formulaic Character of Anglo-Saxon Narrative Poetry," *Speculum* 28 (1953): 446–67, whose conclusions are largely refuted by Larry D. Benson, "The Literary Character of Anglo-Saxon Formulaic Poetry," *PMLA* 81 (1966): 334–41: also T. A. Shippey, *Old English Verse* (London, 1972), 89–98. For an attempt to apply the theory to Middle English, see R. A. Waldron, "Oral-Formulaic Technique and Middle English Alliterative Poetry," *Speculum* 32 (1957): 792– 804: Benson's objections apply equally here. See further A. C. Baugh, "Improvisation in the Middle English Romance," *Proceedings of the American Philosophical Society* 103 (1959): 418– 54, and "The Middle English Romance: Some Questions of Creation, Presentation, and Preservation," *Speculum* 42 (1967): 1–31; Thorlac Turville-Petre, *The Alliterative Revival* (Cambridge, 1977), 14–17; J. A. Burrow, *Medieval Writers and Their Work* (Oxford, 1982), 24–36.

later, with notable consequences, in the form of much seemingly wayward variation, for textual criticism, while the longer Middle English romances continue into the fifteenth century to show signs of improvisatory variation that may be attributed to performers with an equal disregard for textual authority even where the scribes were reasonably punctilious.[16] It is hard to imagine, however, that the prospect of having their work recorded in writing could have failed to affect authors' attitude to their practice. And, since scribes and their work by their mere existence demonstrate at least a transitional stage in this development, the concept of more and less original readings and versions can never be ruled out of consideration.

On the precedence of the authorial text, I see no reason to retreat from my earlier position that "even where it is anachronistic to postulate an authoritative text, the original version of a literary work acquires a de facto authority by the mere fact of the author's having troubled to compose it, being evidence of a creative intelligence, however mediocre, and of the taste of an intended audience, however uncultivated."[17] This formulation, I believe, may provide a basis for assessing the status of derivative versions as well. Aside from authorial revision or collaborative authorship, there is a range of possibilities running from the reproduction *literatim* of the exemplar to the creation of an entirely new composition only loosely based on it. In the latter case the nature of authorial intention in no way differs from that in the original composition; as a text in its own right the new product assumes exactly the same de facto authority as the other.[18] The case is not so clear-cut with a redactor who sets out to produce a new version of an existing text; on the other hand there is always in such cases the assumption of a specific audience, and a creative intelligence still operates to some extent. Less clear-cut still are the cases where a copyist tidies up inconsistencies in a text[19] or alters it more or less systematically on the basis of personal interests or prejudices, though without anything so contrived as a formal redaction in mind. In these cases we can still, to a limited

---

16. On the occurrence of wayward variation on a large scale and the combination of circumstances that may have favored it, see my "Regression to the Commonplace," 65–69; on improvisatory variants, see Baugh, "Improvisation." But against too ready an assumption of the continuing influence of the techniques of oral composition on scribal practice even so early as the Old English period, see Douglas Moffat, "Anglo-Saxon Scribes and Old English Verse," *Speculum* 67 (1992): 805–27, especially at 810–13. On the development of literacy in England, see M. T. Clanchy, *From Memory to Written Record: England, 1066–1307* (London, 1979; 2d ed. 1993).

17. "Regression to the Commonplace," 69–70.

18. The same principle guarantees the authority of the original text where there is reason to suppose an anterior tradition.

19. See Elspeth Kennedy, "The Scribe as Editor," *Mélanges de langue et de littérature du moyen âge et de la Renaissance offerts à Jean Frappier* (Geneva, 1970), 523–31.

degree, speak of a creative intelligence: in the first an audience is still implied, to the extent that coherence is sought for its benefit; in the second there need be none, except in the trivial sense that the scribe is his or her own audience. Next, there is the scribe who makes unsystematic alterations to a text for little reason beyond a distrust of complexity or a reaction against the otherness of what is being copied and a desire to assert his or her personality at its expense.[20] Last of all there is the scribe who produces an inaccurate text by not bothering to pay attention to the copy.

These six degrees of alteration are not, of course, discrete steps but arbitrary divisions of a continuous gradation; and insofar as we have to do with degrees of intention, which can perhaps never be said to be entirely wanting, creative intelligence cannot be said to disappear suddenly at any one point on the scale. But occasional difficulties over borderline cases need not invalidate the classification—any more than a difference of opinion as to where red ends and orange begins would invalidate the general principle of a spectrum of colors— or impair its usefulness; and an effective lower limit to the operation of creativity is set in practice where a consistent intention ceases to be detectable. As we descend through our six stages, the intrinsic interest of the text, at least for the general reader, diminishes rapidly. The fifth and sixth cases afford little of consequence; they are significant chiefly for the psychology of scribes, a subject of strictly limited interest, and as object lessons in the types of scribal alteration. The second, third, and fourth, however, like the first, are of potential interest to the student of literature for the de facto authority with which they are endowed to the extent that the scribe has taken on some of the functions of an author. For that reason they are a proper object of study for the textual critic, both in themselves and for the conclusions that can be drawn from comparisons between them and from the study of the progressive developments that may have given rise to them.

The traditional task of the editor, that of reconstructing as far as possible the original version of the text, or such subsequent versions as can be supposed to be the product of a deliberate process of redaction, thus remains a legitimate objective, if no longer the only possible one. It remains so because the intentions of anyone who has taken the trouble to compose a poem afresh or to reshape systematically an existing one are of interest in a different way from the tinkerings of copyists unmotivated by any coherent creative purpose, and, from the point of view of the student of literature, at whom most editions are inevitably directed and whose main concerns are content and style, of greater

---

20. Jacobs, "Regression to the Commonplace," 64–65.

interest as well. Where there is a great deal of scribal variation, as is most notoriously the case with the romances, the recovery of the author's or systematic redactor's version may not be easy, or even possible. But where, on the basis of a comparison of the readings of existing versions and an understanding of the known habits of scribes, it is possible to assert with some plausibility what the reading from which the variants derive is likely to have been, it is an abdication of editorial judgment to refrain from suggesting it. The possibility of being wrong is the inevitable price of saying anything of more than trivial interest or significance.

The dangers of error or arbitrary judgment may be mitigated by a few simple qualifications. The general principles on which variants are to be selected should be made clear at the outset, the evidence on which the conclusions are based should be set out in full, and any conjectural emendation should be clearly signaled as such and explained, if the reasons for it are not already obvious, in the commentary. Where all readings are clearly corrupt and no correct reading suggests itself, the editor should not be ashamed to admit to perplexity; where the tradition is so divergent throughout as to render a plausible reconstruction of an original text impossible, as will often be the case with the romances,[21] it may be necessary to print texts, edited according to the same principles, of two or more versions. Both these special cases represent a pragmatic response to insuperable problems, as does the sometimes necessary practice where there is nothing to choose between readings or following whichever version is in general most reliable or relying on a stemma, and are to be clearly distinguished from the pursuit of relativism for its own sake.

On a more theoretical level, the polarity between scribes and authors is resolved not by blurring the distinction between the two but by recognizing it as a question less of persons than of functions, which can in some cases be exercised simultaneously. To the extent that there is an authorial intention there is an author and a text; where there is none, the activity is purely scribal, the variants are in the nature of things beyond the purview of literary scholarship, and it remains appropriate to think in terms of correct and incorrect, original and unoriginal readings and of scribal corruption. At the higher levels of rewriting these terms need to be used with caution; priority, derivativeness, and revision are more appropriate concepts, for the readings of a derivative version may well be viewed as correct in its own terms and provide a benchmark for the evaluation of secondary derivatives, and so on possibly through a sequence

---

21. See Baugh, "Improvisation," for this situation in *Beves of Hamtoun, Guy of Warwick,* and *Richard Coeur de Lion;* there are certainly other instances. See further Jennifer Fellows's contribution to this volume.

of versions. With this small concession made to relativism, it might be said that the main culturally determined peculiarity of English textual traditions before Chaucer is the predominant anonymity of authors and the phenomenon of cumulative composition: not so much absence of authorship, indeed, as excess of it. The medieval English author, in short, is a reality, not a romantic figment, and we need not feel embarrassed in continuing to investigate his activities. *Auctorem expellas furca, tamen usque recurret.*[22]

---

22. The implications of my argument may extend well beyond medieval textual criticism. If, as strong relativism implies, the concepts of the author and of a definitive text were culturally determined to a high degree, then their general validity would be undermined even in those contexts within which it is commonly accepted. I suggest the contrary: that such arguments are themselves culturally determined, rooted as they are in the traditional insularity of English studies, and it is they that lack general validity.

Author, Author, Author . . . : An Apology for Parallel Texts

Jennifer Fellows

Recent debate over the theory and practice of textual criticism as applied to Middle English literature has tended to focus primarily on the way in which the author's role is conceived and on how far modern notions as to a single "correct" authorial text can appropriately be invoked in dealing with a manuscript culture where the circumstances surrounding the production of literary artifacts were very different from those that obtain in the age of the printed word.[1] At what point can a medieval work be said to be "published"? To what extent does each variant manuscript represent a separate act of publication, a "textual moment" with its own peculiar authority? What status should be accorded to authorial second thoughts—if, indeed, these can be distinguished from the activities of interventionist scribes? Given that authors would, by and large, have little control over the forms and contexts in which their work was disseminated after it had left their hands and that, each manuscript being a unique production, the medieval reader would in all probability have access to no more than a single moment in a textual tradition,[2] is it perhaps more pertinent to an understanding of medieval culture to concentrate on what was actually read than to pursue the elusive chimaera of original authorial intention?

Until comparatively recently, editorial theory, for medieval as for other texts, was dominated by Lachmannian principles, originally formulated to deal with classical and biblical texts.[3] Latterly, however, the applicability of such

---

1. See *Crux and Controversy in Middle English Textual Criticism,* ed. A. J. Minnis and Charlotte Brewer (Cambridge, 1992), especially the contribution by Tim William Machan, "Middle English Text Production and Modern Textual Criticism," 1–18.

2. See Machan, "Middle English Text Production," 16.

3. See John M. Bowers, "Hoccleve's Two Copies of *Lerne to Dye:* Implications for Textual Critics," *Papers of the Bibliographical Society of America* 83 (1989): 440. On Lachmannian

principles in the editing of medieval vernacular works has increasingly been called into question; the inception of this movement toward the rejection of traditional recensional methods may perhaps be dated to the appearance of George Kane's magisterial edition of the A text of *Piers Plowman* in 1960— with all the fierce textual-critical debate that that edition, together with the Kane-Donaldson B text (1975), has generated.[4]

In *Piers Plowman* textual studies the question of authorial revision has inevitably taken center stage. At least three principal versions of the poem have been universally recognized since they were first identified by W. W. Skeat in 1866.[5] Within each of these traditions there is a huge amount of divergence between individual manuscripts, which will sometimes agree, against one another, with manuscripts belonging to one of the other versions. But while much editorial effort has been expended in attempting to distinguish between authorial and scribal alteration and in determining the precise nature of the relationships between the three (or four)[6] versions, no one, so far as I know, has ever seriously questioned the appropriateness of editing these versions as separate poems, each of which is seen as representing Langland's own intentions at different stages, or has suggested that the editor's aim should be to restore the *earliest* authorial text as representing something "purer" and better of which all subsequent versions are debasements or corruptions. Indeed the B text—normally considered to be intermediate chronologically between A and C and therefore to represent neither Langland's first nor his final intentions—is generally considered to be poetically superior to the other versions.

---

recension, see L. D. Reynolds and N. G. Wilson, *Scribes and Scholars: A Guide to the Transmission of Greek and Latin Literature,* 3d ed. (Oxford, 1991), 211–16; on its shortcomings as a method of editing Middle English texts, see Jennifer Fellows, "Editing Middle English Romances," in *Romance in Medieval England,* ed. Maldwyn Mills, Jennifer Fellows, and Carol M. Meale (Cambridge, 1991), 5.

4. *Piers Plowman: The A Version,* ed. George Kane (London, 1960; 2d ed. 1988); *Piers Plowman: The B Version,* ed. George Kane and E. Talbot Donaldson, 2d ed. (London, 1988). For critiques of the editorial method of these two volumes, see, e.g., Lee Patterson, *Negotiating the Past: The Historical Understanding of Medieval Literature* (Madison, Wis., 1987), 77–113; Charlotte Brewer, "George Kane's Processes of Revision," in Minnis and Brewer, *Crux and Controversy,* 71–96.

5. Walter W. Skeat, *Parallel Extracts from Twenty-Nine Manuscripts of Piers Plowman . . .* (London, 1866). Now see *A Parallel-Text Edition of the A, B, C, and Z Versions, 1: Text,* ed. A. V. C. Schmidt (London, 1995). Also cf. Derek Pearsall's review of the above edition in *Speculum* 73 (1997): 517–18.

6. There is still much controversy regarding the status of the so-called Z text: see *Piers Plowman: The Z Version,* ed. A. G. Rigg and Charlotte Brewer (Toronto, 1983). A recent contribution to the debate is Ralph Hanna III, "Studies in the Manuscripts of *Piers Plowman:* MS. Bodley 851 and the Dissemination of *Piers Plowman,*" *Yearbook of Langland Studies* 7 (1993): 1–25.

What I wish to argue here is that the situation is intrinsically no different in the case of many anonymous Middle English works and that, insofar as scribes take upon themselves the role of authors, we should accord their rewritings the same editorial respect as we do Langland's or any other single named author's.[7] My primary focus will be on the popular romances, and most of my examples will be drawn from *Sir Bevis of Hampton*[8]—both because it is the romance text with which I am most intimately familiar and because it represents in extreme form what is widely held to be the "uneditability" (in traditional terms) of Middle English romance.

The editorial approach that I shall advocate—the parallel text—has long been favored by many of those who have sought to edit Middle English romance, but in the absence of any substantial theorization of this procedure it is hard to say how often this is the outcome of pragmatic rather than ideological considerations, the editor making the best of unsatisfactory circumstances by presenting what material is available where sufficient textual evidence for the reconstruction of the archetype is lacking.

In the case of *Bevis* I would argue that to edit the romance in any other way is not only impracticable but inappropriate. *Bevis* survives in six and a bit manuscripts (ranging in date from the mid-fourteenth to the late fifteenth or early sixteenth century)[9] and a large number of printed editions.[10] The relationships between these extant versions are extraordinarily complex and suggest that a substantial corpus of texts of the romance has failed to survive;[11] but if we exclude from consideration the fragmentary Caius and Trinity manuscripts and the Chetham's version (which is a textual hybrid, probably based in part on a printed edition),[12] it is clear that we are left with three distinct manuscript redactions (or reworkings), represented by the Auchinleck manuscript (A), by the Cambridge manuscript (C), and by the Egerton and Naples manu-

---

7. Other examples of authorial revision include Chaucer's of the Prologue to *The Legend of Good Women* and Hoccleve's of *Lerne to Dye;* on the latter, see Bowers, "Hoccleve's Two Copies."

8. All references to the text of *Bevis* will be to Jennifer Fellows, *"Sir Beves of Hampton: Study and Edition,"* 5 vols., Ph.D. diss., University of Cambridge, 1980 (hereafter *Bevis*).

9. These are Edinburgh, National Library of Scotland, Advocates' ms. 19.2.1 (the Auchinleck ms.); Cambridge University Library, ms. Ff.2.38; Cambridge, Gonville and Caius College, ms. 175; Manchester, Chetham's Library, ms. 8009; Naples, Biblioteca Nazionale, ms. XIII.B.29; London, British Library, ms. Egerton 2862; and Cambridge, Trinity College, ms. O.2.13, which contains only a single episode from the romance and may be an excerpt rather than a fragment.

10. Listed in *Bevis,* 1:25–35.

11. Ibid., 1:36–46.

12. Ibid., 1:40–43.

scripts (S and N). The printed editions represent a further redaction, probably made specifically for the press sometime in the last few years of the fifteenth century.[13]

If we accept Judith Weiss's conclusion that the Anglo-Norman *Boeve de Haumtone* is the source of the Middle English *Bevis,*[14] and assume therefore that readings in any of the Middle English redactions that correspond closely to those of *Boeve* must have been those of the original *Bevis,* then we can see that none of the surviving Middle English redactions is appreciably closer to that original than any other. A and C differ substantially in a number of episodes: in the accounts of Bevis's interview with Terri and of the subsequent events leading up to the hero's imprisonment in Damascus, A corresponds more closely to the supposed original than does C, while in those of the boar fight and of the battles against, respectively, the foresters, Bradmond, and Yvor, C stands closer to it than does A.[15] A and C also give variant accounts of the battles with the Saracens on Christmas Day, with Graunder, with the giant of the castle, with the lions, with the dragon, and with the citizens of London, as well as of the separation of Bevis and Josian subsequent upon the hero's banishment. In these cases closeness to the original is less easy to determine, either because there is no equivalent episode in *Boeve* or because none of the extant Middle English redactions stands appreciably closer to *Boeve* than another[16]—though observable tendencies in A, which I shall describe below, suggest that there is more creative reworking here, in at least some of these episodes, than there is in C. The redaction represented by the closely related pair SN shows less creativity, tending to agree either with A or with C in its nonoriginal features. Broadly speaking, the tendency for SN to agree with A against C is more characteristic of the early part of the romance (up to Bevis's arrival in Cologne), while correspondence between SN and C occurs more frequently in the story's later episodes. Probably the SN redaction is ultimately the product of conflation.[17]

---

13. See Jennifer Fellows, *"Bevis redivivus:* the printed editions of *Sir Bevis of Hampton,"* in *Romance Reading on the Book: Essays Presented to Maldwyn Mills,* ed. Jennifer Fellows, Rosalind Field, Gillian Rogers, and Judith Weiss (Cardiff, 1996), 251–68, at 254.

14. Judith E. Martin, "Studies in Some Early Middle English Romances," Ph.D. diss., University of Cambridge, 1968, 107–14.

15. See *Bevis,* 2:1562–69, 1706–25, 1905–42, 882–97, 934–86, 1122–53, 5306–5419, and the relevant commentary (5:61–62, 65, 69, 36–37, 38, 46–47, 170–72).

16. Ibid., 2:650–829, 2322–2401, 2488–2557, 3114–93, 3294–3699, 5478–5889, 4603–98, and the relevant commentary (5:28–33, 80–84, 87–89, 105–6, 112–21, 174–80, 148–58).

17. Ibid., 1:38.

The interrelationships between the various extant versions of the Middle English *Bevis* are, then, constantly shifting and changing, and it can be seen that even if "correctness" is equated with closeness to a notional "Ur-text," no one text is consistently more correct than any other: each redaction contains peculiar features that, on the basis of comparison with the Anglo-Norman *Boeve,* can be adjudged original. On the other hand, there are certain episodes common to all Middle English versions that have no counterpart at all in the Anglo-Norman poem, the most striking examples being the fight with the dragon, and Bevis's single-handed decimation of the citizenry of London.

There are, of course, many passages in *Bevis*—especially near the beginning of the romance—where functional correspondence between the extant texts is sufficiently close for familiar patterns of scribal "corruption" or "debasement" (or whatever morally loaded term one wishes to use) to be observable. Such typical scribal habits have been categorized by Nicolas Jacobs as "lexical glosses," "syntactical glosses," "clarification and expansion," "alterations irrespective of sense," and "smoothing and flattening"—all of which he places under the general heading of "regression to the commonplace."[18] But it would be a grossly simplistic misrepresentation of the extant Middle English versions of this particular romance to suggest that they are, in their totality, simply dim reflections of a brighter, better *Bevis.* For in this instance one cannot completely separate scribal activity from some supposedly purer authorial intention—the redactors, who may or may not be the same people as the scribes of the manuscripts that we have, *are* the authors, each of whom has to some extent "rethought" the romance and left his own peculiar mark on it.

By comparing the Middle English redactions both with one another and with their ultimate source, *Boeve,* one might be able to reconstruct the Middle English original, or at least the common archetype of the extant redactions, with reasonable accuracy as to its general outlines. But, given the number of gaps in the material evidence regarding textual transmission,[19] such a reconstruction would necessarily be extremely hypothetical and its end product a highly artificial construct—bearing, perhaps, little relation to anything that might have been available to a medieval reader. Furthermore, even if the readings of the Middle English archetype of *Bevis* could be established with far more certainty than is in fact possible, the reconstructed archetype would, to my mind, be of far less interest than are the relationships between the

---

18. Nicolas Jacobs, "Regression to the Commonplace in Some Vernacular Textual Traditions," in Minnis and Brewer, *Crux and Controversy,* 61–70, at 62.

19. Cf. the stemma tentatively proposed in *Bevis,* 1:36.

redactions that we have—with all that they can tell us about fourteenth- and fifteenth-century tastes and preoccupations.

How, then, is such a text to be edited? There is, I think, no wholly satisfactory answer. The method adopted by Eugen Kölbing, when he edited *Bevis* for the Early English Text Society in the 1880s and 1890s,[20] was to print in full the Auchinleck text and to present the readings of the other manuscripts (except for those of ms. Chetham 8009, which is printed as a separate text at the foot of the page) as variants. There are two main disadvantages of this method: the first is that, whatever disclaimers are made, one text is implicitly exalted to a position of authority. Kölbing himself is well aware of the difficulties involved in the choice of a base-text, remarking in his notes and introduction that the Auchinleck text is not always the closest to the romance's Anglo-Norman source,[21] but his procedure is nevertheless misleading. His edition has all the trappings of a critical text established by recension, but it is in principle much nearer to a parallel-text edition, in that his base-text is not emended from other manuscripts even where those manuscripts are demonstrably more "correct" or closer to the Anglo-Norman source. The second principal disadvantage of this mode of presentation lies in the sheer bulk and complexity of the textual apparatus, with all the resultant difficulty of working out what any version other than the base-text actually *says*—yet none of them is by any means negligible in terms of textual interest.

In many ways the Auchinleck *Bevis* is the most interesting of them all. For reasons that I have suggested in the preceding paragraph, most readers of the romance will regard this text as the norm and will not recognize its anomalies. However, it is precisely in those episodes in which the Auchinleck *Bevis* stands alone against the Anglo-Norman *Boeve* on the one hand and the remaining Middle English redactions of the romance on the other that its interest primarily inheres. There are five principal episodes of this kind: (1) Bevis's encounter with Terri on his journey to Damascus; (2) the dragon fight; (3) Josian's seven-year separation from Bevis and her sons; (4) the single combat against King Yvor; (5) Bevis's battle against King Edgar's treacherous steward and the citizens of London. All these episodes occur in some form in all extant versions of the Middle English *Bevis,* and numbers 1, 3, and 4 are also in *Boeve.* But the redactor of the Auchinleck version has reworked them substantially, and through a comparison with other versions certain patterns of altera-

---

20. *The Romance of Sir Beues of Hamtoun,* ed. Eugen Kölbing, 3 vols., EETS, e.s. 46, 48, 65 (London, 1885–94).

21. Ibid., xl, 219–360 passim.

tion can be detected. Thus there is a marked preference for French-based vocabulary in episodes 1, 3, and 4 (though none of it betrays the influence of *Boeve*); a particular interest in the character of Josian, who becomes a more active and resourceful figure, in episodes 3 and 5; and a concern to emphasize that Bevis is both an Englishman and a Christian knight—especially in episodes 2, 4, and 5. Episode 3, in which the Auchinleck Josian first hides her beauty by means of a disfiguring herb and later assumes the role of a minstrel in order to support herself and her friend and helper Saber while the latter is ill, also suggests that the redactor was familiar with French romances, such as *Aucassin et Nicolette* or the *Roman de Silence,* as well as with the French tongue.[22]

Several of these features accord with preoccupations evident in the Auchinleck manuscript as a whole, with its emphasis on didactic, patriotic, and, perhaps, women's interests,[23] and suggest that in this instance there is at least a possibility that redactor and scribe are one. At all events, the Auchinleck *Bevis* clearly represents a systematic reworking of the romance—what, in short, may reasonably be termed "authorial" revision. The salient characteristics of this version can, however, be identified only if we have at least some conception of the norm from which it is departing. Since that norm is not represented by any single manuscript version, such a conception can, in turn, only be attained by extensive comparison of the extant Middle English redactions both with their ultimate source, the Anglo-Norman *Boeve,* and with one another. It is to facilitate such comparison, and because of the intrinsic interest of individual redactions such as the Auchinleck, that I would advocate the parallel text as the most appropriate way of presenting a work (or works?) such as *Bevis.*

Bevis is not, of course, the only text for which such an editorial method might be considered the most appropriate. The parallel-text edition has found increasing favor in the past thirty-odd years as a way of dealing with "uneditable" Middle English romances: A. J. Bliss's *Sir Orfeo,* Maldwyn Mills's

---

22. I have given an account of the salient characteristics of the Auchinleck *Bevis* in a paper delivered at the fourth conference on Romance in Medieval England, King Alfred's College, Winchester, 5–7 April 1994.

23. On the unity in conception of the Auchinleck manuscript as a whole, and the way in which its contents are grouped by subject matter and/or theme, see Timothy A. Shonk, "A Study of the Auchinleck Manuscript: Bookmen and Bookmaking in the Early Fourteenth Century," *Speculum* 60 (1985): 71–91; Geraldine Barnes, *Counsel and Strategy in Middle English Romance* (Cambridge, 1993), chaps. 3 and 4. Felicity Riddy suggested that the Auchinleck manuscript might be regarded as a "woman's manuscript" in a paper delivered at the third conference on Romance in Medieval England, University of Bristol, 31 March–2 April 1992.

Lybeaus Desconus, O. D. Macrae-Gibson's *Of Arthour and of Merlin,* and Frances McSparran's *Octovian* are but a few examples of the application of this method.[24] Parallel texts were also used by Julius Zupitza toward the end of the nineteenth century for *Guy of Warwick,*[25] a text where the editorial problems are very similar to those presented by *Bevis.* The method does, however, have some obvious disadvantages. The parallel-text edition is cumbersome in use—which text is the reader to follow?—and there are practical problems relating to the difficulties and expense of printing[26] (which perhaps goes some way to explain why no new edition of longer "uneditable" romances such as *Bevis* and *Guy* has been published during this century). But the objection most commonly put forward is really a moral one: all too often the editor is seen as abrogating certain functions and leaving the reader to make decisions and choices that should have been made for him/her: that such an editor "in effect cease[s] to edit" and that "granted that we need working editions which do not consist of parallel transcriptions of all surviving manuscripts, some degree of editorial judgment is a desideratum" represent a fairly common kind of response to parallel-text editing.[27]

Yet it is more in appearance than in reality that the editor of a parallel-text edition is any more pusillanimous,[28] lacking in judgment, or motivationally dispossessed[29] than any other sort of editor—at least, that should be the case in an ideal editorial world. If the decision to present two or more texts of a work in parallel is an informed one based on careful assessment of the manuscript evidence and its nature—of the interrelationships between extant versions, and the status that may appropriately be accorded to each—then editorial judgment has not been suspended even if it does not manifest itself so clearly on the printed page, in the form of square brackets and all the baggage of the tradi-

---

24. *Sir Orfeo,* ed. A. J. Bliss, 2d ed. (Oxford, 1966); *Lybeaus Desconus,* ed. M. Mills, EETS 261 (London, 1969); *Of Arthour and of Merlin,* ed. O. D. Macrae-Gibson, 2 vols., EETS 268, 279 (London, 1973–79); *Octovian,* ed. Frances McSparran, EETS 289 (London, 1986).

25. *The Romance of Guy of Warwick,* ed. Julius Zupitza, 3 vols., EETS, e.s. 42, 49, 59 (1883–91; rpt. as 1 vol., London, 1966) (contains the Auchinleck and Caius texts in parallel); *The Romance of Guy of Warwick: The Second or 15th-Century Version,* ed. J. Zupitza, EETS, e.s. 25, 26 (1875–76; rpt. as 1 vol., London, 1966).

26. Cf. also Rosamund Allen, "Some Sceptical Observations on the Editing of *The Awntyrs off Arthure,*" in *Manuscripts and Texts: Editorial Problems in Later Middle English Literature,* ed. Derek Pearsall (Cambridge, 1987), 13 n. 37.

27. See Nicolas Jacobs in this volume; Paul Hartle (reviewing *The Wars of Alexander,* ed. Hoyt N. Duggan and Thorlac Turville-Petre), in *Medium Aevum* 60 (1991): 112.

28. Cf. Derek Pearsall, "Authorial Revision in Some Late-Medieval English Texts," in Minnis and Brewer, *Crux and Controversy,* 46.

29. Or, in plain English, lazy.

tional apparatus criticus, as would be the case in a critical edition. Ideally, however, an important part of a parallel-text edition should be a clear statement of its rationale and of the textual features that are held to justify the procedure adopted;[30] for this editorial method is not an equally appropriate one for all medieval texts, or even for all Middle English romances. If the relationships between extant versions of a work suggest an ongoing process of corruption or debasement—due perhaps to incompetence on the part of scribes or to circumstances beyond their control such as physical damage to an exemplar—rather than systematic redaction, then an appropriate aim of the editor (perhaps *the* appropriate aim) will be to attempt to restore the common archetype that can be inferred from those versions. Rosamund Allen has persuasively argued this to be the case for *King Horn* and for *The Awntyrs off Arthure,*[31] and Nicolas Jacobs sees comparable processes at work in the textual tradition of *Sir Degarre.*[32] The parallel text is not, then, proposed as a panacea for all editorial ills, but simply as one among a number of editorial approaches, whose suitability must be assessed on the merits of the individual textual case.

Nor, if the parallel-text method is adopted, is it enough for the editor to take a strictly noninterventionist stance and simply present diplomatic transcriptions of manuscript texts. The primary function of an editor is, after all, to edit and to provide readers with a readable text or texts. Even if a scribe is equated with the redactor and accorded authorial status, this does not justify an excessive and undiscriminating scribolatry[33] or mean that his or her work is necessarily free from error or inconsistency: no one who has ever made a fair copy from their own rough drafts or who has subedited the work of others will imagine that even a holograph manuscript will by definition represent exactly what the author intended at all points. To counsel perfection, then: the ideal to be aimed at in the presentation of parallel texts is correction rather than improvement, the identification and elimination of obvious error, the clarification of obvious nonsense, the establishment of the "right" reading for that particular

---

30. A defense of the parallel-text edition is offered in Dan Embree and Elizabeth Urquhart, "*The Simonie:* The Case for a Parallel-Text Edition," in Pearsall, *Manuscripts and Texts,* 49–59.

31. *King Horn: An Edition Based on Cambridge University Library MS Gg.4.27(2),* ed. Rosamund Allen (New York, 1984), 1; Allen, "Some Sceptical Observations."

32. Jacobs, "Regression to the Commonplace." See also his *The Later Versions of Sir Degarre: A Study in Textual Degeneration,* Medium Aevum Monographs, n.s. 18 (Oxford, 1995).

33. Some of the disadvantages of excessive respect for the individual manuscript are pointed out in Anne Hudson, "Middle English," in *Editing Medieval Texts: English, French, and Latin written in England,* ed. A. G. Rigg (New York, 1977), 38, cited in Allen, "Some Sceptical Observations," 12 n. 31.

text or redaction. If we respect the variant intentions of scribes or redactors and, where appropriate, recognize the fruits of their labors as being in effect alternative *authorial* versions, we shall perhaps be better able to evaluate their work within the context of medieval culture as a whole.

A Bibliographical Essay on Editing Methods and Authorial and Scribal Intention

Douglas Moffat
with Vincent P. McCarren

In the first two essays in this volume, Nicolas Jacobs and Jennifer Fellows address the fundamental practical problems that most editors of Middle English must face if they choose to produce a scholarly edition. What is the relationship of the variant readings in the copies of manuscripts that survive, and what is the relationship of the copies themselves? Are these relationships close enough or clear enough that the editor might contemplate establishing an archetypal text from which existing copies derived, or perhaps even an authorial text? Or are the differences between them such that one must conclude that new redactions have been created or even new works? The type of edition that the editor chooses to make depends on the answers to these questions, and the final product will be judged on how they are handled. Editors of a work surviving in a unique manuscript, or those engaging in a facsimile or diplomatic edition, are to some degree free from such concerns, but these questions impinge on their task as well.

This essay provides a broad bibliographical context for the issues raised by Fellows and Jacobs. It is divided into three parts. The first briefly describes and assesses the kinds of editing methods typically employed by editors of Middle English. The second addresses the problematical question of authorial intention as it applies to Middle English, while the third directs the reader to a number of statements about Middle English scribes and scribal practice. Editors' perceptions of the relationship between authorial intention and what is called, in deliberate counterpoint, scribal intention, necessarily underlie their

The original intention was that Vincent McCarren and I would write this essay jointly. Unfortunately illness prevented a full collaboration. Besides contributing the section on Recension, Vince discussed the topic of this essay with me for many profitable hours and carefully read various drafts. I am most grateful for his assistance.

analysis of variants, as a number of other contributors to this volume demonstrate. Therefore, editors must think seriously about this relationship early in the editorial process.

A number of books and articles about textual scholarship and editing have been particularly helpful in writing this essay. Often they are referred to in specific contexts below, but they deserve to be introduced here as well because of their general usefulness. First of all, the thought-provoking essays by Jacobs and Fellows not only provide the occasion for this essay but also inform many of its ideas. D. C. Greetham's *Textual Scholarship* is required reading for anyone interested in this subject; it contains much that relates directly to Middle English, and this information is placed in a broad historical and theoretical context.[1] Charles Moorman's *Editing the Middle English Manuscript,* while not adequate for the task it sets itself, contains some useful pointers.[2] Anne Hudson's "Middle English" in *Editing Medieval Texts* is a short but insightful piece that raises many important issues.[3] The names of A. S. G. Edwards, Ralph Hanna III, and Derek Pearsall appear frequently in what follows; for general questions of editing, see Edwards's "Observations on the History of Middle English Editing" and "Editing Middle English," Hanna's "Producing Manuscripts and Editions," and Pearsall's "Editing Medieval Texts" and "Theory and Practice in Middle English Editing."[4] Though not primarily concerned with Middle English, G. Thomas Tanselle's "Classical, Biblical, and Medieval Textual Criticism and Modern Editing" is certainly

---

1. D. C. Greetham, *Textual Scholarship: An Introduction* (New York, 1994). This work's bibliography, divided by subject, is in itself invaluable. Also remarkable for its combination of breadth and brevity is Greetham's "Challenges of Theory and Practice in the Editing of Hoccleve's *Regement of Princes,*" in *Manuscripts and Texts: Editorial Problems in Later Middle English Literature,* ed. Derek Pearsall (Cambridge, 1987), 60–86.

2. Charles Moorman, *Editing the Middle English Manuscript* (Jackson, Miss., 1975).

3. Anne Hudson, "Middle English," in *Editing Medieval Texts,* ed. A. G. Rigg (New York, 1977), 34–57. Criticisms of this often-cited article can be found in D. C. Greetham, "The Place of Fredson Bowers in Medieval Editing," *Papers of the Bibliographical Society of America* 82 (1988): 53–69.

4. A. S. G. Edwards, "Observations on the History of Middle English Editing," in Pearsall, *Manuscripts and Texts,* 34–48, and "Editing Middle English," in *Scholarly Editing,* ed. D. C. Greetham (New York, 1995), 184–203; Ralph Hanna III, "Producing Manuscripts and Editions," in *Crux and Controversy in Middle English Textual Criticism,* ed. A. J. Minnis and Charlotte Brewer (Cambridge, 1992), 109–30, reprinted in Hanna's *Pursuing History: Middle English Manuscripts and Their Texts* (Stanford, 1996), 63–82; Derek Pearsall, "Editing Medieval Texts: Some Developments and Problems," in *Textual Criticism and Literary Interpretation,* ed. Jerome J. McGann (Chicago, 1985), 92–106; and "Theory and Practice in Middle English Editing," *Text* 7 (1994): 107–26.

among the best elucidations of the relationship between the editing of classical, medieval, and postmedieval works.[5] David F. Hult's "Reading It Right: The Ideology of Text Editing" focuses on Old French but is more generally illuminating as well.[6] Finally, Tim William Machan's *Textual Criticism and Middle English Texts* must be acknowledged as a defining book in the area of Middle English textual scholarship.[7] As will become clear, I disagree fundamentally with him on some issues, but my ideas have been much clarified by examining his.

Recension

Throughout the nineteenth and most of the twentieth century editors of Middle English tended to employ the approach to editing known variously as recension, stemmatics, or the Lachmannian method, if they used any method at all (see Blake in this volume). The last mentioned here acknowledges the preeminence of Karl Lachmann as a developer and exponent of this procedure, which became the standard method for editing classical texts in the nineteenth century. Recension has been described many times in the literature on textual criticism;[8] perhaps the most succinct description is that of L. D. Reynolds and N. G. Wilson:

> The object of recension is to reconstruct from the evidence of the surviving manuscripts the earliest recoverable form of the text that lies behind them. Unless the manuscript tradition depends on a single witness, it is necessary (1) to establish the relationships of the surviving manuscripts to each other, (2) to eliminate from consideration those

5. G. Thomas Tanselle, "Classical, Biblical, and Medieval Textual Criticism and Modern Editing," *Studies in Bibliography* 36 (1983): 21–68.

6. David F. Hult, "Reading It Right: The Ideology of Text Editing," in *The New Medievalism,* ed. Marina S. Brownlee, Kevin Brownlee, and Stephen G. Nichols (Baltimore, 1991), 113–30.

7. Tim William Machan, *Textual Criticism and Middle English Texts* (Charlottesville, Va., 1994). Machan has published many articles as well, but this book contains the arguments of most of these. The book's bibliography is very extensive.

8. Ludwig Bieler, *The Grammarian's Craft: An Introduction to Textual Criticism,* in *Folia* 2 (1947): 94–107 and *Folia* 3 (1948): 23–32 and 47–55; C. O. Brink, *English Classical Scholarship: Historical Reflections on Bentley, Porson, and Housman* (Cambridge, 1986); E. J. Kenney, *The Classical Text: Aspects of Editing in the Age of the Printed Book* (Berkeley, 1974); Paul Maas, *Textual Criticism,* trans. Barbara Flower (Oxford, 1958); Martin L. West, *Textual Criticism and Editorial Technique* (Stuttgart, 1973).

which are derived exclusively from other existing manuscripts and therefore have no independent value . . . and (3) to use the established relationship of those which remain (ideally expressed in the form of a *stemma codicum* or family tree) to reconstruct the lost manuscript or manuscripts from which the surviving witnesses descend.[9]

Leonard Boyle offers a slightly different perspective:

> Ideally there are three stages in the Recensionist procedure. The first stage uncovers the text that is common to all the witnesses. The second tackles the problem of what is not common. The third . . . turns the text established in the first and second stages from the witnesses into an edited text which, with the aid of conjecture, emendation, etc., goes beyond them.[10]

The first two stages are traditionally presented as a systematic and objective comparison of the evidence. Conventionally this comparison focuses on what are perceived as nonauthorial errors in the surviving copies, those errors caused either by scribal blunder or manuscript damage. The theory is that two manuscripts must be related that share such an error (one not likely to have been committed independently). If it can be further demonstrated that one of these manuscripts is derived from the other, by its containing, for example, an additional error, this derivative or more recent manuscript can be safely eliminated from the process of establishing the text. The goal is to discover the archetype, the copy from which all other copies derive, or at least the surviving witnesses that are closest to the lost archetype. The latter would be the typical situation in Middle English.

While the ideal formulation of recension as a method does not rule out conjectural emendation, its foundation is this systematic establishment of filiation between the surviving witnesses of the work. However, many classicists and medievalists have questioned how truly systematic these first stages of recension are and how applicable the whole method is to actual situations. Giorgio Pasquali, the leader of the "New Philology" of the 1930s, did not spurn

---

9. L. D. Reynolds and N. G. Wilson, *Scribes and Scholars: A Guide to the Transmission of Greek and Latin Literature,* 3d ed. (Oxford, 1991), 207–8.

10. Leonard E. Boyle, "Optimist or Recensionist: 'Common Errors' or 'Common Variations'?" in *Latin Script and Letters, A.D. 400–900: Festschrift presented to Ludwig Bieler,* ed. J. J. O'Meara and B. Naumann (Leiden, 1976), 264–74; quotation from p. 207. See also Boyle's "'Epistulae Venerunt Parum Dulces': The Place of Codicology in the Editing of Medieval Latin Texts," in *Editing and Editors: A Retrospect,* ed. Richard Landon (New York, 1988), 29–46.

recension completely, since it was necessary for the classification of manu-scripts. However, he cast doubt on the likelihood of successful systematic application of the method to all textual situations. Each work had to be handled within its own manuscript tradition, and each required special editing tech-niques.[11] Pasquali's dictum *recentiores non deteriores* calls into question a central tenet of recension, that manuscript dissemination primarily follows a line of vertical descent. He argued that the textual critic had to be prepared to face the reality of a much more complex manuscript tradition that contained not only vertical but horizontal dissemination brought about by conflation and contamination. The medievalists Joseph Bédier and George Kane developed their alternative editorial methods, best-text and direct editing, in order to handle just this complexity.[12] These methods will be discussed below.

Exponents of the eclectic approach to editing, most notably A. E. Housman, argued that, because of the complexity of manuscript transmission, the individ-ual critic's judgment had to be placed above applications of an overly simplis-tic system. This approach relies heavily upon what has fittingly been called *divinatio*. D. R. Shackleton Bailey describes it in the following way:

When a novice or a non-critic tries to solve a textual crux, he will generally start with the corruption—juggling with the letters, trying out various paleographically acceptable substitutions. If the corruption is simple and graphical he may stumble on the true reading, though he may very well fail to recognize it as such. The critic on the other hand generally gets his clue from the context. He is faced with a pattern of thought, part of which has been broken. He has to adjust his mind to that pattern, to run it into the mold of the author's as represented in this

---

11. Giorgio Pasquali, *Storia della tradizione e critica del testo* (Florence, 1934). See also S. Timpanaro, *La genesi del metodo del Lachmann* (Florence, 1963). For a facile and informative presentation of the humanistic method of textual scholarship, see Sesto Prete, *Observations on the History of Textual Criticism in the Medieval and Renaissance Periods* (Collegeville, 1970). For a discussion of the criticism of recension and of various attempts to modify its procedures, see Greetham, *Textual Scholarship,* 323–30.

12. Bédier attacks recension in "La Tradition manuscrite du *Lai du l'Ombre:* réflexions sur l'art d'éditer les anciens textes," *Romania* 54 (1928): 161–96, 321–56. Kane's position on recen-sion can be found in *Piers Plowman: The A version: Will's Vision of Piers Plowman and of Do-Well* (London, 1960; 2d ed. 1988), 55, and George Kane and E. Talbot Donaldson, *Piers Plowman: The B version* (London, 1975; 2d ed. 1988), 17–18 n. 10. See also Donaldson, "The Psychology of Editors of Middle English Texts," in *Speaking of Chaucer* (New York, 1970), 102–18; George Kane, "John M. Manly and Edith Rickert," in *Editing Chaucer: The Great Tradition,* ed. Paul Ruggiers (Norman, Okla., 1984), 207–29, in which he attacks the recensionist underpinnings of the Manly-Rickert edition of *The Canterbury Tales;* and N. F. Blake, "Editorial Assumptions in the Manly-Rickert Edition of *The Canterbury Tales,*" *English Studies* 64 (1983): 385–400.

particular passage. Once that is done, and the correct pattern, so far as it emerges from the context, is established, then, with the help of such indications as the corrupt piece itself provides, and subject to the control of touchstones which knowledge and experience automatically apply, the missing link may suggest itself, often with little conscious effort. The power to run the mind on to a literary context, reacting to and retaining compositely and in due proportion each successive impression—that is as near as I can get to the secret of *divinatio*.[13]

Or, to quote Housman, critics know the true reading of their author "with the marrow of their bones, which is the same stuff as his."[14] The eclectic position has many affinities with the direct method used by some Middle English editors.

The idea that recension provides a systematic method of editing in and of itself is probably indefensible for most, if not all, Middle English works that survive in multiple copies. There is considerable evidence for horizontal dissemination of Middle English works. The more popular the work, the more likely its manuscript tradition would have deviated from a strictly vertical descent, which is a precondition of the recensionist method.[15] However, the idea that recension should be abandoned as a method of organizing a variety of manuscript witnesses is untenable. Paul Oskar Kristeller argues for its continued usefulness, providing one employs the concept of shared error judiciously, applying it to "obvious errors" only.[16] S. S. Hussey stresses recension's practical advantages:

If two or three manuscripts regularly share the same common errors, such as the same examples of eyeskip, this surely argues a genetic relationship, and, given the impracticability of citing all variant readings from all manuscripts in a modern edition, it should be sufficient to cite the best manuscript from each group, plus any variation of significance within the group.[17]

---

13. D. R. Shackleton Bailey, *Profile of Horace* (Cambridge, Mass., 1982), 108.

14. A. E. Housman, ed., *M. Annaei Lucani, Belli Civilis, libri decem* (Oxford, 1926), vi.

15. Besides Kane and Kane and Donaldson's discussion of the *Piers Plowman* manuscripts, see Anne Hudson, "The Variable Text," in Minnis and Brewer, *Crux and Controversy,* 49–60.

16. Paul Oskar Kristeller, "The Lachmann Method: Merits and Limitations," *Text* 1 (1984, for 1981): 11–20.

17. S. S. Hussey, "Editing *The Scale of Perfection:* Return to Recension," in Minnis and Brewer, *Crux and Controversy,* 97–108; quotation from p. 105.

Ralph Hanna not only sees the practical virtues of recension but also its theoretical implications:

> While I concur with Kane-Donaldson that no constructed *stemma* can edit a text, no other method provides a way to historicize textual generation and to link this behaviour to specific human work. And Kane-Donaldson's total rejection of the value of attestation—the stemmatic discovery that multitudinous shared readings may represent in the last analysis only a single, historicizable production decision—seems to me less than compelling. Not only do they reject as impossible any historically plausible construction of the evidence by attending to potential vertical descent of readings, but they surrender any interest in the historical development of the text and thus tend to remove it from history altogether.[18]

While it seems unlikely that recension as an editorial method can be rehabilitated for Middle English, wholesale rejection of it as a way of examining textual evidence is too extreme.

Best-Text Editing

Best-text editing developed as a medievalist response to the theory and practice of recension. Joseph Bédier, with whom the method is associated, argued that the recensionists tended, despite the evidence, to create bipartite stemmas even in cases where the evidence indicated a more complex tradition.[19] Further, Bédier recognized that the reality of horizontal as well as vertical dissemination irretrievably complicated the genetic relations of medieval texts. However, whereas eclecticists like Housman and proponents of Middle English direct editing, to be discussed below, postulate a recoverable authorial text, Bédier and the adherents of best-text editing accept the loss of the original composition. The role of editors is not to present the modern reader with a "hypothesis" of the author's original[20] but with the best surviving text somewhat "cleansed"

---

18. Hanna, "Producing Manuscripts and Editions," 126.
19. Bédier, "La Tradition manuscrite." For an assessment of Bédier, see Mary B. Speer, "In Defense of Philology: Two New Guides to Textual Criticism," *Romance Philology* 32 (1982): 335–44, and "Old French Literature," in Greetham, *Scholarly Editing*, 382–416, esp. 394–404. See also Greetham, *Textual Scholarship*, 324–25.
20. Kane and Donaldson, *Piers Plowman*, 212.

of obvious, explicable scribal error.[21] The notion that the modern critic can recover the original form of a medieval work from scribal copies is regarded, from the point of view of best-text editing, as misguided, even hubristic.

Best-text editing has been most frequently used for Old and Middle French works, but it has Middle English advocates as well. Moorman argues that eclectic editing of the sort practiced by George Kane depends on an intimate and assured knowledge of the fine points of Middle English language, metrics, and scribal habits. Therefore, because we are still largely ignorant in these areas, he declares that the only responsible approach to editing is best-text.[22] John Bowers argues that the evidence against monogeneous descent of Middle English works constrains the editor to the best-text method. He points out that this method should not result, however, in refusal to give information about the text.[23] Variant readings included in a textual apparatus and conjectural suggestions included in explanatory notes ought to be part of a best-text edition. But these variants and conjectures should not impinge on the establishment of the text itself; only obvious mechanical errors should be corrected and clearly marked as corrected in the text.

The question arises, then, how does one select the best text of a given work? Presumably this is achieved through an examination of codicological, linguistic, and literary evidence in all the extant copies, from which one copy will emerge as the most worthy of being edited, because of its relative fidelity to the imagined original. However, best-text editing has been attacked on theoretical grounds for these very procedures. Specifically, it is difficult to understand why the information gathered and the judgment exercised in the preliminary selection process cannot be profitably extended to the establishment of the text itself.[24] In other words, why at the point of actually establishing the text does the best-text editor, in effect, surrender responsibility to the chosen manuscript's scribe(s)?

---

21. Eugène Vinaver, "Principles of Textual Emendation," in *Studies in French Language and Medieval Literature Presented to Professor M. K. Pope* (Manchester, 1930), 351–69; rpt. in *Medieval Manuscripts and Textual Criticism,* ed. Christopher Kleinhenz (Chapel Hill, 1976), 139–59. See especially 157–59.

22. Charles Moorman, "One Hundred Years of Editing the *Canterbury Tales,*" *Chaucer Review* 24 (1989): 99–114.

23. John M. Bowers, "Hoccleve's Two Copies of *Lerne to Dye:* Implications for Textual Critics," *Papers of the Bibliographical Society of America* 83 (1989): 437–72, esp. 461.

24. Donaldson, "Psychology"; Greetham, *Textual Scholarship,* 235; Ralph Hanna III, "Problems of 'Best-Text' Editing and the Hengwrt Manuscript of *The Canterbury Tales,*" in Pearsall, *Manuscripts and Texts,* 87–94, and "The Hengwrt Manuscript and the Canon of *The Canterbury Tales,*" *English Manuscript Studies: 1100–1700* 1 (1989): 64–84, reprinted in Hanna, *Pursuing History,* 140–55.

Ralph Hanna has further attacked the idea that presenting an "authentic," although cleansed, medieval text, rather than a hypothetical and potentially unauthentic one, puts the audience of the best-text edition more truly in the position of a medieval audience.[25] He points out that there is a great deal of evidence to suggest that medieval scribes, and presumably other readers, were not always satisfied with the readings of a single manuscript. Furthermore, there is no question but that best-text editors used (or ought to have used) their own modern judgment during the selection process, and that the edition's users, in turn, although ostensibly placed in the position of true medieval users, will have to rely on their modern judgment in assessing the results. Another anomaly in the "authenticity" argument concerns the correction of even the most obvious blunders. In order to be authentic, should not the text be as faithful a transcription as possible, "warts and all," of the chosen text?

Edwards and Hanna both point out that best-text editing has been influential, in effect, in the editing of *The Canterbury Tales*.[26] The Ellesmere manuscript for, among others, Skeat and Robinson, and the Hengwrt manuscript for, among others, Donaldson, Blake, and the Variorum Chaucer, have served with varying degrees of acknowledgment as best text. The argument that the same scribe copied both manuscripts greatly complicates this situation (see "Scribal Intentions" below). While the lengthy and complicated debate about the manuscript tradition and the editing of *The Canterbury Tales* cannot be taken up here, the reader is encouraged to look at the work on this question done by Norman Blake, Ralph Hanna, Charles Owen, and Joseph Dane.[27] One feature of the *Canterbury Tales* debate that is instructive for editors of other Middle English works is the fact that designation of a particular copy of a work as the best text can be a matter of considerable contention. (See also Blake in this volume.)

One situation in Middle English where best-text editing might prove a good option is when no adequate edition exists of a work extant in many copies. The best-text method could expedite the appearance of a *provisional* critical edition, especially if the editor could justify restricting consideration to a selection

---

25. Hanna, "Problems," 88–89.

26. Edwards, "Editing Middle English," 188–89; Hanna, "Problems" and "Hengwrt Manuscript."

27. N. F. Blake, *The Textual Tradition of the "Canterbury Tales"* (London, 1985); Joseph Dane, "Copy-Text and Its Variants in Some Recent Chaucer Editions," *Studies in Bibliography* 44 (1991): 164–83; Hanna, "Problems" and "Hengwrt Manuscript"; Charles A. Owen, Jr., *The Manuscripts of the "Canterbury Tales"* (Cambridge, 1991). See also John H. Fisher, "Historical and Methodological Considerations for Adopting 'Best-Text' or *Usus Scribendi* for Textual Criticism of Chaucer's Poems," *Text* 6 (1994): 165–80.

of manuscripts, perhaps by a judicious series of trial collations. Obviously questions would arise as to the initial selection procedure, but if this procedure could be defended and the edition's provisional nature were explicitly declared, the advantage of making the text available in a modern edition ought to outweigh the problem of incompleteness. Derek Pearsall's edition of the C-Text of *Piers Plowman* is a good example of such an edition.[28] However, this sort of edition is not to be confused with the presentation of a single version of a text carried out prior to the some considerable examination of the extant copies, no matter how numerous. For example, Morris's edition of *The Pricke of Conscience* might legitimately be called a partial best-text edition.[29] He did print what he believed was the linguistically most authoritative version of the 11 copies he examined. However, he provided sparse annotation and did not, of course, use the other 104 extant copies.

Hanna has argued that what he calls, perhaps with some irony, a "responsible" best-text edition could be an option for an editor who would produce a critical edition of a Middle English work.[30] Such an edition would present the text of the copy judged to be best "in aggregate." A clear indication of how this selection was made would be included in the edition, and the best text's readings would have to be defended in every case where variants from other copies, or a suspicion of error, existed. It would require, therefore, a full textual and explanatory apparatus. In such an edition the best text would not only serve as copy-text narrowly defined but also would be granted explicit presumptive authority as well.[31] Tanselle makes a similar recommendation for extending the idea of copy-text to ancient and medieval works.[32]

The best-text option might be considered, therefore, when editors judge that one copy of the work stands out for various reasons as the best surviving text of the work, but that the distinction between scribal and authorial writing fundamental to direct editing cannot be made with sufficient frequency or assurance in order to establish an authoritative text. Rather than attempting, then, to

---

28. William Langland, *Piers Plowman: The C-text,* ed. Derek Pearsall, 2d ed., Exeter Medieval English Texts and Studies (Exeter, 1994).

29. *The Pricke of Conscience,* ed. Richard Morris (Berlin, 1863).

30. Hanna, "Producing Manuscripts and Editions," 128.

31. The classic formulation of the theory of copy-text is found in W. W. Greg, "The Rationale of Copy-Text," *Studies in Bibliography* 3 (1950–51): 19–36. See also Fredson Bowers, "Greg's 'Rationale of Copy-Text' Revisited," *Studies in Bibliography* 31 (1978): 90–162. For application, and misapplication, of the theory to the editing of Middle English, see Dane, "Copy-Text," and Greetham, "Place of Fredson Bowers."

32. Tanselle, "Classical, Biblical," 50–52.

establish the text on the basis of a series of questionable judgments as to what is authorial and what scribal, editors could print the best text, emending it against the other witnesses where certainty or at least probability of error can be achieved. Full annotation, including defense of the best text's readings themselves, ought to be included, as Hanna recommends. The romance *The King of Tars* is an example of a work that would be susceptible to such an edition. Its most recent editor, Judith Perryman, makes a convincing case that the Auchinleck version ought to be preferred on various grounds to the other two copies, but she also argues that its authority cannot be demonstrated for many of the numerous variant readings.[33] However, while she does provide variant readings in her textual apparatus, Perryman takes a very conservative line, rarely emending the Auchinleck readings or defending them in her apparatus.

Edwards points out that best-text editing is not an option for works existing in a single copy. Even if the editor intended to adopt the highly conservative stance advocated by Vinaver, comparison and judgment of multiple copies is crucial to the method. Where there is only one text, there can be no "best" text. The editor of a work found in a unique copy must employ other strategies and justify policies of intervention or nonintervention on other theoretical bases. If scribal tendencies can be discerned in this single copy, one might intervene on that basis. However, it seems more likely that only clear linguistic, stylistic, or literary criteria would justify substantial intervention in such a text. A convenient analysis of the application of a variety of such criteria to a text that occurs in two copies, *The Wars of Alexander,* is provided by Thorlac Turville-Petre.[34] Although technically no "best" text is available when only two texts survive either, editors of such works are often in a much better position than editors with one copy only. The presence of even a partial second copy of *The Wars of Alexander* enabled Duggan and Turville-Petre to discern the categories of analysis the latter discusses, which in turn allowed them to prepare a critical edition of the work.[35] Failing the discovery of a closely translated source, a metrical system, or some similar means of gaining leverage on the unique copy, the editor is probably best advised to adopt a conservative approach. In fact, faced with a particularly inscrutable or badly damaged text, editors may defensibly conclude that a purely transcriptional, that is, diplomatic, edition is

---

33. Judith Perryman, *The King of Tars,* Middle English Texts, 12 (Heidelberg, 1986).

34. Thorlac Turville-Petre, "Editing *The Wars of Alexander,*" in Pearsall, *Manuscripts and Texts,* 143–60.

35. Hoyt N. Duggan and Thorlac Turville-Petre, *The Wars of Alexander,* EETS, s.s. 10 (Oxford, 1989).

their only option, although ideally such a text should be accompanied by thorough explanatory annotation.[36]

Direct Editing

In the first paper of this volume Nicolas Jacobs argues for an editorial method that has no generally accepted name. It is known variously as direct, deep, or eclectic editing. The last term casts it into relationship with the eclectic approach to classical editing already mentioned, which is most commonly associated with A. E. Housman.[37] There are clearly affinities between direct editing and the eclectic approach to classical editing, but there are significant differences as well. They share a skepticism of automatic reliance on any systematic analysis and codification of the copies of a work, specifically recension, that purport to provide a basis for arriving at authoritative readings. No such limited codification should override careful consideration of every questionable passage or reading, weighing of variants, and dismissal of all the variants, should critical judgment suggest that the author wrote something different. The most significant difference between the classical and medieval strains of eclecticism would seem to lie in the emphasis each places on the analysis of scribal variants. Editors of a Middle English work must allow for the linguistic proximity of scribe and author, which is much closer than that of scribe and author within the realm of classical literature. Sheer incomprehension of the vernacular is less likely to occur (although certainly possible), and by the same token, plausible alteration is more likely. Editors using the direct method for a Middle English work cannot, therefore, content themselves with ferreting out purely mechanical or unconscious scribal errors; rather, a broader range of motivations for scribal alteration of the exemplar must be considered, such as psychological, social, literary, and theological. Such editors choose a manuscript to serve as a base text for a variety of reasons—for example, a perceived relative lack of error, linguistic homogeneity or proximity to the author's dialect, completeness—but this manuscript is granted no presumptive authority, and its readings are considered as liable to be wrong as those of any other witness.

The best short statements about direct editing are found in George Kane's "'Good' and 'Bad' Manuscripts: Texts and Critics" and E. Talbot Donaldson's

---

36. Edwards, "Editing Middle English," 186–87. The "transcriptional" edition par excellence of a Middle English work is E. J. Dobson's *The English Text of the Ancrene Riwle Edited from B.M. Cotton MS. Cleopatra C. vi,* EETS 264 (London, 1972).

37. See Greetham, *Textual Scholarship,* 323–24 and 333–35.

"The Psychology of Editors of Middle English Texts."[38] In the former essay Kane, with whom the method is most closely associated, presents the goal of the critical edition as the effort to recover "the physical features of his poem as they stood in the exemplar first copied by another hand than the author's."[39] The editorial procedure in Kane's view has essentially two operations: one, the identification of mechanical error and "unconscious variation" in the scribal copies; two, the differentiation between authorial and scribal writing and the occasional supplanting of the latter by means of conjectural emendation.[40] One might say that the examination of the scribal impact on the text replaces the initial stages of recension. Instead of examining error in order to discover filiation of the surviving copies, one examines individual variants in those copies to discover the direction of variation in each case. One proceeds through the text one lemma at a time. Kane developed this method in order to tackle the problems of editing *Piers Plowman,* and it is in the introductions to his edition of the A-text of that work and his edition of the B-text with Donaldson that the fullest explication of the principles and procedures of direct editing are to be found.[41]

If one accepts Kane's description of the editorial process unreservedly, one accepts as well its limited applicability to Middle English, as Kane himself more or less intimates. In order to carry out the second of the operations mentioned above editors need to have many extant copies, because it is primarily through the comparison of these that they will establish the crucial distinction between the *usus scribendi* of the author and of the scribes.[42] Moreover, and for the same reason, the work should be of considerable length. It would seem to follow that the large number of Middle English works that exist in only one or a few copies, or are quite short, would not be susceptible to direct editing as described by Kane. Secondly, the author must be a great craftsman in order that the modern literary critic might differentiate the author's style from the pedestrian alterations of the copyists. This last require-

---

38. George Kane, "'Good' and 'Bad' Manuscripts: Texts and Critics," in *Studies in the Age of Chaucer, Proceedings No. 2, 1986 Fifth Annual International Congress, 20–23 March 1986, Philadelphia, Pennsylvania,* ed. John V. Fleming and Thomas J. Heffernan (Knoxville, 1987), 137–45; Donaldson, "Psychology."

39. Kane, "Good and Bad Manuscripts," 144.

40. See George Kane, "Conjectural Emendation," in *Medieval Literature and Civilisation: Studies in Memory of G. N. Garmonsway,* ed. Derek Pearsall and Ronald Waldron (1969), 155–69; rpt. in *Medieval Manuscripts and Textual Criticism,* ed. Christopher Kleinhenz (Chapel Hill, 1976), 211–25.

41. Kane, *Piers Plowman;* Kane and Donaldson, *Piers Plowman.*

42. Kane and Donaldson, *Piers Plowman,* 130ff.

ment presents a serious obstacle to the method's wide applicability. If one were to accept the traditional assessment of Middle English literature, direct editing would seem to be viable only for the works of Chaucer and for *Piers Plowman.* The *Pearl* poet, though usually judged a great writer, could not be so edited, because his work exists in a unique copy. On the other hand, the writers of works like *Cursor Mundi* or *The Pricke of Conscience,* who each produced poems of considerable length that exist in multiple copies, could not be so edited, because traditionally their craftsmanship has been judged too banal to be clearly distinguished from what scribes themselves might produce. *Usus scribendi* of scribe and author could not, therefore, be distinguished. Of course this line of reasoning begs the question, on what grounds is the traditional assessment of greatness in Middle English literature justified?

There have been two responses to the narrowness of Kane's definition of direct editing. Some have attempted to broaden the technique's applicability, specifically to verse romance.[43] Rosamund Allen, in "Some Sceptical Observations," forthrightly presents the problems encountered in applying direct editing to this genre: such romances do not always occur in many copies, nor need they be particularly lengthy; furthermore, they are products of poets considerably less talented, or perhaps more conventionally talented, than Chaucer.[44] In light of the efforts of Allen and Jacobs, two preliminary acts would seem to be required of editors who would consider direct editing of a text that does not fall strictly within the limits established by Kane. First of all, a thorough examination of all manuscript variants must be undertaken in order to establish a taxonomy of scribal alterations peculiar to the work in question, since each work will presumably elicit different responses from the individual scribes (see "Scribal Intention" below). Mechanical application of the categories of scribal alteration posited for other texts would be methodologically questionable. Secondly, careful thinking about what might constitute the authorial *usus scribendi* would be needed for any given work. A good deal of

---

43. Besides Nicolas Jacobs's essay in this volume, see his "Regression to the Commonplace in Some Vernacular Textual Traditions," in Minnis and Brewer, *Crux and Controversy,* 61–70; "The Process of Scribal Substitution and Redaction: A Study of the Cambridge Fragment of *Sir Degarre,*" *Medium Aevum* 53 (1984): 26–48; "The Second Revision of *Sir Degarre:* The Egerton Fragment and Its Congeners," *Neuphilogische Mitteilungen* 85 (1984): 95–107; *The Later Versions of Sir Degarre:* A Study in Textual Degeneration, Medium Aevum Monographs, n.s. 18 (Oxford, 1995). Also very important in this regard is Rosamund Allen's "Some Sceptical Observations on the Editing of *The Awntyrs off Arthure,*" in Pearsall, *Manuscripts and Texts,* 5–25. For editions of romances carried out on these principles, see Allen's *King Horn* (New York, 1984); Robert J. Gates, *The Awntyrs off Arthure at the Terne Wathelyne* (Philadelphia, 1969); Ralph Hanna III, *The Awntyrs off Arthure at the Terne Wathelyne* (Manchester, 1974).

44. Allen, "Some Sceptical Observations."

attention would have to be given to stylistic analysis. In fact, the whole question of medieval authorship as applied to the work to be edited will have to be thought through, and the reasoning behind the editors' declaration that they can unfailingly or at least frequently differentiate between the style of the author and the scribes will have to be clearly presented (see "Authorial Intention" below).

The second response to direct editing has been more critical, calling into question the application of modern judgment to the techniques and motivations of medieval authors. Adams, Brewer, Fowler, and Machan most thoroughly, but also Edwards, Hudson, Pearsall, and others have critically examined the justification for assured discrimination between authorial and scribal writing, even for an acknowledged great poet like Langland by an acknowledged great critic like Kane.[45] One line of questioning claims that the literary judgment of the modern critic is based in the first instance on postmedieval editions whose texts are themselves questionably established. How can an appreciation of the nuances of style not be affected and even to some extent created by the modern critic's early encounters with these editions? Another point of attack has to do with the apparent gap between medieval and modern literary taste. Lydgate, for example, while not without his partisans among contemporary critics, has not achieved canonical status. But the numerous surviving copies of his works attest to his considerable medieval popularity. If we judge Lydgate to be an inferior poet, is the lack in his artistry or in our understanding? If it is in our understanding, do we not judge Chaucer to be great on the same flawed basis? A defense against such objections could emphasize relatively objective stylistic analysis rather than an appeal to a prima facie "greatness." A clearly delineated source or metrical scheme would be of obvious benefit to the direct editor (see "Best-Text Editing" above) because either would ideally provide a standard measure, as it were, against which to place all the surviving witnesses.

Other questions about direct editing remain. John Bowers has argued for the

---

45. Charlotte Brewer's views are expressed in the following articles: "Authorial vs. Scribal Writing in *Piers Plowman*," in *Medieval Literature: Texts and Interpretation,* ed. Tim William Machan, Medieval and Renaissance Texts and Studies, 79 (Binghamton, 1991), 59–89; "George Kane's Process of Revision," in Minnis and Brewer, *Crux and Controversy,* 71–96; "The Textual Principles of Kane's A Text," *Yearbook of Langland Studies* 3 (1989): 67–90. See also David C. Fowler, "A New Edition of the B Text of *Piers Plowman*," *Year's Work in English Studies* 7 (1977): 23–42; Lee Patterson, "The Logic of Textual Criticism and the Way of Genius: The Kane-Donaldson *Piers Plowman* in Historical Perspective," in *Negotiating the Past: The Historical Understanding of Medieval Literature* (Madison, 1987), 77–113. (The article also appears in McGann, *Textual Criticism,* 55–91.) In Machan's *Textual Criticism,* see especially chap. 2. For the comments of Edwards, Hudson, and Pearsall, see the articles cited by them in notes 3 and 4 above.

unlikelihood of what he calls monogeneous descent for Middle English works.[46] He believes that comparison of the two autograph copies of Hoccleve's *Lerne to Dye* demonstrates that even for a "finished" work the author himself could have produced copies dissimilar in detail. Therefore editors should not assume that a single version of a Middle English text, authoritative in every detail, ever existed. There may be two or more such versions. Bowers overstates the significance of minute variants in authorial copies. It could be argued that not every variant of this sort should be treated as a considered authorial change. But Bowers's evidence should serve to caution editors who believe they can recover every detail of an author's copy. The related issue of authorial revision does complicate matters, however (see "Authorial Intention" below). If various authorial versions have found their way into the manuscript tradition of a work, how can editors discern between them, let alone between authorial and scribal variation? In fact, if the analysis of variants is carried out on the assumption that only one surviving variant at most is authorial, then the categories of analysis, and its results, will be significantly predetermined. Editors will reject genuine authorial variants and create explanations for regarding these as scribal, and into the categories created by these explanations other genuine readings could also be placed. It is ironic that direct editing, which was developed in order to handle the complexities in Middle English texts that recension tended to gloss over, is itself being attacked for its own theoretical and methodological inadequacy to handle complexity.

Parallel-Text Editing

Jennifer Fellows's essay in this volume represents one of the few efforts to articulate a rationale for parallel-text editing in Middle English. Other than Fellows's own "Editing Middle English Romances" and Dan Embree and Elizabeth Urquhart's "*The Simonie:* The Case for a Parallel-Text Edition," commendatory statements have usually been made only in passing in regard to textual situations like the one Fellows details for *Bevis of Hamtoun.*[47] Parallel-text presentation has been an option exercised by editors of Middle English for

---

46. J. Bowers, "Hoccleve's Two Copies."

47. Dan Embree and Elizabeth Urquhart, "*The Simonie:* The Case for a Parallel-Text Edition," in Pearsall, *Manuscripts and Texts,* 49–59; Jennifer Fellows, "Editing Middle English Romances," in *Romance in Medieval England,* ed. Maldwyn Mills, Jennifer Fellows, and Carol M. Meale (Cambridge, 1991), 5–16; A. S. G. Edwards, "Middle English Romance: The Limits of Editing, the Limits of Criticism," in Machan, *Medieval Literature,* 91–104, and also "Editing Middle English"; Pearsall, "Theory and Practice," 111–12.

a very long time, an early example being Madden's edition of Laȝamon's *Brut*.
It has usually been attacked, as Fellows points out, for awkwardness of presentation, for the failure of editors to do much more than offer transcriptions of the
versions,[48] and for the apparent unwillingness of some editors to attempt a
critical edition (see Blake in this volume). These are valid observations about
the history of parallel-text editing in Middle English, but they do not constitute
theoretical attacks.

One case where a parallel-text edition is justified occurs when codicological
damage has resulted in substantial loss of what would otherwise be a preferable
version. This is the case, for example, with *Floris and Blauncheflur* where
earlier copies are damaged and/or incomplete.[49] Damage, or corruption, of
another kind caused Smithers to edit *King Alisaunder* in parallel: he judged the
Lincoln's Inn version to have become so corrupted in the course of oral transmission as to be irreconcilable with the preferred Laud version.[50] Regardless
of whether one accepts Smithers's analysis or not, the situation he recognized
was that, on the one hand, the Lincoln's Inn and Laud texts represented two
versions of the same work and, on the other, that they were not reducible to a
single critical text. Embree and Urquhart, as well as Fellows, present cases
where alternative versions of the same work exist that have been reimagined
and restructured by redactors to such an extent that they have become at least
semiautonomous.

A fundamental issue for editors, then, as both Fellows and Jacobs argue, is
finding the point at which scribal embellishment becomes redaction, which, in
turn, blends into authorial composition. Jacobs suggests toward the end of his
essay that there are discernible categories within the range stretching from
copyist to author but that the gradations within this range can be very fine.
Another approach to finding this point might be to adapt to the medieval
situation Tanselle's idea of horizontal and vertical authorial revision. He uses
the terms to distinguish "attempts to improve the work in terms of its original
conception" (horizontal) from "the revision that shifts the conception and
thereby produces a different work" (vertical).[51] Clearly each editor must
decide if parallel-text editing is justified or a critical edition possible, no matter
what method one might use to establish the text. And further, the possibility

---

48. Allen, "Some Sceptical Observations," 12–13.
49. *Floris and Blauncheflur: A Middle English Romance,* ed. Franciscus Catharina De Vries
(Groeningen, 1966).
50. *King Alisaunder,* ed. G.V. Smithers, vol. 1, EETS 227 (London, 1952).
51. G. Thomas Tanselle, "The Editorial Problem of Final Authorial Intention," *Studies in
Bibliography* 29 (1976): 167–211; quotation on p. 195.

must be considered that two obviously related works, like the northern and southern versions of *Octovian*, might be better treated not in parallel but as two separate editions.[52]

In terms of practice, Fellows advocates a quite conservative approach in which obvious error is corrected but the attempt to discover the reading lying behind what is found in any given text does not lead to conjectural emendation. What she appears to advocate, in fact, is the application of the conservative best-text approach to each of the texts edited, perhaps on the theory that each is the best text of that particular version. The theoretical justification for this approach would be that the decision to offer a parallel-text edition, when not forced on the editor by manuscript damage, is a declaration either that the authorial text is unrecoverable, which is, in fact, the best-text position, or that a variety of authorial, or quasi-authorial, texts exists. Therefore, an attempt to discover and establish *the* authorial text runs counter to the evidence, although offering a corrected version of the various texts does not. Parallel-text editing thus theorized is a markedly different editorial option than recension or direct editing or even best-text editing, to which it would seem to be most closely related. Nevertheless, if one grants recovery of an authorial text, or even a number of them, to be the goal of editing, the parallel-text method remains fundamentally at one with the other traditional options available to the editor of a Middle English work.

Authorial Intention

Each of the four methods briefly discussed above represents an option open to editors depending on their perception of the relationship between the copies that survive for their work. What precisely this relationship is will have to be determined by each editor for the specific work in question, and it is not inconceivable that different editors could come to divergent conclusions and consequently produce quite different editions. Underlying decisions about editorial method and implicated fully in the analysis of the manuscript relations and their variants are the editor's knowledge of and assumptions about the relationship between authorial and scribal intentions. Even conservative best-text critics must deal with this relationship, as must editors of a diplomatic

---

52. Both versions have been edited by Frances McSparran: *Octovian*, EETS 289 (London, 1986) and *Octovian Imperator*, Middle English Texts Series, 11 (Heidelberg, 1979). Discussion of the versions' relationship to each other is found on pp. 48–53 of the former and pp. 32–38 of the latter.

edition, providing they choose to present something more than paleographical and codicological commentary. While an understanding of the particular relationship of author(s) and scribe(s) will undoubtedly develop in the course of examining what they produced, editors should acquaint themselves with various critical positions that have been taken in regard to author and scribe, particularly in the Middle English period.

A variety of editorial options currently being explored for postmedieval works would seem at first sight to offer attractive analogies to parallel-text editing of Middle English. These are editorial theories and practices that try to disclose the dynamic or unstable nature of the literary work as it moves through successive versions. The goal of these new approaches to editing, the most well known of which is genetic editing, is to enable the reader to see the work as a series of stages rather than as a static, finished product.[53] However, the Middle English editor must bear in mind, before considering these options, the limitations of the analogy. The vast amounts of data that characterize the modern, especially the nineteenth- and twentieth-century, textual situation make close scrutiny of the ever-changing text possible. However, virtually no Middle English work survives in this state, and the few that approximate it, for example, the various autograph copies of Capgrave's works, reveal above all how much has been lost.[54] If one compares, for example, the notebooks of James Joyce and the various versions of *Ulysses* to the surviving copies of even *Piers Plowman* or *The Canterbury Tales,* what is most obvious are the gaps in the evidence for the medieval works' development.[55]

A number of textual scholars, most notably Jerome J. McGann and D. F. McKenzie, have recently advocated a fundamental shift of emphasis away from the traditional goal of editing—recovery of the authorial text—to a more social or sociological textual orientation.[56] The author of the "original composition" should be regarded as a contributor to the social meaning of the text along with others who may have altered its "linguistic codes" or established its

53. Hans Walter Gabler, "The Synchrony and Diachrony of Texts: Practice and Theory of the Critical Edition of Joyce's *Ulysses,*" *Text* 1 (1984, for 1981): 305–26; Louis Hay, "Genetic Editing, Past and Future: A Few Reflections by a User," trans. J. M. Luccioni and Hans Walter Gabler, *Text* 3 (1987): 117–33; Donald H. Reiman, "'Versioning': The Presentation of Multiple Texts," in *Romantic Texts and Contexts* (Columbia, 1987), 167–80; Hans Zeller, "A New Approach to the Critical Constitution of Literary Texts," *Studies in Bibliography* 28 (1975): 231–64.

54. See note 101.

55. For references, see Hans Walter Gabler, "The Text as Process and the Problems of Intentionality," *Text* 3 (1987): 107–33.

56. The two most well known and cited books by these two scholars are Jerome J. McGann, *A Critique of Modern Textual Criticism* (Chicago, 1983 rpt. Charlottesville, Va., 1992); and D. F. McKenzie, *Bibliography and the Sociology of Texts* (London, 1986).

"bibliographical codes," to use McGann's terms.[57] Textual scholars ought to be concerned not only with the text that can be most closely associated with the author but also with all the various public shapes it acquired. Interest in a work should be reoriented toward its reception in the social milieu and away from its status as a product of the authorial creative intention. Therefore, presumably, editors should attempt to make editions that reflect this reception and the ongoing and various social life of the work rather than to fix the text as the record of authorial intention at some particular moment. The approach to the editing of medieval Russian chronicles known as textology, which accepts the accretions to the original work as worthy of independent textual status, seems somewhat analogous to the social approach to editing, and there may be some Middle English works, like the *Brut* chronicles, where this sort of approach might prove valuable.[58] A work like Nicholas Love's *Mirror of the Blessed Life of Christ* might also be susceptible to this approach, since the "publication" history of the text as an anti-Lollard tract could justify an edition of the derivative southern version as well as the authorial northern version, which the most recent editor has produced.[59] However, as with genetic editing, the social textual approach is best carried out on the basis of a vast amount of quite tightly integrated data having to do not only with authorial revision but publication history and reception of which medievalists can only be envious.

In fact, even the mainstream ideas of authorial intention associated with the Anglo-American school of textual scholarship can only be approximated in

---

57. Jerome J. McGann, "What is Critical Editing?" *Text* 5 (1991): 15–30; rpt. in Jerome J. McGann, *The Textual Condition* (Princeton, 1991), 48–68.

58. John L. Fennell, "Textology as a Key to the Study of Old Russian Literature and History," *Text* 1 (1984, for 1981): 157–66; Lister Matheson, "Historical Prose," in *Middle English Prose: A Critical Guide to Major Authors and Genres,* ed. A. S. G. Edwards (New Brunswick, N.J., 1984), 210–13.

59. Elizabeth Salter, "The Manuscripts of Nicholas Love's *Myrrour of the Blessed Lyf of Jesu Christ* and Related Texts," in *Middle English Prose: Essays on Bibliographical Problems,* ed. A. S. G. Edwards and Derek Pearsall (New York, 1981), 115–27; *Nicholas Love's Mirror of the Blessed Life of Christ,* ed. Michael G. Sargent, Garland Medieval Texts, 18 (New York, 1992). Also worth noting here are Stephen Knight, "Textual Variants: Textual Variance," *Southern Review* (Adelaide) 16 (1983): 44–54; Harold Love, "Sir Walter Greg and the Chaucerian Force Field," *Bulletin of the Bibliographical Society of Australia and New Zealand* 8 (1984): 73–81; and Stephanie Trigg, "The Politics of Medieval Editing: Knight's Quest and Love's Complaint," *Bulletin of the Bibliographical Society of Australia and New Zealand* 9 (1985): 15–22. Knight's quest is for a text with the "fullest socio-literary potency," and he chooses variants to that end; Love's complaint has to do with Knight's unorthodox methodology; Trigg wittily assesses both papers.

most Middle English situations.[60] The idea that the editor must privilege one moment in the author's relation to his own text by attempting to establish the state of the work at that moment, trying in the process not to incorporate but rather to eliminate nonauthorial influence, cannot be achieved with any certainty by Middle English editors or by editors of medieval and ancient works in general, as Tanselle points out.[61] Relative lack of evidence once again distinguishes the positions of textual scholars working on postmedieval works and the Middle English editor. Whereas an editor of a nineteenth-century work can attempt to sort out what might or might not be authorial revision and the chronology of the states of revision, often with the help of external evidence, the Middle English editor is usually left to inferring about these matters from internal evidence only.[62] This is not to suggest that such approaches are wholly invalid for editors of Middle English but rather to remind editors that significant methodological adjustment will be needed in order to adapt them to the task of editing Middle English.

Editors of Middle English would have a somewhat easier time if it could be shown that Middle English writers did not revise their work. Unfortunately, there is a good deal of evidence to the contrary. Signs of significant revision survive, in fact, for four of the best-known Middle English poems, Chaucer's *Canterbury Tales* and *Troilus and Criseyde,* Gower's *Confessio Amantis,* and *Piers Plowman.* The nature of these revisions has been argued over intensely by textual scholars, though the whole question of revision has been largely ignored by literary critics.[63] Occasionally, as in the past with *Piers Plowman* and in the present with *The Canterbury Tales* and *Confessio Amantis,*[64] it has

---

60. See, for example, Fredson Bowers, "Authorial Intention and Editorial Problems," *Text* 5 (1991): 49–62; James McLaverty, "The Concept of Authorial Intention in Textual Criticism," *Library,* 6th ser. 6 (1984): 121–38; Tanselle, "Editorial Problem." Also see Greetham, *Textual Scholarship,* 352–55, and the entry for *Intentionality* in his index.

61. Tanselle, "Classical, Biblical," 23–25.

62. F. Bowers, in his "Authorial Intention," reveals how much must be inferred for postmedieval textual evidence as well.

63. N. F. Blake, "Geoffrey Chaucer: Textual Transmission and Editing," in Minnis and Brewer, *Crux and Controversy,* 19–38; Ralph Hanna III, "Authorial Versions, Rolling Revision, Scribal Error? or, The Truth about Truth," *Studies in the Age of Chaucer* 10 (1988): 23–40, reprinted in Hanna, *Pursuing History,* 159–73; and "Presenting Chaucer as Author," in Machan, *Medieval Literature,* 17–39, reprinted in Hanna, *Pursuing History,* 174–94; Hudson, "The Variable Text"; Derek Pearsall, "Authorial Revision in Some Late-Medieval English Texts," in Minnis and Brewer, *Crux and Controversy,* 39–48.

64. See Charlotte Brewer, "Editors of *Piers Plowman,*" in *The Medieval Text: Editors and Critics,* ed. Marianne Bloch, Andreas Haarder, and Julia McGrew (Odense, 1990), 45–63; Blake, *Textual Tradition;* Peter Nicholson, "Gower's Revisions in the *Confessio Amantis,*" *Chaucer*

been suggested that these revisions were scribal rather than authorial; however, most scholars believe that a significant number of authorial variants survive for all these works. Nevertheless, lacking external evidence by which to organize this internal evidence chronologically or even designate any specific variant as unequivocally authorial, critics are forced to fall back on highly conjectural theories of scribal and authorial practice and book production: instructive comparison can be made between Blake's explanation of the "publication" of *The Canterbury Tales* and Hanna's.[65] In the case of *Piers Plowman,* Skeat's three-version theory is under significant scrutiny: a fourth authorial version has been proposed, and others are considered possible, while the ability to discriminate between authorial and scribal revision has been called into question.[66] The nature of revision in *Troilus and Criseyde* also continues to be debated.[67]

So Middle English editors find themselves in a paradoxical situation. Looking at the four editing methods discussed above—direct, recensionist, best text, parallel text—one sees a persisting interest in discovering authorial intention and a desire to recover the authorial text. Proponents of the first two think that the editor can go a long way toward realizing this desire, while followers of the last two do not. Parallel-text editing as described by Fellows addresses the further possibility that the unrecoverable authorial text may itself be re-authorized, as it were, by redactors with the subsequent copies acquiring or tending to acquire the status of separate works. Despite these differences, however, all four methods proceed from the assumption that an authorial text once existed. But, in fact, relatively few Middle English authors are known by name, and only scanty biographical details can be added to most of these. Almost no Middle English writers have left autograph copies of their works. Furthermore, verifiable details concerning the composition, revision, and publication of specific works are almost wholly lacking. To put it succinctly,

---

Review 19 (1984): 123–43, and "Poet and Scribe in the Manuscripts of Gower's *Confessio Amantis,*" in Pearsall, *Manuscripts and Texts,* 130–42.

65. Blake, *Textual Tradition;* and Hanna, "Hengwrt Manuscript."

66. Brewer, "Authorial vs. Scribal"; William Langland, *Piers Plowman: The Z Version,* ed. A. G. Rigg and Charlotte Brewer, Studies and Texts, 59 (Toronto, 1983).

67. Kevin K. Cureton, "Chaucer's Revision of *Troilus and Criseyde,*" *Studies in Bibliography* 42 (1989): 153–84; Ralph Hanna III, "Robert K. Root," in *Editing Chaucer: The Great Tradition,* ed. Paul G. Ruggiers (Norman, Okla., 1984), 191–205; Charles A. Owen, Jr., "*Troilus and Criseyde:* The Question of Chaucer's Revision," *Studies in the Age of Chaucer* 9 (1987): 155–72. This and many other questions relevant to editing are discussed in Stephen A. Barney, *Studies in 'Troilus': Chaucer's Text, Meter, and Diction,* Medieval Texts and Studies, 14 (East Lansing, 1993).

editors of Middle English typically seek, or at least desire to find, the authorial composition of an author about whom, in the vast majority of cases, they know practically nothing either as a person or as a writer.

As already mentioned, some textual theorists like McGann have argued that the desire to recover the authorial text, the original composition, should be significantly deemphasized as a goal of editing. They argue that this desire is a modern, or perhaps a Romantic, preoccupation that in fact distorts the true textual history of a work. In regard to medieval works, Bernard Cerquiglini and the New Philologists argue for a renewed interest in the material contexts of medieval literature, what they often call the manuscript culture.[68] As with McGann they emphasize the response of readers to text and context, although they would appear to dispense with the significant emphasis that McGann retains on the author. Similarly motivated relative diminutions of the author can be seen in statements by Robert S. Sturges and by Karl D. Uitti and Gina Greco.[69] But the most extreme repudiation of the modern preoccupation with seeking the Middle English authorial text has been fashioned by Tim William Machan.[70]

Machan acknowledges that there was an "author function" in medieval literary culture, but he argues at length against the applicability of the "human-ist" conception of the author to Middle English writing. For the medievals the conception of the work, its *res,* is essential, not its *verba,* which constitutes any given text of this *res.* "Within this framework, words and their layout are not integral to a given text, which in turn is not integral to a given work."[71] Therefore, even the New Philologists' concentration on the material manifesta-tions of the manuscript culture is, for Machan, misguided. He does insist on maintaining a distinction between individual composition *(dictare)* and scribal production *(scribere),* but the idea of trying to establish an authorial text consisting of the words the author actually wrote would seem to be, from Machan's point of view, a modern academic exercise ultimately irrelevant to an understanding of Middle English literary culture.

---

68. Bernard Cerquiglini, *Éloge de la variante: Histoire critique de la philologie* (Paris, 1989); Stephen G. Nichols, "On the Sociology of Medieval Manuscript Annotation," in *Annota-tion and Its Texts,* ed. Stephen A. Barney (Oxford, 1991), 43–73. See also Nichols's "Introduction: Philology in a Manuscript Culture" and various other contributions to the "New Philology" issue of *Speculum* 65 (1990).

69. Karl D. Uitti and Gina Greco, "Computerization, Canonicity, and the Old French Scribe: The Twelfth and Thirteenth Centuries," *Text* 6 (1994): 133–52; Robert S. Sturges, "Textual Scholarship: Ideologies of Literary Production," *Exemplaria* 3 (1991): 109–31.

70. Machan, *Textual Criticism.*

71. Machan, *Textual Criticism,* 162.

The idea that the editor should *not* seek an authorial text, since such a text was not of special interest to the putative author, obviously challenges the preconceptions of most editors of Middle English, regardless of the method they might adopt in editing. Even best-text editors, as Machan himself points out, believe in the idea of an authorial text that once existed, although now unrecoverable. Only a purely transcriptional or diplomatic edition of a single manuscript might not appear at least to gesture toward an original composition lying somewhere behind the surviving copy. It is too early to ascertain the influence that these radical ideas, not only of Machan, but of the New Philologists and the social textual critics, will have on editing itself. However, I would like to offer a few observations on their suitability to the Middle English situation.

McGann, Uitti and Greco, and Machan all seem to believe that computer technology provides, or will provide, the opportunity for their new visions of textual relations to be realized in something that will replace conventional codex editions.[72] Traditional textual criticism developed along with and, so the argument goes, because of print technology and therefore reflects the nature of this technology; computer technology will enable a new, more accurate or comprehensive perception of the medieval manuscript culture to be realized. Peter Baker's essay in this volume gives some sense of how this technology will be employed to present textual information and how the electronic edition will have a flexibility unachievable in book form. One wonders, however, what the users of such editions will want or tolerate. Baker offers the hypothetical example near the beginning of his essay of a reader of lines 127–40 of Chaucer's *Parliament of Fowls* linking by means of hypertext not only to related passages in Dante's *Inferno* but to an edition with commentary of the whole *Commedia*. One question that arises from this example is, would a reader interested in examining this sort of literary relation be interested as well, at the same time, in sorting through the variants and the relations of manuscripts of either work? Even if the reader were primarily concerned with variant readings in the *Parliament* passage, or with a particular copy of the work, would they not want as well the editor's judgment as to what constituted, or might have constituted, the authorial text? A further question raised by Baker's example in regard to replicating the medieval manuscript environment

---

72. Jerome J. McGann, "A Response to T. H. Howard-Hill," *Text* 5 (1991): 47–48; Machan, *Textual Criticism,* 190; Uitti and Greco, "Computerization." See also Murray McGillivray, "Towards a Post-Critical Edition: Theory, Hypertext, and the Presentation of Middle English Works," *Text* 7 (1994): 175–99.

is, to what extent does the immediacy of hypertext at all mimic the situation of the relatively isolated medieval reader, or writer, for that matter?

A further methodological problem for an editor involves the process of establishing a text while ignoring an authorial one. One of the main objectives of McGann and a number of other textual scholars in recent years has been to open a dialogue between textual and literary critics. Important collections of essays have appeared that try to bridge this gap between the two camps of literary study, including McGann's *Textual Criticism and Literary Interpretation,* Cohen's *Devils and Angels,* and, focusing on Middle English, Pearsall's *Manuscripts and Readers in Fifteenth-Century England,* Machan's *Medieval Texts,* and Minnis and Brewer's *Crux and Controversy.*[73] An unintended but useful effect of this movement has been a growing realization that textual criticism and editing need not, perhaps cannot, be so closely related to one another as has generally been accepted. This is one of the main points of T. H. Howard-Hill's criticisms of the social textual approach: it offers no practical means to establish a text that replaces the authorial one.[74] Derek Pearsall has also questioned the necessity of connecting textual criticism and editing, allowing that there may be basically two kinds of editions needed: one to satisfy the theoretical aims of some textual scholars, and one for the much larger audience of readers who would probably be more interested in something approximating the authorial text.[75] To judge from his remarks, Pearsall would frequently put himself in the latter group, and Edwards also has recently reiterated the fundamental interest in the authorial text.[76]

Even without these problems of audience and methodology that a de-emphasis of the authorial text raises, seeking the authorial text remains theoretically defensible, even for Middle English. Attempts such as McGann's to situate the author in a social context and to concentrate on the social practices that combine to give the author's work its particular public manifestations must necessarily obscure from view those features or qualities of the author that made him or her stand out from that society. In the case of Machan's theory of a typical medieval Englishman or woman fulfilling the "author function," these

---

73. McGann, *Textual Criticism;* Machan, *Medieval Literature;* Philip Cohen, ed., *Devils and Angels: Textual Editing and Literary Theory* (Charlottesville, Va., 1991); Derek Pearsall, ed., *Manuscripts and Readers in Fifteenth-Century England: The Literary Implications of Manuscript Study* (Cambridge, 1983). Many of the essays in Minnis and Brewer, *Crux and Controversy,* are relevant to this question.

74. T. H. Howard-Hill, "Theory and Praxis in the Social Approach to Editing," *Text* 5 (1991): 31–46.

75. Pearsall, "Theory and Practice," 117.

76. Edwards, "Editing Middle English," 199.

features or qualities would appear to be dismissed altogether. They would include the craft or technique of the poet, the significant bilingual skill of the translator, or the expertise in the language of a technical subject, in each case acquired after many years of training and practice. Such special qualities enable the author or redactor not only to engage with an ongoing literary tradition but, through sustained application of this talent, to participate in this tradition, perpetuating or changing it, and probably both simultaneously. To be sure, those scribes who make occasional, intermittent alterations in the text, the illuminators and rubricators, those engaged in the various tasks associated with the physical production of the manuscript and later the printed book, participate as well in the perpetuation and change of literary tradition. Their contributions deserve study as do the "market forces" that affect these contributions, not the least being the contemporary audience's reception of the work in its manuscript context. The perceived cultural impact of the work is also worthy of study. But without the individual author or redactor's sustained application of his or her particular talent, the work does not get written and the subsequent "socialization" of the text does not take place. On that ground alone the authorial text can be privileged and made the focus of an edition. This is not to say that different foci might not be found. Some works can be edited in a variety of ways in order to exemplify different features of their textual history, as has already been suggested. But an editorial decision to rule out any attempt to recover the authorial text on theoretical grounds would require considerable explanation.

My position is not dissimilar to the one adopted by Tanselle in response to Morse Peckham, who argues that a

> writer produces utterances because he is a human being. It is a condition of being human. We do not know why human beings produce utterances, nor even how.[77]

Peckham can see no logical reason therefore to privilege the author's efforts over any other contributor's to the discourse we associate with him. Tanselle responds most fully to Peckham's position in his "Greg's Theory of Copy-Text and the Editing of American Literature," but succinctly summarizes his position in "The Problem of Final Authorial Intention":

---

77. Morse Peckham, "Reflections on the Foundations of Modern Textual Editing," *Proof* 1 (1971): 122–55; quotation on p. 139.

> I would . . . claim that the initiator of a discourse can be identified as a
> historical figure (whether or not his name is known . . .), distinct from
> others because he is the initiator; that an interest may attach to this
> initiator; and that the task of attempting to segregate his contributions to
> the discourse from those of others is therefore one legitimate scholarly
> pursuit.[78]

Every extended passage of Middle English, however mundane, represents for
us a historical event, because of the comparative rarity of such evidence, and
the initiators of these events, whose names are mostly lost, are our authors.

In the context of Middle English, the ability to be such an initiator constitutes a talent that we find worthy of study. I do not refer to an exalted
individual talent consciously exercised within or against a great literary tradition. The particular talent that distinguishes the author and redactor of the
Middle English work consists of nothing more, or less, than an ability to
constrain language, even at the level of the word, to convey a thought or
feeling, no matter how conventional the thought, the feeling, or the language
itself might be. Coupled with this must be the motivation both to use this
primary talent in a sustained way and to cause the resulting composition to be
inscribed. This is as mundane and capacious a definition of authorship as one
could likely have: it includes writers as diverse as Chaucer and the appallingly
inadequate translator of the *Letter from Alexander to Aristotle*.[79] But it ex-
cludes nonauthors, those who lacked the talent, motivation, or means to write
works that have come down to us. The crucial point is not that the author or
redactor is great, that the technique is flawless, that the grasp of French or Latin
is sure; nor is it that the responses of others to the author's work are unimportant. Rather, Middle English authors are those who have committed themselves
through recorded use of language to a degree of participation in literary culture
that can only be inferred for most of those who make up their audience.

Even though medieval writers knew that copies of their works would likely
be altered, it is unlikely that any of them who, for example, struggled to
translate a French or Latin text into Middle English would have been indifferent to changes in their wording. It seems unlikely that a rhyming or allitera-

---

78. G. Thomas Tanselle, "Greg's Theory of Copy-Text and the Editing of American Literature," *Studies in Bibliography* 28 (1975): 167–229, esp. 215–19, and "Final Authorial Intention,"
209, n. 68.

79. Thomas Hahn, "The Middle English *Letter of Alexander to Aristotle:* Introduction,
Sources, and Commentary," *Mediaeval Studies* 41 (1979): 117–45.

tive poet would be indifferent to a copyist marring rhyme or alliteration in their works. While Machan's idea of the primacy of *res* over *verba* is an interesting one, to suggest that writers as craftsmen, even indifferent or bad ones, would regard one word as just as good as another is incredible.

If this position on the author is compelling, then it renders the recovery of the authorial text not only desirable but *theoretically* possible. It would remain a desirable goal because the author (or redactor), unlike others who can participate in the text after the (or an) authorized copy is relinquished, is responsible for initiating the sustained particular engagement with the literary tradition that the work represents (even if the work is commissioned, since the concern of the editor is for the particular forms of the text). It would be theoretically recoverable because the author's necessary interest in and ability to constrain language to accomplish the task results in a work that reflects that interest and ability: a text in which language, even at the level of the word, has been purposefully (if not brilliantly) chosen. This is not to suggest that Middle English authors had fixed spelling systems, or that they would not revise their works with each copy that they made and relinquished, or that they did not make mistakes. The point is not that a single text, fixed by the Middle English author in every detail, can be recovered by an editor, for in many cases we would not even know if we had recovered it, but that the attempt to recover an authorial text continues to be a legitimate aim of Middle English editors. That certain texts have been so altered in transmission that the authorial text is beyond recognition or recovery does not mean that the effort to recover that text should not be contemplated.

How, then, might an editor go about seeking the elusive authorial text? Some might find Steven Mailloux's idea of inferred intentionality an attractive theoretical position from which to begin. He defines it as follows:

> Inferred intentions characterize the critic's description of the convention-based responses that the author, as he is writing, understands he will achieve as a result (at least in part) of his projected reader's recognition of his intention.[80]

Mailloux endeavors to shift the focus of the authorial intention debate away from the final authorial intention of Tanselle to intention during the process of composition. He emphasizes with this definition the conventionality of authorial writing, the analysis of which provides the critic with the opportunity to infer the author's intentions in employing these conventions. Because of the

---

80. Steven Mailloux, *Interpretive Conventions: The Reader in the Study of American Fiction* (Ithaca, 1982), 99.

conventionality of much Middle English writing, this would seem to be a promising position. However, inasmuch as language forms the basis of linguistic conventions, Middle English editors find themselves in a less fortunate position than their modern counterparts. Even though the *Middle English Dictionary* and the *Historical Thesaurus* are both near completion, they will only provide the basis for future studies of Middle English lexicology and affective stylistics, which are much needed.

Judgment of variants lies at the heart of the matter, but when based solely on literary taste it is an act fraught with uncertainty, or what's worse, unjustified certainty. Hans Zeller writes persuasively of the tendency over time to change one's mind about readings, and particularly to become more tolerant of what might be authorial. Donaldson writes amusingly of the same phenomenon, likening the editor to a husband who simply can't make up his mind whom to stay married to.[81] Certain procedures, however, do seem worthy of trial. The Turville-Petre article mentioned above and the Duggan and Turville-Petre edition of *The Wars of Alexander* provide examples of how various literary techniques and practices peculiar to the author might be used, during long years of labor, to establish a text much closer to the authorial one than any of the surviving witnesses.[82] For verse, a discernible metrical or rhythmical system would be an obvious boon to the editor. However, the delineation and application of such a system must be executed with great caution.[83] Since so much of Middle English writing is translation, comparison to a source text is another technique available to the editor that would seem to offer the opportunity to recover the authorial text. However, the editor must not only find a source that is verbally close to the Middle English work but also clearly ascertain the abilities and intentions of the author as a translator.[84] The method, from the editing of classical literature, for choosing among variants known as

---

81. Zeller, "New Approach," 259; Donaldson, "Psychology," 103.

82. Turville-Petre, "Editing *Wars of Alexander*"; Duggan and Turville-Petre, *The Wars of Alexander.*

83. Derek Pearsall, "Chaucer's Meter: The Evidence of the Manuscripts," in Machan, *Medieval Literature,* 41–57. See also his "Text, Textual Criticism, and Fifteenth-Century Manuscript Production," in *Fifteenth-Century Studies,* ed. R. F. Yeager (Hamden, 1984), 121–36, especially 125. For a rigorous application of metrical theory to textual problems, see Hoyt N. Duggan, "Alliterative Patterning as a Basis for Emendation in Middle English Alliterative Poetry," *Studies in the Age of Chaucer* 8 (1986): 73–105. See also Thorlac Turville-Petre, "Emendation on the Grounds of Alliteration in *The Wars of Alexander,*" *English Studies* 61 (1980): 302–17.

84. D. C. Greetham, "Models for Textual Transmission of Translation: The Case of John Trevisa," *Studies in Bibliography* 37 (1984): 131–55; Ralph Hanna III, "Editing Middle English Prose Translations: How Prior Is the Source?" *Text* 4 (1988): 207–16. Also see Hamel in this volume.

difficilior or *durior lectio,* while perhaps applicable to some works, has been examined and found wanting for many genres of Middle English writing.[85] While seeking the authorial text, the editor must be prepared to face the prospect that it is not recoverable in every detail, and that a best-text or parallel-text approach would be advisable, and that in the case of a work surviving in only one copy, even a very conservative edition might be the best achievable.

Scribal Intention

Regardless of the type of edition one chooses to attempt, it is essential to try to come to terms with the particular habits and practices of the scribes who have made the copies. Unfortunately, information on Middle English scribes is widely scattered, and as yet there is no consensus on their position in the dissemination of Middle English writing. This essay will conclude with an effort to acquaint the reader with some of the material on this subject and on book production in medieval England.

Obviously scribes played a key role in book production in medieval England. But until recently there has been little specific study of book production as a whole or, consequently, of the precise nature of the scribal role. The typical site for book production in the early Middle English period was a scriptorium attached to a religious institution,[86] and such scriptoria continued to be important sources throughout the period. Peter J. Lucas's "A Fifteenth-Century Scribe at Work under Authorial Scrutiny" might give us some indication of the differentiation of roles in the scriptorial setting, although one should not be overhasty to generalize from this one example.[87] In the fourteenth and fifteenth centuries book production in England became much more diverse, as the various essays in Griffiths and Pearsall's *Book Production and Publishing* make clear.[88] From this collection the essays by A. S. G. Edwards and Derek Pearsall and by Julia Boffey and John J. Thompson are particularly informative

---

85. Robert Adams, "Editing and the Limitations of *Durior Lectio,*" *Yearbook of Langland Studies* 5 (1991): 7–15; Edwards, "Middle English Romance," 94; Pearsall, "Theory and Practice," 111.

86. See Malcolm Parkes, *Scribes, Scripts, and Readers* (London, 1991); and Florence Edler de Roover, "The Scriptorium," in *The Medieval Library,* ed. James Westfall Thompson (Chicago, 1939), 594–612.

87. See note 101.

88. Jeremy Griffiths and Derek Pearsall, eds., *Book Production and Publishing in Britain: 1375–1475* (Cambridge, 1989).

on scribal activity in relation to book production in this later period. Boffey and Thompson provide a great deal of information about specific scribes.[89]

One of the most influential essays in regard to scribal involvement in book production is A. I. Doyle and Malcolm Parkes's "The Production of the Copies of the *Canterbury Tales*," which argues that the two most authoritative *Canterbury Tales* manuscripts, Hengwrt and Ellesmere, were copied by the same scribe from different exemplars, yielding remarkably different codicological and textual results.[90] The subsequent debate over this thesis between R. Vance Ramsey and M. L. Samuels points up the degree to which the evidence in this area is open to varied interpretation.[91] Also instructive in this regard are the different hypotheses of Blake, Hanna, and Owen about the development of the *Canterbury Tales* manuscripts[92] and the debate over the relationship of *The Equatorie of the Planets* to Chaucer, although this last debate does not primarily concern book production.[93]

For discussion of scripts and bibliographical references thereto, see Edwards's "Manuscript and Text" in this volume. On the tendency of fourteenth- and fifteenth-century scribes to change the dialectal features of their English exemplars, see Michael Benskin and Margaret Laing's "Translation and *Mischsprachen* in Middle English Manuscripts."[94] Also interesting in this

---

89. A. S. G. Edwards and Derek Pearsall, "The Manuscripts of the Major English Poetic Texts," in Griffiths and Pearsall, *Book Production,* 257–78; Julia Boffey and John J. Thompson, "Anthologies and Miscellanies: Production and Choice of Texts," in Griffiths and Pearsall, *Book Production,* 279–315.

90. A. I. Doyle and M. B. Parkes, "The Production of the Copies of the *Canterbury Tales* and the *Confessio Amantis,*" in *Medieval Scribes, Manuscripts, and Libraries: Essays Presented to N. R. Ker,* ed. M. B. Parkes and A. G. Watson (London, 1978), 163–210.

91. R. Vance Ramsey, "The Hengwrt and Ellesmere Manuscripts of the *Canterbury Tales:* Different Scribes," *Studies in Bibliography* 35 (1982): 133–54; M. L. Samuels, "The Scribe of the Hengwrt and Ellesmere Manuscripts of *The Canterbury Tales,*" *Studies in the Age of Chaucer* 5 (1983): 49–65; R. Vance Ramsey, "Paleography and Scribes of Shared Training," *Studies in the Age of Chaucer* 8 (1986): 107–44.

92. See note 27 above.

93. On this debate, see the following, among many others: A. S. G. Edwards and Linne R. Mooney, "Is the *Equatorie of the Planets* a Chaucer Holograph?" *Chaucer Review* 26 (1991): 31–42; Pamela Robinson, "Geoffrey Chaucer and the *Equatorie of the Planets:* The State of the Problem," *Chaucer Review* 26 (1991): 17–30; Larry Benson, "Chaucer's Spelling Reconsidered," *English Manuscript Studies* 3 (1992): 1–28; Stephen Partridge, "The Vocabulary of *The Equatorie of the Planets,*" *English Manuscript Studies* 3 (1992): 29–37.

94. Michael Benskin and Margaret Laing, "Translation and *Mischsprachen* in Middle English Manuscripts," in *So Mony People Longages and Tonges: Philological Essays in Scots and Mediaeval English Presented to Angus McIntosh,* ed. Michael Benskin and M. L. Samuels (Edinburgh, 1981), 55–106; (substantially reprinted in vol. 1 of the *Linguistic Atlas of Late Mediaeval English*). See also various essays in *Middle English Dialectology: Essays on Some Principles and Problems,* ed. Margaret Laing (Aberdeen, 1989).

regard is Anne Hudson's "Tradition and Innovation in Some Middle English Manuscripts" as well as articles by G. L. Brook and T. M. Smallwood, who each provide examples of double copying by a single scribe of a passage from the same exemplar.[95] This material is primarily of linguistic interest (see Lucas and Mills in this volume), but Benskin and Laing do give some indication of how the kind of analysis they discuss can yield textual evidence.[96]

For an analysis of the process of copying itself with a discussion of the errors that may result at any point in this process, see Vinaver;[97] H. J. Chaytor adds important points on the aural aspect of copying not treated by Vinaver.[98] Editors who have adopted the direct method of editing have provided exhaustive catalogs of scribal error and variation that they have discovered in the manuscripts of the specific works they treat.[99] Kane provides a succinct analysis of his estimation of scribal motivation and performance in *Piers Plowman* in his essay "The Text" in *A Companion to Piers Plowman.*[100]

Finally, specific scribes known to be responsible for more than one manuscript have been identified, some even by name, and studies have been written on their habits. Though focused on individual scribes, a number of these studies further reveal the general range of scribal intention in the Middle English period. Perhaps most important in this group is John Capgrave, who was an author, scribe, and "publisher." Peter J. Lucas has devoted a number of articles to Capgrave's work as a scribe, and his "Scribe and Publisher" stands as a particularly fine example of the kinds of evidence potentially available and how it can be analyzed.[101] Robert Thornton has also attracted a good deal of

---

95. Anne Hudson, "Tradition and Innovation in Some Middle English Manuscripts," *Review of English Studies,* n.s. 17 (1966): 359–72; G. L. Brook, "A Piece of Evidence for the Study of Middle English Spelling," *Neuphilologische Mitteilungen* 73 (1972): 25–28; T. M. Smallwood, "Another Example of the Double-Copying of a Passage of Middle English," *Neuphilologische Mitteilungen* 87 (1986): 550–54. See also J. Bowers, "Hoccleve's Two Copies."

96. Benskin and Laing, "Translation and *Mischsprachen,*" 85.

97. Vinaver, "Principles of Textual Emendation." R. W. Burchfield discusses a particular source of error in early Middle English texts in "A Source of Scribal Error in Early Middle English Manuscripts," *Medium Aevum* 22 (1953): 10–17.

98. H. J. Chaytor, "Reading and Writing," in *From Script to Print: An Introduction to Medieval Vernacular Literatures,* 2d ed. (London, 1966), 5–21.

99. See notes 41 and 43 above.

100. George Kane, "The Text," in *A Companion to* Piers Plowman, ed. John Alford (Berkeley, 1988), 175–200.

101. Peter J. Lucas, "John Capgrave, O.S.A. (1393–1464) : Scribe and 'Publisher,'" *Transactions of the Cambridge Bibliographical Society* 5 (1969): 1–35, and "An Author as Copyist of His Own Work: John Capgrave," in *New Science out of Old Books: Studies in Manuscripts and Early Printed Books in Honour of A. I. Doyle,* ed. Richard Beadle and A. J. Piper (Aldershot, 1995), 227–48. The latter contains bibliographical references to Lucas's other writing on Capgrave. See also "A Fifteenth-Century Scribe at Work under Authorial Scrutiny: An Incident from John Capgrave's

attention both as a scribe and as collector.[102] John Shirley, Thomas Hoccleve, and the as yet unidentified "Lydgate scribe" are other important late Middle English scribes who each are responsible for a body of work.[103] Also unidentified but very interesting is the scribe responsible for Huntington HM 114, which contains a highly conflated copy of *Piers Plowman*.[104] This scribe might be regarded as a redactor, as might the scribes/*disours* discussed by Maldwyn Mills.[105] A number of scholars have investigated scribal participation, or attempted participation, in the works they were copying. Of particular note in this area are Elspeth Kennedy's "The Scribe as Editor," John J. Thompson's "Textual Instability," Peter Nicholson's "Poet and Scribe," Kate Harris's "John Gower's *Confessio Amantis*," and Barry Windeatt's "The Scribes as Chaucer's Early Critics,"[106] as well as the direct editors mentioned above.[107]

Scriptorium," *Studies in Bibliography* 34 (1981): 66–95. Many of these articles are reprinted in Lucas's *From Author to Audience: John Capgrave and Medieval Publication* (Dublin, 1997).

102. Hoyt N. Duggan, "Scribal Self-Correction and Editorial Theory," *Neuphilologische Mitteilungen* 91 (1990): 215–27; Mary Hamel, "Scribal Self-Corrections in the Thornton Manuscript," *Studies in Bibliography* 36 (1983): 119–37; George R. Keiser, "Lincoln Cathedral MS 91: Life and Milieu of the Scribe," *Studies in Bibliography* 32 (1979): 158–79; John J. Thompson, *Robert Thornton and the London Thornton Manuscript* (Cambridge, 1987), and "The Compiler in Action: Robert Thornton and the 'Thornton' Romances in Lincoln Cathedral MS 91," in Pearsall, *Manuscripts and Readers,* 113–24.

103. A. I. Doyle, "More Light on John Shirley," *Medium Aevum* 30 (1961): 93–101; Jeremy Griffiths, "A Newly Identified Manuscript Inscribed by John Shirley," *Library,* 6th ser., 14 (1992): 83–93. See also A. S. G. Edwards, "Lydgate Manuscripts: Some Directions for Future Research," in Pearsall, *Manuscripts and Readers,* 15–26, esp. 19–21; J. Bowers, "Hoccleve's Two Copies"; H. C. Schulz, "Thomas Hoccleve, Scribe," *Speculum* 12 (1937): 71–81; Edwards, "Lydgate Manuscripts"; and Kathleen Scott, "Lydgate's Lives of SS Edmund and Fremund: A Newly Discovered Manuscript in Arundel Castle," *Viator* 13 (1982): 335–66.

104. Ralph Hanna III, "The Scribe of Huntington HM 114," *Studies in Bibliography* 42 (1989): 120–33.

105. Maldwyn Mills, "A Medieval Reviser at Work," *Medium Aevum* 32 (1963): 11–23.

106. Nicholson, "Poet and Scribe"; Kate Harris, "John Gower's *Confessio Amantis:* The Virtues of Bad Texts," in Pearsall, *Manuscripts and Readers,* 27–40; Barry Windeatt, "The Scribes as Chaucer's Early Critics," *Studies in the Age of Chaucer* 1 (1979): 119–41. See also Elspeth Kennedy, "The Scribe as Editor," in *Mélanges de langue et de littérature du Moyen Age et de la Renaissance* 112, tome 1 (Geneva, 1970), 524–31; John J. Thompson, "Textual Instability and the Late Medieval Reputation of Some Middle English Religious Literature," *Text* 5 (1991): 175–94.

107. Also worthy of note are Norman Davis, "A Scribal Problem in the Paston Letters," *English and Germanic Studies* 4 (1951–52): 31–64, and "A Paston Hand," *Review of English Studies,* n.s. 3 (1952), 209–21; A. I. Doyle, "An Unrecognized Piece of *Piers the Ploughman Creed* and Other Works by Its Scribe," *Speculum* 34 (1959): 428–35, and "The Work of a Late Fifteenth-Century Scribe, William Ebesham," *Bulletin of the John Rylands Library* 39 (1957): 298–325; Peter J. Lucas, "William Gybbe of Wisbech: A Fifteenth-Century English Scribe," *Codices Manuscripti* 11 (1985): 41–64; C. A. Luttrell, "Three North-West Midland Manuscripts," *Neophilologus* 42 (1958): 38–50; C. van Buuren Veenebos, "John Asloan, an Edinburgh Scribe," *English Studies* 47 (1966): 365–72.

Perspectives on the Editing of Literary Texts

Reflections on the Editing of Middle English Texts

N. F. Blake

I wish to consider how Middle English texts, particularly literary texts, have been edited over the last hundred years or so. I will focus especially upon *The Owl and the Nightingale (O&N), Sir Gawain and the Green Knight (Gawain)*, and *Piers Plowman (Piers)*. The reason for the choice of these texts is determined partly because they are among those commonly read by undergraduates or postgraduates and partly because they survive in a differing number of manuscripts and so might be thought to present a range of problems in editorial procedure. *O&N* is extant in two manuscripts, *Gawain* in only one, and *Piers* in numerous manuscripts that are thought to represent three and possibly four different authorial versions of the poem.

We need to remind ourselves that the editing of Middle English manuscripts was for a long time associated with philological study, which required relatively conservative editions so that each text could be studied as close to its surviving form as possible. (This conservatism did not mean that editors necessarily confined themselves only to a single manuscript if more than one manuscript of a text survived, because establishing the "original" form of the text was important to philological enquiry.) The Early English Text Society, for example, was established in 1864 "for the purpose of bringing the mass of Old English Literature within the reach of the ordinary student."[1] While it is true that "philology" at this time encompassed the historical study of language, literature, and culture in general, the Society's belief was that the "ordinary student" clearly directed his antiquarian interests, in the first instance, toward language, philology as it is more narrowly defined, rather than toward literature:

---

1. From a statement published with the 1896 reprint of *Early English Alliterative Poems,* ed. Richard Morris, EETS 1 (London, 1896).

During the thirty-three years of the Society's existence, it has produced, with whatever shortcomings, an amount of good solid work for which all students of our Language, and some of our Literature, must be grateful, and which has rendered possible the beginnings (at least) of proper Histories and Dictionaries of the Language and Literature, and has illustrated the thoughts, the life, the manners and customs of our forefathers.[2]

While it would be unfair to suggest that the Society's early editors always ignored literary merit, their perception that their audience was primarily interested in language necessarily influenced the kind of linguistically conservative edition they produced. Moreover, the Society's audience-directed goal of producing works for the "ordinary student" meant that theoretical concerns regarding editing and textual criticism were perhaps of less importance, at least to some editors, than simply getting a text out to the readers.

The prestige of the Society encouraged editors of Middle English texts generally to maintain a conservative view of their texts as regards both accidentals and substantials, though attitudes to the former changed over time. Moreover, the Society's volumes soon began to be used by readers for the *Oxford English Dictionary,* who were anxious to discover both the earliest occurrence and the peculiar spellings of each word so that its history could be presented fully in the dictionary. The close relationship between EETS and *OED* further established the format of the Middle English edition as conservative and with a primary focus on language.

This conservative, philologically-oriented attitude has persisted for many years in the editing of Middle English texts and still prevails among some editors. The discussions of editorial technique, which have figured so prominently in textual studies of the last thirty years, have made little impact on the way in which Middle English texts have been edited.[3] Not surprisingly, medievalists have contributed very little to this debate; that Middle English texts are different from other texts appears to be accepted even by those who are outside medieval studies.[4] Further, besides being unconcerned with theoretical issues

---

2. Ibid.

3. G. Thomas Tanselle, "Recent Editorial Discussion and the Central Questions of Editing," *Studies in Bibliography* 34 (1981): 23–65; and Peter L. Shillingsburg, "An Inquiry into the Social Status of Texts and Modes of Textual Criticism," *Studies in Bibliography* 42 (1989): 55–79.

4. Cf. for example the comment by Fredson Bowers: "The days are long since gone when it is practicable for a publisher to issue an edition that is designed only for the professional scholar (medieval literature necessarily excepted) and does not seek among its purchasers the general literate reader with an interest in the work being printed, including collegiate students at an early stage in their training" ("Regularization in Critical Texts," *Studies in Bibliography* 42 [1989]: 81.)

of textual scholarship, editors have largely lost touch with the capabilities and expectations of the "ordinary student," which have changed dramatically since the mid-nineteenth century. General agreement seems to remain that the orthographic details of a text's language must be retained, even when an edition is intended for undergraduates, who are apparently seen only as future scholars to be trained from the beginning in philological technique. The fear of yielding an inch in this matter has been prompted by the anxiety that any relinquishing of standards would open the floodgates to the study of texts in modernized versions or translations. It may well be that many Middle English teachers contrast what they consider desirable for the study of their own texts with the modernization typical in editions of Shakespeare's works. Perhaps because of this, there are few studies of Shakespeare's language, for he is seen as a dramatist to be read for literary appreciation and not one to be quarried for information about the language. Yet even while the old conservative attitude persists, almost all Middle English scholars read and teach Chaucer in editions that have introduced some standardization, and base scholarly enquiries on such editions. Perceived literary excellence has in this one instance overcome ingrained conservatism, though possibly to the detriment of Chaucer scholarship.[5]

An average edition of a Middle English text will include a description of the manuscripts in which that text survives and a discussion of their interrelationship to justify what manuscript is chosen as the base for the edition. In addition there may be a section on "The Text" that will explain what features of presentation have been adopted. Often this section is very brief and may not discuss why certain features have been chosen rather than others. Editors do not, as a rule, justify their text presentation, and it is rare to find any theoretical discussion of editing in editions. To be fair to editors, this may be because publishers do not give them enough room for such discussions, but it is not certain that many editors of Middle English texts have ever had much interest in this question. It is only George Kane's edition of *Piers Plowman: The A Version* that contains an extensive discussion on the principles and theory of editing.[6] Apart from Kane's work, there is a lengthy discussion about metrical emendation by Hoyt Duggan, who with T. Turville-Petre was then preparing an edition

---

5. On this general point see N. F. Blake, "Geoffrey Chaucer: Textual Transmission and Editing" and Derek Pearsall, "Authorial Revision in Some Late-Medieval English Texts," in *Crux and Controversy in Middle English Textual Criticism,* ed. A. J. Minnis and Charlotte Brewer (Cambridge, 1992), 19–38 and 39–48.

6. George Kane, *Piers Plowman: The A Version* (London, 1960; rev. ed. 1988), 115–72 on "Editorial Resources and Methods."

of *The Wars of Alexander*.[7] It is perhaps significant that both these major forays into editorial practice were concerned with alliterative poetry, and particularly with its metrics, because the question of whether alliteration in Middle English poetry had any regularity is one that has troubled editors for some time. With poetry that was rhyming and based on metrical feet and with prose, the problems have never seemed so significant—or rather editors have not treated them as such. It may also be that Manly and Rickert's attempt to solve the textual problems of *The Canterbury Tales* was so complicated and apparently arbitrary that it deterred future editors of poems like this from attempting any sustained editorial work.[8]

The editing of Middle English texts has often followed the so-called Lachmann method, by which an editor would produce a critical edition based on a consideration of all extant manuscripts with the purpose of exposing and eliminating errors. The aim of an edition based on this method is to recover the archetype of the surviving manuscripts. Its underlying assumption is that the scribes who had copied the manuscripts were generally careless and meddling, and so the archetype has to be reconstructed through the distorting mirror of the scribal tradition. Given the silence of Middle English editors on their methods, however, it is often unclear whether their goal was truly the recovery of this archetype or, in fact, the author's original work itself. If the goal was the latter, however, a strict application of Lachmann's stemmatic approach would always leave them short.[9] Indeed, can we really assume that the medieval author produced a definitive text that was then corrupted by the scribes? This is by no means certain.[10] Modern experience suggests that authors may leave their text unfinished or its precise contents uncertain.[11] Authors will often correct their text as they go along or in response to certain pressures, like the views of friends or publishers.

In the medieval period, we need to be conscious of the possible relationship

---

7. Hoyt N. Duggan, "Alliterative Patterning as a Basis for Emendation in Middle English Alliterative Poetry," *Studies in the Age of Chaucer* 8 (1986): 73–105. Hoyt N. Duggan and Thorlac Turville-Petre, *The Wars of Alexander*, EETS, s.s. 10 (Oxford, 1989).

8. John Matthews Manly and Edith M. Rickert, *The Text of the "Canterbury Tales," Studied on the Basis of All Known Manuscripts*, 8 vols. (Chicago, 1940), and see Pearsall, "Authorial Revision," 39–40.

9. On the recent application of Lachmann's method to a Middle English editing problem, see S. S. Hussey, "Editing *The Scale of Perfection:* Return to Recension," in Minnis and Brewer, *Crux and Controversy*, 97–108.

10. See the views expressed in Tim William Machan, "Middle English Text Production and Modern Textual Criticism," in Minnis and Brewer, *Crux and Controversy*, 1–18.

11. Compare what is said about this in Jerome J. McGann, *A Critique of Modern Textual Criticism* (Chicago, 1983).

that might have existed between an author and his scribe. It is unlikely that an author presented a scribe with a fair copy that he found no difficulty in copying.[12] An author probably produced a draft on wax tablets or odd scraps of paper or parchment that the scribe would then have had to copy into a presentable and readable text. Often the scribe must have puzzled over what the author meant, what order the lines should be in, whether certain words were meant to be deleted, and whether certain marginal corrections or additions should be included. It may have happened frequently that a scribe would consult with the author as to the author's intentions, and from this it is not hard to imagine that the scribe might have made suggestions for improvement to the text. We tend to be mesmerized today by the little verse that is attributed to Chaucer and contains an attack on the copying abilities of his scribe Adam.

> Adam . scryveyne / if euer it þee byfalle
> Boece or Troylus / for to wryten nuwe /
> Vnder þy long lokkes / þowe most haue þe scalle
> But affter my makyng / þowe wryte more truwe
> So offt adaye . I mot þy werk renuwe /
> It to . corect / and eke to rubbe and scrape /
> And al is thorugh . þy necglygence and rape /[13]

This poem is not to be taken as indicative of the whole Middle English period. Indeed, all we know about Chaucer himself suggests that he may well have been far more casual about the text of his works than these lines suggest. He certainly does not appear to have taken the same interest in them that Gower did in his. There are no authoritative versions of any Chaucer poem or prose text that indicate that he had issued definitive versions.

Indeed, the whole concept of a definitive version of a text based on the author's original or even final intentions may well be an anachronism for this period. Authors may have released preliminary versions of a text followed by later revised ones.[14] There is also the problem of whether an author constantly

---

12. For the view that Chaucer's working copies of his poems, especially *The Canterbury Tales,* may have been in a confused state, see Aage Brusendorff, *The Chaucer Tradition* (Oxford, 1925); and N. F. Blake, *The Textual Tradition of the "Canterbury Tales"* (London, 1985).

13. *A Variorum Edition of the Works of Geoffrey Chaucer,* vol. 5, *The Minor Poems,* ed. George B. Pace and Alfred David (Norman, Okla., 1982), 136–37.

14. See on this point R. K. Root, "Publication before Printing," *PMLA* 28 (1913): 417–31, though his evidence is drawn largely from Italy. N. F. Blake has reopened the question whether Chaucer did issue any versions of *The Canterbury Tales* in his lifetime in "Geoffrey Chaucer and

revised the text, and if so how many of these versions were copied by scribes. We often tend to assume that additions or deletions to texts are made only by interfering scribes, but the example of *Piers* makes it clear that an author could revise a poem constantly. The same could be said to apply to Gower, who produced different frameworks for *Confessio Amantis;* and it is often thought to be true of Chaucer, who may well have produced alterations to both *The Canterbury Tales* and *Troilus and Criseyde* as well as to the different prologues of *The Legend of Good Women.*[15] To establish a text based on the author's original or even final intentions presupposes that such a concept made sense in this period. If scribes were as casual as they are often thought to be, then authors were likely to be resigned to the ephemeral nature of what they wrote.

Moreover, the developing nature of the English language in the absence of a standard meant that scribes were usually more than simple copyists. Texts could be written in various dialects, and they could be rewritten to make them suitable for other dialects or for later stages of the language, as happened, for example, with *Cursor Mundi.* So the question of establishing the dialectal origin of the text is important. If a work survives only in a later form of English and in a different dialect from that in which the original text may have been composed, as is the case of Usk's *Testament of Love,* a modern editor would be unlikely to try to reconstitute the original spelling and dialect. We should also remember that there are very few holographs in Middle English, and we lack criteria that can identify them with certainty. For example, the *Ayenbite of Inwyt* in the extant manuscript, British Library ms. Arundel 57, has been extensively corrected by someone who may be the author.[16] Dr. Gradon comments on these corrections and additions in this way:

> The evidence afforded by the corrections and additions to the manuscript is difficult to interpret. The corrections from a more usual to a more characteristically Kentish spelling could be taken to suggest that the scribe was copying from an exemplar which did not have the Kentish spellings. It seems to suggest, at least, that they were not part of the original orthographic system. . . . Some of the manuscript corrections are also difficult to understand except on the assumption that Dan Michel

---

the Manuscripts of *The Canterbury Tales,"* to be published in the *Journal of the Early Book Society* in 1997.

15. See further N. F. Blake, "Geoffrey Chaucer," and "Caxton's Copytext of Gower's *Confessio Amantis," Anglia* 85 (1967): 282–93 and references there.

16. For a discussion of these corrections see Pamela Gradon, *Dan Michel's Ayenbite of Inwyt,* vol. 2, EETS 278 (Oxford, 1979), 8ff.

was merely the copyist. . . . On the other hand, the gaps in the manuscript, and the glosses and emendation of French words, seem rather to suggest an author's copy. . . . All the author tells us is that the manuscript was written *of his oȝene hand,* which could mean as well that he merely copied it as that he translated it. (10–11)

It is difficult to tell, then, precisely whether this is a scribal or an authorial copy.

It is time now to consider how the texts are presented in a modern edition, and I will start with *O&N,* which is extant in only two manuscripts. These are Cotton Caligula A.ix and Jesus College 29, of which the Cotton manuscript is the earlier and its scribe considered to be the more conservative. The modern edition used most frequently by students in England is that by Eric Stanley, originally edited for Nelson's Medieval and Renaissance Library and subsequently reissued by Manchester University Press.[17] Stanley outlines the editorial principles of the series:

[W]orks of early literature are to be presented to the modern reader in a single text, not a conflate of many texts, nor many texts printed parallel with an expressed preference for one. Ideally the modern reader should be able to approach the work as an educated contemporary reader might have done. A reader may forget the existence of MSS other than that chosen by the editor as the basis for his edition; but the editor cannot, and must not. He must use the evidence of the variant readings to correct and elucidate the chosen MS, for an inferior MS may contain readings that make sense, where the chosen MS makes none; and a doubtful reading in the chosen MS may be explained by a differently doubtful reading in another MS. (5–6)

A reader of this paragraph might be surprised with the text as presented in the edition proper, which is based on the Cotton manuscript. Variant readings from the Jesus manuscript are presented at the foot of the page, and so the modern reader cannot forget the existence of the other version.

In fact, Stanley's "modern reader" of an edited Middle English work that survives in two manuscripts like *O&N* will have many expectations of what an edition will be like, quite apart from the question of whether he or she should forget the existence of different versions. This modern reader, perhaps an updated form of the EETS's "ordinary student," will usually expect the "best"

---

17. Eric Gerald Stanley, *The Owl and the Nightingale* (London, 1960). I quote from this issue.

version available of the text he or she is reading, with as many difficulties as possible ironed out. The medieval reader, on the other hand, would typically have to make the best of whatever text he or she could get hold of. A reader may not have been aware that other manuscripts existed and, if they did, whether they contained a similar, or a widely differing, version. Whereas a medieval reader would have had to accept the text in the format employed by the available copy, most modern readers prefer a familiar format. Verse and stanza breaks should be marked as they are in modern poetry; prose should exhibit modern punctuation and paragraphing; both verse and prose should be lineated. Upon encountering a difficulty, the modern reader looks for notes or a glossary to help understand the text; a medieval reader would simply have to make as much sense as possible of what appeared. The modern reader might even expect the text to be presented in some form of standardized or even modernized spelling, although in this regard he or she would usually be disappointed, as we have already discussed. But, by and large, modern editions have fulfilled these expectations.

Stanley's edition of *O&N* is unusual in choosing one manuscript only to form the basis of his edition. Since there are only two extant versions, and both are thought to be independent, if not immediate, copies of the original, most editors have used that as a convenient reason for providing the reader with a parallel-text edition. In that sense, one could say that many editors have not bothered to provide an edition as such, but have simply provided edited transcripts of the extant manuscripts. This is certainly true of the Early English Text Society edition, which tries to reproduce what is little more than a diplomatic edition of both manuscripts.[18] The editors, or rather Grattan, who finished the edition, claim as justification:

> If we possessed a minimum of three independent MSS., it might be possible to construct a text which should differ little in essentials from the original MS., even though it differed in spellings and in dialectal colouring. But a good many years of work upon a text, which survives in many MSS. have convinced the present editor that, where there are only two MSS. to work from, the number of "certain" or "nearly certain" restorations is so far outweighed by the number of merely "possible" emendations as to make a "restored" text an illusion. (ix)

---

18. J. H. G. Grattan and G. F. H. Sykes, *The Owl and the Nightingale,* EETS, e.s. 119 (London, 1935; rpt. 1959).

Grattan does not explain what he means by a restored text, and the reason for his procedure seems to be little more than saying that, as there are only two manuscripts, it is impossible to adjudicate between them which contains the better reading. This suggests that he would be influenced by weight of numbers in determining a preferable reading, taking shared readings as a sign of authority. What he would have done in the case of nonagreement is unclear, and the possibility of uniform agreement in error should not be overlooked. In this edition there is an attempt to maintain the spelling, punctuation, and layout of the two manuscripts, though naturally many adjustments have to be made because of modern printing types. This procedure Grattan regards as suitable for an edition for the Early English Text Society, though he accepts that it might be possible to produce a single-text edition for the "general reader," who would not be served by a diplomatic edition (ix–x).

The other two major editions of the poem, by Wells and Atkins, both print the two manuscripts, but offer no reasons for this editorial procedure.[19] Indeed, neither justifies printing the two versions side by side, for both editors appear to understand that this was the normal thing to be expected. Wells claimed that "[t]he MSS. are printed as much in facsimile as possible" (2), with any reading that makes sense left as it stands. Abbreviations are italicized, and punctuation, capitalization, and word division are editorial. Where there are corrections in the manuscripts, the original reading is given unless it fails to make sense. Atkins, for his part, was interested in providing as reliable a text as possible with a complete reexamination of the manuscripts. The texts are represented as in the manuscripts with any changes noted carefully. Most attention was paid to the Cotton manuscript, as the earlier of the two. No attempt is made to normalize the spelling systems, for the forms found in each of the two orthographies have "their historical value" (vi). However, both Wells and Atkins are prepared to make emendations to make sense of the text, and Atkins was particularly anxious to "deal with the poem as a piece of literary art, illustrative of the culture of the age which produced it" (vi). This concern departs from the strictly philological orientation discussed above, but it does not seem to have altered the way a text should be edited. Atkins obviously sees no contradiction in offering a text that, on the one hand, preserves minute details relevant to the development of the language and, on the other, is also meant to be read as a piece of literature illustrative of the culture of its time. In fact, the spelling

---

19. John Edwin Wells, *The Owl and the Nightingale* (Boston, 1907); and J. W. H. Atkins, *The Owl and the Nightingale* (Cambridge, 1922).

"systems" of the two manuscripts, so zealously preserved by the editors, inevitably impede literary enjoyment of *O&N* for most modern readers.[20]

On the whole the editions of *O&N* demonstrate the conservatism of Middle English editing already discussed. Where a text exists in two manuscripts, many editors are prepared to edit both of them and thus save themselves the trouble of trying to recreate a conjectural archetype.[21] In the case of *O&N* this decision occurs despite the fact that the Cotton manuscript is accepted as the earlier and the better manuscript by most scholars. Moreover, editors tend to retain the spelling conventions of the manuscripts exactly, though in recent editions some letter forms, like *wynn* and long *s,* may be replaced by their modern equivalents. The texts are presented as documents that are valuable for historical language research. Although language scholars have increasingly encouraged students to look at actual manuscripts, or facsimiles and microfilms which are more accessible, in order to appreciate the representation of medieval language, most editors still feel there is much to be gained by reproducing the original spelling system of the manuscripts they edit.

With *Gawain* different problems arise. There is only one extant manuscript of the poem, and it is written in a Northwest Midlands dialect, which is not the ancestor of Modern Standard English and usually proves difficult to understand for modern readers. Editorial decisions are perhaps more sharply focused, therefore, on the presentation of a difficult text, particularly in matters of spelling and accidentals, and the necessity of emendation because of perceived faulty sense or meter. In other words, editors have to decide how much modernization they will include in their edition and how much emendation is required.

I will focus on three editions, those by Davis, Waldron, and Burrow.[22] Generally, emendation on the basis of meter is not attempted, and Davis says quite explicitly, "No emendations have been made on purely metrical grounds, for the details of the original metrical form are too uncertain" (xxviii). All three

---

20. An attempt to produce a normalized (but not modernized) spelling of part of the poem was made by C. T. Onions, "An Experiment in Textual Reconstruction," *Essays and Studies* 22 (1936): 86–102.

21. I have not taken into account all the editions that have been produced. For example, Gadow's 1909 edition in *Palaestra* is based only on the Cotton manuscript. Naturally, selections have tended to be based on a single manuscript because of the lack of space. The ability to produce both texts is now restricted since publishers may not allow space for parallel editions.

22. *Sir Gawain and the Green Knight,* ed. J. R. R. Tolkien and E. V. Gordon, 2d ed. by Norman Davis (Oxford, 1967); *Sir Gawain and the Green Knight,* ed. R. A. Waldron (London, 1970); and *Sir Gawain and the Green Knight,* ed. J. A. Burrow (Harmondsworth, 1972). As can be seen, all three editions appeared within a short span of years.

editors present their texts with modern punctuation and capitalization; paragraphing is not an issue, as the poem is written in stanzas. As far as spelling is concerned, the three editions go from very traditional to quite modernized. This can be seen by comparing a few lines (20–22) from each edition:

Ande quen þis Bretayn watz bigged bi þis burn rych,
Bolde bredden þerinne, baret þat lofden,
In mony turned tyme tene þat wroȝten.

(Davis)

Ande when this Bretayn was bigged bi this burn rych
Bolde bredden therinne, baret that lofden,
In mony turned tyme tene that wroghten.

(Waldron)

And when this Bretayn was bigged by this burn rich,
Bold bredden therinne baret that loveden,
In mony turned tyme tene that wroghten.

(Burrow)

Davis retains the spelling of the manuscript, expands abbreviations silently, and regularizes word division. He does not try to suggest that the alliteration consisted of two half-lines that should be separated. The other two editors follow most of these decisions except for the retention of the original spelling. Waldron replaces obsolete characters with modern ones and respells certain words on the principle that "alterations should, if possible, be a helpful step toward modern spelling" (28). Thus *hwe* becomes *hue* 'colour', but *hwen* becomes *hewen* '(they) cut'; and *loȝe* as "laughed" becomes *loghe,* but as "low" it becomes *lowe.* But no further modernization is attempted, so that *ande, bi,* and *rych* are retained. Burrow carries the process of modernization a stage further by adopting two principles: "Firstly, some obsolete characters and usages have been modernized. . . . Secondly, wherever the scribe spells a word in several different ways, a single spelling has been selected and used in every case, except where rhyme, metre or alliteration require more than one form (e.g. *wothe* 1576, *wathe* 2355, both in rhyme)" (7). Thus the choice of *and* for *ande* and of *by* for *bi* is not a case of overt modernization, but simply the selection of one of two or more spellings found in the text, though the choice is always in favor of the modern one where possible. Hence the retention of *rych* rather than the substitution of modern *rich* is simply a reflection of the absence of the spelling *rich* in this text. The process is one of standardization, not of modernization. This procedure is presumably motivated by potentially divergent aims: to make the text as user-friendly as possible and to insist that readers are aware of the different spelling systems found in Middle English. But neither Waldron nor Burrow reflects the true spelling system of the manuscript, and both run the risk of creating a false impression of medieval spelling among their users. It is not certain that they gain anything from stopping at this halfway stage rather than going out for a complete modernization of the spelling in the manuscript, even though such a procedure is not without its own problems.[23] The pull of historical linguistics is so strong in England that the solution of the modernized text is rarely offered; the tendency is to make a translation.

The last text to be considered, *Piers,* is the one that has caused most problems for editors. It exists in at least three, and possibly four, versions, and apart from the possible fourth version, the so-called Z-text, all versions exist in a number of manuscripts. All four versions are the work of the same author, William Langland, except for a continuation to the A-text by John But. The problems that arise for an editor of *Piers* are, first, which version to choose for the edition; second, how to decide which manuscript or manuscripts to follow as the base text and what weight to give to that base manuscript in editorial decisions; and third, how much attention to pay to readings in the other versions when editing a text of a single version. After these problems, there come the more standard issues that we have considered in relation to *O&N* and *Gawain* as to how to present the text for modern readers. Let us consider these problems in turn.

An interesting feature of editorial work on *Piers* is that the B-text has always been considered the best from a literary point of view. Consequently when a single version has been edited for general use, this has usually been a B-text, though editions of the A- and C-texts have appeared as independent editions and not as part of a three-text edition. This decision is unusual in that it runs counter to the accepted wisdom of editing, which suggests that editors should produce either the author's original or the final version of a text. The intermediate version(s) would normally be considered to have less status precisely because it or they represented neither first nor final intentions. For it is the author's final intentions that are most often regarded as significant. If an

---

23. This is very evident in modernizations of Shakespeare; see, for example, N. F. Blake, "Modernizing Language and Editing Shakespeare," *Poetica* (Tokyo) 34 (1991): 101–23.

author revises a text, as Langland did with the B-text to produce the C-text, this suggests a feeling of dissatisfaction with what needed to be rewritten to reflect final intentions. Skeat, however, suggested of the C-text that "there is a tendency to diffuseness and to a love for theological subtleties,"[24] and this judgment may be one reason why this text has received less critical favor. More recently there has been an attempt to improve the critical response to the C-text. Pearsall has suggested that the revision in the C-text "seems to have been prompted by an urgent desire to clarify the meaning of the poem and to reshape certain sequences, perhaps partly as a result of the trend of contemporary events and the new context in which they placed the poem."[25] We ignore that decision by the author when we prioritize the second above the third version, for we seem to suggest that his attempts to provide greater clarity in his work are unhelpful, if not unnecessary. Our own critical assumptions are regarded as a better yardstick than the author's intentions. It may be a reasonable decision, but we need to remember that we are offering certain prejudgments about the poem by editing it in this way. In this case we may assume that the tradition of favoring the B-text is so established that it is difficult to dislodge it as the primary version of the poem for students to read and on which critical discussions should focus, whatever editorial theory may suggest.

The second problem presented by a text like *Piers* is the choice of a manuscript to serve as the basis for the text. Traditionally the choice would have followed from a stemmatic analysis that would have led to the manuscript that best reflected the archetype, even if it had occasionally to be emended against the other manuscripts for particular readings. Where a poem exists in several versions, as is true of *Piers,* it is a traditional assumption that each of those versions had an archetype that the editor should try to reconstitute as far as is humanly possible. With the A-text there has been general agreement as to which manuscript to choose as base, but this has as much to do with its completeness as with the satisfactory nature of its text. The manuscript is Trinity College Cambridge ms. R.3.14.[26] With the B-text there has been less agreement, since Skeat and Bennett followed Bodleian Library ms. Laud Misc. 581, whereas Kane-Donaldson and Schmidt chose Trinity College Cambridge

24. W. W. Skeat, *The Vision of William concerning Piers the Plowman by William Langland,* 10th ed. (Oxford, 1923), xi.

25. D. Pearsall, *Piers Plowman by William Langland: An Edition of the C-Text* (London, 1978), 10.

26. For a description and discussion of the manuscripts see Kane, *Piers Plowman.*

ms. B.15.17,[27] which "is the earliest of the B-MSS (about 1400) and although its text is far inferior to that of MS L[aud] it has the advantage of a regular spelling and grammatical system close to that of Langland's day."[28] The C-text has been edited only once in a separate edition by Pearsall.[29] He chose as his base manuscript Huntington Library ms. HM 143 (X) rather than the one used by Skeat, now Huntington Library ms. HM 137 (P); Skeat was not familiar with the former manuscript. P was subject to scribal interference, improvement, and sophistication, whereas X represents the textual tradition far more accurately. The three base manuscripts are chosen on rather different premises: the base for the A-text was chosen for its completeness; those for the B-text either because one represents the assumed archetype best or because the other is the earliest extant manuscript and contains a reasonably consistent orthography and grammar (even though they are not necessarily Langland's); and that for the C-text because it is a good representation of the textual tradition to which it belongs, which is in turn a good one. There is nothing necessarily amiss with these variations, but it does suggest that the establishment of a base text can be somewhat erratic. There is certainly no agreement among Middle English scholars how the base manuscript should be selected.

It is only Kane in his edition of the A-text who has provided detailed discussions of the editorial procedure. He rejects following the base manuscript slavishly, for there is no best manuscript; there are only a number of less corrupt manuscripts. The base manuscript may be allowed to provide the preferred forms for language and spelling, but it should not be allowed to dictate the text's substantive readings. It is his contention that as *Piers* was a living text, it encouraged the scribes to make substitutions in response to the developing social and political situation. Furthermore, its meter, consisting as it does of unrhymed lines with an indeterminate number of syllables, may have encouraged scribes to rewrite lines more freely than was true when scribes copied stanzaic, rhyming, and syllabic poetry. Thus any attempt to reconstruct the archetype must take cognizance of all extant manuscripts, because even a so-called bad manuscript may have retained what was the original reading. At

---

27. W. W. Skeat, *The Vision of William concerning Piers the Plowman, in Three Parallel Texts,* 2 vols., (Oxford, 1886; rpt. 1954); J. A. W. Bennett, *Langland, Piers Plowman: The Prologue and Passus I–VII of the B Text* (Oxford, 1972); G. Kane and E. T. Donaldson, *Piers Plowman: The B Version* (London, 1975; 2d ed. 1988); and A. V. C. Schmidt, *William Langland: The Vision of Piers Plowman, a Complete Edition of the B-Text* (London, 1978). Since this essay was written Schmidt has produced a second, completely revised edition (1995), but the changes do not basically alter what is written here.

28. Schmidt, *Vision of Piers Plowman,* xxxix; cf. 2d ed. lxxx.

29. Pearsall, *Piers Plowman.*

the same time, one needs to bear in mind that the scribes were sensible and sensitive, so that what are often intelligent readings may come from the scribal tradition and not from the author. This does not alter the fact that scribes could also change the text for purposes of simplification of the meaning or for elaboration of the alliteration. Each passage must be judged on its own merits, and since no two editors are likely to think alike, it means that the text of any one version of the poem will be difficult to establish to everyone's satisfaction. An editor must provide the evidence in the apparatus criticus to justify a reading, and each reader will have to form an opinion on each problem. The text is no longer well established, and this naturally provides readers, particularly students, with a real challenge.

The third area of contention concerns the question of how far readings in one version of the poem should influence editorial decisions about the text in another version. Kane changed his mind about this feature of editorial policy, since in his later work he felt that an editor of *Piers* ought to pay more attention to the readings in the other versions. His views have been examined in some depth by Charlotte Brewer.[30] As he wrote in the Kane-Donaldson B-text: "The editor of A now considers that he allowed insufficient weight to readings from other versions in his editing."[31] The reason for this is that if in a given passage the A-text and the C-text agree against what could be assumed to have been the reading in the archetype of the B-text, then either the B-text reading or the A/C-text reading is corrupt. It is more likely to be the former than the latter, and so there must be occasions when the B archetype has to be emended against an A/C-text reading. Hence Kane developed the concept that Langland may have revised his A-text to form the B-text by using a scribal copy of the former that was already corrupt. Not unnaturally, this view has not gone unchallenged, for it ignores the possibility that an author could return to an earlier reading through dissatisfaction with an intermediate revision.[32] This view could also suggest that we are not dealing with three discrete texts of one poem, but with different stages in its genesis. If that were so, it would call into question the preference critics have for the B-text, since that would only be a stage on the way to the final version. It also means that the editing of the A-text may have to be done again, since there are rejected readings in Kane's edition of A that are

---

30. Charlotte Brewer, "George Kane's Processes of Revision," in Minnis and Brewer, *Crux and Controversy*, 71–96.

31. Kane and Donaldson, *Piers Plowman*, 75 n. 15.

32. For details of some of the reviews of Kane's edition see Charlotte Brewer, "Authorial vs. Scribal Writing in *Piers Plowman*," in *Medieval Literature: Texts and Interpretation*, ed. T. W. Machan (Binghamton, 1991), 59–89.

found in B. How much weight could we attach to this type of agreement between versions as against what appears to be the testimony of the manuscripts of a single version when these two are in conflict? This issue has not been resolved, and indeed attitudes toward the state of the text(s) of *Piers* are still in a state of flux. Kane and Donaldson have provided us with the tools to compare the various manuscripts through their extensive apparatus criticus in each volume, but they have not achieved widespread acceptance for their editorial decisions.[33]

As far as presentation of the text of *Piers* in the various editions is concerned, one finds the same differences we noted earlier for *O&N* and *Gawain*. Kane and Kane-Donaldson tend toward the diplomatic style of edition, retaining most Middle English letters and the ampersand in a modernized form, and italicizing abbreviations. They do, however, use modern punctuation, though the punctuation in the B-text is rather more modern than that in A, especially in matters of capitalization. Skeat, Bennett, and Pearsall have adopted a similar procedure, though they expand the ampersand and do not indicate abbreviations; but Skeat went so far as to introduce a dot to indicate the caesura in each alliterative line so that the "half-lines" in *Piers* could be made to echo those found in modern editions of Old English poetry. Schmidt, on the other hand, has offered a more modernized text. Obsolete letters are given their modern equivalent; *u/v* and *i/j* are printed in accordance with modern conventions; abbreviations are expanded silently; and readings adopted from manuscripts other than the base are not identified in the text of the edition, but can be discovered through the apparatus criticus. Punctuation, paragraphing, and capitalization are editorial, though they pay due regard to what is in the base manuscript. A fairly full apparatus criticus is given at the foot of each page. The result is an edition that is much more user-friendly than the others, though the extensive glossing and the apparatus criticus continue to signal the difficulty of the text to the reader.

Perhaps this brief review may create the rather depressing impression that not only have editors of Middle English texts paid rather scant attention to the theoretical advances in editorial procedure, but also that there is still a long way to go before it is likely that any consensus about how to edit a Middle English text will be achieved. It is readily accepted that the way texts are produced has an important bearing on criticism of Middle English literature,[34] but this does not seem to have encouraged scholars of Middle English to arrive at any

---

33. The C-text is being edited as volume 3 for the Athlone edition by George Russell, and although the text has apparently been established for some years now, the volume has yet to appear.

34. See particularly Machan, "Middle English Text Production."

standard editorial procedures or principles for textual presentation.[35] Besides familiarizing ourselves with current debate on editorial theory, we must bear in mind who the audience might be for any edition and to shape the edition for that audience. Who are today's "ordinary" students? Are they a homogeneous group for whom a single kind of edition will be satisfactory? The development of computer editions and the increasing availability of facsimiles provide the opportunity for editors to consider what purpose is to be served and what audience reached by any one edition. Until we begin thinking in these terms, we will continue to produce a variety of editions based on uncertain principles. Perhaps we should also bear in mind that Shakespeare studies are moving in the opposite direction to Middle English, for there the recognition that there may be separate authorial versions of a text like *King Lear* has led to the production of editions that are based on a single witness rather than on a conflation of both or several. But in Shakespeare studies this shift has been marked by a full discussion of the principles and implications involved; in Middle English we seem, on the other hand, to be drifting without a clear idea of where we are going in editorial decisions. It is time we came to terms with the problems involved and reached decisions that editors can work within.

---

35. There have, of course, been several studies devoted to the problems of editing Middle English texts, among which may be cited Charles Moorman, *Editing the Middle English Manuscript* (Jackson, 1975); Anne Hudson, "Middle English:" in *Editing Medieval Texts, English, French, and Latin written in England,* ed. A. G. Rigg (New York, 1977), 34–57; *Manuscripts and Texts: Editorial Problems in Later Middle English Literature,* ed. D. Pearsall (Cambridge, 1987). These volumes contain numerous further references.

Averting Chaucer's Prophecies: Miswriting, Mismetering, and Misunderstanding

Helen Cooper

The correct transmission of Chaucer's text was a problem within his own lifetime, and has remained one ever since. If his complaints about the errors committed by his "owne scriveyn" are to be taken at face value, Adam's "negligence and rape" threatened to corrupt his writings at the root.[1] His immediate sufferings at the hands of a careless scribe were not necessarily worse than those of other authors; but by virtue of their very popularity, Chaucer's works invited a whole series of further kinds of damage in addition.

> And for ther is so gret diversite
> In Englissh and in writyng of oure tonge,
> So prey I God that non myswrite the,
> Ne the mysmetre for defaute of tonge;
> And red wherso thow be, or elles songe,
> That thow be understonde, God I biseche![2]

Chaucer was referring primarily to geographical variations in English dialect; but he was writing with one eye on posterity as well as one on the present—the lines come immediately after those in which he kisses the steps of the great classical poets—and he was aware too that the language was changing over

---

1. *Chaucers Wordes unto Adam, his owne Scriveyn,* in *The Riverside Chaucer,* general ed. Larry D. Benson, 650; all quotations from Chaucer are taken from this edition unless otherwise specified. For full bibliographical details of this and all the other editions of Chaucer I discuss, see "Editions Cited" at the end of this essay; I have consulted all those listed except for Caxton and Stowe, though some of Stowe's material is contained in the facsimile of Thynne's edition. In the case of *Chaucers Wordes,* the early textual tradition is unusually thin (a single manuscript, Trinity College, Cambridge, R.3.20), but there seems no reason to doubt its authenticity: see N. F. Blake, "Geoffrey Chaucer: Textual Transmission and Editing," in *Crux and Controversy in Middle English Textual Criticism,* ed. A. J. Minnis and Charlotte Brewer (Cambridge, 1992), 19.

2. *Troilus and Criseyde,* V.1793–98.

time, even within his own lifespan. The history of Chaucer's text over the next four centuries is a history of miswriting on account of "diversite in Englissh and in writyng of oure tonge," of mismetering and misunderstanding. It was not until the late eighteenth century that the process began to be reversed; and if modern editors can solve most of the problems of linguistic misunderstanding, the potential for cultural misunderstanding increases year by year.

We have to take Chaucer's word for it that Adam Scriveyn was an author's nightmare: there are no manuscripts of his poetry surviving from his lifetime.[3] We can be sure, however, that at least so far as his greatest work was concerned, Chaucer was a scribe's nightmare. The Hengwrt manuscript, one of the very earliest surviving texts of the *Canterbury Tales,* constitutes a record of one copyist's wrestling with intractable and disordered material. He apparently received it as a series of loose and unrelated quires, probably in successive batches, to sort and order as best he could; the sheets were themselves torn or illegible in places; one tale, the Cook's, stopped inexplicably after only a few lines, perhaps at the end of a sheet, so that it appeared that the rest ought to be around somewhere. So the scribe had to fill in the ends of some lines in the Friar's Tale later (III.1311–20), presumably from another exemplar; and he left a space for the rest of the Cook's Tale if ever it turned up and continued his work on a new quire, going back to add in the margin, "Of this Cokes tale maked Chaucer na more."[4] He was right, however, to think that he might be missing some copy: he never received the Canon's Yeoman's Prologue and Tale and the Merchant's Prologue, or at least not while he was working on this manuscript. He also seems never to have worked out a decisive order for the quires containing the tales he had transcribed, and any order he did have in mind was wrecked by their misbinding.

If Chaucer and Adam Scriveyn had found *Boece* and *Troilus* difficult, the problems were as nothing compared with the *Tales.* For most of Chaucer's works, a modern editor has at most sixteen manuscripts to deal with, sometimes only one. For the *Tales,* there are over fifty that are more or less complete, in addition to fragments and separately copied tales; and the early printed editions sometimes draw on manuscripts that are now lost. The sheer number might not have mattered if Chaucer had left his own holograph in anything like finished form; but he did not, and the variations in everything from verbal detail to the order of the tales are substantial. Caxton published the *Tales* within

---

3. I leave aside the vexed question of whether *The Equatorie of the Planets* is by Chaucer, and, if it is, whether the manuscript is his own holograph. Fisher is the only editor so far to include the work in a complete edition of Chaucer.

4. Details of Hengwrt are taken from the facsimile edited by Paul G. Ruggiers.

two years of setting up his printing press at Westminster, probably as the first of his folio editions of Chaucer's various works; and his preface to the second edition indicates his innocent enthusiasm for the project—"innocent," because the new edition was the result of his becoming a sadder and a wiser man.

> Of whyche bookes so incorrecte was one brought to me vi yere passyd, whyche I supposed had ben veray true & correcte. And accordyng to the same I dyde do enprynte a certayn nombre of them, whyche anon were sold to many and dyverse gentylmen. Of whome one gentylman cam to me and said that this book was not accordyng in many places unto the book that Gefferey Chaucer had made.[5]

He therefore went through his first edition comparing it with the new manuscript offered him and making alterations, "for to satysfye th'auctour where as tofore by ygnoraunce I erryd in hurtyng and dyffamyng his book in dyverse places." This process, of using a previous printed edition as a base text and writing corrections in the margins or interleaved sheets, is one that has been constantly replicated down the centuries. Thynne worked from one or more of Caxton's, de Worde's and Pynson's editions; Stowe and Speght worked from Thynne's; Urry from Stowe and Speght, and Tyrwhitt from Speght and Urry, despite their wider collation of manuscripts; Wright from Tyrwhitt, even though he was using a "best text" method, collating Tyrwhitt's edition against Harley 7334; Skeat from Wright, despite changing to the Ellesmere manuscript as his base. Even Manly and Rickert, in their massive attempt to return to all the manuscripts, worked from Skeat, insofar as they used his *Student's Chaucer* as their base text on which to note all variants.[6]

The publication by the Chaucer Society, under the direction of that most remarkable of all Chaucerians, F. J. Furnivall, of eight of the major manuscripts of the *Tales* has enormously assisted editors since the late nineteenth century, but even now there is no fully reliable critical edition of the work. In 1908 Eleanor Prescott Hammond, in her magisterial *Chaucer: A Bibliographical Manual,* summed up the strictures that had been passed on Skeat's great six-volume edition:

---

5. *Caxton's Own Prose,* ed. N. F. Blake (London, 1973), 62.

6. See *Editing Chaucer,* ed. Paul G. Ruggiers (Norman, Okla., 1984), 25–26 (Beverly Boyd on Caxton); 46–47 (James E. Blodgett on Thynne); 99 and 270–71 n. 23 and 24 (William L. Alderson on Urry); 123 (B. A. Windeatt on Tyrwhitt); 149–50 (Thomas W. Ross on Wright); 208 (George Kane on Manly and Rickert). The book constitutes a fine history of the editing of Chaucer from Caxton down to F. N. Robinson. A recent survey of the present state is given by John H. Fisher, "Animadversions on the Text of Chaucer, 1988," *Speculum* 63 (1988): 779–93.

In the method of text-construction, a weakness appears under which editions of Chaucer must labor until his editors recognize, as classical editors long ago recognized, that for a definitive edition the use of all the available evidence is indispensable . . . . An edition of the Canterbury Tales based upon the seven MSS (out of more than fifty) which the Society had issued when Skeat prepared his text, cannot be considered as final. (145)

It was to remedy this "radical weakness" in all previous editions of the *Tales* that John M. Manly and Edith Rickert set out to compare all the textual evidence and reconstruct by recension the archetype of all surviving manuscripts. The heroism of their attempt, and their ultimate failure, have been devastatingly documented by George Kane.[7] Their eight-volume edition appeared in 1940, two years after Edith Rickert's death and in the same year as Manly's; and one cannot help feeling that it was the effort of producing a critical edition of the *Tales* that killed them. Censures of the Hammond kind have gone very quiet since their edition appeared, partly because their faith in strictly scientific recension has been shown to be untenable;[8] and it is tacitly agreed that editors of the *Tales* may legitimately lower their sights. Even the Variorum project explicitly disclaims any pretensions to producing a full critical text, instead basing itself, as Skeat and Robinson had done, on a single manuscript (Hengwrt rather than their Ellesmere) with variants from nine others, including all those Skeat himself used, and the earliest printed editions. This core is supplemented by other manuscripts of the same family when the collated manuscripts have lacunae, and by selected variants from other manuscripts as recorded by Manly and Rickert. The aim is thus "to provide the

---

7. "Manly and Rickert," 207–29. Kane has proceeded to produce, with Janet Cowen, an edition of the *Legend of Good Women* (East Lansing, Mich., 1995) that adheres to his sense of the necessary rigor of editorial principles, such as he has applied to *Piers Plowman* editing. The work has, however, still not solved some of the key issues concerning the text of the poem, in particular that of authorial revision, and it still relies on the editors' sense of what readings are Chaucerian rather than on strict stemmatics: for a full discussion, see the review by Peter Robinson in Canterbury Tales *Project Occasional Papers II* (1997), 135–45.

8. For criticisms of the method, which was first decisively attacked by Joseph Bédier in 1913, see Kane's "Manly and Rickert," 208–13, and George F. Reinecke's "F. N. Robinson" in *Editing Chaucer,* 239; and also E. Talbot Donaldson, "The Psychology of Editors of Middle English Texts" and "Canterbury Tales, D 117: A Critical Edition," in his *Speaking of Chaucer* (London, 1970), 102–30. For a reassertion of its importance (though one which does not adequately answer these criticisms), see Charles Moorman, "One Hundred Years of Editing the *Canterbury Tales,*" *Chaucer Review* 24 (1989): 99–114.

collations of those manuscripts that have attracted commentary" and so "to provide a text upon which the commentary should depend."[9]

Manly and Rickert's edition has generally been taken as a cautionary tale on the impossibility of recovering a "critical text"; moreover, even they did not claim to be establishing what Chaucer wrote, only a common ancestor of all the manuscripts. It seems likely, however, that there never was an authoritative Chaucerian text of the *Tales* (though N. F. Blake has vigorously promoted the cause of the Hengwrt manuscript as the unique authentic witness to the text);[10] the work is unfinished, not just in that its continuity is fragmentary and its announced plan of storytelling unfulfilled, but in that the text itself was left in various provisional states of possible correction and alteration. If that is so, all the resources of computer analysis and hypertext that are now being brought to bear on the work will bring us no closer to a "definitive" edition, though they might confirm such an idea to be an impossibility. It may yet be that electronic methods will recover "what Chaucer actually wrote" where traditional approaches have failed;[11] but by making the full range of manuscript readings and misreadings accessible to every Chaucerian critic, they might also allow a process of pick-your-own-text without any of the established editorial controls, such as could invite critical anarchy.

For all their failure to fulfill their intention, Manly and Rickert performed

---

9. "General Editors' Preface" by Paul G. Ruggiers, Donald C. Baker, and Daniel J. Ransom, in each volume of the Variorum edition of the *Tales;* and see also Baker's introduction to Ruggiers' facsimile of Hengwrt, xvii–xviii.

10. See in particular his edition of Hengwrt, and *The Textual Tradition of the Canterbury Tales* (London, 1985).

11. The quotation is from the first (August 1993) Newsletter issued by *The Canterbury Tales Project*, a scheme headed by Norman Blake and Peter Robinson that aims eventually to publish on CD-ROM all the manuscripts and pre-1500 prints of the *Tales* in both unregularized and regularized form. So far the Wife of Bath's Prologue has appeared (edited by Peter M. W. Robinson, 1996; publication of the whole series is being undertaken by Cambridge University Press). The work signals a major advance over Manly and Rickert's in sophistication, accuracy, and the sheer bulk of information it makes available; but its function is to enable scholars to carry out their own processes of editing with all the information to hand, as well as to offer editorial answers. The results of Peter Robinson's cladistic analysis (an advanced form of stemmatic recension) of the material made available through the CD-ROM are at the time of revising this article about to appear as "A Stemmatic Analysis of the Fifteenth-Century Witnesses to the Wife of Bath's Prologue," Canterbury Tales *Project Occasional Papers II* (1997), 42–108. He offers a much fuller and more sophisticated analysis of manuscript descent and relations than has previously been possible, though it often clarifies problems rather than moving the answers beyond hypothesis. One interesting suggestion to emerge from the project is that Hengwrt may offer a record of Chaucer's own system of punctuation: see Elizabeth Solopova, "The Survival of Chaucer's Punctuation in the Early Manuscripts of the *Canterbury Tales,"* forthcoming in *Proceedings of the 1996 York Medieval Texts Conference,* ed. Alastair Minnis.

vast services to the scholarly world, some intentional, others not. Their corpus of variants may never have the grounds of selection explained, but it is still there to be drawn on; there may be minor inaccuracies in some of their manuscript descriptions, but it is still the work of first recourse. They intended their work to be definitive, and so never to need repeating; in the event, the sheer enormity (in the British even more than the American sense) of their task has freed editors from any sense of obligation to compete, and so enabled them to concentrate on other matters.

It may be such a diversion of interest that has encouraged the widespread assumption that by now the text of Chaucer's works is a known quantity.[12] The canon, after being steadily swollen throughout the sixteenth century, has been refined and cut back until it is reasonably secure, with just a handful of remaining works that are agreed to be doubtful.[13] Chaucer's language and allusions have largely been explained, again with a few agreed cruxes (most of which constituted a good proportion of Tyrwhitt's disarming two-page list of "Words and Phrases not understood" appended to his glossary),[14] and always with the possibility of further refinement as more is learned about his intellectual and social culture. That so many recent editors—Donaldson and Baugh, for instance—omit any detailed discussion of textual matters encourages such a lack of awareness of textual problems; some editors give no indication of textual origins or difficulties at all. R. A. Shoaf's students' edition of *Troilus,* for instance, notes that it is "from the text of A. C. Baugh" on the title page, but does not so much as mention manuscripts in its editorial material; and presumably even he as editor was unaware that the text of Baugh's 1963 *Chaucer's Major Poetry* is effectively the same as that published by Robinson in 1957, down to the detail of the punctuation.[15] *Editing* is an especially

---

12. The controversy over Hengwrt is the main exception, but Blake's views have not acquired enough adherents to make a great impression on Chaucerian editing in general; most recent editors go at most for what Ralph Hanna III called "soft Hengwrtism" in contrast to Blake's fundamentalist "hard" version ("The Hengwrt Manuscript and the Canon of *The Canterbury Tales," English Manuscript Studies* 1 (1989): 64–84, esp. 65). B. A. Windeatt's establishment of the text of *Troilus* took place largely without wider controversy, although he overturned the views of R. K. Root (*The Textual Tradition of Chaucer's Troilus,* Chaucer Society 1st series, 99 [1916; rpt. New York, 1969]); but see Blake, "Geoffrey Chaucer," 26–30.

13. The latest discovery, the *Equatorie of the Planets,* is the only one on which passions can still be roused; even the relegation to the "doubtful" section of the delightful *Merciles Beaute,* accepted as genuine by Skeat, did not raise protests. The final dismissal of most of the spurious works has paradoxically coincided with a renewed interest in them, and especially in the extra Canterbury tales; *Beryn* and *Gamelyn* were the last items to be added to the spurious canon, by Urry in 1721.

14. *The Canterbury Tales of Chaucer,* 5:285–86.

15. The similarity was pointed out in J. A. Burrow's review of Baugh: "In many passages I have found their texts absolutely identical, down to the last comma and final e" (*Essays in*

ambiguous word where Chaucer is concerned, covering everything from the labors of Manly and Rickert to Shoaf's provision of glosses on an established text.

The appearance of textual certainty can nonetheless be deceptive. Few readers ever realize that the roundel at the end of the *Parliament of Fowls* does not appear in that form in any manuscript, and is completely omitted by most; the longest manuscript version is an eight-line stanza found only in Gg.4.27, which contains none of the repetitions and was furthermore added in by a later hand. The standard text is Skeat's conjectural restoration on the model of the "prettiest" roundel he could find.[16] On occasions where textual commentary does give abundant warning of difficulties, doubtful elements of a text will still be used as foundations for critical arguments even by established Chaucerian scholars. Probably the favorite is to ignore the discontinuities of all the orders of the fragments of the *Canterbury Tales* and to treat the work as a seamless whole, with tales that in modern editions are printed adjacent to each other across unbridged fragment boundaries being treated as if they bore the same relationship to each other as tales within fragments.[17] Much more subtle errors

---

Criticism 14 [1964]: 308). The most significant change is the organizational one of tale order in the *Canterbury Tales,* of moving Group B2 (Robinson's VII) to follow B1, in the "Bradshaw shift." The detail of the correspondence at the verbal level is obscured by Baugh's claim in his preface to be offering "critical texts" based on manuscripts named for each poem, which are the same as those used by Robinson. My own spot checks of several hundred lines from *Troilus,* the *Canterbury Tales,* and the *Parliament of Fowls*—concentrated around areas where a manuscript-based text might be expected to differ, such as where Robinson gives conjectural emendations, brings in readings from other manuscripts, or, in the *Tales,* alters readings from his first edition to adopt some of Manly and Rickert's—have shown up one modernized spelling and one dropped comma in *Troilus;* one spelling change that is clearly intentional ("Seint" for Robinson's "seinte" at I (A) 3483, 3486); and one small difference of reading ("by" for Robinson's "for" at IX (H) 157) in the *Tales;* and nothing in the *Parliament of Fowls* despite its textual complexities.

16. Skeat found his "prettiest example" of a roundel in Machaut: "I follow this as a model, both here and in 'Merciless Beaute'; merely warning the reader that he may make either of his refrains of a different length, if he pleases" (1:525). Vincent DiMarco, in the *Riverside Chaucer,* is the one modern editor who makes an attempt to alert his readers to the conjectural nature of the text by printing the repeated lines in square brackets; few editors' notes between Skeat's and DiMarco's give a full indication of how extensive the restoration is. A recent discussion of manuscript evidence for this passage can be found in Ralph Hanna III's "Presenting Chaucer as Author," in *Medieval Literature: Texts and Interpretation,* ed. Tim William Machan, (Binghamton, 1991), 29ff.

17. There is a strong case to be made for believing IV and V to have been linked by Chaucer, almost as strong a one for linking IX and X, and a weaker one for thinking that Chaucer may have intended to follow I with II and VI with VII (for a recent discussion, see Helen Cooper, "The Order of Tales in the Ellesmere Manuscript," in *The Ellesmere Chaucer: Essays in Interpretation,* ed. Martin Stevens and Daniel Woodward [San Marino and Tokyo, 1995], 245–61); but there is no editorial case at all to be made for regarding the others as connected. Furnivall, who christened Fragment VII as B2 and joined it to B1, never formally edited Chaucer, even though later editors

can derive from an editorial presentation of the text that is never noted as being such. No twentieth-century edition of the *Tales* indicates that the division of the Knight's Tale into four parts is unique to the Ellesmere manuscript; even Manly and Rickert keep the text divisions, presumably because they were already present in their working copy of Skeat's *Student's Chaucer.* There is no indication of their absence, or of alternative divisions of the tale, in their corpus of variants; to find them one has to locate their collection of tale divisions at the end of volume 3. So it came about that even so great a scholar as R. E. Kaske expounded in a lecture to the Medieval Academy the earthly nature of the Knight's Tale as against the spiritual nature of the Man of Law's Tale as symbolized in their division into four and three parts, unaware that Hengwrt divides the Knight's Tale into three, other manuscripts divide it into two or five, and most manuscripts do not divide either tale at all.[18] Editions of Chaucer, in summary, are not safe as a basis for certain kinds of critical work, and it may be impossible to tell when one crosses the boundary into danger.

As crucial as an editor's choice of words and textual layout, yet at the same time invisible or silent to most readers from its sheer familiarity, is punctuation. Manly and Rickert's text of the *Tales* is unpunctuated, which gives it a greater air of authenticity (though to an extent a spurious one, since the manuscripts are by no means devoid of pointing); but it also means that any other editor who wishes to use their text still has a constant series of radical decisions to make, about whether subordinate clauses or phrases belong to the preceding or following sentence, about where a speech ends, about classifying words as different parts of speech. These problems can affect the choice of words for an edited text as well as their interpretation, and can again have their roots in the scribes' own difficulties with the same issues. So line 594 of the *Parliament of Fowls* in Vincent DiMarco's edition for the *Riverside Chaucer* reads

"Ye queke," seyde the goos, "ful wel and fayre!"

in which *queke* is a second-person verb and the line has the goose addressing the duck, "You quack both well and handsomely." The manuscripts, presum-

---

from Skeat to Baugh have adopted the order; it represents far and away the most massive editorial intervention in any Chaucerian text. The conjectural reading "Wife of Bath" as the name of the next speaker in the Man of Law's Epilogue is critically attractive, and so is adopted by both Donaldson and Fisher; but there is not the slightest manuscript evidence to associate the link with the Wife's *present* tale.

18. See further Helen Cooper, *The Oxford Guides to Chaucer: The Canterbury Tales* (Oxford, 1989), 62, 73–75, 126, 129.

ably puzzled by whether to take *queke* as a verb or an exclamation, offer a range of variants including "Kek kek" for "ye queke" and "doke" for "goos." On this basis a number of editors, including Robinson, print a version of

"Ye, queke!" yit seyde the doke, ful wel and fayre,

in which the duck, as ducks partly do, says "Yes, quack!" and the adverbs become part of the narration and not part of the speech. A reader will never be aware that there is a problem; yet the abundance of speech in Chaucer's works and the complexities of his syntax mean that similar cruxes occur on every page of an edition.

Textual accuracy and editorial practice overlap again in the vexed area of *mismetering*—how Chaucer's lines should be scanned. Again, the problem goes back very early, to language changes under way in his own lifetime. No Tudor reader of fifteenth-century manuscripts had, or could have had, any idea that Chaucer might have written regular decasyllables: Caxton did not read him so, nor did any sixteenth- or seventeenth-century editors or readers. Urry's *Works of Geoffrey Chaucer* of 1721 was the first that attempted to restore metrical regularity, by adding syllables if necessary, and guiding the reader's pronunciation by printing a sounded *e* as *i* before a consonant, or with an accent if terminal. So the first eight lines of his General Prologue run

When that Aprilis with his Shouris sote,
The drought of March had percid to the rote,
And bathid every veyn in such licour,
Of which vertue engendrid is the flour.
When Zephyrus eke, with his swetè breth
Enspirid hath, in every holt and heth
The tender croppis; and that the yong Sunn
Hath in the Ramm his halvè cours yrunn . . .

This, as the critics were quick to point out, is not Chaucer; but the motive behind the attempt was a good one, however mangled the results. Urry had not yet understood all the grammatical principles behind the final *-e,* and accented them very much to suit; but later editors have frequently practiced a more informed version of the same procedure. *Aprilis* may not be Middle English, but Skeat and the first edition of Robinson smoothed Ellesmere's "Aprill" to read "Aprille"; and Robinson, like Urry, printed "halve" in both his own editions for the same reasons, despite the complete lack of manuscript support (the *Riverside* restores Ellesmere's "half"; Skeat had compromised with "halfe"). A. W. Pollard, in his Globe edition of 1898, dotted a sounded *e* and provided accents for differently stressed words to guide the general reader for whom the edition was intended and who would have been brought up on the mellifluousness of Tennyson.

An editor's beliefs about the regularity of Chaucer's lines will in turn govern the nature of the final text. Tyrwhitt had restored manuscript spellings, Skeat and Robinson smoothed them out; readers brought up on Robinson will react to a smooth line as more "Chaucerian," and therefore more likely to be correct, than a rough one. This is not necessarily wrong, even though the reasoning is circular; Barry Windeatt's work has confirmed that Chaucer did aim at an ancestor of the iambic pentameter as the norm for his verse, at least in the *Troilus*.[19] But this does not mean that the spelling and pointing of the early manuscripts exclude a much greater range of rhythmic variation in the line than strict metrical regularity would allow; "strict metrical regularity" was in any case not a requirement of the decasyllable before the late seventeenth century. An anglophone world that can accept "Friends, Romans, countrymen, lend me your ears" as an iambic pentameter should not have undue difficulty with Ellesmere's

Whan that Aprill with hise shoures soote

or Hengwrt's

Whan that Aueryll with his shoures soote,

even though no edited text has printed either.[20] Again, Chaucer has gone ahead of the editors in his awareness of the problem: his comment in the *House of Fame* on how the shorter lines of that poem may "fayle in a sillable" (1098) suggests that he was fully aware of the differences between the stress basis of English prosody and the syllable counts of continental metrics.[21] Robinson's retreat from "Aprille" to "Aprill" in his second edition represents a proper conversion from anachronistic standards of correctness to the freer rhythms we associate with Shakespeare; but extensive modernization that results in an

---

19. See Windeatt's edition of *Troilus*, 55–64; and also Derek Pearsall, "Chaucer's Meter: The Evidence of the Manuscripts," in MacHan, *Medieval Literature*, 41–57.

20. The apparent exception is N. F. Blake's edition of Hengwrt, but he does not so much edit as transcribe the text. The editors who take Ellesmere as their base still omit the final -*e* on "hise."

21. Headless octosyllabics have always been common in the English practice of the form: Milton's "Haste thee, nymph, and bring with thee" represents standard usage.

equivalent of the dislocated rhythms of the early printed editions does Chaucer no service.

The miswriting and mismetering of Chaucer's text concern most modern readers less and less, especially since the norms of metrical regularity have largely disappeared from contemporary culture. Misunderstanding of all kinds has, however, burgeoned, and editors have spent correspondingly more time on addressing the problem. There has almost always been some modernization of Chaucer's spelling (thorns and yoghs are very seldom reproduced, for instance), and editors from Caxton to Donaldson have discreetly gone further in bringing Chaucer forward. Speght was the first to provide a glossary, in 1598, but a sound glossary requires both more philological expertise than was available until Tyrwhitt began to provide it in the late eighteenth century, and also an accurate text to work from. Speght's definition of *momblishnesse* as "taulke" was foredoomed: his text was a corruption of the French "ne m'oublie-mies"—and the line, furthermore, comes from a poem, *The Assembly of Ladies,* that is now known not to be Chaucer's anyway.[22] Tyrwhitt was enough of a scholar to restore word forms to his text on the basis of manuscript evidence even though the word itself had long disappeared from the language: so "outhees" at last reappeared at *CT* 1:2012 in place of "on theft," with a correct explanation as "outcry." Urry's glossary superseded Speght's, and Tyrwhitt's that of Urry; Skeat's is one of the glories of his edition, and in generosity and detail has not been matched since. Most modern editions aimed at students provide explanatory glosses on the page so as to make continuous reading easier: this is the practice adopted by, for instance, Cawley, Donaldson, Baugh, and Fisher (who also supplies a separate glossary), and also by editions in all other respects as far apart as the *Troilus*es of R. A. Shoaf (where the glosses appear in the margin and at the foot of the page) and B. A. Windeatt (where they appear in the third column of each opening, along with other critical and explanatory material). The first two editions of Robinson had no explanations on the page and an inadequate glossary—inadequate not so much because of missing words, but by the omission of line references for different meanings and of many grammatical markers and different orthographic and morphological forms. The *Riverside Chaucer* both added explanatory glosses at the foot of the page and revised the glossary to take account of the earlier weaknesses. It still does not aim at completeness, however, as it confines itself to words Chaucer uses recurrently; and so Tyrwhitt's "outhees" drops out, to appear only in the page gloss.

---

22. Derek Pearsall, "Thomas Speght," in Ruggiers, *Editing Chaucer,* 81.

The majority of editions produced this century have concentrated on increasing understanding of Chaucer's works in the broader cultural sense, though what different editors think necessary for such a purpose has varied both with the individual and over time. Manly's 1928 *Canterbury Tales,* originally intended "for use in senior high school and elementary college work" but becoming increasingly ambitious as he worked on it, contains a study of the manuscripts, full notes, an etymological glossary, and a substantial section on Chaucer's language (pronunciation, morphology, and idioms); but most particularly his introduction is aimed at overcoming "ignorance of the customs, beliefs and ideals" of Chaucer's age. So there is a substantial section on "Chaucer's England" covering rural life, towns, London and its merchant princes, money, and so on—an old-historicist version of just those topics that the new historicists have rediscovered. The scholarship and historical emphasis of the edition notwithstanding, he omits both *Melibee* and the Parson's Tale. British readers seem to be more patient with these—A. C. Cawley includes both in his popular Everyman edition—but that Chaucer's prose is not what anyone now wants to bother with is assumed from the title forward in both Donaldson's *Chaucer's Poetry: An Anthology for the Modern Reader* and Baugh's *Chaucer's Major Poetry.* Baugh limits his introduction to Chaucer's life, a particularly clear summary of his grammar and syntax, and versification; there are no notes, but his generous foot-of-page glossing covers basic explanations beyond simple word definitions. Donaldson similarly provides a life, a more historical account of the language, and fine little introductory essays on each poem. The life-language-critical introduction method of presenting the text is also adopted by Robinson and Fisher in their complete editions and by R. A. Pratt in his *Tales;*[23] Fisher is particularly generous with bibliographical information, and Robinson supplies the explanatory apparatus that above all established his edition as the one of first resort. "To say anything against the notes would be to come out against God, home, and mother," as George F. Reinecke put it;[24] the multiple editorship of the *Riverside Chaucer* revision has barely managed to keep up the standard, however necessary it was for updating Robinson's information.

The same-page glossing added to the *Riverside* has increased its user-friendliness for students; the idea that the ordinary reader (or what Manly called "sensible men in general" [*Tales,* vi]) might read Chaucer in the original

23. Pratt bases his text on Robinson with variants from Manly and Rickert, chosen most often to give preference to readings attested by the manuscripts over Robinson's smoothing of meter; the effect is to bring his text closer to that of Hengwrt.

24. "F. N. Robinson," 248.

has not been much heard of recently. The conception of what students might want or need does however vary enormously. At one extreme is Shoaf's *Troilus,* with its marginal glosses and twelve-page introduction, designed to minimize the appearance of distance between Chaucer and any other author one might read. At the other is the remarkable *Book of the Duchess* by Helen Phillips, also described as being for undergraduate use, which provides information not only on Chaucer's life and language but on the ideas and literary and cultural background of the poem, and also explanatory and textual notes, extracts from and translations of sources, and a glossary; major changes of textual affiliation, between Fairfax 16 and Thynne, are signaled in the margin of the poem itself, so that students cannot help but learn that texts are made and not found; and, most unusual of all, the problem of rhythm (a larger issue than meter alone) is tackled by giving extra spaces in the line to mark the pauses indicated by medieval pointing, supplemented by light modern punctuation.

Other gaps in a modern appreciation of Chaucer are addressed by other editors. D. S. Brewer, in his *Parlement of Foulys,* takes *language* to mean not just grammar but more particularly rhetoric, a word that was anathema early this century. Unusually, he does not modernize yoghs and thorns, and keeps some abbreviations such as the ampersand, so that his text looks much more like most editions of other Middle English authors. He, like Phillips, provides a generous amount of literary context for the poem, and this too marks a significant change of attitude in recent years. Manly had dismissed "the mere knowledge that Chaucer got the materials for a certain tale from this source or that" as "useless lumber" without the full study of accurate texts (*Tales,* vii); but the stress on grounding Chaucer's works in some kind of literary context is increasing. Windeatt devotes one of the four parallel columns of his fine *Troilus* to source texts given in the original, the *Filostrato,* Petrarch, and Chaucer's *Boece.* Shoaf allots two and a half sentences to Boccaccio, but a whole page, a twelfth of his introduction, to Andreas Capellanus's rules of love. V. A. Kolve and Glending Olson's edition of selected *Tales* gives as much space to "sources and backgrounds" as to the poems themselves. Their most generous selection of "backgrounds"—eleven in all, including Jerome's *Against Jovinian* and an extract on Lechery from the Parson's Tale—is provided for the Wife of Bath's Prologue, and that too marks a new emphasis in Chaucer criticism, whereby he is studied not just for his own sake as a great poet but for the ways in which he epitomizes or opens up areas of current cultural interest—antifeminism in this instance; elsewhere class struggle, emergent economic thought, or dissidence. Current cultural agendas come close to appropriating the text altogether in Peter G. Beidler's edition of the Wife of Bath's Prologue and Tale for the series

Case Studies in Contemporary Criticism: the series aims not just to use a spectrum of modern theoretical approaches to illuminate literary works, but to use those works as case studies to illustrate theory.

Kolve and Olson's and Beidler's editions are designed less for the individual student than for the classroom—indeed they are designed *as* classrooms: the materials for discussion and pointers toward conclusions are all provided, by means of reprints of ten seminal essays in Kolve and Olson, by a series of specially commissioned essays in Beidler. The CD-ROM of the Wife of Bath could provide a different kind of classroom, for exercises in textual editing or at the very least in the problematics of producing an edited text, but one where the results are much less directed. It is one of the ironies of the electronic age of editing that its first result is to turn the very meaning of "editing" inside out: the editorial team is now concerned with using their expertise not to select the one most significant variant to which to give canonical status in an edition, but to find the means of recording every last variant from which such selection might be made—a process not of fine discrimination but of maximized accumulation. It is the new point from which "editing" in the old sense will have to start all over again.

Yet Chaucer, for all his increasing difficulty as readers are dispossessed of the familiarity with the Bible and the classics that he assumes, is not yet the preserve only of scholars—or even of students. There are abundant ways in which his importance to the cultural literacy of the anglophone world is represented and maintained, even before one looks to media that do not retain his text, from films to the tourist paraphernalia at the visitor center in Canterbury. So there is a Chaucer coloring-in book that reproduces the woodcuts from the early printed editions complete with black-letter texts; and the roundel from the *Parliament of Fowls* was given unprecedented exposure to millions of London commuters and visitors when it was chosen as one of the hundred "Poems on the Underground." It is one of the ironies of the history of editing Chaucer that his most widely disseminated poem should be a conjectural reconstruction of a stanza never known in any form to most of his medieval readers.

Editions Cited

Baugh, Albert C., ed. *Chaucer's Major Poetry.* New York, 1963.
Beidler, Peter G. *Geoffrey Chaucer: The Wife of Bath.* Case Studies in Contemporary Criticism. Boston and New York, 1996.
Benson, Larry D., general ed. *The Riverside Chaucer.* Boston, 1987.

Blake, N. F., ed. *The Canterbury Tales by Geoffrey Chaucer Edited from the Heng-wrt Manuscript*. London, 1980.

Brewer, D. S., ed. *Geoffrey Chaucer: The Parlement of Foulys*. 1960; rpt. Manchester, 1972.

Cawley, A. C., ed. *Geoffrey Chaucer: Canterbury Tales*. Everyman edition, 1958; rev. ed., London, 1990.

Caxton, William, ed. *The Canterbury Tales*. 1477; 2d ed. 1483.

Cowen, Janet, and George Kane. eds. *Geoffrey Chaucer: The Legend of Good Women*. East Lansing, Mich. 1995.

Donaldson, E. Talbot, ed. *Chaucer's Poetry: An Anthology for the Modern Reader*. 1958; 2d ed., New York, 1975.

Fisher, John H., ed. *The Complete Poetry and Prose of Geoffrey Chaucer*. 1977; 2d ed., New York, 1989.

Kolve, V. A., and Glending Olson, eds. *Geoffrey Chaucer: The Canterbury Tales: Nine Tales and the General Prologue*. New York, 1989.

Manly, John M., ed. *The Canterbury Tales*. New York, 1928.

Manly, John M., and Edith Rickert, eds. *The Text of the Canterbury Tales*. 8 vols. Chicago, 1940.

Phillips, Helen, ed. *Chaucer: The Book of the Duchess*. Durham and St. Andrews Medieval Texts 3. Durham and St. Andrews, 1982; rev. ed., 1993.

Pollard, Alfred W., ed. *The Works of Geoffrey Chaucer*. Globe edition. London, 1898.

Pratt, Robert A., ed. *The Tales of Canterbury Complete*. Boston, 1966.

Robinson, F. N., ed. *The Works of Geoffrey Chaucer*. 1933; 2d ed., Boston, 1957.

Robinson, Peter M. W., et al., eds. *The Wife of Bath's Prologue on CD-ROM*. Cambridge, 1996.

Root, R. K., ed. *The Book of Troilus and Criseyde*. Princeton, 1926.

Ruggiers, Paul, ed. *The Canterbury Tales: Geoffrey Chaucer: A Facsimile and Transcription of the Hengwrt Manuscript*. Introductions by Donald C. Baker and by A. I. Doyle and M. B. Parkes. Norman, Okla., 1979.

Shoaf, R. A., ed. *Geoffrey Chaucer: Troilus and Criseyde*. East Lansing, Mich., 1989.

Skeat, Walter W., ed. *The Complete Works of Geoffrey Chaucer*. 6 vols. 1894; 2d ed., Oxford, 1899.

Speght, Thomas, ed. *The Workes of our Ancient and Lerned English Poet, Geffrey Chaucer*. 1598; 2d ed., 1602.

Stow, John, ed. *The Workes of Geffrey Chaucer*. 1561.

Thynne, William, ed. *Geoffrey Chaucer: The Works, 1532, with supplementary material from the editions of 1542, 1561, 1598 and 1602*. Facsimile ed. D. S. Brewer. Menston, 1969.

Tyrwhitt, Thomas, ed. *The Canterbury Tales of Chaucer*. 5 vols. 1775–78.

Urry, John, ed. *The Works of Geoffrey Chaucer*. 1721.

Windeatt, B. A., ed. *Geoffrey Chaucer: Troilus and Criseyde*. London, 1984.

Wright, Thomas, ed. *The Canterbury Tales of Geoffrey Chaucer: A New Text*. Percy Society, 24–26, 3 vols. 1847–51.

Editing and the Teaching of
Alliterative Verse

A. S. G. Edwards

I am concerned here with the use of editions in the classroom, and with one particular class of text, alliterative verse. As will be apparent, many of the points I make here have an applicability that extends beyond such verse. But alliterative poetry does provide distinct difficulties of linguistic and stylistic accessibility that the teaching and editorial roles should—ideally—be more closely integrated than for other kinds of Middle English texts.

We lack much general theoretical discussion of the editing of Middle English alliterative verse. The examples of George Kane's A text of *Piers Plowman*[1] and the Kane/Donaldson B text[2]—which place great weight on the conjectural recovery of what are believed to be original readings—are sometimes invoked as procedural models of wider methodological implication. But Professor Kane has been careful not to draw broader conclusions about the applicability of the methods he decided were required for editing *Piers*. Indeed, it is hard to see how they could be profitably extended, since the textual situation even for most other alliterative texts is markedly different from that confronting the editor of *Piers* in terms of both the number and quality of surviving witnesses.

Apart from one or two special cases, like *Piers Plowman* and the alliterative *Siege of Jerusalem* or the *ABC of Aristotle,* much alliterative poetry survives in unique or very small numbers of manuscripts,[3] often manuscripts that are pretty execrable in form and corrupt in content. Even where there is a multi-

---

1. *Piers Plowman: The A Version,* ed. George Kane (London, 1960).

2. *Piers Plowman: The B Version,* ed. George Kane and E. Talbot Donaldson (London, 1975).

3. For a general survey of the manuscripts of alliterative poetry see A. I. Doyle, "The Manuscripts," in *Middle English Alliterative Poetry and Its Literary Background,* ed. David Lawton (Cambridge, 1972), 88–100.

plicity of witnesses, as with such works as *The Pistill of Susan* or *The Awntyrs of Arthur,* the problems are not necessarily any the less, since the possible multiple authorship of, for example, the *Awntyrs*[4] makes the establishing of a distinctive authorial *usus scribendi*—and hence of some form of direct editing—an undertaking open to question on methodological grounds. In other instances the possibility of any form of interventionist editing can be limited due to the intractability of the surviving materials, as with the fragmentary *Mum & the Sothsegger,*[5] the fragments of which may not in fact be from a single work, or with the unique Vernon text of *Joseph of Arimathie,* which, it has been argued, may be an incomplete rough or first draft.[6]

The various hypotheses that have been advanced about the actual forms of composition of alliterative texts do little, in general terms, to lessen the pessimism that might be felt about the possibility of an interventionist approach to recover originality.[7] One may question how far is any form of deep critical editing possible or even appropriate for many such texts because of both the paucity of materials that has survived and the inexorable tendency of alliterative diction toward stock collocations and formulas. These suggest that banality, not originality, was, at times, the initial compositional impulse, as, for example, William Holland has demonstrated in the case of *Arthur & Merlin.*[8] To this may be added Hoyt Duggan's arguments that on occasions texts may themselves be inherently collaborative, involving both poet and performer in the way that, for instance, a play text often can be.[9] Even if such collaboration cannot be conclusively established, this line of argument seems in a number of instances very probable and not wholly encouraging to an editor, since the

---

4. See the most recent discussion of the editorial problems of this poem by Rosamund Allen, "Some Sceptical Observations on the Editing of *The Awntyrs off Arthure*," in *Manuscripts and Texts: Editorial Problems in Later Middle English Literature,* ed. Derek Pearsall (Cambridge, 1987), 5–25.

5. See the edition by Mabel Day and R. Steele, EETS 261 (London, 1934).

6. See the most recent edition, *Joseph of Arimathea: A Critical Edition,* ed. David Lawton, Garland Medieval Texts, 5 (New York, 1983).

7. Terms like *direct* or *deep* or *interventionist* are generally employed to indicate forms of editorial engagement that are committed to conjectural restoration. For discussions of the underlying assumptions of such editing see *Piers Plowman: The A Version,* ed. George Kane, 115–72; Kane's essay on "Conjectural Emendation," in *Medieval Literature and Civilization: Studies in Memory of G. N. Garmonsway,* ed. D. A. Pearsall and R. A. Waldron (London , 1969), 155–69; and the introduction to Rosamund Allen's edition of *King Horn,* Garland Medieval Texts, 7 (New York, 1984).

8. William E. Holland,"Formulaic Diction and the Descent of a Middle English Romance," *Speculum* 48 (1973): 89–109.

9. Hoyt N. Duggan, "The Role of Formulas in the Dissemination of a Middle English Alliterative Romance," *Studies in Bibliography* 29 (1976): 265–88.

general tendency of such collaboration is once again likely to be toward the reductive and/or elucidatory, and away from the difficult reading that provides the underlying principle for deep or direct editing. The possibility of significant editorial intervention for a number of alliterative texts can be open to doubt in fundamental ways.

One of the basic problems confronting an editor is of course the relationship of his or her text to that doubt. Or, to put the matter a little more clearly: what is the extent of the editor's responsibility to make the audience aware not only of the indeterminacy of his or her text, but also of the extent of that indeterminacy? Any attempt to answer that question seems to involve the further question: who is the text being edited for? Joseph Donatelli's recent edition of *Death and Liffe* may provide a way of clarifying my point.[10] This is an excellent edition: accurate, informative, and candid. It is also, in textual terms, extremely conservative. Donatelli points out that "the most exasperating words and lines cannot be solved without radical and extensive revision" (14), and he resists the inclination to undertake such revision. One must have sympathy with his predicament. And one can, without difficulty, applaud the care and accuracy with which he presents and analyzes many of the problems of the text, while eschewing radical emendation.

But this conservative approach raises obvious questions about the audience of the edition. We assume that Donatelli has in mind one who is willing to take his work somewhat further on their own—an audience, that is, of fellow scholars who will be prepared to see his text as a series of complex textual problems to which they will add their own scholia of commentary, exegesis, and (perhaps) speculative emendation on the grounds of sense and meter. This is fair enough, given such a sense of audience. It is, of course, an audience of "us," an audience of professional scholars, for whom intelligibility is not a mandatory criterion of the edition. It is, correspondingly, a text of limited usefulness to the "them" whom we teach in undergraduate and possibly even in graduate courses, since its levels of address are not aimed at such constituencies; they might reasonably feel confused, if not aggrieved, by a form of the text that required skills they did not possess. Here the form of the edition defines the audience in ways that exclude most of those whom we might teach.

More generally it points to the problem of the kinds of editions that are appropriate for the teaching—as distinct from the advanced scholarly study—

---

10. *Death and Liffe*, ed. Joseph M. P. Donatelli, Speculum Anniversary Monographs, 15 (Cambridge, Mass., 1989); for more detailed discussion of this edition see my review in *The Yearbook of Langland Studies* 5 (1991): 196–99.

of alliterative poetry. What sorts of editions do we have? And what sort do we really need?

At times editions of alliterative texts are very obviously what may be termed rhetorical documents, ones that set out to affirm a particular method or hypothesis, not so much about particular readings but about the nature of the text itself. For example, in 1920 Israel Gollancz produced his edition of *Winner & Waster,* one designed to demonstrate the hypothesis of the subtitle: *An Alliterative Poem on Social and Economic Problems in England in the Year 1352.*[11] At certain points, Gollancz found the poem's allegory to be inadequate for the satisfactory illumination of the particulars of this hypothesis and felt it therefore necessary to emend. Thus, in line 101, the herald's fairly innocuous "ȝis lorde" becomes "Y serue, lorde," because Gollancz felt the herald was actually the Black Prince and his emendation provides a translation of the Black Prince's motto, "Iche dene." We see here, if you like, the opposite extreme from Donatelli's conservatism, in a willingness to pursue the logic of argument to a point where the text has to be reinvented to fit the hypothesis.[12]

If this example focuses the issue of editorial intervention and its relationship to interpretation in a particularly obvious—and particularly extreme—way, we should clearly remain conscious that any editorial activity constitutes a form of interpretation. And we have been notably fortunate in the distinction of a number of the modern practitioners of that form of interpretation as applied to alliterative texts. But editorial interpretation of the available evidence must be constrained by the nature of that evidence. In certain circumstances much can be achieved. In the recent Duggan/Turville-Petre edition of the alliterative *Wars of Alexander*[13] we see, among much else, how the identification of a source text can provide proper grounds for emendation. But what is the aspiring student to make of the available forms of the *Awntyrs of Arthur,* which have been subjected to a range of editorial strategies, the most notable of which,

---

11. *A Good Short Debate between Winner and Waster,* ed. Israel Gollancz (London, 1920).

12. For another example of such historically driven—and invalid—editorial intervention see the poem "Summer Sunday," often characterized by editors as "A Lament for Edward II (1327);" (I follow the title as it appears in Rossell Hope Robbins, ed. *Historical Poems of the XIVth and XVth Centuries* [New York, 1959], 98–102). Thorlac Turville-Petre has demonstrated that there is no reason to connect the poem with any particular king and that it is probably late rather than early fourteenth century. See " 'Somer Sunday,' 'De Tribus Regibus Mortuis,' and 'The Awntyrs off Arthure': Three Poems in the Thirteen-Line Stanza," *Review of English Studies,* n.s. 25 (1974): 1–14.

13. *The Wars of Alexander,* ed. Hoyt N. Duggan and Thorlac Turville-Petre, EETS, s.s. 10 (Oxford, 1989).

Ralph Hanna's,[14] is also the most controversial in terms of the range, brilliance, and sheer audacity of its editorial interventions. I find myself wondering whether this is the sort of text we can safely put into student hands. It is an extraordinary and quite dazzling editorial achievement. But its emphasis on transmissional/textual problems leads where few of us, let alone our students, have the proper tools to follow. One suspects that the example of Hanna's *Awntyrs* is most likely to be emulated in the form of Miskimin's edition of *Susannah*,[15] in which failures of judgment and method combine to produce an altogether less successful piece of work. And such editions, whatever their achievements or limitations, do not primarily address the needs of a student audience who are inevitably not adequately equipped to grasp that the literary structure they seek to understand is, in fundamental ways, one shaped by modern editorial intervention.[16]

Predictably, therefore, any decision about the kind of text that is most appropriate for classroom use seems to involve the search for a via media that eschews both extreme conservatism and extreme radicalism—one that presents the text responsibly but without taking the implications of the textual evidence to a point where such evidence, rather than the study of the text as a literary work, is likely to be the main focus of enquiry.

This question of the nature and extent of emendation is a fundamental one, of course. If texts often tend to fall, like Donatelli's and Hanna's, at extreme points of the spectrum—either very conservative or very radical—and if such extreme forms do not make them the most appropriate tools for student use, how is a middle way to be prescribed? Some awareness of the needs of particular audiences seems clearly necessary. For teaching purposes demonstrations of either editorial passivity or editorial hyperingenuity seem inappropriate strategies. What is needed is in the first place a capacity to communicate a sense of the reasons why the received text is almost always to be treated with cautious skepticism. In this sense it seems to be both impossible and indeed irresponsible to teach any Middle English literature without some introduction, however brief, to the textual problems of the materials involved. The recognition that "*the* text" is more appropriately seen as "*a* state of *a* text" to

---

14. *The Awntyrs off Arthure at the Terne Wathelyn,* ed. Ralph Hanna III (Manchester, 1974).

15. *Susannah,* ed. Alice Miskimin, Yale Studies in English, 170 (New Haven, 1969).

16. To some extent, as I have already noted, this is an inevitable consequence of any form of editorial activity. I am merely concerned here to emphasize both the degree and the kinds of such intervention. Nor, I would emphasize, am I engaged in questioning its validity—just its relationship to texts we can use in the classroom.

which there may at times be compelling alternatives can provide a helpful restraint on interpretative exuberance on the part of both teacher and student.[17]

This is not in any sense an argument against emendation, but merely an attempt to suggest that in editions intended for student use there are limits on what should be attempted in editorial terms: neither texts that are avowedly interventionist in the degree and kind of their emendations nor those that tend toward the diplomatic are likely to be the best way of introducing students to the problems of alliterative poetry, or any other genre for that matter. When modest conjecture can impose intelligibility upon a text, it ought to be essayed. Such is not always the case even in the most frequently edited of texts. For example, *Sir Gawain and the Green Knight,* line 11: "Tiscius to Tuscan and teldes bigynnes." Some fairly widely used teaching editions (like Cawley's Everyman)[18] pass over the line without comment. Others do note that the name "Tiscius" appears nowhere else in Middle English and that elsewhere the person apparently here denominated is named "Tuscus" or "Tuscius" or "Turnus" or "Tirius."[19] Some editors do go on to raise the possibility that there might be an error here. But no one seems disposed to edit out of existence a figure who seems to exist solely as a scribal vagary and replace him with a credibly endowed alternative. I confess that the grounds for nonintervention here do not seem very compelling, and appear attributable to a form of the pusillanimity we identify as "the tyranny of copy text." Here is an instance where corruption seems very probable and emendation is possible (unlike a number of the instances confronting Donatelli in *Death and Liffe*). An editor might reasonably offer students proper assistance here by attempting to make up his or her mind as to what the text actually means and emending accordingly.[20]

He or she might consider doing so in other respects. I am somewhat surprised that Larry Benson's interesting experiment in normalization in his edition of the alliterative *Morte Arthur* has not commended itself to more editors

---

17. For a parallel assertion of this view in relation to Eddic poetry see T. W. Machan, "Alliteration and the Editing of Eddic Poetry," *Scandinavian Studies* 64 (1992): 216–27, who concludes that "for these poems . . . there is not in fact 'a single *right* editorial goal'" (227).

18. *Pearl [and] Sir Gawain and the Green Knight,* ed. A. C. Cawley (London, 1962).

19. The various responses to the problems of the manuscript form are helpfully enumerated in *The Pearl Poems: An Omnibus Edition,* ed. William Vantuono (New York, 1984), 2:238–39.

20. There are other instances in the text of *Gawain* where scribal error appears to exist but has gone wholly unremarked, as in lines 2101–2 where Gawain's guide assures him that the Green Knight has a "body bigger þen þe best fowre / þat ar in Arþurez hous, Hestor, oþer oþer." Commentary tends to identify Hector as either Hector of Troy (not, in fact, a member of Arthur's court) or the rather obscure Hector de la Mare, hardly one, let alone four, of the best in Arthur's court. The passage invites emendation, as do lines 2411–13, where Gawain blames Morgan le Fay for her role in the plot against him some lines before Bertilak has revealed it.

of alliterative texts who aspire to be student-friendly.[21] His imposition of a degree of orthographic consistency is potentially helpful for the beginning student, even if it does involve both extensive orthographic changes (averaging about five to a line in a trial passage) and a measure of misleading dialectal adjustment, which tends, as he points out, to make the text rather more Midlandish than it is in the manuscript, which is itself possibly a misleading representation of the poem's original dialect. Given that any edition perforce misrepresents the original text in some measure, such pragmatic procedures might merit more consideration for student purposes.[22]

We also need to be conscious of the ways in which other aspects of the editorial process, apart from emendation and dialect, impinge on forms of literary study. Even such a relatively trivial-seeming matter as capitalization can have a crucial bearing on meaning.[23] Another obvious one is punctuation. John Burrow has recently emphasized that "decisions about punctuation determine, continuously, and often fundamentally, the ways in which a text will be understood by its readers,"[24] and has shown how varied have been the interpretations of the opening lines of *Sir Gawain and the Green Knight* based on the different ways it has been punctuated. One noninterventionist school of editing would perhaps urge the irrelevance of such minutiae, since it has been argued that the proper aim of editing is to reproduce the text as it would have been available to a medieval reader, that is, largely or wholly without punctuation, or indeed, without much editorial apparatus at all.[25] If the editor is to be replaced

---

21. *King Arthur's Death: The Middle English Stanzaic Morte Arthur and Alliterative Morte Arthure,* ed. Larry D. Benson (Indianapolis, 1974).

22. Another helpful attempt to adjust orthography in an edition for student purposes is John Burrow's of *Sir Gawain* (Harmondsworth, 1972); he replaces all obsolete graphic forms and attempts to impose a degree of orthographic uniformity on the text (see 7).

23. See, for example, John Burrow, "Reason's Horse," *Yearbook of Langland Studies* 4 (1990): 139–44, where he urges that the capitalization of "Wil" is essential to render *Piers Plowman* C, 4/21–23 intelligible. Jill Mann notes more generally the responsibilities of the editor in this regard in *Piers Plowman:* "It is the editors of the poem who have the unenviable task of bestowing on the 'abstractum agens' the capital letter which baptises it as a full personification" (*Langland and Allegory,* Morton Bloomfield Lectures on Medieval English Literature, II [Kalamazoo, 1992], 15; see also 15–17).

24. "Problems in Punctuation: *Sir Gawain and the Green Knight,* Lines 1–7," in *Sentences: Essays Presented to Alan Ward on the Occasion of his Retirement from Wadham College, Oxford* (Southampton, 1988), 75.

25. For a recent assertion of this argument see Robert S. Sturges, "Textual Scholarship: Ideologies of Literary Production," *Exemplaria* 3 (1991): 109–31; see especially 125: "The problem . . . is that the choice of a given manuscript version determines all future perceptions of the work in question. . . . Because that version is an actual medieval one, the charge of falsification or unconscious modernization is greatly reduced. . . ; this method seems preferable to critical editing for medieval works."

by the facsimile or the facsimile transcription, then our lives will perhaps be simpler, if not easier. But until we achieve this dubious apotheosis, it seems best to remind ourselves of the validity of Professor Burrow's point, and aim for forms of punctuation that seek, for teaching purposes at least, to represent meaning, if perhaps not to circumscribe it. Interestingly, Burrow and Thorlac Turville-Petre were unable to agree on the forms of punctuation to be employed in their recent edition of the opening lines of *Gawain* and adopt what they term "a light and non-committal punctuation"[26] that leaves open the issue of who is the "tulk" of line 9, Antenor or Aeneas. This may be an instance where an editor should appropriately leave interpretation as open as possible, given the clearly defined options. I do not see much evidence of general interest in this problem of punctuation and the relationship of this issue to student editions. To take a simple example from a very good recent edition of *Sir Gawain and the Green Knight:*

> þe lorde luflych aloft lepez ful ofte,
> Mynned merthe to be made vpon mony syþez,
> Hent heȝly of his hode and on a spere henged
> And wayned hom to wynne þe worchip þerof
> þat most myrþe myȝt meue þat Crystemas whyle.

$$(980-84)^{27}$$

To my mind the end of 980 requires some firmer stop, probably a colon, to mark off the series of actions that follow. The sequence becomes clearer with the addition of punctuation to indicate the distinct steps in the series, preferably semicolons:

> þe lorde luflych aloft lepez ful ofte:
> Mynned merthe to be made vpon mony syþez;
> Hent heȝly of his hode and on a spere henged;
> And wayned hom to wynne þe worchip þerof
> þat most myrþe myȝt meue þat Crystemas whyle.

Such punctuation may seem unduly ponderous; but for the student it may eliminate some degree of uncertainty. And it may help to focus the issue.

---

26. J. A. Burrow and Thorlac Turville-Petre, *A Book of Middle English* (Oxford, 1992), 64.

27. I quote from *The Poems of the Pearl Manuscript,* ed. Malcolm Andrew and Ronald Waldron, York Medieval Texts, second series (London, 1978), 244.

Should such student editions aim for such "open" forms of punctuations as those employed by Burrow and Turville-Petre? Or would students benefit from more syntactic guidance in studying a verse form often marked by fairly loose sentence structure?[28]

In some other important respects the editing of alliterative texts is becoming rather more explicit about some aspects of its procedures, particularly in relation to meter. That this is so is in large measure due to the important work of Hoyt Duggan,[29] who has, through extensive analysis, established norms and constraints for Middle English alliterative verse forms. His criteria have yet to be widely tested—although in this, as in other ways, his edition with Thorlac Turville-Petre of the *Wars of Alexander* provides an impressive model. But such testing, and any appropriate refinement of his hypotheses, seem likely to provide the necessary evidence for an analytical approach to metrical problems.

Then there are the protocols of annotation/explication confronting the editor: in what ways do these differ for alliterative texts from those for any Middle English text that is to be responsibly edited? Most distinctively of course they are linguistic—not simply is the need for glossing greater, but the nature of such glossing is likely, more often than in other Middle English texts, not to be restricted to single words but to encompass larger syntactical units.[30] This circumstance raises the question of translation. Some editions have attempted

---

28. There seems relatively little particular discussion of punctuation in alliterative texts; see, however, Ian Bishop's analysis of the implications of punctuation in two passages in *Pearl in Its Setting* (Oxford, 1968), 126–27, on lines 827–28, 803–4; Lister M. Matheson, "*Piers Plowman* B. 13.331 (330): Some 'Shrewed' Observations," Yearbook of Langland Studies 1 (1987): 108–16; on the punctuation of *Piers Plowman* B. 3. 245–46, C. 4. 335–44 see Paula J. Carlson, "Lady Meed and God's Meed: The Grammar of *Piers Plowman* B 3 C 3," *Traditio* 46 (1991): 291–311; on the complexities of punctuating *Piers Plowman* B 20. 382–84 see R. K. Emmerson, "*Piers Plowman* and Prophecy," *Yearbook of Langland Studies* 7 (1993): 43–44. See also (although not concerned specifically with alliterative texts) P. L. Heyworth, "The Punctuation of Middle English Texts," in *Medieval Studies for J. A. W. Bennett*, ed. P. L. Heyworth (Oxford, 1981), 139–58. Malcolm Parkes's *Pause and Effect: An Introduction to the History of Punctuation in the West* (London, 1992) provides a general account of medieval punctuation theory and practice.

29. For a full bibliography of his various studies see his recent edition of *The Wars of Alexander* with Thorlac Turville-Petre (n. 13 above); see also Turville-Petre, "Emendation on Grounds of Alliteration in *The Wars of Alexander*," *English Studies* 61 (1980): 302–17.

30. An obvious example is lines 31–36 of *Sir Gawain and the Green Knight*, and especially line 35 "With lel letteres loken," a passage which can carry different, possibly deliberately ambiguous, meanings. The passage is well discussed in the note on these lines in the Andrew and Waldron edition (see n. 27 above); see also P. J. Frankis, "*Sir Gawain and the Green Knight*, Line 35: 'With Lel Letteres Loken,'" *Notes and Queries*, n.s. 8 (1961): 329–30.

to solve this problem by offering full translations of a work, in either verse or prose.[31] Whatever the merits of the actual translation there is the obvious risk that it, rather than the original text, will become the object of study.[32] In theory, a more satisfactory alternative is the glossing of difficult passages in footnotes. In practice, the perception of the nature and extent of difficulty tends to vary from one edition to the next. Ideally, any editor should aim to alert the student to any passages that pose grammatical and/or lexical problems and explain how such passages should be understood. Even allowing for human variability such a procedure should serve to direct the student's attention to the text, not away from it.

Questions of language are obviously related to style. The fact that alliterative syntax and diction are often highly formulaic, for example, imposes upon the editor the responsibility both for noting the fact of such formulas and the resonances of those units at other points in the narrative; to offer an obvious example: Arthur's initial words to the Green Knight "Wye, welcum iwys to this place" (252) are ironically echoed by the Green Knight in his opening words to Gawain at the Green Chapel, "Iwysse thou art welcom, wye, to my place" (2240).[33] Or the way in which Arthur's response to the Green Knight's contemptuous laughter, when "the blode schot for schame into his schyre face / And lere" (317–18), is juxtaposed with Gawain's acknowledgment of his infidelity, when "all the blod of his brest blent in his face" (2371).[34] But commentary should not be limited to alerting students to such obvious resonances. It also ideally should seek to elucidate the purposive, dynamic nature of the language and syntax[35] of the text as literary artifact, to relate lexis to poetic texture. This is perhaps one of the most widely needed functions of

---

31. Useful bibliographies of translation of the works of the Gawain-poet can be found in Malcolm Andrew, *The Gawain-Poet: An Annotated Bibliography, 1839–1977* (New York, 1979) and William Vantuono, *The Pearl Poems: An Omnibus Edition,* 2 vols. (New York, 1984)—which itself includes verse translations of all the poems.

32. Even the finest translations occasionally obscure or suppress important details of the original. Thus Marie Borroff's translation of *Sir Gawain and the Green Knight* (New York, 1967), which is reprinted in the influential *Norton Anthology of English Literature,* omits from the initial description of the Green Knight the fact that he is shoeless (160). On the significance of this detail see Cecily Clark, *Review of English Studies,* n.s. 6 (1955): 174–77 and Marjorie Rigby, *Review of English Studies,* n.s. 7 (1956): 173–74.

33. Although this one does not seem to be noted in modern student editions; see, however, *Explicator* 29 (1971), item 73.

34. I am indebted to my student Joan Thomas for this point.

35. For an examination of one such function of syntax in *Sir Gawain* see Cecily Clark, "*Sir Gawain and the Green Knight:* Characterization by Syntax," *Essays in Criticism* 16 (1966): 361–74.

commentary: to demonstrate how alliterative verse embodies a literary language that transcends the formulaic to achieve distinctive poetic effects. The quite extensive examination of lexis in alliterative poetry has not generally been applied to the larger poetic context.[36]

The analysis of topical and rhetorical materials and the explication of underlying traditions and conventions (one thinks of such studies as Nicolas Jacobs's of storm topoi in alliterative poetry,[37] or the study of rhetorical *descriptio* in *Sir Gawain and the Green Knight*[38] and the alliterative *Morte Arthure),*[39] are other forms of literary commentary that can be profitably elaborated in the notes for editions aimed at student audiences, audiences likely to be largely unaware (initially) of the implications of such traditions and conventions for valid responses to the text.[40] Such awareness of forms of explicatory and analytic commentary, while obviously generally desirable for the understanding of Middle English literature, becomes all the more important for much alliterative poetry, which, for beginning students, will lack the relative linguistic accessibility of Chaucer, or the texture of specific reference of *Piers* with its extensive quotations from a variety of sources, which has little parallel elsewhere in the alliterative tradition.[41]

Some consideration of the forms in which we make alliterative poetry accessible to our students is obviously appropriate, not least because of the general concern with the relationship between the material forms of a text and its meaning.[42] As I said at the outset, none of the issues I have raised here is

36. For a good recent example of what can be achieved by relating lexis to poetic texture see Ralph Hanna III, "*Piers Plowman* A.5.15: Pyenye," *Yearbook of Langland Studies* 4 (1990): 145–49. It might properly be objected that such forms of annotation as I am urging would swell the bulk of student editions; but this may not be a bad thing. Perhaps some issues would require cross-reference to appropriate sections of the introduction.

37. "Alliterative Storms: A Topos in Middle English," *Speculum* 47 (1972): 695–719.

38. Derek Pearsall, "Rhetorical Descriptio in *Sir Gawain and the Green Knight,*" *Modern Language Review* 50 (1955): 129–34.

39. John Finlayson, "Rhetorical Descriptio of Place in the Alliterative *Morte Arthure,*" *Modern Philology* 61 (1963): 1–11.

40. It goes—I hope—without saying that one of the important functions of commentary should be to "place" alliterative poems intelligibly in their relation to appropriate literary motifs; but this seems generally to be well handled in modern editions.

41. Much of this material (and a great deal else) has been made accessible to students in the notes in Derek Pearsall's edition of the C-Text of *Piers* (London, 1978), one of the most helpfully annotated modern student alliterative texts.

42. This position was urged initially, and most influentially, by Jerome J. McGann in *A Critique of Modern Textual Criticism* (Chicago, 1983); see also Norman Blake, *The English Language in Medieval Literature* (London, 1977), chap. 3: "The Editorial Process," for some general comments on the implications of editorial activity for distorting our reception of medieval

peculiar to such poetry. But an awareness of the particular problems inhering in such verse may point toward some ways in which we can, through editing, bring the meaning of alliterative texts closer to the students we teach.[43]

literature. Elsewhere McGann notes: "the very physique of a book will embody a code of meaning which the reader will decipher, more or less deeply, more or less self-consciously. To read, for example, a translation of Homer's *Iliad* in the Signet paperback, in the edition published by the University of Chicago Press, in the Norton Critical Edition, or in the limited edition put out by the Folio Society . . . is to read Homer's *Iliad* in four very different ways" (*The Textual Condition* [Princeton, 1991], p. 115).

43. I observe in conclusion that the anthology edited by Thorlac Turville-Petre, *Alliterative Poetry of the Later Middle Ages* (London, 1989) is notably successful in producing editions of alliterative verse of the kind I have been advocating.

I am indebted to Professor Elizabeth Archibald, Derek Pearsall, and James McNelis for comments on drafts of this essay.

Editing Works of a Technical Nature

Editing Scientific and Practical Writings

George R. Keiser

Interest in Middle English scientific and practical writings has been a steady, but rather minor, current in medieval studies since the antiquarian period of the eighteenth and nineteenth centuries. In the past two decades, however, this interest has accelerated, and the apologetic tone of studies in this area has begun to be muted. It has long been clear, from such works as W. C. Curry's *Chaucer and the Medieval Sciences* (1926), that students of literature have much to learn from medieval science, but it has also been apparent that the scientific treatises most worthy of study were those written in Latin. Vernacular scientific writings were to Latin writings as, for a long time, Middle English romances were to continental romances, slavish imitations by lesser minds—in a word, poor relations. Eminent scholars of medieval science reinforced the disdain, as we see in the following observation by J. D. North in his 1976 edition of a vernacular translation of Richard of Wallingford's *Exafrenon:*

> No one, so far as I know, has made a detailed study of scientific writings as a whole in Middle English. There is little incentive to make even a conspectus of works which, written as they usually were by men of something less than the best academic training, tend to be intrinsically uninteresting except from a social or linguistic point of view.[1]

It is significant that in his 1988 book *Chaucer's Universe,* North made extensive use of vernacular treatises on astrology, treating them with a respect that belies his earlier harsh dismissal of such works as "intrinsically uninteresting."[2]

---

1. *Richard of Wallingford* (Oxford, 1976), 2.94.
2. *Chaucer's Universe* (Oxford, 1988). For one of many similar attacks on vernacular treatises, see Sir Frederick Smith, *The Early History of Veterinary Literature and Its British Development* (London, 1919): 1.103–222. For a more sympathetic view of a Middle English veterinary

Two publications that helped to shape a more positive view of English vernacular treatises on science and practical information were Rossell Hope Robbins's 1970 essay, "Medical Manuscripts in Middle English" and the 1974 Michael Seymour et al. edition of John Trevisa's translation of *De proprietatibus rerum* by Bartholomaeus Anglicus.[3] These works were soon followed by editions of several Middle English treatises in the Belgian series, *Scripta,* under the general editorship of Willy Braekman, and two surveys of vernacular prose writings in medicine and science by Linda Ehrsam Voigts and Laurel Braswell(-Means), respectively, both of whom have made many other distinguished contributions in this area.[4] With the importance of editing and studying vernacular treatises on science and practical information now fairly well established, this is an appropriate moment for discussing how to proceed with the vast amount of editorial work yet to be done in this area.

The prospective editor of a treatise on science must recognize that the enterprise of editing should be an extended and challenging exercise in judgment, requiring an earnest commitment to scholarship. The first challenge is to locate as many as possible (ideally, all) of the manuscripts in which the treatise under consideration is preserved. Though still not an easy task, locating manuscripts of scientific writings is far easier than in the past because of the development of a number of research tools. Among the most important are new, more comprehensive manuscript catalogs, such as those of the collections at the Huntington and Beinecke Libraries and, of particular value for its descriptions of medical and scientific manuscripts, that of the Wellcome Library.[5] Whereas earlier catalogs often provided cursory and inadequate descriptions of vernacular scientific writings, the new catalogers conscientiously provide specific information about them, even when their identity has not yet been determined.

---

treatise, see G. Keiser, "Medicines for Horses: The Continuity from Script to Print," *Yale University Library Gazette* 69 (1995): 111–28.

3. R. H. Robbins, "Medical Manuscripts in Middle English," *Speculum* 45 (1970): 393–415; M. Seymour et al., *On the Properties of Things: John Trevisa's Translation of Bartholomæus Anglicus, De Proprietatibus Rerum,* 3 vols. (Oxford, 1975–88).

4. L. E. Voigts, "Medical Prose" and L. Braswell, "Scientific and Utilitarian Prose," in *Middle English Prose: A Critical Guide to Major Authors and Genres,* ed. A. S. G. Edwards (New Brunswick, N.J., 1984): 315–35, 337–87. *Scripta: Mediaeval and Renaissance Texts and Studies* (Brussels) was initiated in 1980 and continued publishing until Prof. Dr. W. L. Braekman's retirement in 1993.

5. Barbara A. Shailor, *Catalogue of Medieval and Renaissance Manuscripts in the Beinecke Rare Book and Manuscript Library,* 3 vols. (Binghamton, 1984–92); C. W. Dutschke et al., *Guide to Medieval and Renaissance Manuscripts in the Huntington Library,* 2 vols. (San Marino, Calif., 1989); S. A. J. Moorat, *Catalogue of Western Manuscripts on Medicine and Science in the Wellcome Historical Medical Library,* vol. 1 (London, 1962).

Further help is available from the ongoing project of indexing vernacular prose works, under the general editorship of A. S. G. Edwards, from which we now have the *Index of Printed Middle English Prose* and the completed hand-lists, thirteen as of this writing, of the *Index of Middle English Prose*.[6] The former volume and several of the handlists represent a high level of scholarly achievement. The prospective editor may find the handlist covering the Ash-mole manuscripts at the Bodleian Library especially helpful, not only because this collection contains numerous vernacular scientific miscellanies, but also because the editor of the handlist has included unusually detailed cross-references to texts in other collections. In due time, one hopes, the *Index* will cover the mother lode of vernacular scientific treatises in the British Library's Harley and, especially, Sloane collections. Fortunately, Linda Voigts and Pa-tricia Derry Kurtz provide very full information concerning the British Library and other collections in their forthcoming *Catalogue of Incipits of Scientific and Medical Writings in Old and Middle English*. Now nearly complete, this catalog is already proving an indispensable research tool, thanks to the gener-osity of the collaborators in responding to requests for information from those working in the area.

With these tools available the justification for producing diplomatic or semi-diplomatic editions based on only one manuscript is far less than it was in the recent past. Such editions have been frequent, especially in the *Scripta* series, and there is something to be said for the fact that they have brought very interesting texts to critical attention. Justification for such editions may exist in one instance, the Ph.D. dissertation, for a doctoral student will rarely have sufficient resources to pay the costs for travel to a number of archives and for microfilms of several manuscripts. However, after the dissertation is accepted, the difficult question will arise as to whether such an edition should be pub-lished without extensive revision; for a new Ph.D., especially one seeking a permanent position or facing a tenure decision, the pressures to find a publisher without the delay required for extensive revision will be understandably great.

An editor with a list of manuscripts in hand, ready to assemble and organize information about them, would be well advised to look carefully at Monica H. Green's recent study, "Obstetrical and Gynecological Texts in Middle En-glish."[7] This model of scholarship demonstrates what is essential for the next stage of the project: determining the nature and state of the text each preserves

---

6. R. E. Lewis, N. F. Blake, A. S. G. Edwards, eds., *Index of Printed Middle English Prose* (New York, 1985); publication of the handlists under the general editorship of A. S. G. Edwards began in 1984 and will continue for the foreseeable future (Cambridge).

7. *Studies in the Age of Chaucer* 14 (1992): 53–88.

and defining the relationships among them, if at all possible, with the help of the source(s) from which the English text has been translated or adapted.

Examining the manuscripts of a Middle English scientific treatise will probably bring the editor to a fuller understanding of the truism that every medieval manuscript is unique. Scribes frequently modified what they found in their exemplars, deleting apparently irrelevant or confusing material, or at least abbreviating it, interpolating material from elsewhere to expand undeveloped or more relevant subjects, sometimes reproducing or exacerbating errors in the exemplar or translation. Compounding the difficulty is the fact that scribes copying scientific writings often confronted an unfamiliar, technical vocabulary, Latin or French words imported with at best slight modification, or unfamiliar plant-names.

To determine the relationships among the manuscripts and, eventually, select a base-text for an edition, the editorial task of collating texts may be made more difficult by the fact that the treatise is of considerable length. As so few of these works have been studied previously, the editor may have to make an arbitrary choice of a manuscript from which to begin the collation. Establishing the date and origin of the manuscripts, for which the editor should have some grounding in codicological analysis, will be useful, but even an early manuscript or one copied by a learned, or at least a very competent, scribe can have had an unsatisfactory exemplar. For this initial stage the editor may want to make sample transcriptions from several parts of a manuscript, especially in the case of longer works. Painful as it is to contemplate, the editor must be prepared to abandon the original transcriptions if and when a more satisfactory manuscript comes along.

Where a source exists, the editor has a very valuable tool to use in determining manuscript relations and, eventually, selecting the base-manuscript and testing its readings. Though the search may culminate in futility—which should not prevent an editor from bringing an important and interesting treatise to critical attention—the benefits of knowing the source are sufficient to encourage a search for it at an early stage in the preparation of an edition. To undertake such a search, the editor must become familiar with treatises on the same subject that have received attention, both in the vernacular and in Latin and French. For that the editor must have recourse to histories of medieval science, the annual and cumulative *Isis* bibliographies, manuscript catalogs, and the Thorndike-Kibre *Incipits of Mediaeval Scientific Writings in Latin.*[8]

---

8. *Isis Cumulative Bibliography,* vol. 1, 1913–65, ed. Magda Whitrow (London, 1971); vol. 2, 1966–75, ed. John Neu (London, 1980); vol. 3, 1976–85, ed. John Neu (Boston, 1989); Lynn

Not to be overlooked is the list of incunabular editions of treatises in science and medicine compiled by A. C. Klebs; influential scientific treatises in Latin and French were often printed on the Continent early in the history of printing.[9] Finally, the prospective editor will find that scholars working in the area are among the most valuable resources for information of this kind.

Implicit in the discussion to this point is the idea that for an editor of a vernacular treatise on science or practical information the principal goal will probably be a text as close as possible—textual witness(es) and good judgment permitting—to what came from the compiler's pen and was the origin of the surviving textual tradition. In attempting to recapture what came from the compiler's pen, the editor will be seeking evidence about the intention of the compiler, recognizing that it can never be fully known and that speculations about intention are inevitably founded on risky assumptions. While that attempt is an essential effort to produce a successful edition, the editor should also recognize that as interesting as what may have come from the compiler's pen is what has happened to a text during the history of its transmission and dissemination. Therefore, an editor needs to examine the various states of the treatise that exist in the extant manuscripts for what they reveal about the contemporary reception and understanding of the treatise. This examination may contribute to an understanding of the nature of the treatise and the uses that its compiler intended it to have.

How to judge what came from the compiler's pen and choose the manuscript that best represents it may not be a very easy task. An editor upon whom Dame Fortune smiles will choose as base-text the one that preserves a clear, coherent, and complete translation of its source. A less fortunate editor may find that the most satisfactory text is fragmentary or that the most complete text was copied by an inept or careless scribe. Or, the editor may find that the text exists in different states, owing to a complex history of transmission in which editorial revision of the text has led to rearrangement of the parts, excisions, abbreviations, or expansions. Or, the editor may find that several treatises have been conflated to form an entirely new compilation.

Thorndike and Pearl Kibre, *Incipits of Mediaeval Scientific Writings in Latin* (Cambridge, Mass., 1963). For histories of medieval science, the prospective editor can begin with George Sarton, *Introduction to the History of Science,* 3 vols. (Baltimore, 1927–48) and Lynn Thorndike, *History of Magic and Experimental Science,* especially vols. 1–4 (New York, 1934). More recent, though less comprehensive, is David C. Lindberg, ed., *Science in the Middle Ages* (Chicago, 1978). For other recent works the student should consult the annual bibliographies in *Isis,* as well as the cumulative volumes.

9. A. C. Klebs, *Incunabula scientifica et medica, Osiris* 4 (1938; rpt. Hildesheim 1963).

To some extent the state of the witnesses will affect the editor's choice of a base-text; therefore, the reasons for that choice will inevitably vary. In an extreme case where the editor has to work with a text close to what may have come from the compiler's pen but was copied by an inept scribe, the extent of the emendation required for the edition may be so great as to justify turning to a less satisfactory witness, if one exists. Should the most satisfactory exemplar be fragmentary, the editor may have to turn to another text, at least for the missing portions. For his edition of the herbal *Agnus Castus* Gösta Brodin faced an unusual, but not a unique situation: all of the manuscripts were incomplete. Thus, to reconstruct a complete version of the herbal he supplemented the base-text with substantial portions of four other manuscripts.[10] In the case of a revised work, publication costs permitting, the editor should give serious thought to a parallel-text edition. When I edited *The Boke of Stones,* a Middle English lapidary extant in two manuscripts, the earlier one fragmentary, the later one a revision, the work was short enough to permit a parallel-text edition.[11] The alternative, of incorporating the lost material from the revised version into the base-text, seemed undesirable. Reproducing both texts in full had the additional virtue of illustrating two forms of English prose separated by a half-century.

For a text that is made up of various treatises the editor may wish to present a base-manuscript that best represents the efforts of the compiler who put the several treatises together, or the editor may want to go back and recover the individual treatises, if that is more desirable and still possible. The likelihood is that the conflation has an intrinsic interest and deserves an edition of its own. Here again a parallel-text edition may be possible, or the editor may want to make use of an appendix or two to present other versions of material in the compilation. In her facsimile edition of *The Boke of St. Albans* (1485; RSTC 3308) Rachel Hands included a transcription of a manuscript text of the hunting treatise that had been incorporated into the printed work.[12] Yet another manuscript version had been printed previously, and the accessibility of the three texts is highly desirable, for each casts light on the other. Into his edition of *The Boke of St. Albans* (1496; RSTC 3309) Wynkyn de Worde interpolated a text of *The Treatyse of Fysshynge wyth an Angle,* portions of which are extant

---

10. *Agnus Castus: A Middle English Herbal,* Essays and Studies on English Language and Literature, 6 (Uppsala, 1950). For his edition of *Thomas Norton's Ordinal of Alchemy,* EETS 272 (London, 1975) John Reidy reconstructed the text from two different manuscripts.

11. G. Keiser, ed., *The Middle English "Boke of Stones": The Southern Version,* Scripta, 13 (Brussels, 1984).

12. *English Hawking and Hunting in "The Boke of St. Albans"* (London, 1975).

in two manuscripts. These fragments have been edited, the better-known one in a volume with an edition of Wynkyn's version, prepared by Sherman Kuhn. In still another edition of Wynkyn's text W. L. Braekman included parallel and related texts of fishing material from which the *Treatyse* was compiled.[13] The opportunity for study of the fishing and hunting treatises was greatly enhanced by having the related texts available within the same book.

An unhappy prospect for an editor is that conditions beyond his or her control may necessitate choosing a base-text that is less than satisfactory. Access to the most satisfactory text is not always possible: the manuscript may be in private hands; the costs of traveling to and settling in at its location may be prohibitively expensive; photographic reproduction of a quality from which to make a transcription, for any one of several reasons, may not be possible. In such instances, the base-text will have to be one that is in some respects less than fully satisfactory, and the editor may have to settle for providing variants from a better exemplar (if even that is possible).

Prior to preparing the text, the editor will have to make decisions about the scope and nature of the edition. Modern editorial procedures, like so much else in modern criticism, are a subject of ongoing debate. Anne Hudson's 1977 tripartite division of editions—unemended, critical, and eclectic—still seems valid, as does this observation: "there can be no 'formula' for the ideal edition, but the editor must make his own decisions about the presentation of the text in light of the evidence available."[14] While this observation refers to writing of all kinds, Hudson's emphasis on the ongoing exercise of editorial judgment in preparing an edition is certainly relevant to the editing of scientific and practical writings, and this editorial judgment should be based on the full and complete examination of the state of the text in the various witnesses that I have been urging.

For the editor of a translation an essential aspect of that exercise of judgment will be the use of the source to test the readings in the vernacular version. That editor will need to be aware that having the source, especially for a closely translated text, can lead to an overconfident belief that a conscientious modern editor is always more capable of discerning, understanding, and reproducing a translator's intention than a contemporary scribe. It is a short journey from this

---

13. John McDonald, assisted by Sherman Kuhn and Dwight Webster, *The Origins of Angling* (New York, 1963); G. Keiser, "The Middle English *Treatyse of Fysshynge wyth an Angle* and the Gentle Reader," *Yale University Library Gazette* 61 (1986): 22–48; *The Treatise on Angling in "The Boke of St. Albans" (1496)*, ed. W. L. Braekman, Scripta, 1 (Brussels, 1980).

14. Anne Hudson, "Middle English," *Editing Medieval Texts*, ed. A. G. Rigg (New York, 1977), 51.

belief to the conclusion that disagreements between the English text and the source inevitably attest to scribal corruption. The result may be an edition characterized by hypercorrection, which does not represent what came from the compiler's pen and what influenced generations of early readers. In testing disagreements between the English text and the source, the editor must not overlook the possibility that the translator misread the source or relied upon a different text than that on which a modern edition of the source is based. That edition, like the one the editor of the English text will produce, is an idealized construct, the sum of numerous editorial judgments about alternate readings that may or may not appear in a record of variants. Very desirable, but certainly not always possible, is access to manuscripts of the source, especially those from the same period and place as that in which the translator worked. Even with such access, only an unwise editor discounts the idea that a vernacular treatise is a deliberate adaptation of the source, incorporating additional (mis)information and other conscious revisions.

The Seymour edition of Trevisa's translation of Bartholomaeus Anglicus illustrates the problems that arise when editors make use of a source to enforce radical restoration of a text, by means of an abundance of conjectural emendations. Its discussion of editorial method defines the understanding of intention by the editors: "it has been assumed, on the basis of evidence contained in the translation, that Trevisa was an intelligent and competent Latinist who generally (and sometimes literally rather than idiomatically) followed the Latin text before him without question, though occasionally interpolating his own comment" (1.xv). Trevisa's intention, it appears, was to produce something just a cut above what Samuel Workman called "stencil translation."[15] The assumption that the intelligent and competent Latinist was translating word-by-word leads to another assumption: the existence of a word in the Latin text, for which no corresponding word is found either in the base-text or any of the extant witnesses, justifies the manufacture of a reading.

Such ambitious editorial work led to numerous problematic readings in the Trevisa edition; from a few of these the editors withdrew some support in the volume devoted to textual commentary, published thirteen years after the two volumes of text. For example, the editor of Book XVI, Trevisa's lapidary, conceded "the emendation may be unjustified" (3:162) in instances where the reading *inuenitur* in the Latin text had been used to justify emending "is" to "is [yfounde]." The concession is reluctant, and the editor is silent about another,

---

15. Samuel K. Workman, *Fifteenth Century Translation as an Influence on English Prose* (Princeton, 1940).

similar reading, where *inueniuntur* led to the emending of "beþ" to "beþ [yfounde]." Such emendations, which seem to defy a claim of editorial aware-ness that "in translating recurrent syntax and phrasing in his source he [Tre-visa] developed certain habits of syntax and idiom" (1:xv), may amount to little more than examples of editorial fussiness when viewed individually. Taken together, however, they can characterize Trevisa's habits as translator in a way that is some distance from the reality.

Reaction to the active editing of Seymour and his associates has not always been enthusiastic. Responding to the controversy, in particular to a somewhat unfavorable review, David Greetham wrote an eloquent rationale for their editorial practices. From his own experience in editing Book XV, Trevisa's geography, Greetham generalized about the editorial treatment of translated works by constructing "models which can be employed in evaluating the conditions to be found in the translated and translating languages and texts."[16] Greetham's study is a very impressive intellectual exercise, and it deserves careful study by an editor of a translated scientific treatise. However, an editor evaluating readings in a translation should consider that a translator may be engaged in an act more complex than Greetham's models suggest. Further-more, the uncertainties of the witness(es) to the text and those of the wit-ness(es) to the source often require editorial judgments of greater complexity than a series of models would suggest (and that is implicitly clear in Greet-ham's study).[17]

One example from an English lapidary, the *Boke of Stones,* illustrates the complexities. The two extant manuscripts contain this statement: "The bokes telleþ vs þat þe gentil rubye fyn and clene is lord of stones and is also water of wateres." Coming upon that last phrase, which defies sense, an editor will be tempted to emend the text to read "gem of gems," as is found in manuscripts of the French source. The emendation might be reasonable if paleographical confusion of *water* and *gem* were likely. As it is not, the reading must be what came from the compiler's pen, the likely reason for which is apparent in

---

16. "Models for the Textual Transmission of Translation: The Case of John Trevisa," *Studies in Bibliography* 37 (1984): 132. Though Greetham does not mention a review by Anne Hudson, *Review of English Studies* 28 (1977): 203–4, three pages (145–47) of the article are a response to a reading proposed by Hudson. Another review of the Seymour edition worthy of attention is that of Klaus Bitterling, *Anglia* 98 (1980): 492–99.

17. Though neither is concerned with scientific writings, two other studies of translations deserve the prospective editor's attention: Tim William Machan, "Editorial Method and Medieval Translations: The Example of Chaucer's *Boece,*" *Studies in Bibliography* 41 (1988): 188–96; C. W. Marx, "Problems of Editing a Translation: Anglo-Norman to Middle English," *The Medieval Translator, II,* Westfield Publications in Medieval Studies, vol. 5 (London, 1991), 253–67.

manuscripts of the source. While some versions read, "C'est la gemme des gemmes" (Bibliothèque nationale, mss. fr 2008, 2009), others read "Ce est la iame des iames" (Bibliothèque nationale, ms. fr 12786). It is conceivable that the translator's manuscript of the source had a variant form, "Ce est la iaue de iaues," but it seems more probable that the translator misread "iame" as "iawe" or "iaue."

The decision to retain the reading "water of wateres" is based in great part on paleographical considerations, but also on assumptions about the critical acumen of the translator of the lapidary, which are less complimentary than those Greetham and his associates made about Trevisa. Such assumptions will have a part in the decisions to emend or not to emend, for the editor is not only attempting to recapture what came from the translator's pen, but also reconstructing the version of the source used by the translator and the translator's understanding of that version. That awareness may prevent the editor from producing a modern improvement on the translator's text, a text that is more the editor's than the translator's.

This example illustrates the desirability of having access to more than one manuscript of the source of a translated work. This general principle holds true not only for works translated from a Latin or French source, but for English treatises that are compiled, in whole or in part, from other English writings. The vernacular lapidary in Peterborough Cathedral ms. 33 is a compilation that draws upon texts of at least two vernacular works, the *Boke of Stones* and Trevisa's Book XVI. When Evans and Serjeantson edited the "Peterborough Lapidary" and the *Boke of Stones,* which they called "The London Lapidary of King Philip," they knew only the revised version of the latter work in Bodleian ms., Douce 291, not the version found in Newberry Library, ms. 32.9. Therefore, they were unable to recognize the extent of the Peterborough compiler's indebtedness to the *Boke of Stones.* Similarly, until the Seymour edition of Trevisa appeared, it was not clear how extensively the Peterborough compiler had borrowed from that work. Indeed, even this edition of Trevisa, because it lacks a record of variants, is inadequate for determining the extent of that indebtedness because the Peterborough compiler was borrowing from a text different from that which served as the base-text for the edition.[18]

These complex relations among the Middle English lapidaries lead to a larger point concerning the importance of editorial judgment. If hypercorrec-

---

18. G. R. Keiser, "The Sources of the Peterborough Lapidary," *Cultuurhistorische Caleido-scoop,* ed. C. DeBacker (Gent, 1992), 343–48.

tion represents one extreme, the other is a failure to temper editorial rigor with flexibility in establishing readings in editions of scientific writings, even when the witnesses may not support emendation. For example, the Newberry and Douce texts of the *Boke of Stones* share a clearly erroneous reading in the phrase "an heer of wolle of shepe þat is white lombe." As the source indicates, the penultimate word should be *with*, not "white," and the Peterborough text's "with" is surely the correct reading (which I mistakenly refrained from emending when I edited the text). By itself the evidence of the Peterborough Lapidary, copied long after the two known versions of the *Boke of Stones,* might seem to be of dubious value, but in combination with the source, it supports emendation.

The question of how much weight to give to a later, derivative version of a text comes more sharply into focus in the case of a Middle English translation of the Second Anglo-Norman Prose Lapidary, which Evans and Serjeantson edited from an Elizabethan commonplace book, British Library ms., Sloane 2628. A much earlier text has now emerged, in a late-fourteenth-century manuscript, British Library, Egerton 827, which is far closer to the Anglo-Norman version. Yet in numerous instances the Elizabethan version preserves a reading, or at least a sense, much closer to the Anglo-Norman version. How an editor evaluates the evidence of a later manuscript, especially one preserving a text revised by an editor or scribe, and how much to rely on it for emendations are questions that can be answered only on a case-by-case basis.[19] In each instance possible contamination from scribal use of the source or an independent translation must be considered if the editor is to avoid producing a more accurate translation than the original translator produced.

Finally, the editor of a scientific or practical treatise has a specific responsibility to prepare a critical apparatus that assists readers unacquainted with such writings, as most will be, to understand the treatise. In deciding how best to fulfill this responsibility the editor will want to look closely at the apparatus in recent editions of scientific writing. If it seems beneficial and relevant to do so, the editor should adapt or incorporate features of that apparatus. One very recent edition, *Practical and Popular Science,* seems to deserve special notice in this regard. An anthology of a dozen Middle English treatises of different nature, each prepared by a different editor (or pair of collaborators, in two cases), this volume illustrates a range of possible approaches to critical appa-

---

19. G. Keiser, "An Unnoticed Middle English Version of the Second Anglo-Norman Prose Lapidary," *Manuscripta* 38 (1994): 74–79.

ratus and, indeed, to many other matters of concern to editors of scientific writings.[20]

First, in devising critical apparatus, the editor should recognize that readers unfamiliar with medieval science need to be introduced to the learned and popular traditions from which the treatise emerges. For very useful models the prospective editor would do well to look carefully at John Reidy's edition of the *Ordinal of Alchemy,* the edition of Latin and Middle English versions of a phlebotomy text by Linda E. Voigts and Michael R. McVaugh, and F. M. Getz's edition of the vernacular adaptation of Gilbertus Anglicus's *Compendium medicinae.*[21] It is also advisable to investigate early modern treatises on the same subject to determine how long the learning in the treatise or, perhaps, the treatise itself continued to endure.

To assure a better understanding of those traditions and their endurance an editor should consider providing technical information, which may require the assistance of academic colleagues in the natural sciences. My own experience suggests that these colleagues will have little reluctance in sharing their learning and, indeed, will be delighted to find themselves acknowledged in the edition. When I edited a manuscript of the *The Treatyse of Fysshynge wyth an Angle,* a colleague in the Department of Entomology graciously (and eagerly) identified the baits recommended in the treatise. In a more recent study of a veterinary treatise I have relied on the help of an excellent student from our College of Veterinary Medicine to define the nature of the ailments and to evaluate the potential efficacy of the therapies.

Second, depending on how wide an audience the edition is intended to reach and how difficult the language is, the editor might consider a translation parallel to the text, as in Sherman Kuhn's edition of the Middle English fishing treatise, which was directed to readers of *Sports Illustrated,* or Beryl Rowland's edition of a gynecological treatise,[22] whose anticipated readers must

---

20. Lister M. Matheson, ed., *Popular and Practical Science of Medieval England* (East Lansing, Mich., 1994).

21. *Thomas Norton's Ordinal of Alchemy,* lii–lxxv; Linda E. Voigts and Michael R. McVaugh, eds., "A Latin Technical Phlebotomy and Its Middle English Translation," *Transactions of the American Philosophical Society,* 74 (1984): 1–25; F. M. Getz, ed., *Healing and Society in Medieval England* (Madison, 1991), xviii–xli. A caveat concerning the problematic nature of the latter edition is necessary: see reviews by Tony Hunt, *Medical History* 37 (1993): 206–7, and G. Keiser, *Journal of the History of the Behavioral Sciences* 30 (1994): 71–74. Worth noting is the fact that Voigts and McVaugh provide, in an appendix, a text of another Middle English phlebotomy, translated from the same source as the one that is their central concern.

22. *Medieval Woman's Guide to Health: The First English Gynecological Handbook* (Kent, Ohio, 1981); regarding the problematic nature of this edition, see the review by L. E. Voigts and Jerry Stannard, *Speculum* 57 (1982): 422–26.

have included students and teachers in women's studies programs. Presumably because the publishers of their work envisioned a learned audience that included many nonspecialists, Voigts and McVaugh provided a lengthy summary of the Latin version of their phlebotomy treatise (56–61).

Third, if the treatise is a translation and if a source is used for emendations, an edition should have a detailed explanation of why the editor selected the particular text of the source used for emendation, as well as the editor's conclusions about the translator's handling of the source. The brevity of the phlebotomy treatise permitted Voigts and McVaugh to include a full text of the Latin source, and they carefully explained that from thirty possible manuscripts they selected a fourteenth-century text close to that of the English translation, rather than one closer to the original version of circa 1200 (9–10). In my edition of the *Boke of Stones* I thought it advisable to give an account of several manuscripts of the French source (xiii–xvi) and to present rather detailed explorations of their several texts in the commentary on the English text (45–79). In their earlier edition Evans and Serjeantson based their commentary on a late version of the source, which contributed to a mistaken impression of the English translator's handling of the source (133–46).

Fourth, as the manuscript miscellanies that preserve Middle English writings on science and practical information are often very interesting, some codicological analysis is desirable. As much as any other kind of Middle English writings, scientific treatises can be better understood in their context, and the manuscript miscellanies provide an excellent opportunity for explaining and illustrating that context. At the very least an account of the contents of the miscellanies, as well as a description of *ordinatio* and finding devices, can reveal a great deal about the nature and range of contemporary readers of the treatise. From this information the editor can proceed to a better explanation of the history of transmission and state of the text in the various witnesses.[23] This explanation should include some information about scribal techniques (use of abbreviations, for example) and the scribe's response to the technical language and other special terms.

Fifth, while an extensive record of variants will contribute to a cluttered appearance and perhaps distract some readers, a reasonably complete account of the most important variants can serve numerous purposes. Without it the

---

23. In her monumental edition of Anglo-Norman agricultural treatises, *Walter of Henley* (Oxford, 1971), Dorothea Oschinsky does a remarkable job of describing the state of the texts in the witnesses and of defining the relationships among accretive and otherwise modified texts. This edition certainly deserves the attention of a prospective editor of vernacular writings on science and information.

reader cannot evaluate the judgment of the editor or study the state of the text in the witnesses. Because it limited the record of variants to those relevant to emendations, the Seymour edition of Trevisa is an especially attractive and readable text. However, as Anne Hudson has noted, a text that lacks a record of variants "can only be used by one interested in its content: any study of the text's linguistic history, of any traces of change in translational method, or of scribal interest in its matter, is quite impossible" ("Middle English," 41). As noted above, the absence of a record of variants made it difficult for me to judge how indebted the compiler of the Peterborough Lapidary was to Trevisa's Book XVI. Only when I consulted the more complete record of variants in the dissertation from which Book XVI of the Seymour edition was derived did it become possible to see that the Peterborough compiler had borrowed extensively from a text rather different from that used for the edition.[24]

Finally, as the manuscripts themselves attest, charts and illustrations are extremely helpful, and at times altogether necessary, for reading many works of science and information. Surprisingly few recent editions make use of illustrations or even direct their readers to other books containing relevant illuminations from contemporary manuscripts. Reidy's *Ordinal of Alchemy* is better for the inclusion of one of a program of six illuminations from the base-text. The use of sketches of birth-figures based on illuminations in the manuscript adds to Rowland's gynecological treatise, but the reasons for using modern sketches rather than the manuscript illuminations themselves, especially in a volume with numerous illustrations of less relevance, are as unclear as many other matters in this edition. For more ideal models one must turn to the charts in North's edition of Richard of Wallingford, the manuscript illuminations in Voigts and McVaugh's phlebotomy treatise, and the surprisingly extensive and helpful array of charts, diagrams, and reproductions of illuminations accompanying many of the treatises in *Practical and Popular Science.*

In devising critical apparatus for scientific and practical writings, the editor should go as far as the publisher allows and expertise permits, not fearing a reviewer's disapproval, so long as the apparatus fulfills the all-important purpose of making the edited text more easily accessible and comprehensible. Making these writings accessible, in the fullest sense of the word, to all students of later medieval England is the responsibility of and indeed the greatest challenge to their editors.

---

24. Unfortunately, the long-delayed third volume has no detailed record of variants, and for such information the student of Trevisa must return to the manuscripts. It should be noted, however, that criticism of this edition does not overshadow the fact that having an edition of Trevisa available, even one that does not fulfill all hopes, is reason for gratitude.

Editing Astrological and Prognostic Texts

Linne Mooney

The principal difficulty in editing astrological and prognostic texts is finding them. Locating merely a single instance of such a text is easy, for they are ubiquitous in medieval English miscellanies and scientific manuscripts. But finding further copies or versions of this single instance often involves a significant commitment of time and effort—and a great deal of perseverance.

Reference tools necessary for this pursuit are not many, but fortunately they are increasing. The *Index of Middle English Verse (IMEV)*, its *Supplement,* and the handlists of the *Index of Middle English Prose*—currently appearing at the rate of about one per year—are works of first resort.[1] Rossell Hope Robbins's 1939 article "English Almanacks of the Fifteenth Century," which first identified many Middle English astrological and prognostic texts, remains useful, as do the articles of Förster and the books of Swainson and Wright.[2] Among more recent studies are Irma Taavitsainen's *Middle English Lunaries: A Study of the Genre* and Laurel Means's "Electionary, Lunary, Destinary, and Questionary: Toward Defining Categories of Middle English Prognostic Material."[3] Finally,

---

1. Carleton Brown and Rossell Hope Robbins, *The Index of Middle English Verse* (New Haven, 1943); Rossell Hope Robbins and John L. Cutler, *Supplement to the Index of Middle English Verse* (Lexington, Ky., 1965); A. S. G. Edwards, general editor, *The Index of Middle English Prose,* vols. 1–13 (Woodbridge, 1983–97).

2. Rossell Hope Robbins, "English Almanacks of the Fifteenth Century," *Philological Quarterly* 18 (1939): 321–31; Max Förster, "Beiträge zur mittelalterlichen Volkskunde," *Archiv für das Studium der neueren Sprachen* 120 (1908): 43–52, 296–305; 121 (1908): 30–46; 125 (1910): 39–70; 127 (1911): 31–84; 128 (1912): 55–71, 285–308; 129 (1912): 16–49; 134 (1916): 264–93; Förster, "Kleinere mittelenglische Texte," *Anglia* 42 (1918): 145–224; Charles Swainson, *A Handbook of Weather Folklore* (Edinburgh, 1873); A. R. Wright and T. E. Lones, *British Calendar Customs,* 3 vols. (London, 1938–40).

3. Irma Taavitsainen, *Middle English Lunaries: A Study of the Genre,* Mémoires de la Société Néophilologique de Helsinki, 47 (Helsinki, 1988); Laurel Means, "Electionary, Lunary, Destinary, and Questionary: Toward Defining Categories of Middle English Prognostic Material," *Studies in Philology* 89 (1992): 367–403.

Popular and Practical Science of Medieval England, ed. Lister M. Matheson, offers a number of models for editions of astrological and prognostic texts, not only in the sections on astrology (3–59) and prognostication (61–183) but also in medical texts with astrological and prognostic content, "Diet and Bloodletting: A Monthly Regimen" (245–61) and "A Zodiacal Lunary for Medical Professionals" (283–300).[4]

Even with those tools that are currently available, there are frequently gaps in our knowledge of the texts where astrological and prognostic materials are concerned. In the manuscripts, texts of astrological or prognostic content are frequently brief, and they often occur with several individual texts occurring in sequence, so that catalogers have tended to group them, giving only the incipit of the first. For instance, the *Index of Middle English Verse* and its *Supplement* failed to record verse prognostications for the year based on the Dominical Letter in San Marino, Huntington HM 64, ff. 94–95 ("An hoote wynter, a tempestly somer, / Plenty of corne, of frute goode caster") because they were interspersed with verse prognostications based on the day of the week on which Christmas falls (*IMEV* 1905) on those folios. That is, the prognostications for the year in which the Dominical Letter is *A* follow the lines giving prognostication for the year in which Christmas falls on a Monday (lines 47–58 of *IMEV* 1905), those for the year in which the Dominical Letter is *B* follow those for when Christmas falls on a Sunday (lines 33–46 of *IMEV* 1905), and so on. Very similar verse prognostications based on the Dominical Letter survive in Cambridge, Magdalene, Pepys 1236, f. 66[v], another item not recorded in *IMEV* or its *Supplement.* Even as meticulous a cataloger as was M. R. James in preparing the catalog of *The Western Manuscripts in the Library of Trinity College, Cambridge* tended to group astrological and prognostic texts.[5] For instance, his entry for ms. O.2.40 grouped together six prose astrological texts, each having separate heading and colophon, under a single entry, "On 152 sqq. a tract in English on '*separaciones applicaciones etc. planetarum,*' with names in cypher" (3:144). He did not give any incipits. Since other reference tools, like *The Index of Middle English Verse* or Wells's *Manual,* depended upon the library catalogs as sources for their entries, the catalogers' omissions are not corrected there.[6]

---

4. Lister Matheson, ed., *Popular and Practical Science of Medieval England* (East Lansing, Mich., 1994).

5. M. R. James, *The Western Manuscripts in the Library of Trinity College, Cambridge: A Descriptive Catalogue,* 4 vols. (Cambridge, 1900–1904).

6. John Edwin Wells, *Manual of the Writings in Middle English, 1050–1400* (New Haven, Conn., 1916; *Supplements* 1–9, 1919–51). For *Index of Middle English Verse,* see note 1.

Besides occurring in sequence, brief Middle English texts of this content are also frequently written singly onto the margins or flyleaves of manuscripts, or added between major texts of very different content. In such locations they are often omitted from mention by editors of the manuscripts and by catalogers. In the case of flyleaf additions, they have even been left off of microfilms of the manuscripts. For instance, a Middle English medical or astrological fragment on melancholy written on a pastedown inside the back cover of Trinity College, Cambridge O.2.5 is not only omitted by James but also does not appear in the microfilm of that manuscript. Distinguishing individual texts that have been herded indiscriminately into a group by modern catalogers requires the perseverance mentioned above; discovering stray texts left unmentioned by such catalogers may require a bit of luck as well.

Until the *Index of Middle English Prose* is complete, one creative way to find other versions, or sources, of a Middle English astrological or prognostic text is to translate its first lines into Latin and consult the *Catalogue of Incipits of Mediaeval Scientific Writings in Latin,* edited by Lynn Thorndike and Pearl Kibre.[7] Using this method I discovered references to Latin versions of one of those Middle English astrological texts from Cambridge, Trinity College ms. O.2.40 that James had grouped together for his entry. The Middle English text began on folio 152,

The houre of þe sun ys fortunat in all begynnyg but for goyng to þe kyng or to oder myȝthty men & namely not in þe sonne downegoyng nor to do on new cloþs nor lat no blode nor gyf oute no substance for marchandes nor begyn no fundacyon of beyldyng or townes nor by no bestys.

Neither the *Index of Printed Middle English Prose* nor any of the handlists of the *Index of Middle English Prose* published to date listed this incipit.[8] Something close to the Latinized text of the incipit was found, however, in Thorndike and Kibre, column 639: "Hora solis infortunata est in omni re . . . ," there identified as either Dorotheus Sidonius, *De electionibus in horis* or Haly Aben Ragel, *De iudiciis.* Dorotheus's text, found in Cambridge, Pembroke College 204, ff. 76ᵛ–77 and Munich, Staatsbibliothek lat. 59, ff. 277ᵛ–278, turned out to be the Latin original for the Middle English text; and thus I discovered that

---

7. Lynn Thorndike and Pearl Kibre, *A Catalogue of Incipits of Mediaeval Scientific Writings in Latin* (Cambridge, Mass., 1963).

8. R. E. Lewis, N. F. Blake, and A. S. G. Edwards, *An Index of Printed Middle English Prose* (New York, 1985). For *Index of Middle English Prose* see note 1.

the Middle English text is one of the few surviving witnesses of this work by Dorotheus. I have as yet been unable to locate further Middle English versions.

Identifying or finding sources for Middle English astrological and prognostic texts may also be complicated by the medieval scribes' habit of compiling information from several sources in a single encyclopedic compendium of the subject. This was a problem I encountered when editing a text on astrological medicine ("A Middle English Verse Compendium of Astrological Medicine"),[9] where excerpts, paraphrases, and translations from several sources are held loosely together by rhyme. A clumsy compiler, like the author and/or scribes of the compendium I edited, gives clues to the separate sources for his compilation. In the case of the "Compendium," changes in person and number, or in rhyme scheme, and omissions or additions of portions with distinct subject matter in one or the other of the two surviving manuscript versions of the text, indicate at least seven distinct sources for portions of the received text. A more careful medieval compiler leaves more work for the modern editor to determine the boundaries between originally separate materials. Natural breaks in the subject matter, sometimes cued by the medieval author or compiler (e.g., "Nowe turne we to . . . "), suggest possible divisions in source materials. Medieval citations of author or source (e.g., "Ion of Burgoyn says thus in his treticys," "In Ionis lyf of Beuerley that may thou lere") suggest others. Once the distinct portions of the text are defined, the editor can move forward in identifying sources for each of them.

Another editorial difficulty that arises from medieval works of this sort is how to treat additions or omissions of significant portions of the text in various manuscripts. The clearest editorial procedure here is to provide a base text that closely follows the fullest and most nearly authorial version of the text, and indicate additions or omissions of the other manuscripts in textual notes. This is not the procedure I followed in editing the "Compendium" text mentioned above, where I indicated lines unique to the base manuscript by a letter (*A* for Ashmole) in the margin, and interspersed in the base text the additions unique to the only other surviving text, indicating them by another letter (*S* for Sloane) in the margin. Such decisions may be left to the best judgment of editors, based on their reading of the texts (in the case of the "Compendium," the composite nature of the text seemed to allow such treatment, which would do injustice to other editions); but editors should also bear in mind the desirability of present-

---

9. Linne R. Mooney, "A Middle English Verse Compendium of Astrological Medicine," *Medical History* 28 (1984): 406–19.

ing to their readers a base text in a form as close to the medieval original as possible.

Perhaps it is unnecessary to say that an understanding of the cultural and scientific contexts of astrological and prognostic texts is required to edit them. Much work in this area has been done by John North (esp. *Chaucer's Universe*), J. C. Eade *(The Forgotten Sky)*, and others on the astronomical/astrological references in works of Chaucer—much of which applies to astrological works in general.[10] North provides a good beginning glossary of astronomical/astrological terms in his series of articles, "Kalenderes Enlumyned Ben They."[11] For the English cultural context of astrological texts, editors should read Hilary Carey's book, *Courting Disaster: Astrology at the English Court and University in the Later Middle Ages;* or for a broader history of astrology, S. J. Tester's *A History of Western Astrology.*[12]

Knowledge of medieval science will be helpful in understanding the peculiar features that frequently occur in this genre of writing. For instance, these texts are likely to include sigils, illustrations, or ciphers. Sigils, or sigla—symbols representing the words for names of planets, signs of the zodiac, elements, and so forth—often occur in tables, where they are preferred for their size over writing out a word like *Sagittarius* in full. They are also sometimes embedded in texts, where their occurrence would serve as do ciphers to limit the number of readers who could understand the text. Their interpretation is sometimes difficult for modern readers as well. Editors will have no difficulty in recognizing that the sigil of a crescent represents the moon; but would not automatically recognize a sigil that looks sometimes like an Arabic number 4, sometimes like Arabic 21, and sometimes like a crooked modern capital *H* as representing "Jove" or "Jupiter." Cappelli's *Dizionario di Abbreviature latine*

---

10. John North, *Chaucer's Universe* (Oxford, 1988; rpt. 1990); J. C. Eade, *The Forgotten Sky: A Guide to Astrology in English Literature* (Oxford, 1984). Other texts by North are "Kalenderes Enlumyned Ben They," *Review of English Studies,* new ser. 20, no. 78 (1969): 129–54; no. 79 (1969): 257–83; no. 80 (1969): 418–44. "The Alphonsine Tables in England," in *Prismata: Festschrift für Willy Hartner,* ed. Y. Maeyama and W. Saltzer (Wiesbaden, 1977), rpt. *Stars, Minds, and Fate: Essays in Ancient and Medieval Cosmology,* ed. John North (London, 1989), 327–59; *Richard of Wallingford,* 3 vols. (Oxford, 1976); "The Western Calendar—'Intolerabilis, Horribilis et Derisibilis': Four Centuries of Discontent," in *Gregorian Reform of the Calendar: Proceedings of the Vatican Conference to Commemorate Its 400th Anniversary, 1582–1982,* ed. G. V. Coyne, et al. (Vatican, 1983), 75–113.

11. J. North, "Kalenderes Enlumyned Ben They."

12. Hilary M. Carey, *Courting Disaster: Astrology at the English Court and University in the Later Middle Ages* (London, 1992); S. J. Tester, *A History of Western Astrology* (Woodbridge, Suffolk, 1987).

ed italiane is of some assistance with these, especially the appendix of "Segni Convenzionali," 406–12, since the same sigils were used for English as for Latin texts.[13] For a more complete dictionary of sigils, one should consult Fred Gettings's *Dictionary of Occult, Hermetic, and Alchemical Sigils.*[14] Even with these reference tools to assist, the editor will sometimes need to use his or her imagination in interpreting sigils, since medieval scribes sometimes altered the sigils out of ignorance or carelessness (as with the three appearances of the sigil for "Jupiter" described above); and sometimes several quite distinct sigils were used to designate a single word or idea, as Linda Ehrsam Voigts points out in her article, "The Character of the *Carecter:* Ambiguous Sigils in Scientific and Medical Texts" (92–93).[15] Medieval scribes also recognized that many of their readers could not read the common astrological sigils, and so wrote glossaries to them in the manuscripts themselves. One such is found in the late-fifteenth-century Middle English astronomical/astrological manuscript, Trinity College, Cambridge O.7.2ᵉ, on folios 14–14ᵛ.

Illustrations also sometimes take the place of sigils or text in Middle English astrological or prognostic texts—like the modern picture texts for early readers where, for example, a circle with rays emanating from it takes the place of the word *sun.* Since each scribe established his or her own "language" of illustrations, there can be no guide or dictionary for interpreting them, and editors must consider the context in which the illustrations occur and use their imagination. Illustrations are sometimes employed to represent the crops, weather, or political effects forecast in prognosticatory texts, as in the two lunaries/almanacks, Oxford, Bodleian, Rawlinson D.393 and Ashmole 8, illustrated by Taavitsainen, 142–143. Illustrations also appear in political prognostications, usually representing elements from the coat of arms of the persons involved. To decipher such heraldic symbols, one might consult A. C. Fox-Davies and T. C. Jack, *A Complete Guide to Heraldry.*[16]

Ciphers may be found in astrological and prognostic texts where apparently the author or scribe wished to limit the circulation of information to those who knew or could discover the cipher. Ciphers are usually peculiar to each scribe, as well, so there are no guides or dictionaries to assist the editor. The scribe of Trinity College, Cambridge O.2.40, William Wymondham, an Augustinian

---

13. A. Cappelli, *Dizionario di Abbreviature latine ed italiane* (Milan, 1929; rev. 1967).

14. Fred Gettings, *A Dictionary of Occult, Hermetic, and Alchemical Sigils* (London, 1981).

15. Linda Ehrsam Voigts, "The Character of the *Carecter:* Ambiguous Sigils in Scientific and Medical Texts," in *Latin and Vernacular Studies in Late-Medieval Texts and Manuscripts,* ed. A. J. Minnis (Cambridge, 1989), 91–109.

16. Arthur Charles Fox-Davies and T. C. Jack, *A Complete Guide to Heraldry* (London, 1909).

canon of Kirby Bellars, Leicestershire, wrote the names of planets in cipher in his astronomical/astrological texts, by substituting for each vowel the letter that next follows it in the alphabet, e.g. on folio 153Aᵛ, "As þe mpnf ys in apposition with sbturnf þᵗ ys ewyl thyng to begynne & to playn or speke of any machandes," where he substitutes *p* for *o* and *f* for *e* in *mone,* and *b* for *a, f* for *e* in *saturne.*

One particularly important aspect of editing astrological and prognostic texts is the handling of the charts and figures one concludes are integral to the text. They must be reproduced with care. Charts comprising columns of figures are relatively easy to reproduce for camera-ready editions with whatever word-processing software one uses on the computer, but illustrations and diagrams pose a problem. They range in complexity from simple geometric diagrams like the birth-chart horoscope figures of early astrology and the quadrant figures of early astronomical texts to the complex drawings that accompany prognostications about the dispositions of men. Some examples of the more simple diagrams are the eclipse figures accompanying early astronomical kalendars like John Somer's or Nicholas of Lynn's; or the diagrams accompanying astronomical texts like Chaucer's *Treatise on the Astrolabe.* An example of a more complex drawing is the "Zodiac Man," a representation of the human body, with small figures of the signs of the zodiac drawn covering those parts of the body that each was thought to influence—often found in conjunction with John Somer's and Nicholas of Lynn's kalendars.[17] It may be a comfort to modern editors to note that medieval scribes or scriptoria were also troubled by these figures and often left blank space for them that was never filled, presumably because no artist could be found—or afforded—to fill them in. Fully eight copies of John Somer's kalendar leave a blank space in the middle of the Latin text about the influences of the zodiac ("Aries. Cave ab incisione . . . ," Thorndike and Kibre, col. 129) for the drawing of the zodiac man that was never filled in. Computer technologies are just now making possible the reproduction of such figures for camera-ready copy, whereas until now editors have had to call upon artists or photographers to reproduce them. In any case, they ought to be presented to the reader as fully and accurately as possible.

The edition of the manuscript text complete, one might also wish to examine early printed versions of it, for clarification of a reading or just to consider the text's continued production and distribution. Fortunately, tracing astrological and prognostic texts into early print is assisted by the work of Bernard

---

17. Nicholas of Lynn, *Kalendarium,* ed. Sigmund Eisner (Athens, Ga., 1980); John Somer, *Kalendarium,* ed. Linne R. Mooney (forthcoming).

Capp, whose study of *English Almanacs, 1500–1800: Astrology and the Popular Press* appeared in 1977.[18] Particularly useful are Capp's first two chapters, the first, a general introduction to astrology and almanacs (15–22), the second, on "The Development of the Almanac" (23–66). E. F. Bosanquet's *English Printed Almanacks and Prognostications to 1600* and its supplements are invaluable for identifying early printed almanacs, and Pollard and Redgrave's *Short Title Catalogue,* second edition, in the entry for "Almanacks, Prognostications, and Kalendars" (items 386–532.11; vol. 1, pp. 15–30) reorganizes and supplements Bosanquet's lists.[19]

Finally, the editors of Middle English texts of astrological and prognostic content must bear in mind the audience for whom they are editing the text. For editions that will appear in journals for the history of science or technology one might assume a readership familiar with the terms of astronomy/astrology and prognostication; but for editions in journals of literature or history, one cannot and should not assume such familiarity. A glossary of terms like *house, mansion, trine,* and *ascension,* or even *conjunction, opposition, Dominical Letter,* and *Golden Number* is an obvious desideratum. As already mentioned above, John North included such a glossary in the first portion of his series of articles, "Kalenderes Enlumyned Ben They." Extensive explanatory notes, explaining unfamiliar terms or operations, or an introduction that explains the theories behind the operations (or both), are other approaches to this problem. With such aids, the editor makes his or her text accessible to a wider readership among scholars of medieval English literature, history, and history of science.

Reference Works Specific to Editing Astrological and Prognostical Texts

Bober, Harry. "The Zodiacal Miniature of the *Trés Riches Heures* of the Duke of Berry—Its Sources and Meaning." *Journal of the Warburg and Courtauld Institutes* 11 (1948): 1–34.
Bosanquet, Eustace F. *English Printed Almanacks and Prognostications: A Bibliographical History to the Year 1600.* Bibliographical Society Illustrated Monographs, vol. 17. Oxford, 1917.

---

18. Bernard Capp, *English Almanacks, 1500–1800: Astrology and the Popular Press* (Ithaca, N.Y., 1977).

19. Eustace F. Bosanquet, *English Printed Almanacks and Prognostications: A Bibliographical History to the Year 1600,* Bibliographical Society Illustrated Monographs, 17 (Oxford, 1917); Bosanquet, "English Printed Almanacks and Prognostications . . . to . . . 1600: Corrigenda and Addenda," *Library,* 4th ser., 8 (1928): 456–77; Bosanquet, "Notes on Further Addenda to English Printed Almanacks and Prognostications . . . to . . . 1600," *Library,* 4th ser., 18, no. 1 (1937–38): 39–66.

————. "English Printed Almanacks and Prognostications . . . to . . . 1600: Corrigenda and Addenda." *Library,* 4th ser., 8 (1928): 456–77.

————. "Notes on Further Addenda to English Printed Almanacks and Prognostications . . . to . . . 1600," *Library,* 4th ser., 18, no. 1 (1937–38): 39–66.

Capp, Bernard. *English Almanacks, 1500–1800: Astrology and the Popular Press.* Ithaca, N.Y., 1977.

Cappelli, A. *Dizionario di Abbreviature latine ed italiane.* Milan, 1929; rev. 1967.

Carey, Hilary M. *Courting Disaster: Astrology at the English Court and University in the Later Middle Ages.* London, 1992.

Cheney, C. R. *Handbook of Dates for Students of English History.* London, 1970.

Eade, J. C. *The Forgotten Sky: A Guide to Astrology in English Literature.* Oxford, 1984.

Förster, Max. "Beiträge zur mittelalterlichen Volkskunde." *Archiv für das Studium der neueren Sprachen* 120 (1908): 43–52, 296–305; 121 (1908): 30–46; 125 (1910): 39–70; 127 (1911): 31–84; 128 (1912): 55–71, 285–308; 129 (1912): 16–49; 134 (1916): 264–93.

————. "Kleinere mittelenglische Texte." *Anglia* 42 (1918): 145–224.

Fox-Davies, Arthur Charles, and T. C. Jack. *A Complete Guide to Heraldry.* London, 1909.

Gettings, Fred. *A Dictionary of Occult, Hermetic, and Alchemical Sigils.* London, 1981.

MacKinney, Loren C. *Medical Illustrations in Medieval Manuscripts.* London, 1965.

Matheson, Lister M., ed. *Popular and Practical Science of Medieval England.* East Lansing, Mich., 1994.

Means, Laurel. "Electionary, Lunary, Destinary, and Questionary: Toward Defining Categories of Middle English Prognostic Material." *Studies in Philology* 89 (1992): 367–403.

————. "'Ffor as moche as yche man may not haue þe astrolabe': Popular Middle English Variations on the Computus." *Speculum* 67 (1992): 595–623.

Mooney, Linne R. "A Middle English Verse Compendium of Astrological Medicine." *Medical History* 28 (1984): 406–19.

Nicholas of Lynn. *Kalendarium.* Ed. Sigmund Eisner. Athens, Ga., 1980.

North, John. "The Alphonsine Tables in England." In *Prismata: Festschrift für Willy Hartner,* ed. Y. Maeyama and W. Saltzer. Wiesbaden, 1977; rpt. *Stars, Minds, and Fate: Essays in Ancient and Medieval Cosmology,* ed. J. D. North. London, 1989. 327–59.

————. *Chaucer's Universe.* Oxford, 1988; rpt. 1990.

————. "Kalenderes Enlumyned Ben They." *Review of English Studies,* n.s. 20, no. 78 (1969): 129–54; no. 79 (1969): 257–83; no. 80 (1969): 418–44.

————. *Richard of Wallingford.* 3 vols. Oxford, 1976.

————. "The Western Calendar—Intolerabilis, horribilis et derisibilis'; Four Centuries of Discontent." In *Gregorian Reform of the Calendar: Proceedings of the Vatican Conference to Commemorate Its 400th Anniversary, 1582–1982,* ed. G. V. Coyne, et. al. Vatican, 1983. 75–113.

Pickering, F. P. *The Calendar Pages of Medieval Service Books.* Reading, 1980.

Powicke, Sir F. Maurice, and E. B. Fryde. *Handbook of British Chronology.* 2d ed. London, 1961.

Robbins, Rossell Hope. "English Almanacks of the Fifteenth Century." *Philological Quarterly* 18 (1939): 321–31.

Saxl, Fritz, and Hans Meier, gen. eds. *Catalogue of Astrological and Mythological Illuminated Manuscripts of the Middle Ages: Manuscripts in English Libraries.* Ed. Harry Bober. Verzeichnis astrologischer und mythologischer illustrierter Handschriften des lateinischen Mittelalters, 3 (London, 1953).

Severs, Jonathan Burke, and Albert E. Hartung, gen. eds. *A Manual of the Writings in Middle English, 1050–1500.* New Haven, Conn., 1967–.

Singer, Dorothea Waley, Annie Anderson, and Robina Addis. *A Catalogue of Latin and Vernacular Alchemical Manuscripts in Great Britain and Ireland, Dating from before the XVI Century.* 3 vols. Brussels, 1928–31.

Singer, Dorothea Waley, and Annie Anderson. *A Catalogue of Latin and Vernacular Plague Tracts in Great Britain and Eire in Manuscripts Written before the Sixteenth Century.* London, 1950.

Somer, John. *Kalendarium.* Ed. Linne Mooney. Forthcoming.

Swainson, Charles. *A Handbook of Weather Folklore.* Edinburgh, 1873.

Taavitsainen, Irma. *Middle English Lunaries: A Study of the Genre.* Mémoires de la Société Néophilologique de Helsinki, 47. Helsinki, 1988.

Tester, S. J. *A History of Western Astrology.* Woodbridge, Suffolk, 1987.

Thorndike, Lynn. *Latin Treatises on Comets between 1238 and 1368 A.D.* Chicago, 1950.

Thorndike, Lynn, and Pearl Kibre. *A Catalogue of Incipits of Mediaeval Scientific Writings in Latin.* Cambridge, Mass., 1963.

Tuckerman, B. *Planetary, Lunar, and Solar Positions.* Vols. 1 and 2, 600 B.C. to A.D. 1649. Memoirs of the American Philosophical Society, 56 (1962) and 59 (1964).

van Wijk, W. E. *Le Nombre d'Or: Étude de chronologie technique, suivie du texte de la Massa Compoti d'Alexandre de Villedieu.* The Hague, 1936.

Voigts, Linda Ehrsam. "The Character of the *Carecter:* Ambiguous Sigils in Scientific and Medical Texts," in *Latin and Vernacular Studies in Late-Medieval Texts and Manuscripts,* ed. A. J. Minnis. Cambridge, 1989. 91–109.

Wells, John Edwin. *Manual of the Writings in Middle English, 1050–1400.* New Haven, Conn., 1916; Supplements 1–9, 1919–51.

Wordsworth, Christopher. *The Ancient Kalendar of the University of Oxford from documents of the Fourteenth to the Seventeenth Century.* Oxford Historical Society Publications, 45. Oxford, 1904.

Wormald, Francis, ed. *English Benedictine Kalendars after A.D. 1100.* 2 vols. Henry Bradshaw Society, vols. 77, 81 (1938, 1943–44).

Wright, A. R., and T. E. Lones. *British Calendar Customs.* 3 vols. London, 1938–40.

Editing Middle English
Culinary Manuscripts

Constance B. Hieatt

The principal requirements for an editor of Middle English culinary texts are a broad understanding of culinary techniques; a good grounding in Old and Middle English and Old French (from which many culinary terms are borrowed), coupled with an inveterate etymological bent; a wide knowledge of other medieval English and continental culinary materials; and a healthy dose of skepticism about the reliability of the scribes, former editors, and even dictionaries.

The editor must bear in mind that most scribes were clerics, not cooks, and that most editors and lexicographers—at least those of a generation or so ago—were equally unlikely to have spent much time in the kitchen. Even the most astute paleographer can be easily misled if she or he does not know that, from a practical point of view, certain readings appear absurd and demand explanations that may not be immediately forthcoming. As for paleography itself, perhaps it should go without saying that you cannot edit medieval culinary recipes if you are unable to read the scribal hands of the period, and that, furthermore, you must be conscientious in checking all transcriptions against the manuscript(s) before going into print.

This was, however, not a truth universally acknowledged among the early editors of this genre. The first editor of *The Forme of Cury,* Samuel Pegge, was apparently fairly accurate in his transcriptions, but his 1790 edition contained uncorrected flaws;[1] and when Richard Warner produced a new edition in 1791, he evidently consulted no manuscripts at all, and, far from correcting the errors of Pegge and others, introduced new ones that can only be attributed to careless copying of his printed originals (see *CI,* 22–23). Most of the nineteenth-

---

1. See Constance B. Hieatt and Sharon Butler, eds., *Curye on Inglysch: English Culinary Manuscripts of the Fourteenth Century (Including the* Forme of Cury), EETS, s.s. 8 (London, 1985), 22. This edition will be referred to hereafter as *CI.*

century editors had higher standards, but not all: Mrs. Alexander Napier's *A Noble Boke off Cookry*[2] is so thick with misreadings that one early student of the subject wrote, "I found it easier to make a fresh transcript than to correct the errors in the printed copy: they were too numerous."[3]

Mrs. Napier's inaccuracies begin with the title, which is written twice on fol. 1ᵛ of the manuscript: the first, more complete, version of the title gives the spelling "book," and the second "bok"; neither one spells the word "boke." Minor, it might be remarked, but ominous, nevertheless. The first line of the first recipe in the collection yields an example of the serious misreadings that render this edition totally unreliable: "a potage for somer sessone" calls for filets of "vele" (veal), but Mrs. Napier reads "befe" (beef). In many scribal hands, *v* and *b,* and even *l* and *f,* may look very similar, but here it is not at all difficult to see what the scribe wrote—and anyone familiar with medieval dietary theories will know that beef is *not* the appropriate meat for this dish.

That others have failed, or dodged, their responsibilities as paleographers does not necessarily mean that future editors must undertake a formal course of study in that subject. In any case, the failings of others should serve as a warning of pitfalls to be avoided. First, one should never accept anyone's readings on trust. Thomas Austin was an excellent editor,[4] but he did misread a word once in a while, as I have found when checking his edition against the manuscripts. My late colleague Sharon Butler and I frequently found reason to doubt our own (and each other's) earlier readings. Even the most cautious and thoroughly experienced editors get embroiled in difficulties and disagreements, largely because the hands of the fifteenth-century scribes who copied most extant medieval recipe collections are often very difficult to read and sometimes careless in their execution. After all, these collections were usually in volumes not intended to be pored over studiously, much less admired, but to be used as practical references—or records of the personal interests of the original owner.

I will give examples from a manuscript which I have only recently edited: B.L. ms. Harleian 5401.[5] Dr. Butler left me her transcription of the titles in this

---

2. (London, 1882); hereafter, *NBC.*

3. John Hodgkin, in a letter dated 14 December 1915 to Henry Guppy, librarian of the John Rylands University Library of Manchester; the letter is still in that library, where it is kept with Rylands English ms. 7, the Manchester manuscript of *The Forme of Cury.*

4. Editor of *Two Fifteenth-Century Cookery Books,* EETS 91 (London, 1888; rpt. 1964). This edition will be referred to hereafter as *CB.*

5. "The Middle English Culinary Recipes in MS Harley 5401: An Edition and Commentary," *Medium Aevum* 65 (1996): 54–71.

manuscript, and when I compared my readings with hers, I found a remarkable number of disagreements. This collection has a number of very strange titles, including such bafflements as "Re salsike" (fol. 96ᵛ), as I first read it; Dr. Butler read this as one word. After further investigation, I found that this is actually a recipe we edited in an earlier manuscript, where it has the title "Rys alkere":⁶ so possibly the Harleian 5401 title ought to be read as *res alsike*. But, as we remarked in *CI* (211), *Rys alkere* is an unsatisfactory title since rice is not a distinctive ingredient in the recipe. The later title is probably also wrong, and I cannot explain either "alkere" or "alsike." Nor was I certain whether another title in Harleian 5401 (on fol. 97ʳ) was to be read as "a farreseour," a stuffing (<A-N "farsure"), or "a faire saus," which are the conflicting readings we came up with: but since the recipe is for a mixture to be cooked "in a poket of a pike," I thought a stuffing was more likely to be indicated. And I now see that the spelling is actually "faireseour."

But the reader should note my initial grounds for preferring Dr. Butler's reading of "a farreseour" as more likely than my own "faire saus": that is, culinary common sense tells me one is more likely to put a "stuffing" rather than a "sauce" in the belly of a fish. But that doesn't really settle the question, unfortunately. One consideration is that the two were sometimes one and the same in medieval recipes. A well-known example is the "Sauce Madame" that was evidently popular in England with roast goose. The cook was directed to stuff the goose with herbs, fruit, and garlic, and, when the bird was done, dilute the stuffing with wine, season it, and serve as a sauce.⁷

The second factor that kept me from certainty that the title of this recipe in Harleian 5401 must have indicated a stuffing rather than a sauce is that the scribes who transcribed such recipes were often completely in the dark themselves, and given to all sorts of misreadings. Some of these are largely matters of mistaking the letters written by a previous scribe for other similar letters, as when a scribe evidently mistook *k* for *w*—an understandable confusion in many fourteenth-century hands—and wrote that to make "Furmente," a sort of wheat pilaf that was usually served with venison, the wheat is to be boiled until

---

6. *CI* II.83, 78.

7. See *CI*, 104–5, and *An Ordinance of Pottage* (hereafter referred to as *OP*), ed. Constance B. Hieatt (London, 1988), 81; the recipe also occurs in *NBC* and probably in other English collections. An identically titled recipe in a French source, however, is a true sauce, not a stuffing, although partially cooked in a dripping pan under the goose: see *Le Viandier de Taillevent*, ed. Jérôme Pichon and Georges Vicaire (Paris, 1892; rpt. Lusarches, n.d.), 176. This recipe from the fifteenth-century printed edition is not in Terence Scully's more recent edition of the manuscripts, i.e., Terence Scully, ed., *The Viandier of Taillevent* (Ottawa, 1988).

it is brown (*CI,* 125). Dr. Butler and I did not consider burned porridge appetizing, so we preferred the reading of a manuscript that says to boil the wheat until it is broken.

The same error occurs in reverse in several manuscripts of *The Forme of Cury* in its recipe for a fritter called "Nysebek" (*CI,* 138), which mistakenly calls for sour dock (sorrel): a pretty peculiar substitute for sourdough! We can hope no one tried to follow the wrong version of the recipe. Both of these scribal errors imply culinary ignorance, but it would be a rare scribe who knew how to boil grains or make fritters. Similarly we find *k* mistaken for *w* in a recipe for sausage "hedgehogs" ("Hirchones," *CI,* 139), where we are told to decorate the "hedgehog" with pastry "prews" instead of "pricks."

Early editors did not hesitate to explain away such scribal errors. Warner glosses "prews" as "perhaps flat cakes, or balls," although his directions for sticking such objects into the sausage would surely give pause to anyone actually contemplating making this particular decorative dish. He is equally unperturbed by the word Pegge gives as "curose" in the directions for the final preparation of "Sambocade," an elderflower tart (see *CI,* 138). "Bake it up with curose" is glossed, "with care." In fact, "curose" is a misreading of the manuscript's "eurose" (<A-N *eue rosat, eawrose,* etc.), rosewater: a normal last-minute flavoring added to a sweet dish in a kitchen where such extracts as vanilla (a New World product unknown in fourteenth-century Europe) were not available—and one still much used in modern Europe, at least east of England.

Perhaps the funniest of Warner's glosses is "hot water" for "ew ardant" (distilled spirits, aqua vitae, or brandy) in a recipe for a pastry castle (*CI,* 142–43) that was evidently meant to be presented dramatically aflame. One might have thought that even a kitchen ignoramus could imagine the disastrous effects of pouring hot water over a pastry castle. More serious basic problems, however, can be seen in his gloss of the title of the "hedgehog" recipe. Pegge's source manuscript gave this title as "Hert rowce"; Warner transcribed this as "Hert rowee" and glossed it as "hart roes," although when the recipe says to make the sausage in the shape of an "urchin" he correctly glosses "hedgehog." It doesn't seem to have puzzled him that hedgehogs do not bear much resemblance to harts, or roe deer.

Dr. Butler and I had two signal advantages over Pegge and Warner when we edited this recipe. The first was our prior acquaintance with the great fourteenth-century French collections, the *Viandier* and the *Ménagier de Paris,* both of which give recipes for *heriçons* or *herissons,* sausage hedgehogs—an adaptation of which had long been a favorite recipe of ours; the other was our discovery of three variant manuscripts that gave the title as "Urchons," "Hirchones," and "Hyrchounys." It was not difficult to see how one of these words, either the original French or an English derivative retaining the *h*, could have been corrupted to "hert rowce" by a careless—or uncomprehending—scribe.

A manuscript that is unparalleled is, of course, always going to be harder to edit than one for which there are other witnesses that may offer helpful variants. And whether there are parallel Middle English manuscripts or not, parallels in French recipes can offer truly enlightening help. And not only *French* recipes: the more the editor knows about Continental (and, indeed, Arabic) recipe collections, the better. A case where no French collection could have been much help is the recipe in *OP* (79) for a curd-cheese fritter. This is entitled "Samacays," and when I first saw it I realized that the ingredients were very similar to those of the tart filling in the similarly titled "Sambocade" (mentioned above in connection with the word *eurose*), except that nothing resembling elderflowers is called for in the fritter recipe.

But elderflowers are what gives "Sambocade" its name: from Lat. *sambucus*. I wondered whether "Samacays" had originally been an elderflower fritter. I became sure that it was when I found a similar fritter recipe in a Latin collection dating from the beginning of the fourteenth century; this recipe calls for *flores sambuci,* elderflowers.[8] I later found, further, that it may go back to an Arabic original (see my note in *OP,* 23). This is not at all surprising, since several other dishes in this Latin collection are of Arabic origin.[9] One of these is "Mamonia" (407); the original Arabic dish was called *ma'mūniyya.*[10]

Thus Austin was doing little more than guessing (wrongly) when he explained the etymology of the popular dish called "mawmene" (variously spelled) in England as "apparently derived from the Fr. *malmener,* the meat being teased small" (136). Not all Middle English culinary words are derived from French, and there does not seem to be any French recipe for mawmene, although it appears in Italian collections—apparently derived from the tradi-

---

8. "Fristellis," in the *Liber de Coquina,* ed. Marianne Mulon, in "Deux traités inédits d'art culinaire médiéval," *Bulletin philologique et historique* (1971 for 1968), 411. The elderflowers are likely to have been lost from the English recipe because they were designated by an Anglo-Norman term no longer comprehensible to later English copyists; cf. *OP,* 15.

9. Several of these are discussed in Maxime Rodinson, "*Romania* and Other Arab Words in Italian," trans. Barbara Inskip, with additional notes by Professor Rodinson, *Petits Propos Culinaires (PPC)* 34 (1990): 31–44. The original article appeared in *Romania* 71 (1950), 433–49.

10. See Maxime Rodinson, "Ma'mūniyya East and West," trans. Barbara Inskip, *PPC* 33 (1989): 15–25. The original article was published in *Études d'orientalisme dédiées à la mémoire de Lévi-Provençal* (Paris, 1962), 2:733–47.

tion of the *Liber de Coquina,* which seems to be of Italian origin. It remains that Austin's explanation of the etymology of *mawmene* was the only one advanced until very recently, with the exception of the *OED*'s equally wrong suggestion that the word might be related to *malmsey.*

Of course, the *OED* is not the only standard work of reference that may sometimes be misleading. When it informs us that the original, basic, Middle English meaning of *parboil* is "to boil thoroughly" it is simply echoing Cotgrave—and agreeing with all the French dictionaries.[11] But it should have been obvious years ago that there is something wrong with this definition: for example, in recipes telling us to parboil the fish before frying or grilling it. A "thoroughly boiled" fish would have disintegrated before it could be put on/in the grill or frying pan. This word in culinary manuscripts, both French and English, always occurs in a context calling for further cooking: which certainly points to the modern meaning of *parboil*—that is, give it a preliminary boiling before finishing the cooking in a further step, often involving a different method of cooking. The *Forme of Cury* recipe for "Cawdel of samoun" (*CI,* 123) would seem to settle the issue: it says, "perboile hem a lytell." To "thoroughly boil" something just "a little" sounds like a contradiction in terms, although the amount of time needed for that preliminary boiling may vary from a few minutes for a vegetable to some hours for a ham.

In general, experienced cooks can trust their culinary instincts in matters like this. Cooking techniques have not changed much, however our tools and kitchen apparatus may have been improved. You can "seethe" your "furmente" in a cauldron or a microwave, and grinding an almond produces similar results whether you use a mortar and pestle or a food processor.[12] Cooks, then as now, were inventive in improvising ways to gain a desired result, although they could not whip cream or beat egg whites stiff in an era long before the invention of the eggbeater.[13] On the other hand, the study of medieval culinary

---

11. Randle Cotgrave, *A Dictionarie of the French and English Tongues* (London, 1611; facs. rpt. Columbia, S.C., 1950).

12. For suggestions on adapting medieval culinary directions, see *OP,* 113–17, and Hieatt, Hosington, and Butler, *Pleyn Delit: Medieval Cookery for Modern Cooks,* 2d ed. (Toronto, 1996), xx–xxiii. Archeologists and historians have now begun to give us studies of the implements and techniques of the medieval kitchen; an account focusing on the earlier period, but actually drawing on records from as late as the fifteenth century, is the chapter on "Methods of Cooking" in Ann Hagen, *A Handbook of Anglo-Saxon Food: Processing and Consumption* (Pinner, Middlesex, 1992). Information on this subject—along with other aspects of English culinary history—will be found throughout C. Anne Wilson's *Food and Drink in Britain* (London, 1973).

13. Whisks did not begin to come into common use until the sixteenth century; thus a strainer

vocabulary still has a long way to go:[14] *seethe,* for example, may not have had exactly the same meaning as *boil* in early English. In some contexts, it looks as if *seethe* may mean "simmer," which is not the same thing as "cook it in a rolling boil."

Editors will have to tread warily in glossing such terms until more definitive word studies are available, but a competent cook should not need further documentary evidence to assure him/her that in the fifteenth century *perboile* meant more or less what *parboil* means today. And, of course, a scholar who is not a competent cook is not qualified to edit culinary manuscripts. But even one who has truly mastered the art of cookery, and who finds Middle English manuscripts easy to read and has read widely (in various languages) in the culinary literature of medieval Europe and beyond, must remember that there is a lot more reading to be done and kept up with.

Nor is this an easy chore: current scholarship in this field will not be found conveniently indexed in any annual bibliography. There are, to be sure, a handful of journals that are worth keeping an eye on, some of them unlikely to be familiar to most Middle English scholars—such as *Petits Propos Culinaires,* known as *PPC.*[15] And of course one can and should pick up bibliographical information from other people's footnotes and bibliographies, as in any other area of study. But a great deal of work in this area appears in less predictable publications, especially conference proceedings. To be alerted to such sources of information, you must be in contact with a rather special grapevine; attending conferences where you can meet others with an interest in the general area is almost indispensable.

But if all of this sounds discouraging, I am happy to add that, at long last, the field in general is now being taken seriously by historians[16] (and even some

---

was the convenient means of making a smooth blend of egg yolks—or other "batters," etc. For the earliest English reference I have found to anything resembling a modern whisk, see *CI,* V.11 (p. 150), ll. 2–4.

14. The only fairly full study of the subject in general remains M. S. Serjeantson, "The Vocabulary of Cookery in the Fifteenth Century," in *Essays and Studies by Members of the English Association* 23 (1937): 25–37. This may still be useful if approached with caution, but it is, of course, seriously out-of-date.

15. *PPC* is published in London by Prospect Books, Ltd., with three issues a year.

16. Examples include Christopher Dyer, "English Diet in the Later Middle Ages," in *Social Relations and Ideas: Essays in Honour of R. H. Hilton,* ed. T. H. Aston et al. (Cambridge, 1983); *Manger et Boire au Moyen Age,* ed. Denis Menjot, 2 vols. (Nice, 1984); and C. M. Woolgar, ed., *Household Accounts from Medieval England,* 2 vols. (Oxford, 1992–93). Also cf. the most recent works on medieval cookery in general: Terence Scully, *The Art of Cookery in the Middle Ages* (Woodbridge, Suffolk, and Rochester, N.Y., 1995) (see review by C. Hieatt in *Speculum* 73 [1997]:

philologists—although those of us in the latter category seem to be an endangered species nowadays), and much more help is available today than was the case only a few years ago. For example, there is the *Répertoire des manuscrits médiévaux contenant des recettes culinaires,* a detailed catalog of such manuscripts with complete information about the reference works listing them and works in which they are discussed, edited, or translated.[17] Of course, this information is complete only to the extent of what was then known by those of us who compiled the *Répertoire:* we would not dream of calling it "definitive." It is not, because there are not enough of us, nor enough of a tradition behind us. We badly need some qualified new recruits to carry on a study that is just beginning to pay off.

We look forward to welcoming our successors. In some cases, a lack of background in one of the necessary areas can be overcome by collaboration with another scholar with different strengths, although as the veteran of half a dozen such collaborations, I must admit that a certain amount of friction is inevitable. No two scholars work at exactly the same pace.

But, as in marriage, there is much to be gained for those who can control their occasional exasperation. My late collaborator Sharon Butler, who had a firm grasp of Latin as well as Old and Middle English, also had an incomparable ability to mimic the hands of medieval scribes. Her imitations of dubious words were a great help when we had to come to a final decision on how to transcribe them. I never would have dared to edit Anglo-Norman recipes without the help of that well-trained Anglo-Normanist Robin Jones: my brief exposure to Old French in graduate school forty years ago did not equip me to understand, let alone discuss, linguistic finer points. My work in editing early Northern European recipes in collaboration with the late Rudolf Grewe had the happy bonus of giving me access to Dr. Grewe's extensive knowledge of medieval Arabic culinary literature, among other things.[18]

567–69) and J. L. Flandrin and M. Montanari, eds., *Histoire de L'Alimentation* (Paris, 1996).

17. In *Du manuscrit à la table,* ed. Carole Lambert (Montreal, 1992), 315–88.

18. Dr. Grewe died before we could complete work on the book, so this edition is not yet in print; with the help of his computer disks and papers, I hope to be able to finish it by the end of 1997.

Editing Glossographical Texts: To Marrow and to Marrow and to Marrow

Vincent P. McCarren

A. S. Way, the nineteenth-century editor of the *Promptorium Parvulorum,* one of the three major glossaries produced in England during the fifteenth century, remarked in his introduction: "The MSS. of the Medulla [another of the three] are more numerous than those of the Promptorium; they vary in their contents in a remarkable degree; it might indeed seem that each transcriber made such modifications of the text as pleased him, or that he engrafted upon it the additional words and explanatory glosses which he found inserted by any previous hand."[1] Michael Lapidge supports this perception: "Of all texts, glossaries are the most prone to scribal interference: to selective copying, interpolation, omission, and so on."[2] Yet, however descriptive and penetrating either of the above observations are, perhaps the words of Lindsay and Thomson offer greater breadth: "Glossaries are . . . hasty make-shifts, the mere result of massing the word-collections that were available at this or that monastery and then re-arranging the mass. In fact, there was often no 'compiler' properly so called. The original glossary was not made (by mental effort); it grew (by the mechanical fusion of the different parts of a volume which had been made a receptacle for *glossae collectae* of various authors); the derivative glossaries exhibit only the mental effort of selecting or recasting or combining previously published items."[3] To attempt to establish a text in these understated circumstances can be bewildering. Because of the great variation of versions within a given manuscript tradition, i.e. one version of the text including a

---

1. *Promptorium Parvulorum sive Clericorum,* ed. (from Hrl. 221) Albert Way (London, 1865), xxi–xxii.
2. M. Lapidge, "The School of Theodore and Hadrian," *Anglo-Saxon England* 15 (1986): 54.
3. W. M. Lindsay and H. J. Thomson, *Ancient Lore in Medieval Latin Glossaries,* St. Andrew's University Publications, 13 (Oxford, 1921), viii.

number of lemmata and glosses that some other versions omit, it would be futile to attempt to 'create' a stemma for such a text.[4]

However, in the doing the rewards are great. In the process of transcription and collation of any of the manuscripts of the principal glossaries of the period you will observe at least three recurrent points of interests. First, the discovery of hitherto unattested Middle English words that broaden the philological dimensions of the period; secondly, new Latin words and Greek, and novel senses of words, regularly appearing, in turn, extending the parameters of these languages; finally, unique variant spellings occurring frequently, due in large part to recitative copying and auditory memory, offering additional linguistic and phonological evidence in both Latin and Middle English to significantly influence the direction of medieval lexicography.

Interlinear insertions or marginalia, that is, glosses in their original state, are elements that qualify or in some way define the words within a given literary context. Sense can be determined with reasonable accuracy because of the accompanying narrative. It is only when these equivalencies are removed from their context and assumed under an artificial category of *glossae collectae* that we are introduced to the acontextual and subliterary field of glossography. Obviously, "the glossary" formed a collection of words and phrases reflecting virtually every aspect of theoretical and practical life, since its substance is derived from supralineal and marginal inserts made in copies of every conceivable type of "literary" transmission. In these glossaries Latin and Middle English predominate; transliterated Greek and Hebrew also make their appearance. The interchange of these languages in such a work reflects the culmination of a linguistic tradition that dates from the early centuries A.D., that is, Jerome, the Old and New Testaments, Isidore,[5] and Festus,[6] through the Latin, Greek,[7] and Old English glossaries of the seventh, eighth, and ninth centuries,[8] and on into the eleventh-, twelfth-, and thirteenth-century word lists and glossaries such as the *Elementarium* of Papias,[9] and the *Magnae Derivationes* of

4. M. Lapidge, "Textual Criticism and the Literature of Anglo-Saxon England," *Bulletin of the John Rylands Library* 73 (1991): 30.

5. *Isidori Hispalensis Episcopi Etymologiarum Sive Originum Libri XX,* ed. W. M. Lindsay, 2 vols. (Oxford, 1911).

6. *Sexti Pompei Festi De Verborum significatu quae supersunt cum Pauli Epitome,* ed. W. M. Lindsay (Leipzig, 1913).

7. *Corpus Glossariorum Latinorum,* ed. G. Goetz, 8 vols. (Leipzig, 1888–1923).

8. B. Bischoff, et al., eds., *The Epinal, Erfurt, Werden, and Corpus Glossaries,* Early English Manuscripts in Facsimile, 22 (Copenhagen, 1988).

9. Papias, *Elementarium doctrina rudimentum,* Editio princeps (Milan, 1476). See V. de Angelis, *Papiae Elementarium,* Littera A, vols. 1–3 (Milan, 1977–80). Also see G. Cremascoli, "Ricercho sul lessicografo Papia," *Aevum* 43 (1969): 31–55.

Hugutio of Pisa,[10] as well as bears witness to the remarkable dialectal phenomenon that mirrored the changes in the Middle English language throughout the area during the fifteenth century.

In other genres there is a maintainable perspective, a series of verbal clues or literary insights into the meaning of a textually corrupt word or phrase. In editing a glossary we are dealing with the "bare bones" of a language (or two or three or four), words stripped of whatever contextual meaning they might have had, and often left in a corrupt state.

It is usually at this point that an editor of a glossary must weave together every stitch of linguistic talent with a view toward solving the textual riddle that so willingly presents itself, never losing sight of the fact that "every textual problem imposes its own terms of reference and demands to be approached on its own individual premisses. There can be no question of 'a' method, only of the method . . . that is proper to all investigators of a historical character."[11] For example, consider the entry and gloss: "Bilixan: haubrek on [read: or] cloþ with two þredes weuen," as it appears in the *MED* under the lexical entry *hauberk* n. meaning "a coat of mail." There is an immediately identifiable problem: the ending *-an* of the word *Bilixan*. Latin does not allow for an inflexional ending in *-an*. Greek does, but in the accusative singular; not something to be entertained here.

Format is "all" in a glossary,[12] so if one scans the folios of the photostatic copy or the microfilm it becomes apparent that the English indefinite article *an* is used frequently enough. *An* as an abbreviation of *anglice* would be abnormal. That is generally abbreviated as *a* with raised *e,* or in some cases *an* with raised *ce,* never just *an*. What seems not to have been noticed, however, is that there is a punct before *a* as well as after *n* in the manuscript, indicating that the scribe was aware of some syntactic demarcation; not so the *MED* editor. The next step would be to remove *-an* and deal with what is left of the word: *Bilix*. If this word exists, then a case can be made for reediting the word by suggesting a

---

10. Hugutio's "Derivationes" has been handed down in some two hundred manuscripts but, to date, has not been edited. For the most complete listing of the "Derivationes" see G. L. Bursill-Hall, *A Census of Medieval Latin Grammatical Manuscripts* (Stuttgart, 1981). For an introduction into his work, see also Wolfgang Muller, "Huguccio of Pisa: Canonist, Bishop, and Grammarian," *Viator* 22 (1991): 121–52; esp. 137ff. Also for a synopsis of his work see Claus Riessner, *Die "Magnae Derivationes" des Uguccione da Pisa und ihre Bedeutung für die romanische Philologie* (Rome, 1965). For more detail on the place of Papias and Hugutio in glossography see Olga Weijers, "Lexicography in the Middle Ages," *Viator* 20 (1989): 139–53.

11. E. J. Kenney, *The Classical Text* (Berkeley, 1974), 138.

12. See Brian Merrilees' seminal work on lexicographical metalinguistics, "Metalexicographie medievale: La fonction de la metalangue dans un dictionnaire bilingue du Moyen Age," *Archivum latinitatis medii aevi: Bulletin Du Cange* 50 (1991): 33–70.

change in the entry word of the citation. The word does exist and is of common occurrence with the lexical meaning "a kersey" (see *Cath. Angl.* Add. ms. 15562: "Carsay: bilex"), a coarse woolen cloth. This justifies the one side of the equation, the Latin entry, and supports the other side, the gloss or interpretation: "an haubrek, cloþ with two þredes weuen." Hence the "contract" has been kept; the entry equals the gloss in sense and vice-versa. That is the litmus test. Now one can reedit with confidence.

The central problem for an editor of a medieval glossary is determining meaning within limited and, in many cases, confused contexts.[13] The general structure is the entry word or lemma explained by what is currently called the interpretation or, more traditionally, the gloss. Two of the three glossaries discussed in this essay have English entries followed by Latin interpretations *(Catholicon Anglicum*[14] and *Promptorium Parvulorum); the third (Medulla Grammatice)*[15] offers the reverse, Latin followed by English interpretation (although not infrequently Latin-Latin appears). In general, these glossaries provide an entry followed by a noun's genitive case, an adjective's double or triple terminations, or the verb's second singular form. Where appropriate, labels such as *grece* and/or *latine* and, in some cases, *ebraice* are provided and *id est* is inserted between entry and gloss(es) (serving the function of a colon) to show equivalences. Lexical equilibrium is to be expected. If not, the following kind of editorial error occurs by the hand of the editor and at the expense of the scribe. The editor of the Harley 1738 ms. of the *Medulla* provides the reading: "Antea: þens." Impressed by the temporal adverb, he should have pursued its meaning: *formerly, earlier. Þens* will not offer that meaning. The core of the problem seems to have been the misreading of the þ for *y* coupled by the mis-separation of letters. The *a* does not belong to the entry but rather the gloss. Hence, *ayens* determining the entry as *ante,* meaning, quite naturally, "before, in front of, against."

---

13. Two of the major works of the twentieth century concerned with medieval glossography will emphasize these points: *English Glosses from British Library Additional Manuscript 37075,* ed. T. W. Ross and E. Brooks Jr. (Norman, Okla., 1984); Firminus Verris, *Dictionarius/ Dictionnaire Latin-Français de Firmin Le Ver,* ed. B. Merrilees and W. Edwards, Corpus Christianorum, Continuatio Mediaevalis (Turnhout, 1994).

14. *Catholicon Anglicum,* Add. ms. 15562, ?c1475. Also *Catholicon Anglicum* (from ms. 168 in library of Lord Monson), ed. S. J. H. Herrtage (London, 1881).

15. Mss. Additional 24640, 33534, 37789; Bristol Univ. DM 14; Canterbury D.2; Downside Abbey 26540; Harley 1000, 1738, 2181, 2257, 2270; Holkham misc. 39; Lincoln 88, 111; Pepys 2002; Rawlinson C 101; St. John's College (Cambridge)72 C 22; Shrewsbury XVI; Stonyhurst XV (A.1.10). Fragments: mss. Bristol Univ. DM 1; Brasenose College (Oxford) UBS.2.87–8; Gloucester GDR/Z1/31; Rawlinson D.913.

So the first consideration for an edition of such a text is to provide yourself with a reasonably accomplished command of Latin and Middle English. Nor, obviously, should a functional "feel" for Greek be dismissed, or a gentle inclination toward Hebrew. But just how ideal can one's "world of languages" be? What is really important is finding yourself with the opportunity of corroborating your linguistic conclusions. Have enough confidence in your own ability so that there is no hesitation on your part to "pounce" upon your colleagues better versed in some of the languages than you, if only to allow them to restrain you from devising an "unholy" error. You might think of them collectively as Socrates' "demon." They'll be delighted to help because the material, for one thing, is ever new. This admonition is of twofold importance: to help you interpret what the scribe gets right; and what the scribe gets wrong. Such an entry and interpretation as: "Aduoco, as: to clepe to" or "Cornu: an horne" would cause no difficulty. But consider how you might react by being confronted with the task of editing the following entry in the *Medulla Grammatice:* "Semita: half a wey." Pause a moment; think about what is awkward and how to deal with it. What do other manuscripts say? Use the tradition, and for the most part, stay within it. *Divinatio,* the art of "precise" conjectural emendation, belongs to the very few. The Pepys manuscript indicates corroboration: "halff a way, a path" (but with no comment from the editor).[16] On the other hand, the Canterbury,[17] Harley 1738,[18] and the St. John's (Cambridge) manuscripts provide the expected reading: "a path." This is the proper lexical entry and gloss (see *A New Latin Dictionary* [Lewis and Short] and/or *The Oxford Latin Dictionary*). Why the error? Well, in the Stonyhurst manuscript this entry is preceded by "Semis: dimidium" and followed by "Semitonus: half a tone"; and "Semiuir: half a mon"!

Now to an example that is a little more elusive. The Stonyhurst manuscript of the *Medulla* reads: "Abdomen, ge .i. pinguedo, le." What is being conveyed here is that *Abdomen* is a Greek word, that is, (equivalent to), *pinguedo,* which is a Latin word. But *Abdomen* is not Greek. What probably happened was that the scribe, having seen on the exemplar "Abdomen grece .i. pinguedo le," conceived of *grece* as the resolved form of the abbreviation: *ge.* Not so,

---

16. "Pepys MS. 2002 Medulla Grammatice: An Edition," ed. J. F. Huntsman, Ph.D. diss., University of Texas at Austin, 1973.

17. "The Medulla Grammatice Latin-English Dictionary" (Canterbury D.2), ed. J. Marie Van Zandt-McCleary, Ph.D. diss., University of Chicago, 1958.

18. The Latin-Middle English Glossary *Medulla Grammatice,* B.M. Harl. ms. 1738, ed. F. A. Tremblay, Ph.D. diss., Catholic University of America, 1968.

however. *Grece* means *gres(e* in Middle English which, in turn, is our very own *grease*. Indeed, lexicographical editing can be a slippery business.

Martial, in his *Epigrammaton libri,* book 2.8, addresses himself to the issue of scribal inadequacy with characteristically piercing brilliance (I could not avoid the verse):

> Good reader, do not blame the bard
> For phrases too obscure or hard,
> Or if the grammar seem to halt;
> Believe me that's the scrivener's fault.
> He knew your eagerness to read
> And sacrificed too much to speed.
> If me you blame instead of him,
> Your intellect must need be dim.[19]

But at what risk did the scribe act to support his claims? Any less rigorously than we? Consider the Stonyhurst manuscript reading "Camur g(rec)e, wrong" followed immediately by "Camurus a um curuus." I looked to the Harley 2257 manuscript which provides: "Camur g(rec)e wronge la(tin)e followed again immediately by "Camurus ra rum .i. curuus." I add the second entries in both manuscripts because their glosses clarify the individual situations as well as support the *Oxford Latin Dictionary* entry: *Camur(us).* Is *Camur* a Latin word and not a Greek one? The *OLD* quotes Vergil as its principal documentation: *Georgics* 3.55: "camuris . . . cornibus" and glosses the word as "curved or arched inward" and suggests the Greek Καμάρα as the likely etymon (see under Καμάρα in *LSJ* and its *Revised Supplement*). Also see the entry in *A Latin Dictionary,* ed. by Lewis and Short, under *Camur* which gives a variety of explanations, two of which suggest that *Camur* is found in *Isidore* XII, 1, 35 and XV, 8, 5. Checking both of these readings what seems to be of considerable interest is that Isidore (Lindsay, Oxford, 1911) gives both entries in the Greek: XII, 1, 35: "Καμουρ enim verbo Graeco curvum significat;" and XV, 8, 5: "Καμουρ enim Graece curvum est." Can it be argued that *Camur* is both Latin and Greek? Not likely, I think. The Καμουρ of Isidore plus references to Prudentius and Macrobius (see *Lewis and Short*) are much later than Vergil which is chronologically the earliest entry on record. But you see the scribes' problem. They opted for the Greek entry and transliterated it, which is the normal course in this tradition, but, you might say, they placed chronology in

---

19. *Martial, The Twelve Books of Epigrams,* trans. by J. A. Pott and F. A.Wright, Broadway Translations (London, 1924), 47–48.

an inferior position. But just so much did the scribe have to work with in comparison with the multifarious lexica we now have! It's a point that demands a perspective. Am I more correct in considering the lemma as Latin and not intended as Greek? Or not? I think so (above is my evidence), but you might disagree. The obligation of the editor is to bring forth all the evidence and let the reader choose. In this case the real Greek source is probably Καμάρα, but that is not what we are discussing. Everything points to the gloss "wrong(e," which in Middle English means "curved" or "crooked." What can be said is that the Harley 2257 manuscript is incorrect in labeling "wronge" as Latin. Hence my conclusion is that the Stonyhurst manuscript is more correct, or should I say, almost right.

However, it has been my experience that the greater number of textual problems are due principally to a failure on the part of editors to acknowledge responsibility for their text. In the introduction to the Van Zandt-McCleary edition of the Canterbury manuscript of the *Medulla* (one of the unpublished dissertations) the editor briefly accounts for readings from the Stonyhurst manuscript by relying upon a series of readings from a *Historical Commission Report* rather than verifying the readings of the easily accessible manuscript itself (never, if possible, acquiesce in another's reading, no matter how reliable you think it may be; always check the manuscript for yourself). She writes: "The following extracts may perhaps serve to indicate the nature and dialectal character of this curious manuscript."[20] Regrettably six of the seven entries were misread, with multiple misreadings in a few instances. In one case an unsupportable hapax legomenon was created, which is bad business practice.[21] We have enough ghost words in the language.

Peter Haworth, a scholar of the 1920s, possesses the dubious distinction of having put into print a fragment of the *Medulla* without knowing it, or so it

---

20. Van Zandt-McCleary, *Medulla Grammatice,* xxvii.
21. Ibid.: Archula, a little whicche (misreading of ms.: litel).
    Arista, an ale of corne (misreading of ms. corn).
    Asciola, a litel thixel.
    Catulus, a whelp, or a chetou (misreading of ms. cheton: see *MED chiton*) or a kyndyl.
    Coclia, heizt, a rund trou, and (ms. has ampersand) a shille (misreading of ms. schille) of a fishe.
    Emarcio (should be corrected to -*eo*), es (transcriber omits it from the ms.), to drie, or welwe.
    Fex, cis (transcriber omits it from the ms.), dartes (should have been corrected to *darstes;* referring to drastes (s.v. *MED*)) of ale or of wyne.

seems.[22] He claimed that the Bristol University ms. DM 1 belonged to the tradition of the *Hortus Vocabulorum.* I've argued elsewhere that it is, in fact, a fragment of the *Medulla Grammatice.*[23] Up to this point there was no edited portion of any part of the *Medulla* published. My intention here is to emphasize that there was no edited text to rely upon as a parallel. All that was available was the Bristol fragment. One must go back to the manuscript. That is all there is in the case of the *Medulla* (the other two major glossaries mentioned above both have single edited versions). The Bristol fragment has 465 entries and interpretations.What was unfortunate was that of this number Haworth's edition revealed between 150 and 200 transcriptional errors that ran the complete paleographical gamut. To "dot one more i" and conclude this segment, it may be worth mentioning that DeWitt Starnes, a deservedly well regarded lexicologist, in his work entitled *Renaissance Dictionaries* compares the language of a folio of the Harley 2257 ms. of the *Medulla* and the printed edition of the *Hortus Vocabulorum.*[24] In one hundred lines of his transcription of the text of this *Medulla* manuscript he commits 34 errors. And this, along with the work of Haworth, is in print; others I've referred to remain unpublished. When a mistake is made in manuscript studies, it becomes text and is about as difficult to remove as it is to discount a tax.

The words of Quintilian (bk. 9.4.39) may serve as a reminder to the careless or untrained: "The unskilled are likely to alter forms they find in archaic texts, and in their desire to inveigh against what they consider the scribes' ignorance they confess their own."[25] The following example emphasizes editorial pretension upon simple scribal practice. R. T. Meyer, in one of the few articles having anything to do with the *Medulla,*[26] inserts his reading of an entry and gloss from the Stonyhurst manuscript as follows: "Abra .i. ancilla libera .i. liberta (leg. liberata)." But there is no need for *(leg. liberata)* since the word before it is not *liberta* but *liberata.* Hence, "Abra .i. ancilla libera .i. liberata" should be the reading (that is, just what the scribe had).

In the Herrtage edition of the *Catholicon Anglicum* there is a similar example: the entry *a Scowrge* is glossed by a series of words: "flagrum, flagellum,

22. P. Haworth, "The First Latin-English Dictionary. A Bristol University Manuscript," *Transactions of the Bristol and Gloucestershire Archaeological Society* 45 (1923): 253–75.

23. V. P. McCarren, "The Bristol University MS DM 1, A Fragment of the *Medulla Grammatice:* An Edition," *Traditio* 48 (1993): 173–235.

24. De Witt T. Starnes, *Renaissance Dictionaries* (Austin, 1954), 32–34.

25. "Quae in veteribus libris reperta mutare imperiti solent, et dum librariorum insectari volunt inscientiam, suam confitentur."

26. R. T. Meyer, "The Relation of the Medulla to the Earlier English Glossaries," *Dictionary Society of North America,* 1979, 141–50.

quaragena, scutica (? sentica A), scorpio, scorpius, tauria." The point revolves around (?sentica A). A = Add. ms. 15562, a variant manuscript unedited. The problem is solely a paleographical one. The *-en* of *sentica* is easily rendered *-cu,* directing one to the correct reading: *scutica.* The editor erred by not paying more attention to the similarity of the word in his edition: *scutica,* and also failed to take into account that *sentica* is at best something like a "thorny brier," which would serve as the raw material for a whip *(scutica).* Chances are the scribe knew more about the text and its language than we do. As a rule, with the regular cautions, give the scribe the benefit of the doubt. At least Herrtage queried his own reading. What would have been further beneficial would have been to turn to the other sources. The *Promptorium Parvulorum* (450) reads: "Scorge: flagellum, scutica"; the *Medulla* reads: "Scutica: a wyppe other a ʒerde." This probably would have convinced him of *scutica,* not *sentica.* In this line of work one needs all the help one can get.

Consequent upon this failure of editors to acknowledge responsibility for their text, one might argue for four primary duties of the editor of a text: first, as has been mentioned, gather up a knowledge of the language(s) in which the tradition of the text is transmitted. If not, please don't touch. It would seem an obvious requirement, but it isn't taken seriously enough, and the results prove disastrous. Secondly, acquire sound paleographical skills by way of the appropriate manuals,[27] in order to help produce accurate transcriptions, overcoming the awful business of abbreviations and the general nature of the fast hand, for which the Germans have coined an appropriate onomatopoetic word, *verschleifung.* Then, third, an understanding of the style, habits, and inclinations of the scribe of the particular manuscript; and finally, a familiarity with the entire textual tradition. If these admonitions are heeded, then any other problems can be, more or less, dealt with by periodic attention to the words of Nietzsche: (to translate) "Philology is that venerable art which demands one thing above all from its worshipper, to go aside, to take one's time, to become silent, to become slow. . . . just by this it attracts and charms us most in the midst of an age of 'work,' that is of haste, of indecent and sweating hurry that wants 'to have done' with everything in a moment, with any old and new books too—while itself it is not so easily at an end; it teaches to read well; that means

---

27. *Dizionario di Abbreviature Latine ed Italiane,* A. Cappelli (Milan, 1929), rev. 1967; *English Cursive Book Hands, 1250–1500,* M. B. Parkes, rev. ed. (Oxford, 1979); *Handwriting in England and Wales,* N. Denholm-Young, (Cardiff, 1954); *The Record Interpreter,* C. T. Martin (London, 1910); *Manuel de Paleographie,* M. Prou (Paris, 1890); *English Vernacular Hands,* C. E. Wright (Oxford, 1960); *English Court Hand, A.D. 1066 to 1500,* C. Johnson, H. Jenkinson (Oxford, 1915).

to read slowly, deeply, with consideration and carefully, with reservations, with open doors, with delicate fingers and eyes."[28]

But observe what happens when the rules are ignored. Consider the word *cillio.* In the Bristol manuscript fragment of the *Medulla,* the entry and interpretation read: "Cillio: to steryn, caret suppinis." Entry word, interpretation, and a minor comment by the scribe: expected and quite normal glossographical language. The segment appears, among many of the manuscripts of the *Medulla,* in Harley 1738. Yet, the reading given by the editor violates all four principles just referred to. Instead of "caret suppinis" he reads: "cum suppiris." *Caret* is abbreviated quite normally in the manuscript but misread by the editor. *Suppiris* is the ablative case of nothing that exists in the Latin language. It's a word that cannot be functional because it is not Latin, and it appears nowhere else in the tradition. And, what is most alarming is that it could influence some as being close enough to being correct to be acceptable. For example, could it be *suspirium: p* written for *s,* meaning a "deep breath," perhaps a directive for pronunciation? But such directives are not given in this fashion. Hence, the considerable responsibility for intimacy with the text and the genre. What about another quick example in the same manuscript: *Cupedinus,* normalized (a dangerous procedure at best; we should not forget that we are dealing with fifteenth century, not present-day, phonetics) to *Cupidineus* and glossed as "histy"? It's nothing but an unfortunate reading. *Cupio* and derivatives mean "long for," "desire," and paleographically *hi* has the same makeup as *lu,* a vertical stroke and two minims: hence, the correct reading is "lusty."

Apart from the manuscript tradition, however, there is little recourse. There is no printed text, no bibliography to speak of (nothing certainly to "hang your hat on"). However, you can and must avail yourself of lexica, all you can obtain from all periods, because, as you now realize, these modern dictionaries are based, to no inconsiderable degree, upon these earlier glossaries.[29] What about finding yourself in the following position? In the introduction to the Harley 1738 ms. the editor lists fifty-five entries from his manuscript, none of which are favored with interpretations. Next to each he provides the interpretation given by another manuscript (Stonyhurst). However, in doing so, he commits twenty-five errors. He claims, for example, that *insipidus* 'vnsauery' and *auersor* 'fro wytnes' do not appear in the Stonyhurst manuscript; but they do. Consider another entry word, *suffibulum.* The editor claims that the Stonyhurst manuscript reads *suffiblicum* here. But it doesn't. It appears in the manuscript

---

28. A translation of a statement of F. Nietzsche's as found on the page opposite the frontispiece of *The Brut or The Chronicles of England,* ed. F. W. D. Brie (London, 1906).

29. See the list of dictionaries at the end of this essay.

as *suffiblm̄*. The position of the macron near the *l* and above the *m* has its application before as well as after the *l*. Hence, the newly unfounded creation *suffiblicum* must give way to *suffibulum*, which is what the Harley scribe wrote in the first place. So, nothing lost, but fortunately nothing gained.

In dealing with glossaries one's flanks are unprotected; there is no rear- or van-guard of text to offer explanation. Every word absorbs full attention for better or worse. What should you do when you are presented with the following: "Man grece, videre le?" The problem is sense. It makes none. Capitals are notorious, yet there is no note or suggestion anywhere amid the three unpublished dissertations (Canterbury D.2, Harley 1738, and Pepys 2002 mss. of the *Medulla Grammatice*) to indicate that this problem was even recognized. But here is the remarkable irony: the answer is in "the hand." If one checks any of the manuscripts and notices the shape of the *M:* ᕋ, and realizes that *-an* is the infinitive ending in Greek of the -αω class contract verbs, then one probably has tumbled to it already in ʽορᾶν, which, in English means "to see," a perfect parallel to *videre*. The attraction of this entry is that it is a scribal error perpetuated by editors, who know little or no Greek and less paleography. Consider another entry and gloss from the Stonyhurst manuscript: "Graba ge, capud le," which is the commonly accepted reading among the manuscripts. *Graba* seems unrecognizable. Supposedly it means something like "head" or "source." Engage most or all of your orthographic and phonological training, go to Liddell-Scott-Jones and search. *G* and *K* are guttural, but Κεφαλή won't bring us close enough. However, a "capital" notion would be the word: Κρανίον which unfortunately leads us two ways: one, Κράνα (Doric form of Κρήνη): "well-spring or source" (the minims constituting the *n* could easily be mistaken for *u*, which in turn is often normalized as *v*, which in fifteenth-century hands is a letter identical to *b:* ᖯ). Hesychius offers a second and crucially supporting gloss: Κεφαλή. Two, Κάρα, which is the poetic form for Κεφαλή 'head'. The problem, of course, is that both words reflect sounds similar to *graba*, and in the transference from exemplar to copy the strains of pronunciation might have given *graba*. Choose one and put the other in the notes with adequate explanation, including relevant variant readings from other manuscripts. Your readers will be grateful, even if there yet remains some doubt. You will have presented all the evidence.

Then, there is a word of considerable interest to any glossator, which does double duty in highlighting the inability of both scribe and modern editor: *Anthropos* (written *Antrophos*). Although a most reasonable phonetic exchange of *t* for *th* and *ph* for *p,* one is nonetheless tantalized by the variation: *antro* + *phos,* two Greek words meaning "light in a cave" (something our scribes need plenty of from time to time). It is glossed as *homo* and labeled "indeclinabile." What is so indeclinable about *anthropos?* Yet, as caustic as we may wish to be about the scribe at this point, our criticism pales before the Harley 1738 editor's attempt to understand it. He reads: *antraparhos.* And that is quite a reading! *Antru* (with macron over the *u*) is the word immediately below our entry, and our editor mistakenly attached the macron to the *p* of *antrophos* above it, thereby construing *p* with macron beneath it = *par.* He also misread *a* for *o*.

As the foregoing examples point up difficulties intrinsic to the particular glossary, estimate the potential danger of the next example as its crux exceeds its own lexical boundaries. *The Dictionary of Medieval Latin from British Sources,* a paragon of lexical insight, has the entry *antepedare,* meaning "to buck," supported by a single quote. There is another entry, *dumpedare,* presented as a hapax legomenon, with solitary support from the *Catholicon Anglicum.* I came upon this set of curiosities when I was working at the *MED* on the Middle English word *to wynche.* There we use two sources of the *Catholicon* (the tradition contains approximately 180 manuscripts), one manuscript and one printed edition.[30] I checked the manuscript first to avoid any false impression. The entry read: "to wynche: Calcitrare, re-, repercutere, repedare," and then a final word with two curious first letters followed by *-pedare* (obviously another compound). A first glance suggested *du* with a macron over the *u*. However, I don't ever recall the use of *dum* as a verbal compound element. I wondered what Herrtage made of it: *dumpedare.* Very interesting. I checked the *Promptorium* and the *Medulla,* but neither referred to this compound. The former offered: "wyncyn: Calcitro, recalcitro, repedo." The latter provides the Latin as entry word, but only comes as close in sense as *kyke.* So, I looked again, comparing letters from other entries and interpretations. Paleographically *dum* was explainable, but it made no sense: an imperfect figure 8 with two minims and a macron over the minims. In the *Catholicon* the *d* is generally more angular in its left loops. However, the capital *A* seemed right, and with two minims following, rendered *n* not *u* and a macron over the minims, which is equivalent to the abbreviation for *ante,* one reads *Antepedare.* Hence, the entry *dumpedare* should be deleted, and the *Catholicon* quotation in support of it should be transferred to the entry *antepedare.*

In glossary work, however, one is not always working in a vacuum. Our present lexica, the monumental historical dictionaries, have been dependent, rightly or wrongly, upon their forebears, the English-Latin, and Latin-English

---

30. See note 14.

glossaries of the fifteenth century, that is, the ones I have discussed in this essay. Of course, there are many others that have yet to be seen and still others that have not yet been discovered. George Goetz has remarked (in translation): "The number of Latin glossaries scattered throughout European libraries is almost incalculable."[31] The work to be done on Middle English within the vast glossarial corpus is also considerable. For a survey of the primary and secondary glossographical sources volumes two and three of the magnum opus of F. A. Tremblay is indispensable.[32] Aside from the *glossae collectae* much work of revision is well overdue. This requires careful textual comparison with the manuscripts behind the prominent editions, most of which were produced in the latter half of the nineteenth century. I refer to the above-mentioned *Promptorium Parvulorum* of A. S. Way and the Herrtage edition of the *Catholicon Anglicum,* as well as the Wright-Wülcker edition of fifteenth-century glossaries.[33] Note also should be taken of the invaluable information contained in the introductions and appendices of these works.

In assuming the task of editing a glossary or any part thereof, you will gradually realize that, in whatever small measure, you may help determine the future of the language. To support this statement consider the following, final example. A lemma and gloss were rendered by the Harley 1738 transcriber as "Farinatus: an evyl doer." Here, as should be immediately evident, there is no coresponsion between lemma and gloss. The English seems clear, direct, and definite enough. But what can be said of *Farinatus?* It is the perfect passive participle of *farinare* 'to make bread'. Then, does it in this context mean "one having been cerealized?" I have clearly chosen a *hapax* to explain one. I suppose an evil doer might be serialized, but not farinated. So *farinatus,* I'd conclude, is not plausible here. But resorting to feasible phonetic shifts: $f = ph;$ three minims equaling *m* as well as *in;* and *t* often confused with *c* (frequently all it amounts to is a quick flash of an ascender) the reading might be *pharmacus,* which is found with only one citation in *Lewis and Short* as *poisoner* or *sorcerer.* φάρμακος, as found in *Liddell-Scott-Jones,* is far from bountifully supported. So, although there is a lexical source for the Latin word, we are nonetheless fortunate, in the Latin tradition, to have been left with at least one reference to strengthen our resolve about this entry and gloss. Yet, if there had

31. G. Goetz, "Glossographie" in *Realencyclopadie der class. Altertumswiss.,* ed. by Pauly-Wissowa-Kroll, 13 (Stuttgart 1910) cols. 1433–66.

32. *Bibliotheca Lexicologiae Medii Aevi,* compiled by F. A. Tremblay, 10 vols. (Edwin Mellen Press, Canada, U.K., U.S., 1989).

33. *Anglo-Saxon and Old English Vocabularies,* ed. Thomas Wright, 2d ed., rev. by Richard Wülcker (London, 1884).

been uncertainty over the text of Petronius at this point, and this reading of the Harley 1738 editor, along with the readings of the other manuscripts of the *Medulla,* were all we had . . . Well then, you see how close you can be to the "act of re-creation."

Modern Dictionaries of Use in Editing Glossographical Texts

Dictionary of Medieval Latin from British Sources. Ed. R. E. Latham and D. R. Howlett. Oxford, 1975–. [Anglo-Latin: English; 6th to 17th centuries—at present *A–L*].

Dictionnaire Etymologique de la Langue Grecque. Ed. Emile Boisacq. Heidelberg, 1950.

Dictionnaire Etymologique de la Langue Latine. Ed. A. Ernout and A. Meillet. 4th ed. by J. Andre. Paris, 1985.

Dictionnaire Latin-Français des Auteurs Chretiens. Ed. A. Blaise. Strasbourg, 1954. [2d to 8th centuries]

Glossarium Latino-Germanicum Mediae et Infimae Aetatis. Ed. L. Diefenbach. Darmstadt, 1968 (based upon the 1857 edition). [Principally 15th century]

Glossarium Mediae et Infimae Latinitatis. Ed. C. D. Du Cange. Rev. ed., 8 vols. Paris, 1840–57. [Latin: Latin; 5th to 15th centuries]

A Glossary of Later Latin to 600 A.D. Ed. A. Souter. Oxford, 1949. [Latin: English; 180–600 A.D.]

Greek-English Lexicon. Ed. H. G. Liddell, R. Scott, rev. H. S. Jones. 9th ed. Oxford, 1940 (with supplement, 1968). *Revised Supplement,* ed. P. G. W. Glare (Oxford, 1996).

Greek Lexicon of the Roman and Byzantine Periods, ed. E. A. Sophocles. Harvard, 1914. [146 B.C. to 1100 A.D.]

Lateinisches Etymologisches Wörterbuch. Ed. A. Walde; 3d ed. by J. B. Hofmann. Heidelberg, 1938–56.

Lexicon Latinitatis Medii Aevi [Corpus Christianorum]. Ed. Albert Blaise. Turnhout, 1975. [Latin: French; 7th to 18th centuries]

Mediae Latinitatis Lexicon Minus. Ed. J. F. Niermeyer *(ab-laborare)* and J. F. Niermeyer and C. Van De Kieft *(laborare-zucarum).* Leiden, 1954, 1976. [Latin: French, English; 550–1150 A.D.]

Middle English Dictionary. Ed. H. Kurath, S. M. Kuhn, et al., Ann Arbor, 1952–.

Mittellateinisches Wörterbuch. Munich, 1959–. [Latin: Latin; to the end of the 13th century—at present *A–Conductus*]

A New Latin Dictionary. Rev. by C. T. Lewis and C. Short. New York, 1909. [Latin: English; beginnings to 8th century]

Novum Glossarium Mediae Latinitatis. Ed. F. Blatt. Hafniae, Denmark, 1963. [Latin: French; 9th–13th centuries—*L–Passerulus*]

Oxford English Dictionary. Ed. J. A. H. Murray et al., 13 vols. Oxford, 1933.

Oxford Latin Dictionary. Ed. P. G. W. Glare. Oxford, 1968–83. [Latin: English; beginnings to 3d century]

A Patristic-Greek Lexicon, ed. G. W. H. Lampe. Oxford, 1961–68. [1st to 9th cent.
  A.D.]
Revised Medieval Latin Word-List. Ed. R. E. Latham, London, 1965. [Anglo-Latin:
  English; 8th to 16th centuries]
Thesaurus Linguae Graecae CD ROM D. Irvine, Calif., 1992. [Homer to 15th cent.
  A.D.]
Thesaurus Linguae Latinae, Leipzig, 1900–. [Latin: Latin; beginnings to the 7th
  century—*A* to *P* at present]

Elements of an Edition

Manuscript and Text

A. S. G. Edwards

All editions include in their introductory materials some account of the manuscripts and/or printed books upon which they are based. The first issue related to this fact is that such accounts are necessarily bifurcated: different parts of them properly occur at two separate points. First, there will be some description of the witnesses, usually at some point just before analysis of their textual relationships, description with which this chapter is chiefly concerned. Second, there is likely to be just before the text a section generally titled "A Note on the Text" in which specific features will be described of the transcription and presentation of the manuscript that serves as base manuscript.[1] For any comparison of a page of a published edition with the corresponding part of the manuscript on which it is based will reveal the large number of editorial decisions that separate the two forms of the text. These will include such matters as the treatment of manuscript contractions (which in most circumstances are likely to be silently expanded)[2] and any problems associated with their expansion, and the policies employed for treating capitalization and word division. It will also probably be the place to detail specific aspects of the manuscript that bear on the text, such as any anomalous forms of contraction and punctuation. The latter will normally be editorial, but the presence of any forms of scribal notation should be mentioned here. All of these decisions are properly discussed in the "Note on the Text."

---

1. I use the singular here. But it is, of course, conceivable that there will be more than one manuscript as the base one. This situation occurs most obviously when parallel versions of the same work are printed together, as is not infrequently the case with romance texts.

2. There may be particular circumstances where it is appropriate to produce a diplomatic transcript, one that seeks to represent typographically either the forms of contractions employed or the ways they have been expanded. For a recent series of suggestions as to the conventions for representing such diplomatic transcripts see Michelle P. Brown, *A Guide to Western Historical Scripts from Antiquity to 1600* (London, 1990), 5–7. I offer a few criticisms in my review in *Medievalia et Humanistica* 22 (1995): 187–91.

In other respects, the actual appearance of the text in manuscript may differ markedly from its appearance in a modern edition. Some of the ways in which Middle English texts are transmitted in manuscript can involve matters of formal representation that the editor will have to address and describe either in the "Note on the Text" or in the manuscript description. For example, the distinction between verse and prose is not always preserved (or necessarily understood) in scribal copying, and a number of verse texts have eluded identification because they have been written as prose.[3] And other aspects of verse can be ignored by scribes. For example, manuscripts of works in tail rhyme do not always present the bob and wheel in the form modern editors set it out. The systematic recording of any such departures from the manuscript in the edition is an essential part of the editor's responsibility, and since they cannot always be clearly conveyed in the textual apparatus itself, they are best noted here.

The actual manuscript descriptions often vary markedly from edition to edition in the amount and in the nature of the information they offer. What follows is a brief outline of the sort of information that might appropriately be included in a manuscript description to accompany an edition of a Middle English text. Not all this information will be appropriate in all cases. But I hope that my outline will provide some ways of thinking about manuscript description as an aspect of the editorial process. A number of further details and much practical advice may be found in appendix A of this volume.

In seeing the manuscript description in an edition in this way, as part of the "editorial process," I am making a distinction between a description of a Middle English manuscript in an edition and a description of the same manuscript made for other purposes, most obviously as it may exist in a catalog of medieval manuscripts. The aim of a catalog description is to describe the manuscript fully and systematically[4] as a physical structure, in terms of the

---

3. For an interesting recent example see Susanna Greer Fein, "A Thirteen-Line Alliterative Stanza on the Abuse of Prayer from the Audelay MS," *Medium Aevum* 63 (1994): 61–74. The difficulties of differentiating between unrhymed alliterative verse and prose can, at times, be considerable. For some discussion of the problems see Elizabeth Salter, "Alliterative Modes and Affiliations in the Fourteenth Century," *Neuphilologische Mitteilungen* 79 (1978): 25–35.

4. Some study of the methodologies of various important catalogs of medieval manuscripts is desirable. Of course, such catalogs vary in significant respects, but some acquaintance with the following is part of the general education of any medievalist: the various catalogs of M. R. James; G. F. Warner and J. P. Gilson, *Catalogue of the Western Manuscripts in the Old Royal and King's Collections,* 4 vols. (London, 1921); R. A. B. Mynors, *Catalogue of the Manuscripts of Balliol College, Oxford* (Oxford, 1963); N. R. Ker, *Medieval Manuscripts in British Libraries* (Oxford, 1969–); A. C. de la Mare, *Catalogue of the Collection of Medieval Manuscripts Bequeathed to the Bodleian Library by James P. R. Lyell* (Oxford, 1971); Barbara Shailor, *Catalogue of Medieval and*

material(s) of which it is composed, its quiring, its contents, decoration, and scribe(s), and other related matters.[5] In contrast, the editor is concerned with the manuscript in a more specific way, with the textual significance of this physical structure, with what it reveals about the transmission of the text, a concern that may not necessarily extend very searchingly to other unrelated aspects of the whole manuscript. Thus, the editor may not be interested in all the contents of a manuscript, only with a single text in it, and his or her description may reflect this restricted interest. Conversely, because of this interest, he or she may deal with some aspects of the particular text in more detail than a cataloger is likely to, noting, for instance, the omission of even single lines. The editor analyzes aspects of the physical form of the transmitted text for a fuller understanding of the processes of transmission, since such understanding may clarify the circumstances through which the text has been corrupted and also perhaps help to establish the relationship between witnesses so as to enable the elimination of particular ones that can be shown to derive from others that survive.

The actual physical description of the manuscript itself will be most immediately concerned with aspects of its codicology: the various elements of structure, script, and decoration that are involved in its construction, some of which elements can have potential textual significance. Most immediately, the description is likely to seek to establish the physical collation of the manuscript; that is, to determine what evidence there is of loss or misplacement of leaves, and where these leaves were originally located in the sequence of quires or gatherings out of which the manuscript was constructed.[6] Evidence of quire

---

Renaissance Manuscripts in the Beinecke Rare Book Room and Manuscript Library, Yale University, 3 vols. (Binghamton, 1984–92); C. W. Dutschke, *Guide to Medieval and Renaissance Manuscripts in the Huntington Library,* 2 vols. (San Marino, Calif., 1989); Rosamond McKitterick and Richard Beadle, *Catalogue of the Pepys Library at Magdalene College, Cambridge,* vol. 5: *Manuscripts,* part 1: Medieval (Cambridge, 1992).

5. Ker enumerates sixteen points that must form part of a catalog description in *Medieval Manuscripts,* 1:vii–xiii; for a valuable introduction to the various aspects of the medieval manuscript see G. S. Ivy, "The Bibliography of the Manuscript Book," in *The English Library before 1700,* ed. Francis Wormald and C. E. Wright (London, 1958), 32–65. More specific issues of book production in relation to Middle English manuscripts are addressed in various of the essays in *Book Production and Publishing in Britain, 1375–1475,* ed. Jeremy Griffiths and Derek Pearsall (Cambridge, 1989).

6. Such missing leaves can, on occasions, be identified in locations far removed from the manuscript of which they were once a part. See, for example, the fragments of the Auchinleck manuscript of *Kyng Alisaunder* identified by G. V. Smithers, "Two Newly-Discovered Fragments from the Auchinleck MS," *Medium Aevum* 18 (1949): 1–11; "Another Fragment of the Auchinleck MS," in *Medieval Literature and Civilisation: Studies in Honour of G. N. Garmonsway,* ed.

signatures and catchwords and (where appropriate) of watermarks[7] should be analyzed. Such analysis of the sequence and internal structure of quires should also establish such matters of obvious textual relevance as the insertion of cancel leaves to replace excised ones.[8] It will also note any anomalies in the manuscript's construction that may reflect textual problems. Such analysis can yield important results in terms of our understanding of the transmission of the text. At times, it can enable a hypothetical reconstruction of the sequence of a text, as Douglas Moffat has attempted in a closely reasoned analysis of the now separate leaves that make up the "The Worcester Fragments."[9] In other circumstances, it can reveal the actual order of the construction of a manuscript, as John Thompson has done with Lincoln Cathedral ms. 91, the Lincoln "Thornton" manuscript,[10] or as Peter Meredith has with the manuscript of the N-Town Cycle (British Library ms. Cotton Vespasian D viii).[11] In some circumstances, such codicological analysis may require the reconstruction of manuscripts that have been broken up.[12]

Our understanding of the way the text was transmitted can impinge upon broader questions of manuscript construction. It is clear that manuscripts were

---

D. Pearsall and R. A. Waldron (London, 1969), 192–210; and the quire of Huntington ms. HM 268 (Lydgate's *Fall of Princes*) identified by A. S. G. Edwards, "The Huntington *Fall of Princes* and Sloane 2452," *Manuscripta* 16 (1972): 37–40.

7. For an example of the use of paper and watermark evidence see Stephen Spector, "Symmetry in Watermark Sequences," *Studies in Bibliography* 31 (1978): 162–78, who examines it in relation to BL Cotton Vitellius D. viii (the N-town cycle).

8. An example of such a cancel leaf is the first folio of Bodleian Library ms. Arch. Selden. B. 24, the beginning of the text of Chaucer's *Troilus and Criseyde*. Here it seems that a decision was made, after this text had been copied and other contents added to the manuscript, to "upgrade" it by adding demi-vinet borders to both recto and verso and to include an historiated initial in the first letter of the text. For reproduction and discussion see *Bodleian Library MS Arch. Selden. B. 24: A Facsimile,* introduction by Julia Boffey and A. S. G. Edwards, with technical description by B. C. Barker-Benfield (Cambridge, 1997).

9. See *The Soul's Address to the Body: The Worcester Fragments,* ed. Douglas Moffat, Medieval Texts and Studies, 1 (East Lansing, Mich., 1987), 44–50.

10. John J. Thompson, "The Compiler in Action: Robert Thornton and the 'Thornton' Romances in Lincoln Cathedral MS 91," *Manuscripts and Readers in Fifteenth-Century England,* ed. Derek Pearsall (Cambridge, 1983), 113–24.

11. Peter Meredith, "Manuscript, Scribe, and Performance: Further Looks at the N-town Manuscript," in *Regionalism in Late Medieval Manuscripts and Texts,* ed. Felicity Riddy (Cambridge, 1991), 109–28.

12. For some examples of the reconstruction of such manuscripts see Thorlac Turville-Petre, "The Relationship of the Vernon and Clopton Manuscripts," *Studies in the Vernon Manuscript,* ed. D. Pearsall (Cambridge, 1990), 29–44; Kathleen L. Smith (Scott), "A Fifteenth-Century Vernacular Manuscript Restored," *Bodleian Library Record* 7 (1966): 234–41; the description of Huntington Library ms. HM 115 in Dutschke, *Guide;* 1:152–53; the description of Sion College, London ms. Arc. L. 40. 2/E.44 in Ker, *Medieval Manuscripts,* 1:290–91.

often transmitted in the form of fascicles or "booklets." Sometimes these booklets created groups or sequences of texts that became regularly transmitted. This is evident by comparison among the manuscripts of the so-called Oxford group of Chaucer's poems, Bodleian Library mss. Fairfax 16, Tanner 346, and Bodley 638, but the procedure can be demonstrated in other Middle English manuscripts.[13] Understanding such processes of circulation and identifying them in a manuscript description is valuable in providing information about the transmission of the text that may serve to supplement and/or confirm the evidence of textual collation. It may also be helpful in understanding aberrant forms of a text. Thus, the text of Chaucer's *Troilus and Criseyde* in Bodleian Library ms. Digby 181 breaks off in the middle of a verso page (fol. 93[v]) in the middle of Book 3. There is no indication that any more of the text ever existed in this copy. This would seem to suggest that the text of *Troilus* was only available to the scribe in a partial, fascicular form, and that he was ultimately unable to obtain any more of an exemplar. There are other surviving exemplars that similarly confirm the fragmentary circulation of exemplars. Thus, Glasgow University Hunterian U. 1.1. of the *Canterbury Tales* can be shown to derive textually for most of its first half from Cambridge University ms. Mm. 2. 5. After this, it is related to a quite different copy of the *Tales*. One may assume that here as well the exemplar was available to the copyists only in part. In other circumstances, consciousness of the circulation of groups of shorter texts in such booklets that may reflect conscious collocations may have editorial implications.[14] In such respects, an understanding of the codicology of the manuscript has significant textual implications and should be reflected in its description.

Obviously the actual script or scripts will be identified and the implications of the identification discussed. Categorizations should probably take the form established by Malcolm Parkes, since this has achieved the most general currency for Middle English manuscripts.[15] One possible implication is the use of

---

13. See further on this matter Julia Boffey and John Thompson, "Anthologies and Miscellanies: Production and Choice of Texts," in Griffiths and Pearsall, *Book Production,* 279–316. For some analysis of the specifically textual implications of booklet production see Ralph Hanna III, "Booklets in Medieval Manuscripts: Further Considerations," *Studies in Bibliography* 39 (1986): 100–111, and "Two Lollard Codices and Lollard Book-Production," *Studies in Bibliography* 43 (1990): 49–62. Professor Hanna's book *Pursuing History: Middle English Manuscripts and Their Texts* (Stanford, 1996) reprints both these essays, on 21–34 and 48–59 respectively, together with a number of other studies central to the subject of this chapter.

14. See, for example, Julia Boffey's discussion of the circulation of groups of Chaucer's lyrics: "The Reputation and Circulation of Chaucer's Lyrics in the Fifteenth Century," *Chaucer Review* 28 (1993): 23–40.

15. M. B. Parkes, *English Cursive Book Hands, 1250–1500,* rev. ed. (London, 1979).

script as a basis for dating a manuscript, since dating can be a criterion of textual significance. It is worth stressing that paleographers generally stress the limited evidence for dating that is afforded by script alone.[16] A recent instance where such possible evidence of dating has assumed some textual importance is the edition of the Z-Text of *Piers Plowman* by George Rigg and Charlotte Brewer.[17] In their edition the editors argue that this text is a pre-A version of Langland's poem, partly on the grounds of script that "supports a date in the later fourteenth century."[18] This view has been disputed by George Kane,[19] who suggests that "it looks like a s. xiv/xv hand."[20] Whatever one's view, the dispute makes the obvious general point: paleographical evidence is rarely clear-cut and, since it is open to various interpretations, needs to be used with caution.

Aspects of script can be of textual significance. The forms of rubrication often indicate subdivisions of the work into chapters, categories that can, at times, be ways of distinguishing textual subgroups of a text.[21] And the *ordinatio* of the text, its general layout on the page, can be of significance,[22] as, for example, George Keiser has shown in the case of Lydgate's *Lyf of Our Lady,* where it is essential to grasping the devotional design of the work.[23] And elsewhere, the presence of glosses or other annotation can be a clue to textual

---

16. L. C. Hector's comment on dating archival material by handwriting alone has a broader applicability: "The needs of scholarship are usually met if the date allotted to such material on the evidence of its handwriting can be taken to be correct to within fifty years, which by the wise student of archive hands is reckoned to be close palaeographical dating" (*The Handwriting of English Documents,* 2d ed. [London, 1966], 13). It is, of course, quite likely that an old scribe will continue to copy in the forms he was trained in perhaps half a century before.

17. William Langland, *Piers Plowman: The Z Version,* ed. A. G. Rigg and Charlotte Brewer, Pontifical Institute of Medieval Studies and Texts, 59 (Toronto, 1983), with introduction by Rigg and Brewer (Cambridge, 1994). For facsimile edition of ms. Bodley 851, see appendix B in this volume.

18. Rigg and Brewer, *Piers Plowman,* 4.

19. "The 'Z Version' of Piers Plowman," *Speculum* 60 (1985): 910–30.

20. Ibid., 912.

21. See, for example, George Keiser's "Serving the Needs of Readers: Textual Division in Some Late Medieval English Texts," in *New Science out of Old Books: Studies in Manuscripts and Early Printed Books in Honour of A. I. Doyle,* ed. Richard Beadle and A. J. Piper (Aldershot, 1995), 207–26.

22. On this term and its implications see M. B. Parkes, "The Influence of the Concepts of *Ordinatio* and *Compilatio* on the Development of the Book," in *Medieval Learning and Literature: Essays Presented to Richard William Hunt,* ed. J. J. G. Alexander and M. Gibson (Oxford, 1976), 115–44.

23. George R. Keiser, "Ordinatio in the Manuscripts of Lydgate's *Lyf of Our Lady:* Its Value for the Reader, Its Challenge for the Modern Editor," in *Medieval Literature: Texts and Interpretation,* ed. T. W. Machan (Binghamton, 1991), 139–57.

relationships.[24] Hence all these aspects of the manuscript need to be noted, if not exhaustively at least in a way that demonstrates their relevance to the text.

The identification may be possible of not simply the type of script but also of a corpus of work with which the scribe can be associated. We have substantial bodies of holograph material for author/scribes like Thomas Hoccleve[25] and John Capgrave.[26] And increasingly efforts are being made to identify particular scribal bodies of work,[27] some of them by scribes whose careers can be identified in some detail.[28] Such identifications contextualize scribal activity and contribute to a slowly growing understanding of the medieval English book trade. As has become clearer through recent research, this trade was crucially focused around the role of the scribe working in shifting, often rather unsystematic relationships with decorators, artists, and stationers[29] as well as with other scribes.[30] The complexities of such relationships are revealed in the work of the fifteenth-century scribe John Shirley, whose extant copies as well as other manuscripts derived from his exemplars seem to have circulated widely.[31] Identification of such scribal corpora can, in certain circumstances,

---

24. For an example of the editorial implications of glosses see Marcia Smith Marzec, "The Latin Marginalia of Hoccleve's *Regiment of Princes* as an Aid to Stemmatic Analysis," *Text* 3 (1987): 269–84. The glosses in the manuscripts of the *Canterbury Tales* and their textual importance will be the subject of a forthcoming book by Stephen J. Partridge.

25. H. C. Schulz, "Thomas Hoccleve, Scribe," *Speculum* 12 (1937): 71–81.

26. Peter Lucas, "John Capgrave, O. S. A. (1393–1464), Scribe and 'Publisher,'" *Transactions of the Cambridge Bibliographical Society* 5 (1969): 1–35.

27. See the seminal study by A. I. Doyle and M. B. Parkes, "The Production of Copies of the *Canterbury Tales* and *Confessio Amantis* in the Early Fifteenth Century," in *Medieval Scribes, Manuscripts, and Libraries: Essays Presented to N. R. Ker*, ed. M. B. Parkes and A. G. Watson (London, 1978), 163–210. For an assessment of the bibliography on Middle English scribal production, see the final section of Moffat's "Bibliographical Essay" in this volume.

28. See, for example, on the corpus of one such Middle English scribe, A. I. Doyle, "An Unrecognized Piece of *Piers the Ploughman's Creed* and Other Works by Its Scribe," *Speculum* 34 (1959): 428–35; and R. F. Green, "Notes on Some Manuscripts of Hoccleve's Regiment of Princes," *British Library Journal* 4 (1978): 37–41.

29. See, for example, Doyle and Parkes, "Production of Copies"; and A. S. G. Edwards and Derek Pearsall, "The Manuscripts of the Major English Poetic Texts," in Griffiths and Pearsall, *Book Production,* 257–78.

30. See, for example, Alan Fletcher's study of Middle English Wycliffite texts, "A Hive of Industry or a Hornets' Nest? Ms Sidney Sussex and Its Scribes," *Late-Medieval Religious Texts and Their Transmission: Essays in Honour of A. I. Doyle,* ed. A. J. Minnis (Cambridge, 1994), 131–56. Doyle and Parkes note Hoccleve's collaboration as scribe in a manuscript of Gower's *Confessio Amantis.*

31. For the most recent list of Shirley's manuscripts and those deriving from them see Jeremy Griffiths, "A Newly Identified Manuscript Inscribed by John Shirley," *Library,* 6th series, 14 (1992): 83–93.

permit the comparison of the scribe's treatment of multiple copies of the same work, an activity of potential importance for the editor.[32]

At times, the various kinds of decoration in a manuscript can have important editorial implications. One thinks of the issue of fitt division in *Sir Gawain and the Green Knight,* about which editors have tended to follow the example of the poem's first editor, Frederic Madden, in dividing the poem into four fitts. The evidence of the large initials in the unique manuscript suggests, however, that a more complex, nine-part division was intended.[33] In other romance manuscripts there are large initials and other indications of internal divisions.[34] John Burrow has demonstrated how an understanding of the manuscript evidence establishes the formal divisions of Chaucer's *Sir Thopas.*[35] And Carol Meale has shown the ways in which the evidence of such large initials has been ignored in the Winchester manuscript of Malory's *Morte Darthur.*[36] If they are followed, she argues, they provide evidence of significantly different groupings of parts of the text than those reflected in modern editions.

In other ways, the nonverbal elements of a text may need to be noted because of their textual significance. Any description is likely to note illustrations in the text. But some effort to assess their degree of complementariness to the text can be important. In such notable example as the Ellesmere manuscript of the *Canterbury Tales*[37] and Bodleian ms. Douce 104 of *Piers Plowman* the illustrations seem themselves to be a response to a careful reading of the text.[38]

---

32. See Doyle and Parkes, "Production of Copies"; and A. S. G. Edwards's study of the various manuscripts of Lydgate's *Siege of Thebes* copied by Stephen Dodesham: "Beinecke 661 and Early Fifteenth-Century English Manuscript Production," Beinecke Studies in Early Manuscripts, *Yale University Library Gazette* 66 (1991): 181–96.

33. For discussion of the significance of these initials see Laurita L. Hill, "Madden's Divisions of *Sir Gawain* and the 'Large Initial Capitals' of Cotton Nero A. X.," *Speculum* 21 (1946): 67–71; James W. Tuttleton, "The Manuscript Divisions of *Sir Gawain and the Green Knight,*" *Speculum* 41 (1966): 304–10; Michael Robertson, "Stanzaic Symmetry in *Sir Gawain and the Green Knight,*" *Speculum* 57 (1982): 779–85. See also, on the same question in another poem in this manuscript, R. J. Spendal, "The Manuscript Capitals in *Cleanness,*" *Notes and Queries,* n.s. 221 (1976): 340–41.

34. For a valuable general survey of this problem see Philippa Hardman, "Fitt Divisions in Middle English Romances: A Consideration of the Evidence," *Yearbook of English Studies* 22 (1992): 63–80.

35. John Burrow, "*Sir Thopas:* An Agony in Three Fitts," *Review of English Studies,* n.s. 22 (1971): 54–58.

36. In "'The Whole Book': Editing and the Creation of Meaning in Malory's Text," in *A Companion to Malory,* ed. Elizabeth Archibald and A. S. G. Edwards (Cambridge, 1996), 3–17.

37. The most recent facsimile is *The Ellesmere Manuscript of the Canterbury Tales: A Working Facsimile,* with introduction by Ralph Hanna III (Cambridge, 1989).

38. See further *Piers Plowman: A Facsimile of Bodleian Library, Oxford MS Douce 104,* with introduction by Derek Pearsall and catalog by Kathleen Scott (Cambridge, 1992).

In the case of the Chaucer portrait that appears in some early manuscripts of Hoccleve's *Regement of Princes,* it has been convincingly argued that this is part of a conscious strategy to "authorize" Hoccleve's poem, and is therefore an essential part of it.[39] The patterns of illustration in a number of the early manuscripts of Gower's *Confessio Amantis* and in Lydgate's *Troy Book* and *Lives of SS Edmund and Fremund* suggest that consistent sequences of illustrative models were available to producers of these copies.[40]

All of the matters discussed are potentially relevant to what is often the least resolvable aspect of any description: dating the manuscript. We have few tools that can be employed to assist in such an exercise, but they are increasing. Among the most useful are the various catalogs of dated and datable manuscripts compiled by Pamela Robinson[41] and Andrew Watson[42] (though, of course, many of these are not English and even fewer in Middle English). The identification of scribal corpora, discussed above, may also be of relevance, as is the body of scribal colophons already assembled.[43]

One final matter that often gets overlooked or treated too perfunctorily is provenance: the history of the ownership of the manuscript or manuscripts being described. Efforts should be made to identify such owners. This is not merely a matter of antiquarian curiosity but may serve to furnish important information about matters of substance connected with the text itself. For example, the only authority for the occasion of Chaucer's *Book of the Duchess* is the statement added in a sixteenth-century hand to Bodleian Library ms. Fairfax 16, fol. 130 that the poem was "made by Geffrey / Chawcyer at ye request of ye duke of lancastar: piteosly / complaynynge the deathe of ye sayd

---

39. See David Carlson, "Thomas Hoccleve and the Chaucer Portrait," *Huntington Library Quarterly* 54 (1991): 283–300.

40. See Jeremy Griffiths, "*Confessio Amantis:* The Poem and Its Pictures," in *Gower's Confessio Amantis: Responses and Reassessments,* ed. A. J. Minnis (Cambridge, 1983), 163–78; Lesley Lawton, "The Illustration of Late Medieval Secular Texts, with Special Reference to Lydgate's Troy Book," in Pearsall, *Manuscripts and Readers,* 41–69; Kathleen Scott, "Lydgate's Lives of Saints Edmund and Fremund: A Newly-Located Manuscript in Arundel Castle," *Viator* 13 (1982): 335–66.

41. *Catalogue of Dated and Datable Manuscripts, c. 737–1600 in Cambridge Libraries,* 2 vols. (Cambridge, 1988).

42. *Catalogue of Dated and Datable Manuscripts in the Department of Manuscripts in the British Library, c. 700–1600,* 2 vols. (London, 1979); *Catalogue of Dated and Datable Manuscripts in Oxford Libraries, c. 435–1600,* 2 vols. (Oxford, 1984). Comparable catalogs have been prepared for a number of Continental libraries; for details see Leonard Boyle, *Medieval Latin Palaeography: A Bibliographical Introduction,* Toronto Medieval Bibliographies, 8 (Toronto, 1984), 44–47.

43. *Colophons de manuscrits occidenteaux des origins au XVIe siècle,* 6 vols. (Fribourg, 1965–82).

duchesse blanche." Knowledge that this hand, which has provided other notes and attributions, is that of the Elizabethan antiquary John Stow (1525?–1605), who was a noted collector, annotator, and copyist of Middle English manuscripts, as well as an editor of Chaucer, gives some weight to this claim since it is possible that his researches may have given him access to information now lost. John Shirley often provides unusually circumstantial notes about the occasions for particular poems by Chaucer and Lydgate. In other instances identification of an early owner can enable the reconstruction of contexts relevant to the manuscript's compilation, as has been done recently with such important Middle English manuscripts as British Library ms. Harley 2252[44] and Bodleian Library ms. Rawlinson C. 86.[45]

These comments on the editorial relevance of manuscript descriptions may serve to indicate the close relationship between such descriptions and the larger purposes of the edition. A proper understanding of this relationship will enable the editor to present relevant information in a succinct and intelligible manner.

---

44. See Carol M. Meale, "The Compiler at Work: John Colyns and BL MS Harley 2252," in Pearsall, *Manuscripts and Readers,* 82–103.

45. Julia Boffey and Carol Meale, "Selecting the Text: Rawlinson C. 86 and Some Other Books for London Readers," in Riddy, *Regionalism,* 143–70.

The Treatment of Language

Peter J. Lucas

Recent editions of Middle English texts show considerable variety in their treatments of the language of those texts. Some offer full, or relatively full, accounts of at least some linguistic features,[1] others nothing at all,[2] with most falling in between. Whether these offerings predominantly project the abilities and interests of the editors, producing, in the case of Smithers's edition of *Havelok,* what one reviewer has described as a "monument to the former glories of philological learning,"[3] whether they predominantly cater for the presumed interests and needs of readers, or whether they may sometimes reflect the constraints imposed by publishers, is not clear. I propose to consider the provision of treatments of the language from three points of view, (1) orientation, (2) scope and procedure, and (3) manner of presentation. As I shall try to show, preparation of an account of the language of a text is an integral part of the process of editing that text.

It may be helpful to begin by indicating how an editor's analysis of the language of a text may contribute to the wider field of Middle English language

An earlier version of this essay was delivered at the 28th International Congress on Medieval Studies at Western Michigan University, Kalamazoo, in May 1993. I am grateful to the convenors, Vincent McCarren and Douglas Moffat, and to the audience for their comments, and in particular to Hoyt Duggan and Douglas Moffat for their constructive suggestions. I am solely responsible for the views expressed and for any remaining flaws or infelicities.

1. For example, G. H. V. Bunt, *William of Palerne: An Alliterative Romance,* Mediaevalia Groningana, 6 (Groningen, 1985); Peter J. Lucas, *John Capgrave's Abbreuiacion of Cronicles,* EETS, 285 (Oxford, 1983); G. V. Smithers, *Havelok* (Oxford, 1987).

2. For example, Sarah M. Horrall, *The Lyf of Oure Lady: The Middle English Translation of Thomas of Hales' Vita Sancte Marie,* Middle English Texts, 17 (Heidelberg, 1985); David A. Lawton, *Joseph of Arimathea: A Critical Edition,* Garland Medieval Texts, 5 (New York, 1983); David Thomson, *An Edition of Middle English Grammatical Texts,* Garland Medieval Texts, 8 (New York, 1984).

3. Nicolas Jacobs, review of *Havelok,* ed. Smithers (1987), in *Medium Aevum* 57 (1988): 304; cf. S. R. T. O. d'Ardenne, *Þe Liflade ant te Passiun of Seinte Iuliene,* EETS, o.s. 249 (Oxford, 1961), 177–250.

studies. The Middle English period in the development of English may be characterized as one where there was no generally agreed mode of writing it. Whereas Old English had developed a standard,[4] and a standard was to be developed once again by the early Modern English period,[5] Middle English had no fixed spelling system. Earlier philological work of the neogrammarian school concentrated in the main on reconstructing the historical development of Middle English sounds. Subsequent work on phonology has sought to accommodate this part of the scholarly inheritance to articulatory phonetics and, more particularly, to phonemic theory. More recently there has been an emphasis on studying written Middle English language as a medium in itself, and this approach permeates the *Linguistic Atlas of Late Mediaeval English* (1986).[6] The authors of *LALME* are very strict, and rightly so, in insisting on the priority of written evidence per se over any discernible chronological phonic interpretation of it. But they overstate their argument in the comparison of written Middle English with a present-day English-language newspaper: "The letter-units out of which its text is mainly made up may convey different phonic messages to different readers." This truism relates to a present-day fixed spelling system. In Middle English, a period of *un*-fixed spelling conventions, more phonic information is likely to be conveyed by variations in spelling.[7] Some features of the written language will reflect phonological developments; but others will not, and yet may still, as *LALME* shows, have a chronological or regional distribution.

Each Middle English text offers linguistic information about itself, data that relate to the larger picture of the language at the time it was written. This distinction is fundamental, and is based on that formulated by Saussure between the two aspects of *le langage,* what he called *le langue,* the inherited

---

4. H. Gneuss, "The Origin of Standard Old English and Æthelwold's School at Winchester," *Anglo-Saxon England* 1 (1972): 63–83; also W. Hofstetter, "Winchester and the Standardization of Old English Vocabulary," *Anglo-Saxon England* 17 (1988): 139–61.

5. See, e.g., E. J. Dobson, "Early Modern Standard English," *Transactions of the Philological Society* (1955): 25–54, rpt. in *Approaches to English Historical Linguistics: An Anthology,* ed. R. Lass (New York, 1969), 419–39; Manfred Görlach, "The Development of Standard Englishes," in *Studies in the History of the English Language* (Heidelberg, 1990), 9–64; Joseph B.Trahern, Jr. ed., *Standardizing English,* Tennessee Studies in Literature, 31 (Knoxville, 1989).

6. A. McIntosh, M. L. Samuels, and M. Benskin, *Linguistic Atlas of Late Mediaeval English (LALME),* 4 vols. (Aberdeen, 1986), e.g., 1:5–6.

7. For a threefold distinction between *(a)* Spelling Features mainly of Orthographic Interest, *(b)* Spelling Features of Orthographic Interest and having possible or probable Phonic Significance, and *(c)* Spelling Features of Interest largely for their possible or probable Phonic Significance, see Peter J. Lucas, "Consistency and Correctness in the Orthographic Usage of John Capgrave's *Chronicle,*" *Studia Neophilologica* 45 (1973): 323–55, rev. reissue in Peter J. Lucas, *From Author to Audience: John Capgrave and Medieval Publication* (Dublin, 1997), chap. 8.

store of verbal symbols that make up the language user's competence, and *la parole,* the individual act of linguistic performance,[8] for the present purposes the act of writing. In order to build up as complete a picture as possible of the historical and dialectal development of *le langue* Middle English, we need all the information we can get from every Middle English text on the level of *la parole,* that is every Middle English scribal version of every Middle English text. Each scribal version of a Middle English text represents an idiolect (or one or more idiolects superimposed upon one other). Only by accumulating evidence from associated idiolects do we acquire a picture of a dialect and how it developed; only by accumulating evidence from associated dialects do we gain a picture of the language and how it developed.[9] In the fifteenth century the evidence of idiolects in contact becomes particularly important for tracing the spread of standardization in written English, which preceded the development of early Modern Standard English;[10] only a full account of a scribe's linguistic usage will furnish all the information needed.

Very few texts survive in an author's handwriting, showing the author's linguistic usage at the time of writing. That this linguistic usage could change over a period of time can be illustrated from Capgrave.[11] That it could change even as a writer was writing his or her book can be illustrated from Orm's decision to use *e* not *eo* in words with Old English *ĕo* (e.g., OE *heort* 'heart', *lēod* 'people'), a decision made about two-thirds of the way through the work, and then reinforced by going through from the beginning up to line 13852 correcting the *eo*'s to *e*.[12] That an author's linguistic usage could be inconsistent can be illustrated from Hoccleve.[13] However, most copies of Middle English texts are copies at some stage removed from an author's original. Such copies contain various linguistic usages, layered, so to speak, one on top of

---

8. Ferdinand de Saussure, *Course in General Linguistics* (trans. *Cours de linguistique générale*), ed. Charles Bally and Albert Sechehaye, trans. and annot. Roy Harris (London, 1983).

9. Indeed, the features themselves may be considered more important than the dialect: *il y a des caractères dialectaux, il n'y a pas de dialectes,* to quote Paul Meyer. Here I have favored an aggregate model of a dialect rather than a relational one. For discussion see Roy Harris, "Saussure and Linguistic Geography," *Language Sciences* 15 (1993): 1–14.

10. Cf. Peter J. Lucas, "Towards a Standard Written English? Continuity and Change in the Orthographic Usage of John Capgrave OSA (1393–1464)," in *English Historical Linguistics 1992: Papers from the Seventh International Conference on English Historical Linguistics,* ed. F. Fernández, M. Fuster, and J. J. Calvo (Amsterdam, 1994), 91–104; rev. reissue in Lucas, *From Author to Audience,* chap. 9.

11. See Lucas, "Continuity and Change."

12. See R. W. Burchfield, "The Language and Orthography of the Ormulum MS.," *Transactions of the Philological Society* 55 (1956): 56–87.

13. John M. Bowers, "Hoccleve's Two Copies of *Lerne to Dye:* Implications for Textual Critics," *Papers of the Bibliographical Society of America* 83 (1989): 437–72, esp. 454–56.

another. A scribe may have attempted to "translate" the dialect of the exemplar into his or her own, and the extent to which the scribe may have succeeded varied considerably, some copies being almost completely successful in leaving no relict spellings from an earlier linguistic layer, others less so.[14] Some editors, perhaps taking Kane and Donaldson's distinction between the *usus scribendi* and the *usus auctoris* to heart, have responded to this feature of their texts by treating the language of the scribe and the language of the author separately.[15] Of course, in some cases the matter may be more complex, as several scribal layers may be observable. Moreover, there may be a change of scribe in the midst of copying a work, such a change of personnel giving rise to a change of linguistic usage, as, for example, on folio 35 of the Winchester Malory (now BL Additional MS 59678),[16] where the second scribe uses *ye* forms in preference to the first scribe's *thou* forms. Here the linguistic information confirms the paleographical analysis.

Orientation

The primary purpose of an account of the language of a Middle English text should be to elucidate that text. Such elucidation should take account of at least two elements: (1) establishing the text, including the usefulness of linguistic data for that purpose, and (2) analyzing the text.

---

14. See Michael Benskin and Margaret Laing, "Translations and *Mischsprachen* in Middle English," in *So Meny People Longages and Tonges* (Angus McIntosh *Festschrift*), ed. Michael Benskin and Michael L. Samuels (Edinburgh, 1981), 55–106, summarized in *LALME,* 1:19–22; Anne Hudson, "Tradition and Innovation in Some Middle English Manuscripts," *Review of English Studies,* n.s. 17 (1966): 359–72; Peter J. Lucas, "A Fifteenth-Century Copyist at Work under Authorial Scrutiny: An Incident from John Capgrave's Scriptorium," *Studies in Bibliography* 34 (1981): 66–95, rev. reissue in Lucas, *From Author to Audience,* chap. 5. For further discussion by members of the *LALME* team see essays by Angus McIntosh, M. L. Samuels, and Margaret Laing, in *Middle English Dialectology: Essays on Some Principles and Problems,* ed. Margaret Laing (Aberdeen, 1989). Cf. also Mills, in this volume.

15. For example, Maldwyn Mills, *Horne Childe & Maiden Rimnild,* Middle English Texts, 20 (Heidelberg, 1988). For the distinction between the *usus auctoris* and the *usus scribendi* see George Kane and Talbot Donaldson, *Piers Plowman: The B Version,* 2d ed. (London, 1988), esp. 130ff.

16. E. Vinaver, *The Works of Sir Thomas Malory,* 3 vols. (Oxford, 1967 ed.), vol. 1, plate 3, facing p. cii. For a facsimile of the whole manuscript see N. R. Ker, *The Winchester Malory,* EETS, s.s. 4 (Oxford, 1976). Differentiating (or not) what appears to be the work of more than one scribe can be problematical. For discussion of an interesting case see Peter J. Lucas, "William Gybbe of Wisbech: A Fifteenth-Century English Scribe," *Codices Manuscripti* 11 (1985): 41–64, esp. 46–51, rev. reissue in Lucas, *From Author to Audience,* chap. 6. Cf. Mills, 187–88, in this volume.

Establishing the Text

Study of the language of a text should assist any editor who bases his/her edited text on a single manuscript (or more than one manuscript printed in parallel), whether such a "best text" is chosen by the stemmatic or by the "direct" method; if the stemmatic method is used, study of the language of the various versions should assist the process of analyzing textual affiliations. Essentially the process of editing a text has three stages: the transcription, the intermediate text, and the final edited text. The first and the last of these are static: the transcription is fixed by virtue of being a record of what is in the manuscript, and the final edited text is fixed because it is final. The intermediate text, however, will constantly change as the editor makes decisions, and even changes his or her mind as he or she goes along. One of the ways in which these changes will occur is in the treatment of abbreviations and contractions.[17] It is important that in expanding abbreviations and contractions the scribe's spelling habits should not be violated.[18] The same discipline holds for any decision where a linguistic factor is involved, such as emendation: as appropriate, any "improvements" to the manuscript text should be in accordance with the scribe's linguistic habits.

The Usefulness of Linguistic Data for Establishing the Text

Editorial decisions will often depend on many factors, such as the availability of a source text, the use of a predictable metrical scheme,[19] the survival of the text in more than one copy, but some decisions will depend on linguistic criteria alone, which extend right across the linguistic spectrum. The following examples, mostly taken from the *Pearl*-poet, are intended to indicate some of

---

17. Peter J. Lucas, "Computer Assistance in the Editorial Expansion of Contractions in a Middle English Text," *Association of Literary and Linguistic Computing Bulletin* 9 (1981): 9–10.

18. Of course, it could be argued that expansion of the contraction is itself a violation of the scribe's usage. Earlier editions (e.g., A. J. Bliss, *Sir Orfeo* [Oxford, 1955]) used to mark such expansions by the use of italics, but the proliferation of such editorial "clutter" is now generally discouraged in critical editions in the interests of promoting ease of reading fluency. Texts produced for specialist readers, however, might benefit from retaining features of scribal usage that will inevitably be masked in a critical edition.

19. Editors who place considerable reliance on metrical criteria include Smithers, *Havelok* (1987), and Hoyt N. Duggan and Thorlac Turville-Petre, *The Wars of Alexander,* EETS, s.s. 10 (Oxford, 1989).

the possibilities.[20] *Pearl* is a particularly useful text for this purpose because it is possible to trace improvements in some readings as editors have progressively paid more attention to the language: modern editors can avoid the pitfalls of earlier editors of the *Pearl*-poet's work by observing what later editors have done to achieve the improvements.

Spelling/Vocabulary

Sometimes the manuscript data are ambiguous as to its correct interpretation. At *Pearl* 630, since the scribe does not "dot" his ⟨i⟩s, the manuscript reading could be *myȝt* 'power' (so Morris, Gollancz, Osgood, Chase) or *niyȝt* 'night'. From the point of view of sense *niyȝt* is preferable because the day in the vineyard is a metaphor for the life of man, which sinks to the night of death, but without a close study of the scribe's spelling (*niyȝt* occurs also at *Cleanness* 359, 1779, *Gawain* 929) earlier editors did not appreciate the viability of *niyȝt* as a legitimate spelling for *night*. Another example involves the graph ⟨ȝ⟩. In *Gawain* and elsewhere scribes used this graph for *ȝ* and *z*, and unless this practice is kept (as in *Pearl,* ed. Gordon), editors may sometimes need linguistic information to make a decision; in any event a decision will be necessary for a glossary or translation. At *Gawain* 2173 MS ⟨forȝ⟩ was taken by *MED* as *forz* = *force* 'waterfall', the first recorded instance of the word. But an analysis of the scribe's spelling practice shows that after ⟨r⟩ ⟨ȝ⟩ always means *ȝ,* as in *sorȝe* 'sorrow', never *z* (unless here at 2173). So the word is almost certainly *forȝ* (OE *furh* 'furrow') meaning "watercourse" (*Gawain,* ed. Davis, note to 2173).

Spelling/Phonology

Sometimes editors have been tempted to emend "unusual" spellings of familiar words. At *Pearl* 815 and 945 MS ⟨lomp⟩ and ⟨lompe⟩ 'lamb' were emended to *lomb(e)* by earlier editors, and at 1046 MS ⟨lombe lyȝt⟩ 'lantern' was emended to *lompelyȝt*. But *lomp(e)* is an acceptable linguistic variation of *lamb,* probably indicating a variant pronunciation with unvoicing of the final /b/ to /p/ (so Gordon, appendix II.2 and note to 815). MS ⟨lombe⟩ for *lamp* is to be interpreted as a "reverse" spelling, showing ⟨b⟩ for etymological *p*. To reach this conclusion it is necessary to collate all the relevant forms in the text, including those with probable unvoicing of final *d* and *g* as well (e.g., *fonte* 'found' 327,

---

20. C. G. Osgood, *The Pearl* (Boston 1906); E. V. Gordon, *Pearl* (Oxford, 1953); J. R. R. Tolkien, E. V. Gordon, rev. Norman Davis, *Sir Gawain and the Green Knight* (Oxford, 1967); Malcolm Andrew and Ronald Waldron, *The Poems of the Pearl Manuscript* (London, 1978, rev. ed. Exeter, 1987). References to earlier editions may be found in the bibliographies to the editions cited.

þynk 'thing' *Gawain* 1526 etc.), where reverse spellings may also occur (e.g., *coumforde* 'consolation' 369 in rhyme). Gordon, followed by Andrew/ Waldron, is justified by retaining the manuscript readings, but prior to Gordon's analysis of the language editors thought that the scribe had made mistakes here. That such reverse spellings are the result of scribal "mistranslation" of an exemplar can be seen also at *Wars of Alexander* 1199 and 4315, where manuscript ⟨hald⟩ and ⟨stand⟩ are written for *hold* 'true' and *stond* sb. 'time'.[21]

Morphology—Pronouns

Many scribes employ consistent spelling distinctions between personal-pronoun forms. The scribe of the *Pearl* manuscript consistently uses the form ⟨hem⟩ for "them" and ⟨hym⟩ for "him." On the basis of this consistent usage, at *Pearl* 532 MS ⟨hen⟩ is emended by editors to *hem*. Similarly in Capgrave one aberrant form ⟨hin⟩ is almost certainly a slip for *him,* Capgrave's invariable usage elsewhere, rather than evidence for a Middle English reflex of OE *hine*.[22] On the same basis, at *Pearl* 635 and 715 MS ⟨hym⟩ meaning "them" is also emended to *hem*. Particular problems can arise with the third-person pronoun feminine singular. In *Pearl* editors emend MS ⟨he⟩ (691) meaning "she" to *ho* and MS ⟨ho⟩ (479) meaning "he" to *he* in accordance with the scribe's normal usage. In other manuscripts, where ⟨ʒe⟩ appears for "she" (e.g., BL ms. Harley 913), or where "she" appears as both ⟨he⟩ and ⟨she⟩ (e.g., Huntington ms. HM 143), there is no linguistic support for emendation.[23]

Morphology—Verbs

A smudge or blot on the manuscript may require an editor to supply some lost letters. At *Pearl* 25 the manuscript reads

Þat spot of spysez [ ]t nedez sprede.

Some earlier editors read *myʒt,* but a verb with the sense "must" is more appropriate, and Osgood's *mot* is much preferable. It is noteworthy that the preferable reading was supplied by the first editor to make a glossary of the

21. For brief discussion see Duggan and Turville-Petre, *Wars of Alexander* (1989), xxvi.

22. For Capgrave's usage see *Abbreuiacion of Cronicles,* ed. Lucas, lx. On isolated ⟨hin⟩-forms as unlikely evidence of a ME reflex of OE *hine* see Derek Britton, "The Etymology of Modern Dialect *'En* 'Him,'" *Notes and Queries* 239 (1994): 16–18, esp. 17 and n. 6.

23. MS Harley 913 (c.1330–35) contains Irish-English poems; see Angela M. Lucas, *Anglo-Irish Poems of the Middle Ages,* Maynooth Bicentenary Series (Dublin, 1995). HM 143 contains Langland, *Piers Plowman,* C-text; Derek Pearsall, *Piers Plowman by William Langland: An Edition of the C-text* (London, 1978, rpt. Exeter, 1994), finds ⟨he⟩ for *she* "a form so gratuitously confusing that it is emended in the present edition" (21).

poem, which required him to collect all the relevant forms together. At *Pearl* 532 MS ⟨sade⟩ 'said' was emended by some earlier editors to *sayde,* but Gordon in his note to line 532 adduces other examples (at 784, *Cleanness* 210, and in other texts) that justify retention of the manuscript reading (so also Andrew/Waldron). The present tense of the same verb occurs at *Pearl* 689 as MS ⟨saȝ⟩ = *saz* 'says'. Gordon, in notes to lines 532 and 689, adducing *satz* (677), and noting *sayz* beside *saytz,* points out that manuscript ⟨saytȝ⟩ at 836 must be an error for ⟨saȝ⟩, which the scribe knew to be a form for *says* (even though in this context it meant "saw"), so *saz* must be a legitimate form for *says* and should stand. Unaccountably Andrew/Waldron emend at 689 to *sayz.*

Sometimes the exigencies of rhyme or meter indicate forms that are otherwise alien to the scribal idiolect of the manuscript text. At *Pearl* 513 *totz* 'takes' is such a form used only in rhyme. In his *Norbert* Capgrave occasionally used present third-person singular forms in *-is* in rhyme against usual *-ith.*[24] In *Wars of Alexander* Duggan and Turville-Petre restore past-tense plural endings in *-en* where the meter requires the syllable, even though some linguistic inconsistency results.[25] Although meter is the controlling factor here, a full grasp of the linguistic as well as the editorial implications is necessary to reach a decision.

Syntax

At *Pearl* 2 editors found *to clanly clos* uncertain in meaning. Gordon is surely right to argue that the best sense is achieved by taking it as a split infinitive: "to set fairly." To reach this decision some awareness of the historical status of the split infinitive is required.[26] Apparently it first occurs in the *Pearl*-poet, being found also at *Gawain* 88, 1540, 1863. Again, linguistic analysis is necessary to find parallel instances of the usage which can then be set in historical context.

Word-Forms

At *Pearl* 77 editors were uncertain as to whether MS ⟨on slydeȝ⟩ was to be taken as *on slydez* 'slip over (each other)' (so Gordon and Andrew/Waldron) or *onslydez* 'unfold'. Gordon's point (note to 77) that the negative prefix is always

---

24. See Lucas, "Continuity and Change," 95. In his essay in this volume, Mills following general usage, gives the impression that rhyme forms may be regarded as reliable indicators typifying the language of the original. I seriously question this position.

25. For discussion see Duggan and Turville-Petre, *Wars of Alexander,* xliv.

26. See Tauno F. Mustanoja, *A Middle English Syntax* (Helsinki, 1960), 515–16.

spelt *vn-* in this scribe's idiolect is decisive in requiring *on* to be taken as an adverb here.

Analyzing the Text

It follows from the approach outlined above—specifically, that the account of the language should be text-edition orientated—that the linguistic analysis of a text will need to be primarily (but not exclusively) descriptive. As full an account as possible of the scribe's linguistic habits, particularly orthographic (leading to phonological) and grammatical usage, will be invaluable in providing a sound basis on which decisions can be taken regarding the text. These decisions may be both internal, that is, affecting the establishment of the text, and external, that is, affecting what conclusions can be drawn about the text (for example, with regard to manuscript affiliations, dialect, etc.): such conclusions will place the text in its wider context. Linguistic analysis of a scribe's usage is the only means available of trying to recover features of the language of prior redactions and ultimately of the author.

Scope and Procedure

Scope

Although, ideally, as many aspects of a scribe's linguistic usage as possible will be made available, some factors may influence an editor's decision as to what to offer. For example, less might be provided if there is already a treatment of the language of a text elsewhere, though much would depend on the quality of any such prior account.[27] The existence of such a prior treatment might make possible an abbreviated account that focused on a particular manuscript version and its differences from other versions or from the supposed language of "the original." If the language of a text is very similar to that found in other texts, as, for example, is likely with texts associated with the Lollards (Samuels's Type I),[28] and the features of that language have been fully described elsewhere, then a brief summary of the main features and a notice of any idiosyncrasies in the text under consideration should suffice. Much will

---

27. As noted by Mills in this volume, even treatment by *LALME* does not guarantee comprehensiveness.

28. Michael L. Samuels, "Some Applications of Middle English Dialectology," in Roger Lass, *Approaches to English Historical Linguistics* (NewYork, 1969), 404–18, esp. 407–9.

depend on the importance of the dialectal aspect of a text. If there are external criteria to provide localization, a full account of the language is desirable, with possibly a brief notice of those features that are particularly distinctive of that dialect. If it is necessary to discover the dialect by analysis of the linguistic features of the text, then the goal of the presentation may influence the way the evidence is presented. In any event there is everything to be said for presenting as much evidence as possible. An approach that selects only those features that the editor thinks significant tends to offer a "foreclosed" account, which cannot be checked without duplicating a great deal of the groundwork already presumably undertaken by the editor. If the text is from an area or period that is otherwise thinly represented, then, again, the fuller the treatment the better. Particular attention needs to be paid to twelfth-century and fifteenth-century texts, as both these periods were characterized by more rapid, or more fundamental, change than the intervening centuries.[29]

Procedure

An editor will start with a transcription. If done by hand it will be desirable to put it into machine-readable form at the earliest opportunity, unless the text is so short as to make this unnecessary. The next stage is to produce an alphabetical *index verborum* or preferably a concordance, which can be done electronically (see Robinson in this volume). Work on the language can then proceed hand in hand with work on the glossary (see Moffat in this volume). Notes relating to linguistic matters for inclusion in the commentary can also be drafted at this stage. All forms with variant spellings (e.g. *bank/bonk*) will need to be collected together and the etymology noted from one of the standard dictionaries, such as *ODEE, MED, OED*. Sometimes the development of a word (e.g. *chafer* 'beetle', *heffer*) may require further elucidation by using the indexes in books such as Dobson, Jordan, and Luick to locate detailed discussion. The other books in the list appended to this essay will provide compara-

---

29. In the twelfth century changes in the morphological system were particularly marked. In the fifteenth century changes in spelling practice (and phonology) are notable, but there were many other changes right across the linguistic spectrum. For discussion see, e.g., Kemp Malone, "When Did Middle English Begin?" *Curme Volume of Linguistic Studies,* Language Monographs, 7 (Baltimore, 1930), 110–17; Manfred Görlach, "Fifteenth-Century English—Middle English or Early Modern English?" in *In Other Words: Transcultural Studies in Philology, Translation, and Lexicology Presented to Hans Heinrich Meier on the Occasion of his Sixty-fifth Birthday,* ed. J. Lachlan Mackenzie and Richard Todd (Dordrecht, 1989), 97–106, rev. reissue in Manfred Görlach, *New Studies in the History of English,* Anglistische Forschungen, 232 (Heidelberg, 1995), 179–89; and Norman Blake, "Premises and Periods in a History of English," in Fernández, Fuster, and Calvo, *English Historical Linguistics 1992,* 39–46.

tive material or further elucidation of particular details as appropriate. Problems can be isolated and advice sought if necessary. For the language section in the introduction or appendix, detailed information needs to be grouped according to some overall scheme already devised, preferably a descriptive one.

Manner of Presentation

Most recent editions begin their account of the language with phonology, which is placed in a historical framework, so that, for example, spellings with ⟨ou⟩ may be found under OE /uː/. This practice, which originated with editors who were orientated toward providing material for reconstructing the development of Middle English sounds, is still used, for example, by Bunt in his very thorough and (in its own terms) admirable account of the language of *William of Palerne* (1985). But this procedure is not now necessarily the best way to meet the needs of modern readers. As I have already advocated, a descriptive account orientated toward the text itself has many benefits. When starting to compile the linguistic description, therefore, rather than bearing in mind some earlier historical phase of the development of the language, it may be more helpful to begin with the historical-linguistic position reached at the time of the text, and then to illustrate each feature orthographically with reference to the various phonological origins of that feature. I adopted this approach in my edition of Capgrave's *Abbreuiacion of Cronicles,* and the framework organization of phonological features utilized there is available as a comprehensive model for anyone who wishes to follow it.[30] In this method a phonemic approach is adopted without violating the priority that needs to be given to written language (represented by the text) over the spoken language (which can only be reconstructed by applying knowledge gleaned from other texts to the written evidence of the text under scrutiny). Any reader who so wishes can follow the presumed history of the various sounds without necessarily coming to the material with a prior knowledge of their development. For example, OE /aː/ gives ME /ɔː/ (e.g. OE *stān,* ME *stone*) except in northern areas. Historical linguists will know to look for ME /ɔː/ under OE /aː/, but other readers may find it helpful to have it under ME /ɔː/ itself. Some texts near a dialect boundary (or of a transitional date) may show both ME /aː/ and ME /ɔː/ from OE /aː/. In such cases, with a primarily descriptive presentation, both reflexes will be shown separately and each can be cross-referenced to the other, and, as appro-

---

30. Capgrave, *Abbreuiacion of Cronicles,* ed. Lucas, xlv–liii. At §§7.8, 14.7, and 17.5.2 references to OF *ue* should be without the accent over the *e.*

priate, a summary of indicative features at the end could draw attention to the variation in historical development or dialectal significance.[31]

Whether to use linguistic notation or not is another matter for the editor to decide. Phonetic symbols within /phonemic slashes/ may render the material less accessible to readers who are not primarily historical linguists, but their use should certainly not be abandoned if the result is greater precision.[32] IPA symbols are in general use (e.g., in the latest edition of *OED*) and are to be recommended, but whatever system of notation is adopted it should be used consistently.[33]

Besides phonology it is also invaluable to have as much information as possible on morphology, syntax, and possibly some aspects of vocabulary. In morphology the extent of noun paradigms and the forms used, the pronouns, especially personal pronouns, and the verb forms are particularly important, and tabulated presentation is to be recommended as clear and concise; see, for example, Capgrave's *Abbreuiacion of Cronicles,* ed. Lucas, lviii–lxvi. As already indicated it will be necessary to know the characteristic morphological usage of a text or textual version in order to take some decisions in establishing the text, and many morphological features, of course, show a regional distribution. Some recent editions include discusssion of a few aspects of syntax, for example, Smithers's *Havelok* (1987) on separable compound verbs, Gradon's *Ayenbite* (1979) on modal auxiliaries, and Rigg/Brewer's *Piers Plowman: The Z Version* (1983) on elliptical phrase constructions;[34] but these will inevitably be selective. A fuller selection of syntactical features is included by Bremmer in *The Fyve Wyttes* (1987).[35] Similarly with vocabulary the treatment might look at innovative uses, particular kinds of word formation, or heavy borrowing of words of a particular type (e.g., from Latin), but again such features will be ones that strike the editor as of particular importance for one reason or another. If a Middle English work is a translation, some analysis of the vocabulary and the extent to which it is influenced by the source may be productive. For example, of two Middle English translations of *La Somme le Roi,* namely

---

31. Cp. McIntosh et al., "a map relating to 'the word for "stone"'' (stan, ston, etc.) is not a map showing where OE *ā* is retained unchanged and when rounded; it is a map showing where scribes were in the habit of writing *a* and where *o* in this word": *LALME,* 1:6.

32. Cf. Pamela Gradon, *The Ayenbite of Inwyt,* EETS 278 (Oxford, 1979), 20–53.

33. Smithers's inconsistency in this respect (*Havelok,* 1987) is criticized by Jacobs in his review.

34. A. G. Rigg and Charlotte Brewer, *Piers Plowman: The Z Version,* PIMS Studies and Texts, 59 (Toronto, 1983).

35. Rolf H. Bremmer Jr., *The Fyve Wyttes* (Amsterdam, 1987).

Dan Michel's *Ayenbite of Inwyt* and *The Book of Vices and Virtues,* the *Ayenbite* uses much less vocabulary borrowed from French.[36] Editors could provide pointers in this area at least, if not exhaustive studies. An example of an editor who is helpful in this respect is Blayney in her *Translations of Chartier* (1980).[37] As a general rule some indication of the lexicographical importance of the items selected *in relation to the text* is a desideratum.

It is important to set out all the linguistic data first, before attempting to interpret them. Such an analysis will be essential to provide the editor with his/her own perspective before taking into account evidence from outside the text. He/she can assess the level of linguistic consistency or the extent of variation (which may indicate a combination of the scribe's own idiolect with relict forms of an earlier scribe's idiolect), and relate this information to the date of the manuscript and the date of the text, the degree of accuracy shown by the text (as to whether or not it requires much editorial correction), any other manuscript versions, and any other work by the same scribe or the same author. With regard to determining the dialect of a text, it is only through a comparison of forms having a geographical distribution that the regional features can be arrived at. While due attention is paid to the date of the text as well, some features will give a quick indication of the possibilities, for example, the reflexes of OE /aː/, OE /y(ː)/, the treatment of pronoun forms, especially the third-person nominative singular feminine and the third-person plural, and the treatment of verb forms, especially the present third-person singular and the present plural. In deciding these and additional features no doubt the editor may have recourse to *LALME,* especially for the period 1350–1450. The process will be one of gradually introducing more features into the interpretation so that there is increasing refinement in the argument until the probable provenance of the scribe (and, if there are sufficient apparently relict forms, the exemplar) is narrowed down as far as possible. But, even if the result is that *LALME's* findings are confirmed, it is preferable that the analysis is based independently on as full an inventory of linguistic data as possible, rather than merely presenting data chosen to conform to *LALME's* criteria, in which case there is a danger of circular argumentation. *LALME* should be regarded as the

---

36. See Leo Carruthers, *La Somme le Roi et ses traductions anglaises: Étude comparée* (Paris, 1986).

37. Margaret Blayney, *Fifteenth-Century English Translations of Alain Chartier's "Le Traité de l'Esperance & Le Quadrilogue Invectif,"* vol. 2, EETS 281 (Oxford, 1980), 68–70. On the other hand her "tabular analysis" of "vocabulary . . . of great interest" (35–39, 44–46) is somewhat too concise to be as helpful as it might have been.

foundation of modern studies in later Middle English dialectology rather than the whole building. Every edition with a full account of the language of its text is a contribution toward the potential completion of that building.[38]

Finally, what is particularly useful is to have the number of instances of the various features, whether orthographic/phonological, morphological, or other, as, for example, in Capgrave's *Abbreuiacion of Cronicles.* Nowadays, most editions will be processed through a computer, and the gathering of this kind of information is relatively easy, especially if a concordance is used as the foundation for the glossary. In this way the information can be presented in such a way that it can be weighed by the user. Ultimately the material may need to be interpreted or reinterpreted in relation to information from other texts unknown to the editor, or the analysis of which is incomplete, at the time of editing, and the more significant information of weight an editor can supply, the longer his/ her account of the language will be of value.

The Language of Middle English Texts: Some Relevant Books

For bibliography see Tajima 1988 (to 1985) and Burnley and Tajima 1995.

Benskin, M., and M. L. Samuels. *So Many People Longages and Tonges.* A. McIntosh Festschrift. Edinburgh, 1981.
Björkman, E. *Scandinavian Loan-Words in Middle English.* Halle, 1900, rpt. 1973.
Burnley, D., and M. Tajima. *The Language of Middle English Literature.* Annotated Bibliographies of Old and Middle English Literature, 1. Woodbridge, 1995.
Campbell, A. *Old English Grammar.* Oxford, 1959.
Dobson, E. J. *English Pronunciation, 1500–1700.* Oxford, 1968.
Fisher, J. H., M. Richardson, and J. L. Fisher. *An Anthology of Chancery English.* Knoxville, 1984.
Forsström, G. *The Verb 'to be' in Middle English.* Lund Studies in English, 15. 1948.
Friederici, H. *Der Lautstand Londons um 1400.* Jena, 1937.
Jordan, R. *Handbuch der mittelenglischen Grammatik.* Heidelberg, 1968 ed. Also rev. and trans. E. J. Crook, Janua Linguarum, ser. pract. 218. The Hague, 1974.
Kihlbom, A. *A Contribution to the Study of Fifteenth Century English.* Uppsala, 1926.
Laing, M., ed. *Middle English Dialectology.* Aberdeen, 1989.

---

38. For further discussion, where the emphasis is more on conformity to *LALME*'s procedures, see Mills, in this volume. In a recent edition Anne Hudson says: "The laborious analysis of scribal features in later medieval manuscripts has become redundant following the publication of *A Linguistic Atlas of Late Mediaeval English,*" in *Two Wycliffite Texts,* EETS 301 (1993), xxv. It is to be hoped that this statement by a distinguished editor and scholar will not mislead; cf. above, p. 177.

Lass, R., ed. *Approaches to English Historical Linguistics*. New York, 1969.

Long, M. M. *The English Strong Verb from Chaucer to Caxton*. Menasha, Wisc., 1944.

Luick, K. *Historische Grammatik der englischen Sprache*. Leipzig, 1914–29, rpt. Oxford, 1964.

McIntosh, A., M. L. Samuels, and M. Benskin. *Linguistic Atlas of Late Mediaeval English*. 4 vols. Aberdeen, 1986.

Mitchell, B. *Old English Syntax*. 2 vols. Oxford, 1985.

Mustanoja, T. F. *Middle English Syntax*. Helsinki, 1960.

Oakden, J. P. *Alliterative Poetry in Middle English*. Manchester, 1930–35, rpt. 1968.

Pope, M. K. *From Latin to Modern French*. Manchester, 1934.

Reed, D. W. *The History of Inflectional N in English Verbs before 1500*. University of California Publ. in English, 7.4. 1950. 157–328.

Rettger, J. F. *The Development of Ablaut in the Strong Verbs of the East Midland Dialects of Middle English*. Language Dissertations, 18. 1934.

Samuels, M. L. *Linguistic Evolution*. Cambridge, 1972.

Smith, J. J., ed. *The English of Chaucer and His Contemporaries*. Aberdeen, 1988.

Stanley, E. G., and D. Gray, eds. *Five Hundred Years of Words and Sounds*. E. J. Dobson Festschrift. Cambridge, 1983.

Tajima, M. *Old and Middle English Language Studies: A Classified Bibliography, 1923–1985*. Amsterdam, 1988.

Visser, F. Th. *An Historical Syntax of the English Language*. 3 vols. Leiden, 1963–73.

Wyld, H. C. *A History of Modern Colloquial English*. Oxford, 1936.

Using the *Linguistic Atlas of Late Mediaeval English*

Maldwyn Mills

The Nature of the *Atlas*

Some aspects of this work may surprise the reader who consults it for the first time. First, and most obviously, less than a third of the *Linguistic Atlas of Late Mediaeval English* (henceforth *LALME*) is taken up with maps.[1] Second, none of the four volumes that make it up contains linguistic data that are not also substantially present in one or more of the others;[2] what is distinctive is the form in which the common data are presented: various kinds of map, word list, and word index. Third, this is exclusively an atlas of *written* Middle English, with no attempt made to correlate any of the forms recorded—even those very rare ones that involve only vowels or consonant groups—with the sounds that they represent.[3]

Begun in the early 1950s, *LALME* owed a great deal, on the one hand, to the experience gained by Angus McIntosh as one of the directors of the Linguistic Survey of Scotland;[4] on the other, to the perceived inadequacy of previous works in the field. Even the relatively ambitious survey of Moore, Meech, and

---

1. Contrast the dialect atlases of twentieth-century English of Orton and Wright (1974) and Orton, Sanderson, and Widdowson (1978). The mapping in *LALME* is not, however, restricted to England but also takes in four of the Welsh and ten of the Scottish counties.

2. Most restricted in its diffusion throughout *LALME* is a body of data relating to the southern part of Britain, which appears only in 1:541–51 and 4:313–25.

3. McIntosh noted that while some of the variant spellings of the same item certainly implied phonetic differences, it was impossible to infer the exact sounds involved (in Laing 1989b, 2–4: also *LALME* 1:5).

4. See McIntosh 1952, also K. M. Petyt 1980, 93–98. The most substantial presentation of the findings of this survey is in *The Linguistic Atlas of Scotland* (Mather and Speitel 1975–86). The first stage in the collection of data was also in written form (obtained by means of a postal questionnaire), but it was here followed up with face-to-face interviews.

Whitehall (1935) was seen to depend upon too small a number of source texts, drawn from too extensive a period of time; to consider too limited a range of linguistic features, and group them together in a way that obscured their real value. It also served to confirm the traditional—but misleading—divisions of the dialects of Middle English into northern, northeast Midland, and so on. These divisions are abandoned in *LALME*, which stresses instead "a continuum in which the forms of language made up . . . a complex of overlapping distributions,"[5] and the other weaknesses noted are also made good. With rare exceptions, the chronological range is narrowed to 1350–1450 for the northern and Midland texts, and 1325–1425 for the southern,[6] and the number of both texts drawn upon, and linguistic items recorded has become enormously larger.

Fundamental to the *LALME* project—as it had been to that of Moore, Meech, and Whitehall—was a dependence on texts that had explicit links with specific places; these served as "anchor texts" in relation to which others—of less obvious provenance—could be placed on the map grid. Documentary texts were of special importance as potential anchors; since they were more likely to be the work of local scribes, their dialectal form of Middle English (henceforth *language*) was more apt to coincide with that of their attested place of origin.[7] But they had disadvantages of their own as well. Their specialized nature and frequent brevity often seriously limited the range of linguistic information that they offered, while the linguistic value of those from the southern part of the country was often diminished by the influence of the administrative language of London.[8]

Literary (and other nondocumentary) texts would generally offer a much

---

5. *LALME* 1:4a. An assignment of texts to counties, as in Jordan 1934, 2–15 can also sometimes mislead: see Benskin 1991b, 230, 243.

6. *LALME* 1:3. The earlier limit for southern texts allows for the inclusion of the linguistically crucial *Ayenbite of Inwit* (London, British Library, Arundel 57: see *LALME* 1:105a), and for almost all of the Auchinleck manuscript (Edinburgh, National Library of Scotland, ms. Advocates 19.2.1: see *LALME* 1:88). The large-scale extension of the methods of *LALME* to earlier Middle English (i.e. between ca. 1150 and 1300) is not easy, as documents that could be used as anchor texts are thin on the ground, with their scribes less prone to introduce forms from their own language. As in *LALME*, the northern texts are especially difficult to place accurately: see the map in Riddy 1991, 46. Nonetheless, work is going ahead on dialectal variation in Early Middle English, with the aim of producing linguistic maps: see Laing 1991 and Laing 1993, 1–10. See also note 17.

7. *LALME* 1:9b. Two earlier scholars who drew upon nonliterary Middle English texts in their search for firm dialectal criteria are W. Heuser (1914) and G. Kristensson (1967). The first made particular use of the personal and street-names mentioned in London documents of the thirteenth and fourteenth centuries; the second, of the Lay Subsidy Rolls for Lincolnshire and the six northern counties of England (1290–1350).

8. Benskin 1991, 220.

greater variety of linguistic data; what is more, many such texts were found to be as linguistically consistent as such autograph texts as the *Ayenbite,* either because they were literal transcripts of originals already written in an unmixed form of Middle English, or—and more often—were "translations" of the language of their exemplars into the scribe's own language, which was itself homogeneous.[9] McIntosh has judged the second of these possibilities to have been much the more common in the period covered by *LALME.*[10]

At the same time, the greater length of many of these texts meant that they were more likely than the documents already noted to be the work of a plurality of scribes, and if paleographical and orthographical tests showed this to be so, the precise limits of each hand had to be determined, and each of the resulting "scribal texts" investigated separately from the others. Furthermore, manuscripts of this type were always more likely than documentary texts to have been written in a language distinct from that of the place where the copying was actually done. Both of these matters can be illustrated from the well-known Auchinleck manuscript (National Library of Scotland ms. 19.2.1), which is conveniently available in facsimile.[11]

First, the matter of the diversity and identification of scribal texts within a larger manuscript whole. The most rapid leafing through the Auchinleck manuscript shows it to be a collaborative work, but scholars have not always agreed upon the limits of the individual contributions to it. The most convincing analysis was provided by A. J. Bliss, who identified six separate scribes,[12] and whose conclusions were accepted by *LALME,*[13] but other scholars (both earlier and later) reached different conclusions by fusing two scribes into one, or dividing one scribe into two. Kölbing, for example, assigned to his scribes α and γ what are really only two versions of the hand of the principal copyist (Bliss's 1, *LALME*'s A);[14] an examination of the spelling as well as the letter-

---

9. For the importance of these translations see Laing 1989c, ix–x and McIntosh 1989b, 27–28. The concept of translation—though in a very much more limited sense of the word—had already given Rolf Kaiser the starting point of his study of the word geography of Middle English (1937). In this, a comparison of the vocabulary of the principal copies of the *Cursor Mundi* was used as the first step in establishing distinctive groups of northern and southern words (the second on a much smaller scale than the first). A passage in *Cursor Mundi* itself describing a still more radical kind of translation is set at the head of Kaiser's study and is also quoted on *LALME* 1:5a.

10. McIntosh defines these modes of translation, together with a third, intermediate between them, in 1989d, 92; see also *LALME* 1:13.

11. See Pearsall and Cunningham 1977.

12. Bliss 1951, 652–54.

13. See *LALME* 1:88; the hands are here designated by letters of the alphabet, not numerals.

14. Kölbing 1884, 183, 186–88, 190. Cambridge University Library ms. Ff.ii.38—also available in facsimile—offers another example of a seeming change of hand (after the fifth line of fol.

forms of the relevant sections confirms the rightness of Bliss's conclusion.

Second, the possible discrepancy between the scribe's native "language" and that of the place in which he did his copying.[15] Although lacking any written evidence to associate it with London, the Auchinleck manuscript has been widely accepted as the kind of book most likely to have been produced in the capital, and M. L. Samuels has also shown that two of its scribes (Bliss's 1 and 3, *LALME*'s A and C) wrote an early form of London English.[16] In *LALME* 1:88 the first of these scribes is assigned to Middlesex, the second to London, while the copyist responsible for the other really sizable contribution to the book (Bliss's scribe 5, *LALME*'s hand E) is placed in Essex. On the other hand the other two contributors noted at the same point in *LALME* are allocated to Worcestershire and on the Gloucestershire/Worcestershire border respectively. So that, although working in London, these last had emphatically not adopted the language of the capital, but continued to reproduce, quite consistently, their own regional forms of written Middle English.

The documents to be used as anchor texts were next "interrogated" with the help of an elaborate questionnaire. This procedure was of course suggested by research into the living dialects of English and Scottish,[17] but the differences between the two exercises were so marked as to make necessary a number of innovations both in the *LALME* questionnaire itself, and in the use subsequently made of it. The more familiar kind of questionnaire is meant for use with informants of flesh and blood, from whom an even number of responses to particular questions can be obtained, whose present place of residence is known from the outset, and whose past movements about the country may—with tact and luck—be discovered in the course of an interview. But the *LALME* questionnaire could only be addressed to the medieval informants

---

93rb). This was taken at face value by F. E. Richardson (1965, xii), but denied by P. R. Robinson on paleographical grounds (in McSparran and Robinson 1979, xiv) and by McSparran on orthographical grounds (1986, 7). A reproduction of fol. 93r serves as frontispiece to her edition.

15. See *LALME* 1:45 and 2:x. for possible discrepancies—in documents no less than in other kinds of text—between these two. For the close agreement of these two sources of information, see, for example, the discussion of the Egerton text of *The Seege or Batayle of Troye* in Barnicle 1927, xv–xvii and xix–xx; also *LALME* 1:109b.

16. The first of these scribes was by far the most substantial contributor to the manuscript and may have been its compiler. For their languages, see the accounts given by M. L. Samuels of the general development of London English (1988a, 23–24; 1989, 70–75).

17. See Petyt 1980, 88–98. In compiling the *Linguistic Atlas of Early Medieval English,* however, the use of a questionnaire has been replaced by "a new method based on modern techniques of information storage and retrieval" (Laing 1993, 1).

through however much (or little) of their written output had survived;[18] answers were often not available to every item in the questionnaire, and any earlier places of residence that might have enlarged the total linguistic repertory of a given scribe could only be inferred—if at all—by elaborate subsequent analysis.

The questionnaire evolved to cope with these special circumstances and difficulties comprises no fewer than 280 numbered items, all of high frequency and each found in at least two "functional equivalents." By no means all of these items are relevant to the whole of the area mapped (rather more than half relate only to texts from the north of the country; rather more than a sixth, to those from the south). A complete list of these items is given alphabetically in *LALME* 1:557–58, 3:xxiii–xxiv, and 4:xxi–xxii, as well as in the order that is actually followed in the linguistic profiles of volume 3, in 1:552–53, 3:xviii–xix, and 4:xvi–xvii. Only the (greater part of) the second component of this latter, composite sequence (items 65–266) is alphabetically arranged; in the first, the items are mostly grouped according to grammatical category (SHE, HER, IT, THEY, THEM, and THEIR constitute items 4–9).

Words of such high frequency as these make up by far the greatest part of the questionnaire as a whole and sets the methodology of *LALME* apart both from recent investigations into the living dialects of English, and from studies of Middle English word geography. The *Word Geography of England*—to make an obvious comparison—is overwhelmingly concerned to seek out what are palpably different words for the same basic concept, (*daft/gaumless* [M 64]; *only/nobbut* [M 160], etc.), and only very rarely records variants that differ in nothing more than a single vowel or diphthong (*nay/no* [M 71]). *LALME,* on the other hand, is most concerned to record all the different forms of a single word: under item 42 STRENGTH, for example, we find such variant forms as *strengh, strenketh, strenthe;* here what is rare is to find obviously different words for the same item—such as *are* and *be* under item 17 ARE.[19] One consequence is that the body of variants as a whole—which is set out, following the order of the questionnaire, in 4:3–307—can seem a little unexciting and lacking in color. They also contrast with the kind of words presented in the

---

18. For the presence of the same hand in more than one manuscript, see Doyle and Parkes 1978.

19. See McIntosh 1952, 41–43, for the difference between collecting variant forms of "one and the same word," and of collecting "a series of words all with the same meaning."

best known earlier lexical studies of Middle English,[20] also chiefly concerned with distinct (and often distinctive) *words* for the same concepts. The emphasis upon the common rather than the rare in *LALME* was of course deliberate: a means of combating distortions of the total picture produced by widespread loss of data, and of making possible the use of texts limited both in their extent and in their range of vocabulary. It does not, however, prevent some of the forms attested for the high-frequency items from being at once rare and, it would seem, of limited geographical spread.

The emphasis upon words also serves to contrast the methodology of *LALME* with that of most previous studies of the dialects of Middle English, where the main concern was with phonological and morphological features.[21] Individual vowels and consonants, or groups of such, appear only as items 44, 47, and 267–71; morphological, nominal, or adjectival suffixes as items 56–64 and 272–80. Only in the "Appendix of Southern Forms" (4:309–25), which stands quite outside the main questionnaire itself, is there a really significant body of material of this kind; this includes such time-honored dialectal markers as "East Saxon" *a* for OE *ǣ*, and "Kentish" *ia, ya, yea* for OE *ǣ*.[22]

At the same time, while the number of explicitly phonological elements is very small, a good many of the specific variants set out in volume 4 are distinguished one from another by only a segment of the item forms: *g- / y- / ʒ-* in item 135 GATE; *-a- / -e-* in the preterite singular of item 137 GIVE.[23] It is also true that the "southern" items 159 and 206 involve not single words but small groups of words, which contain the same stressed vowel (short and long Old English *y*): item 159 offers variant forms of *dint, kind, mind,* and *stint;* item 206, of *bride, hide,* and *pride,* and in each group we find examples of the familiar regional spellings of *e, i/y,* and *u* for the reflexes of the Old English vowels. Neither of these points, however, seriously affects the primacy of the word in the questionnaire. In the second case, indeed, the words grouped under single items have their variant forms recorded separately and in sequence in the County Dictionary (4:204–5 and 237–38), and while the variant forms may offer alternations of Middle English vowels long held to be dialectally signifi-

---

20. Notably that of Kaiser (1937), whom McIntosh acknowledged as the most important of the earlier researchers in the field of Middle English word geography (1989g, 94–95, notes 1, 8, and 12).

21. See for example the features plotted on map 1 in Moore, Meech, and Whitehall 1935.

22. *LALME* 4:317, and the Dot Maps 1133 and 1156 in 1:543 and 546.

23. Segments of this kind are used as supplementary evidence for localization in Benskin 1991b, 243–46 and elsewhere.

cant, these may not affect all the words containing them equally. Gilliéron's dictum *"Chaque mot a son histoire"* is apt, and cited more than once.[24]

The detailed responses obtained from each scribal text were then set out, following the order of the main (composite) form of the questionnaire, as a "linguistic profile" (henceforth LP).[25] The dominant forms of each numbered item are recorded first, with the less frequent ones enclosed in single brackets, and the rare ones in double brackets; thus in LP 1 (3:230) we find against THEM the sequence "theym, them (thayme, theyme) ((yem, thaym, theme, yam))." The *LALME* preoccupation with written English comes through very clearly in the number of variants recorded that are most unlikely to have reflected phonetic differences: pairs like *it/itt* (though even these might have their diagnostic value in reflecting the practice of different scriptoria). Although some LPs for the north of the country are not given a grid reference, the overwhelming majority of LPs are; and this reference will also be given in each of the two forms of the index of sources supplied in volume 1: a repository list, in which the texts are arranged under the libraries, record offices, and so forth in which they are presently to be found (1:57–171), and a county list, in which they are arranged under the county (or counties) with which they are explicitly associated or to which they can be assigned on linguistic grounds (1:173–287).

After this, each LP was localized with the help of the most proximate of those already placed on the map (by the "fit-technique").[26] McIntosh speaks of "the frequent close correlation of variation of LPs with geographical position" and notes that, for any localized manuscript, "its nearest neighbours in the matrix are likely to have the most closely similar LPs."[27] All LPs assigned a specific location are set out on the six key maps given in 2:383–88 and 4:334–39. On the same relatively large scale as these are the "Item Maps" that are set out in the second volume of *LALME*. These record the distribution of sixty-two items from the LPs, with the actual forms of each item set out in full. It is therefore easy to see not only what are the dominant forms for particular areas, but also how gradually one form may be replaced by another, and how intricately they may overlap and interpenetrate.

---

24. On *LALME* 1:8a, for example, although Benskin later suggested that the principle could be taken too far (Benskin 1991b, 244).

25. As McIntosh recognized (1989c, 44–45, and 1989f, 63), Bliss had effectively provided selective LPs of his own for five of the Auchinleck scribes (Bliss 1951, 654).

26. For the early history of which, see McIntosh 1989b, 26–27.

27. 1989c, 41.

One consequence of this interfusion of forms is that any attempt at superimposing upon the item maps lines defining the boundaries between one form and another ("isoglosses") would have been difficult, subjective, and sometimes misleading.[28] At the same time, if they coexist with the actual item-forms themselves, such isoglosses can give immediate help in clarifying the distribution of the latter. McIntosh produced such a map—and on a very much smaller scale than the item maps—in a separate article predating *LALME,* and reprinted in Laing's anthology.[29] This illustrates the distribution of the principal variants for CHURCH in the Midland counties, and four isoglosses are superimposed on these to mark the approximate limits of *kirk, kirc,* and *che-, chi-,* and *chu-* forms.

In the first volume of *LALME* the same data is presented in the form of (very much smaller) "Dot Maps" (1:305–540).[30] Between 1:305 and 457, each of these covers the whole of the area surveyed; between 1:461 and 517, the northern part of it; between 1:521 and 540 the southern. A further set between 1:541 and 1:551 is concerned with a number of items supplementary to those set out in the questionnaire and the related LPs, and listed in full in an appendix of southern forms (4:309–25). Each dot map records the distribution of a particular form or group of forms of a single item; five (covering the whole of England and the border counties) are needed for CHURCH (item 98), showing the distribution of four distinct types in *ch-* and one in *k-* (1:400–401). In all such maps the black dots (graded in size, to convey frequency of usage) that mark the occurrences of the relevant item are superimposed on a network of gray dots representing the location of all the mapped LPs.

An index to the LPs is supplied in the county dictionary of volume 4; here the totality of variants that have been found for a given item are set out in alphabetical order, with each form followed by a list of the LPs in which it occurs, arranged alphabetically by county. This is invaluable for gaining an idea of the total range, distribution, and relative frequency of the item forms. Thrown into relief here are forms that are so restricted in their distribution as to be diagnostically significant: *ho* as a subtype of item 7 THEY; *nyf(f)* as one of item 46 NOR: see the dot maps on 1:314 and 426.

---

28. See Benskin 1991b, 233–36, prompted by Burton 1991, 178.

29. 1989g, 88. Samuels replaces maps that had also originally combined item-forms and isoglosses with Dot Maps, in 1989, 68–69 and 72–73.

30. For the relation of the dot to the item maps, see *LALME* 2:ix.

Shortcomings, Criticisms, and Verification

The range and scale of *LALME,* its radically novel approach, and the relative speed with which it was completed, made it inevitable that some aspects of it would be less satisfactory than others, making it as a whole—as its authors themselves point out[31]—a provisional rather than a definitive piece of work. Its collaborative nature, and the fact that parts of its methodology evolved over the course of time, have produced anomalies that pose real difficulties for the user (the composite nature of the main questionnaire is the most obvious example). These points were addressed by Benskin in a paper that appeared some five years after *LALME.*[32] Here he has a good deal to say about the "imperfect collaboration" of McIntosh and Samuels in the earlier stages of their work; the different time-scales to which the two scholars worked (with McIntosh less prepared to set deadlines in advance), their different approach toward the documents investigated (with Samuels more selective in his record-ing of item forms), and the different ways in which the data collected was at first set out (as LPs by McIntosh, as word lists by Samuels).[33] It is claimed, however, that these discrepancies were eliminated in the course of time, and that any damage to the unity and accuracy of *LALME* was minimized.

The article in which these points were conceded was a reply to a wide-ranging critique of *LALME* by T. L. Burton (1991), in which—among other criticisms[34]—he raised doubts about the accuracy of some of the southern LPs,

---

31. *LALME* 1:vii, 1:28b, and 2:xivb.

32. Benskin 1991b, 216 (for the evolutionary aspect), 210 (user-unfriendliness), 209–10 (provisional nature).

33. Benskin 1991b, 211–19. The selective approach of Samuels and his bias toward forms that were of diagnostic significance come out in his "Appendix of Southern Forms," and the dot maps associated with it (*LALME* 1:541–51; dot maps 1115–200).

34. As of the conflation of two or more LPs into a single one, as was done for the Hengwrt and Ellesmere copies of *The Canterbury Tales* (LP 6400). The identity of the two hands in which these are written has been generally accepted (see especially Doyle and Parkes 1978, 170, 174), despite minor variations in the spelling (apparent in the parallel excerpts on 172–73 and 188–89 in the same paper). For the view that two scribes writing identical hands were involved, see R. V. Ramsey 1982, 133–54 and 1986, 107–44; for its rejection, see Samuels 1988c, 38–50, and Smith 1988b, 51–69. Conflation of a different kind occurs when two or more LPs are assigned the same point on the grid, as when LPs 5890, 5900, 5910 and 9380, all linked with Canterbury, are duly located there, although their item-forms are not always identical, with LP 5890 (for the *Ayenbite*) espe-cially individual. But differences of chronology account for something here, since this text is not only early, but old fashioned (*LALME* 1:201c).

their assumed provenance, and their use as "primary anchors."[35] Benskin admitted the justice of some of these criticisms, but insisted that while such texts might be unsatisfactory in themselves, they were not typical of Samuels's work as a whole, and had never been used as anchor texts; the most they had done was to support conclusions arrived at by other means.[36] Most of those who use *LALME* will not be able, like Burton, to check for themselves the comprehensiveness of its LPs, or the accuracy with which the forms set out in them have been transcribed. But one or two of its central assumptions can be investigated without going outside the *Atlas* itself, most particularly, those to do with the placing of the LPs. As already noted,[37] it is assumed that those closest to each other on the large key maps should be the ones with the largest number of item forms in common, and both the general truth and the particular modifications of this view are easily investigated. After selecting a handful of adjacent LPs,[38] parallel lists of the items that they all have in common can be drawn up and compared, any seeming anomalies of distribution noted, and their explanation sought in the dot and item maps for the words in question. Such an exercise also has the advantage of familiarizing the reader with some vital aspects of the content and methodology of *LALME*, before making serious editorial use of either.

Using the Atlas

It is now time to look more closely at the ways in which a prospective editor can make use of *LALME*. The first step is to look up each of the manuscripts of the text being edited in the repository list in 1:57–171, and see, first, whether it has been provided with an LP and, if it has, whether the text being edited was one of those consulted in drawing this up. If both of these conditions are fulfilled it might seem that very little remains for the editor to do, but the text should still be surveyed in relation to the item forms collected from the part of Britain to which it has been assigned; it is always possible that variant forms of

---

35. And so were not only inaccurate in themselves but a cause of inaccuracy in others (i.e. the LPs localized in relation to them). See Burton 1991, 169–70.

36. Benskin 1991b, 218–20.

37. McIntosh 1989c, 41.

38. Especially full LPs are to be found in the numerical range 4000–4999, drawn from a belt of varying width in which the northern and southern surveys overlapped, so that what began as separate LPs were conflated (*LALME* 3:xa).

some of these will slip through the net from time to time,[39] especially if the text is from the southern part of the total area surveyed. If an LP is given for the manuscript as a whole, but the text being edited was not one of those consulted in drawing it up, its interrogation by the questionnaire is still more essential; it is always possible that some fresh minority forms will be found,[40] or that our ideas of the relative frequency of those already recorded will be modified.[41]

If one of the manuscripts containing the text is given a brief mention in *LALME* but no LP is provided—most probably because its language is mixed rather than homogeneous—then, obviously, almost everything remains to do. However, some suggestive information will often be found in *LALME;* see, for example, the entry for the first of the two literary manuscripts in the hand of Robert Thornton, under Lincoln Cathedral Chapter Library 91 (A.5.2) (1:98b). This, while providing no grid reference, notes that Thornton was born at Oswaldkirk, Yorks, and that some of the texts at least were copied "in a different language from Thornton's own." The fact that Oswaldkirk is about three miles east of Ampleforth, and four miles south of Helmsley sends us to key map 3, and this shows us that the LPs closest to this spot are the coalescent 7 and 197 (grid reference 458 485). A brief comparison with these other North Riding LPs would certainly be worth making by anyone editing a text from this collection.[42]

If the text has not even been provided with information like the above, then the first step must be to decide whether it is written in a single hand or not, and here, as we have seen, first impressions can be deceptive, and should be carefully checked. The next step is, again, to "interrogate" each scribal text that can be identified.[43] When an LP has finally been drawn up, it may be localized with the help of the "fit-technique" noted earlier. The indispensable guide here

---

39. Such as the form ȝut ("yet"), which appears in line 649 of the text of *Arthour and Merlin* of ms. Douce 236 (in Kölbing 1890, 276–355), but not listed in LP 5350.

40. Forms listed in the LP (531) for Cambridge University Library Ff.ii.38 can be supplemented by the minority forms *wodur* (OTHER: normally *odur*) and *hur* (THEIR: normally *þer, ther),* noted by McSparran (1986, 30–31).

41. The "Kentish" forms *oxi, oxy* of ms. Auchinleck, which are given in single brackets against ASK in LP 6510, seem to be confined to the copy of *Guy of Warwick* found here (one of the four texts consulted for the LP).

42. Essential reading for anyone editing a text from this manuscript is McIntosh 1989e, 179–87.

43. "Researchers who wish to establish the provenance of a text not treated in *[LALME]* will consider first those items common to both versions of the questionnaire: there are over ninety, sufficient in most cases to determine whether the language of a text belongs to the northern or the southern sector" (Benskin 1991b, 228).

has been provided by Benskin, in an article in which the technique is applied to a northern LP (576).[44] This was placed in the East Riding of Yorkshire in *LALME* 3:597–98, but was not then localized with enough precision for it to be assigned a grid reference and entered on the large-scale key maps. The article must be read in full, but it may be noted here that a more precise placing of the LP was achieved in four stages: the consultation of the relevant dot maps for the whole of the area surveyed; of the dot maps for the northern region; of the item maps for the part of the northern region so far established; of those LPs set closest to the area defined. In this case the process leads to a tentative placing in "the area between Beverley and York, towards Pocklington and Market Weighton."

Before this conclusion was reached, however, notice had to be taken of forms in LP 576 that were anomalous through being absent from the most proximate of the LPs surrounding it, but found in others from well outside the area suggested by the greater part of the evidence. In this particular case these anomalies are so few in number, and so very difficult to locate anywhere on the *LALME* grid, that they could be largely ignored; however interesting (and puzzling) in themselves, they do not undermine the location for the text that is indicated by the rest of the evidence. But when they are numerous and seemingly random in their dialectal variety they can pose real problems, since there will be no single place on the *LALME* grid[45]—and certainly no border region[46]—in which they can be accommodated together with the rest of the linguistic data available.

Discrepant forms such as these must be noted, grouped together, and then separately examined by the editor, to ascertain, as far as possible, their own most likely placing on the grid.[47] Their presence in the language of the text— which as a result becomes mixed rather than homogeneous—may have more

---

44. Benskin 1991a, 16–25. It is important to note that, for all the apparent precision with which LPs are set on the large item maps, their location is relative and approximate, not exact. See Kristensson 1981, 4, and McIntosh 1989b, 27.

45. Kristensson noted that the "fit-technique" would work only with texts of which the language was "homogeneous in its totality" (1981, 3).

46. "Border regions" were always popular with earlier students of Middle English as repositories for the more awkward bits of linguistic evidence. As "border-areas" they are accepted as possibilities in *LALME* 1:11–12, but with the reminder that "in the dialect continuum, *every* area is, in respect of some of its features, a border-area."

47. If a minority of forms still contradict the location implied by the majority, these too must be separately grouped and separately investigated.

than one cause; to ascertain which is possible in theory[48] but difficult in practice for any editors who do not possess the linguistic expertise and practical skills of the makers of *LALME*.[49] The most radical and least random type of mixed language is one that is genuinely the creation of a single agent, whether the scribe himself or herself, or an author transmitted without scribal alteration, and arises through personal familiarity with widely separate parts of Britain, and with their dialects. Given the general anonymity of Middle English scribes, an explanation of this kind is normally impossible to confirm by other types of information, but this may be managed if the mixed language can be traced back through the various scribes to the author, and sufficient information concerning that author's life has survived. Exemplary here is the case of John Gower whose linguistic mixture of forms characteristic of southwest Suffolk and northwest Kent correlates very neatly with historical evidence concerning the land holdings of his family.[50]

Another kind of mixture involving comparably disjunctive forms is that which develops in the dialect of London, from 1300 to 1400. M. L. Samuels has noted that before the first of these dates its constituent elements were indeed from contiguous regions, with features from Kent, Surrey, and Middlesex complementing what was predominantly an Essex type of language. But after this it acquired first a "marked East Anglian colouring," and then received an influx of Central Midland features resulting from immigration from Northamptonshire and Bedfordshire. So that in both of these last stages, regions well outside any conceivable border-area would have made important contributions to a mixed type of language.[51]

But the most unpredictable mixture of scribal and exemplary forms is typical of copyists whose approach to their texts stands between the two extremes defined by McIntosh:[52] the more or less exact reproduction of an exemplar, and the more or less thorough translation of its language into the scribe's own. This third, intermediate type of scribe—who like the second, but not the first, is said to have been very common between 1350 and 1450—

---

48. See the distinctions made between genuine and apparent types of *Mischsprachen* in *LALME* 1:14b–23a; also—at more length and more technically—in the antecedent version of these pages in Benskin and Samuels 1981, 75–87.

49. And even their conclusions have sometimes to be left open-ended: see Laing 1989b, 208, and Benskin 1991b, 223.

50. Samuels and Smith 1988, 17. A different kind of mixed language can also be more deliberately produced by a single author wishing to reach a wider audience: see McIntosh 1989d, 237–38, and Kristensson 1981, 8.

51. Samuels 1972, 168–70.

52. See note 10 above.

neither consistently renders the forms of the exemplar unaltered, nor consistently replaces them with his or her own, and "relicts"[53] of the language of this exemplar will be present in the copy made from it in random fashion. If such relict forms are not evenly diffused throughout the copy, but tend to bunch together in parts of it, and if these come just before tangible differences in the color of the ink, or the aspect of the hand, one might suppose their explanation to lie in the fatigue (and consequent relaxation of control) experienced at the end of a long session of copying.[54] Under these conditions the forms let through may indeed have been far removed from the scribe's own; elsewhere they may have been less so, and even been to some extent familiar to him as part of the scribe's total "passive repertoire"[55] of variants.

Especially interesting and diverse is the scribal treatment of words in rhyme position. A translating scribe may here carry through his or her usual practice, and by substituting his or her own characteristic forms will from time to time make the rhyme seem faulty. Where, for example, the original had linked *hyre* and *desyre,* the copy may have substituted *hure* for the first rhyme word. Elsewhere, however, it is quite common for such a scribe to keep the original spelling of the vital words,[56] even when the rhyme itself would have worked equally well in translation.[57] Thus to preserve a rhyme with *valeye,* the scribe might keep the *beye* of the exemplar instead of substituting for it the usual form *both(e).* Here *beye* would most probably have been part of his or her passive repertoire, though it might also be a relict, let in by the eye rather than the ear.

Diverse Interpretations: An Example

The version of the romance of *Arthour and Merlin* found in Bodleian ms. Douce 236 provides *LALME* with its LP 5350 (under Dorset, on 3:88). The text is given in full in Kölbing's edition (1890, 276–355), and its provenance and language are given some attention by Macrae-Gibson in his own much more recent one (1979—only a few years before the appearance of *LALME*). What is interesting is that his conclusions are virtually the reverse of those of *LALME*.

---

53. Such relicts are distinguished from the products of "constrained usage": forms that are not wholly alien to the scribe's own language but variants (if little used ones) within that language, the choice being determined by what he found in his exemplar (*LALME* 1:19; for a specific example from the work of a Chaucerian scribe, see Samuels 1988a, 25).

54. Mills 1988, 33–34.

55. See the discussion in *LALME* 1:14a.

56. See *LALME* 1:17b.

57. McIntosh 1978, 137–39.

Extralinguistic material seems to have counted for a good deal in the latter. At the head of the LP it is noted that "the MS has connexions with Tolpuddle," and on the key map on 2:387 and 4:338 it is placed at exactly this point in Dorset. This is not the first time that the association of this manuscript with Tolpuddle had been taken literally,[58] but Macrae-Gibson was much less inclined to follow suit, noting that the vital reference on fol. 14 is in a much later hand than the body of the manuscript, and that on fol. 22 there is a "note in a sixteenth- to seventeenth-century hand" that, by alluding to Admaston (? Staffordshire), points in a very different direction.[59]

It is also claimed in *LALME* that the manuscript is "copied from a Kent or London original" (so that a marked geographical discontinuity would be implied). This judgment must depend on a collation of relict forms quite separate from those in rhyme position, since these last are diagnostically inconclusive except for *beye,*[60] and the relevant part of the county dictionary (4:134b) shows this to be a western rather than an eastern form of BOTH in late Middle English (and so the wrong way round to support the conclusion expressed). When we turn to the LP, we find that on the whole *u* spellings of words in OE [$y(:)$] are certainly more common than *e* spellings, though *hure* (THEIR) and *furst* (FIRST) are to varying degrees less common than the alternative *here* and *ferst*. In the edition, however, Macrae-Gibson had come to the reverse conclusion, suggesting—if tentatively—that the mixture of scribal forms could suggest a London provenance for the manuscript, and that "a SE/London scribe working from a western exemplar seems more likely than the other way round."[61]

It must be stressed at this point that the evidence from which Macrae-Gibson worked was very different from that set out in LP 5350; much more limited in its range of separate items, much more concerned with the spellings of individual vowels than with those of whole words. But as an editor, he was also deeply involved with textual matters, and was at this point influenced by the fact that Douce 236 has the same (if rather remote)[62] lost common antecedent as the text of *Arthour and Merlin* that is preserved in London, Lincoln's Inn, ms. Hale 150.[63] This text, too, has a marked "western colouring"; since this was not evenly diffused through all the texts in the collection, he suggested that it might derive from "a collection of Western exemplars" and not from the

---

58. See Moore, Meech, and Whitehall 1935, 55.

59. Macrae-Gibson 1979, 42–43.

60. In the LP this *beye* is designated a rhyme word (by suffixed *rh*).

61. Macrae-Gibson 1979, 65.

62. Ibid., 49 (where a stemma is provided).

63. For which see LP 4037 (under Shropshire, on 3:433–34).

scribe himself.[64] This hypothesis of inherited western forms was then extended to the Douce copy, to give the tentative conclusion noted above.

The diversity of these conclusions is at first disheartening, but it is possible that the matter could still be resolved by taking a fresh look at the linguistic and the textual evidence together. From the point of view of language, the amount of material that *LALME* has made available for texts from all the regions involved (London, West Midland, South West) is clearly of the greatest importance, even if the areas around the grid references that are given for the two texts in question are less densely supplied with LPs than are many other parts of the country. When this data has been assimilated, then the difficult matter of establishing the precise relationship of the texts can be attempted once again. As Benskin and Laing point out, although an account of the "dialectal stages in the transmission of a text" is not a substitute for that of its relation to other texts (finally to be expressed in a stemma), yet the two "cohere sufficiently often for the one to pose worthwhile questions in respect of the other."[65] It is also salutary to remind ourselves from time to time that the linguistic scrutiny of a text being edited cannot for long exist in isolation from other forms of scholarly enquiry. No part of editing is an island.

Works Cited

Barnicle, M. E., ed. 1927. *The Seege or Batayle of Troye.* EETS 172. London.
Benskin, M. 1991a. "The 'Fit'-Technique Explained." In Riddy 1991, 9–26.
———. 1991b. "In Reply to Dr Burton." *Leeds Studies in English* 22:209–62.
Benskin, M., and M. Laing. 1981. "Translations and *Mischsprachen* in Middle English Manuscripts." In Benskin and Samuels 1981, 55–106.
Benskin, M., and M. L. Samuels, eds. 1981. *So Meny People Longages and Tonges: Philological Essays in Scots and Mediaeval English Presented to Angus McIntosh.* Edinburgh.
Bliss, A. J. 1951. "Notes on the Auchinleck Manuscript." *Speculum* 26:652–58.
Burton, T. L. 1991. "On the Current State of Middle English Dialectology." *Leeds Studies in English* 22:167–208.
Doyle, A. I., and M. B. Parkes. 1978. "The Production of Copies of the *Canterbury Tales* and the *Confessio Amantis* in the Early Fifteenth Century." In *Medieval Scribes, Manuscripts, and Libraries: Essays Presented to N. R. Ker,* ed. M. B. Parkes and A. G. Watson. London. 163–210.
Heuser, W. 1914. *Alt-London.* Strassburg.
Jordan, R. 1934. *Handbuch der mittelenglischen Grammatik.* Vol. 1. Heidelberg.

64. Macrae-Gibson 1979, 63.
65. In Benskin and Laing 1981, 85.

Kaiser, R. 1937. *Zur Geographie des mittelenglischen Wortschatzes.* Palaestra 205. Leipzig.

Kölbing, E. 1884. "Vier Romanz Handschriften." *Englische Studien* 7:177–201.

———, ed. 1890. *Arthour and Merlin.* Altenglische Bibliothek, 4. Leipzig.

Kristensson, G. 1967. *A Survey of Middle English Dialects, 1290–1350: The Six Northern Counties and Lincolnshire.* Lund Studies in English, 35. Lund.

———. 1981. "On Middle English Dialectology." In Benskin and Samuels 1981, 3–13.

Laing, M. 1989a. "Dialectal Analysis and Linguistically Composite Texts in Middle English." In Laing 1989c, 150–69.

———. 1989b. "Linguistic Profiles and Textual Criticism: The Translations by Richard Misyn of Rolle's *Incendium Amores* and *Emendatio Vitae.*" In Laing 1989c, 188–223.

———, ed. 1989c. *Middle English Dialectology: Essays on Some Principles and Problems.* Aberdeen.

———. 1991. "Anchor Texts and Literary Manuscripts in Early Middle English." In Riddy 1991, 27–52.

———. 1993. *Catalogue of Sources for a Linguistic Atlas of Early Medieval English.* Cambridge.

Macrae-Gibson, O., ed. 1979. *Of Arthour and Merlin.* Vol. 2. EETS 279. Oxford.

Mather, J. Y., and H. H. Speitel. 1975–86. *The Linguistic Atlas of Scotland.* 3 vols. London.

McIntosh, A. 1952. *An Introduction to the Survey of Scottish Dialects.* Edinburgh.

———. 1978. "The Middle English Poem 'The Four Foes of Mankind.'" *Neuphilologische Mitteilungen* 79:137–44.

———. 1989a. "The Analysis of Written Middle English." In Laing 1989c, 1–21.

———. 1989b. "A New Approach to Middle English Dialectology." In Laing 1989c, 22–31.

———. 1989c. "Scribal Profiles from Middle English Texts." In Laing 1989c, 32–45.

———. 1989d. "Some Notes on the Language and Textual Transmission of the *Scottish Troy Book.*" In Laing 1989c, 237–55.

———. 1989e. "The Textual Transmission of the Alliterative *Morte Arthure.*" In Laing 1989c, 179–87.

———. 1989f. "Towards an Inventory of Middle English Scribes." In Laing 1989c, 46–63.

———. 1989g. "Word Geography in the Lexicography of Medieval English." In Laing 1989c, 86–97.

McIntosh, A., M. L. Samuels, and M. Benskin, with the assistance of M. Laing and K. Williamson. 1986. *A Linguistic Atlas of Late Mediaeval English.* 4 vols. Aberdeen.

McSparran, F., ed. 1986. *Octovian.* EETS 289. Oxford.

McSparran, F., and P. R. Robinson, eds. 1979. *Cambridge University Library Ms Ff. 2. 38.* Scolar Press Facsimile. London.

Mills, M., ed. 1988. *Horn Childe and Maiden Rimnild.* Middle English Texts, 20. Heidelberg.

Moore, S., S. B. Meech, and H. Whitehall. 1935. "Middle English Dialect Characteristics and Dialect Boundaries." *Essays and Studies in English and Comparative Literature.* University of Michigan Publications in Language and Literature, 13. Ann Arbor.

Orton, H., S. Sanderson, and J. Widdowson. 1978. *The Linguistic Atlas of England.* London.

Orton, H., and N. Wright. 1974. *A Word Geography of England.* London.

Pearsall, D. A., and I. C. Cunningham, eds. 1977. *The Auchinleck Manuscript. National Library of Scotland. Advocates 19.2.1.* Scolar Press Facsimile. London.

Petyt, K. M. 1980. *The Study of Dialect: An Introduction to Dialectology.* London.

Ramsey, R. V. 1982. "The Hengwrt and Ellesmere Manuscripts of the *Canterbury Tales:* Different Scribes." *Studies in Bibliography* 35:133–54.

———. 1986. "Palaeography and Scribes of Shared Training." *Studies in the Age of Chaucer* 8:107–44.

Richardson, F. E., ed. 1965. *Sir Eglamour of Artois.* EETS 256. Oxford.

Riddy, F., ed. 1991. *Regionalism in Late Medieval Manuscripts and Texts: Essays Celebrating the Publication of "A Linguistic Atlas of Late Mediaeval English."* Cambridge.

Samuels, M. L. 1972. *Linguistic Evolution: With Special Reference to English.* Cambridge.

———. 1988a. "Chaucer's Spelling." In Smith 1988a, 23–37.

———. 1988b. "Langland's Dialect." In Smith 1988a, 70–85.

———. 1988c. "The Scribe of the Hengwrt and Ellesmere Manuscripts of *The Canterbury Tales.*" In Smith 1988a, 38–50.

———. 1989. "Some Applications of Middle English Dialectology." In Laing 1989c, 64–80.

Samuels, M. L., and J. J. Smith. 1988. "The Language of Gower." In Smith 1988a, 13–22.

Smith, J. J., ed. 1988a. *The English of Chaucer and His Contemporaries: Essays by M. L. Samuels and J. J. Smith.* Aberdeen.

———. 1988b. "The Trinity Gower D-Scribe and His Work on Two Early *Canterbury Tales* Manuscripts." In Smith 1988a, 51–69.

The Use of Sources in Editing Middle English Texts

Mary Hamel

One way to begin a discussion of how the editor of a Middle English text should deal with its sources is to consider how medieval writers themselves used sources. According to St. Bonaventure (speaking upon the writing of theology),

> there are four ways of making a book. For someone writes out the words of other men without adding or changing anything, and he is called the scribe *[scriptor]* pure and simple. Someone else writes the words of other men, putting together material, but not his own, and he is called the compiler *[compilator]*. Someone else writes the words of other men and also his own, but with those of other men comprising the principal part while his own are annexed merely to make clear the argument, and he is called the commentator *[commentator],* not the author. Someone else writes the words of other men and also of his own, but with his own forming the principal part and those of others being annexed merely by way of confirmation, and such a person should be called the author *[auctor].*[1]

Bonaventure does not consider the possibility that an *auctor* might write a work entirely in his own words, expressing only his own ideas. And Middle

---

1. "Ad intelligentiam dictorum notandum, quod quadruplex est modus faciendi librum. Aliquis enim scribit alienam materiam nihil addendo, vel mutando; et iste mere dicitur scriptor. Aliquis scribit aliena addendo, sed non de suo: et iste compilator dicitur. Aliquis scribit et aliena, et sua; sed aliena tanquam principalia, et sua tanquam annexa ad evidentiam; et iste dicitur commentator. Aliquis scribit et sua, et aliena; sed sua tanquam principalia, aliena tanquam annexa ad confirmationem: et talis debet dici auctor" (*S. Bonaventurae opera omnia,* ed. A. C. Peltier [Paris, 1864], 1:20). Translation from A. J. Minnis and A. B. Scott, "Commentary on Peter Lombard's *Sentences:* Extracts from Exposition of the Prologue," in *Medieval Literary Theory and Criticism, c. 1100–c.1375: The Commentary Tradition,* rev. ed. (Oxford, 1991), 229.

English writers stopped short of being, properly speaking, "authors": as Tim William Machan has remarked, "The use of the vernacular" prevents "Chaucer or the many anonymous Middle English writers . . . from being *auctores*";[2] indeed, according to Alistair Minnis, "No 'modern' writer could decently be called an *auctor* in a period in which men saw themselves as dwarfs standing on the shoulders of giants, i.e. the 'ancients.'"[3]

Few if any Middle English texts, then, were "original" in the sense "not derived from something else";[4] the expectation was that any Middle English work *would* be derivative to a greater or lesser degree. The Middle English writer was most often, in fact, the direct translator of a single text in French or Latin or the compiler of several related texts in one or both of those languages. Even the most inventive of medieval writers (such as Chaucer) borrowed plots, motifs, and other elements from a wide range of sources and was in addition an inveterate alluder to or quoter of earlier writers' texts and literary traditions; and Chaucer was not unique in this habitual intertextuality. Therefore the examination of sources is an essential task for the editor of a Middle English text, simply in order to understand what the text in question is.

There are three main issues that arise in the editor's work with sources. First, how does one identify the source or sources of a given work? Second, how can sources, once identified, be used to help establish and emend the text? Third, what can the study of sources add to the editor's ability to understand the circumstances, author, and audience of the text?

The Identification of Sources

For the first issue, the most basic question to consider is what we mean by *source*. The term denotes not so much an earlier text from which the text one is studying is derived as the relationship of derivation itself.[5] Thus defined, the word covers a range of possibilities:

---

2. "Middle English Text Production and Modern Textual Criticism," in A. J. Minnis and Charlotte Brewer, eds., *Crux and Controversy in Middle English Textual Criticism* (Cambridge, 1992), 7.

3. *Medieval Theory of Authorship: Scholastic Literary Attitudes in the Later Middle Ages* (London, 1984), 12.

4. *The American Heritage Dictionary of the English Language,* 3d ed. (Boston, 1992), s.v.

5. "Nothing is constituted as a 'source' by its nature. . . . the so-called 'derivative' text actually creates the source . . . making it something it had not been at its inception by entering into a relationship with it": Katherine O'Brien O'Keeffe, "Source, Method, Theory, Practice: On Reading Two Old English Verse Texts," *Bulletin of the John Rylands University Library of Manchester* 76 (1994): 57–58.

1. the Latin, French, or other text that has been translated into Middle English prose that demonstrates a phrase-by-phrase, sense-by-sense, or even word-by-word correspondence, with the Middle English writer apparently acting as an interpreter of linguistic meaning only (an example might be the French prose source of Chaucer's *Melibee*);[6]

2. the Latin, French, or other text that is translated into English verse, with the English writer adding versification and other stylistic variations to his basic translation (for example, the Chaucerian *Romaunt of the Rose*);

3. the text in prose or verse (from whatever language) that provides the structure, characters, a number of verbal correspondences, and some stylistic elements for a Middle English work, with the English writer freely adapting the materials not only by English versification (if a poem) but also by condensation, rearrangement, and the addition of other materials, and by the use of various rhetorical strategies and devices (examples here can range from *The Wars of Alexander* to Chaucer's *Troilus and Criseyde*);[7]

4. the texts that offer subsidiary material to amplify the English writer's adaptation of a primary source (e.g., Chaucer's use of Boethius, Petrarch, and others in the *Troilus*);

5. the multiple texts (in whatever language) that provide models for some elements of dialogue, structure, description, or theme in a complex English work (as Chaucer's *Franklin's Tale,* for example, adapts only plot structure from its "primary" source in Boccaccio's *Filocolo* but develops other elements independently, using sources such as the *Roman de la Rose,* Boethius's *Consolatio,* Jerome's *Adversus Jovinianum,* and Chrétien's *Cligès,* among others);[8]

---

6. Chaucer's text is "a close translation . . . with few deviations" from the French *Livre de Melibée:* Sharon Hiltz DeLong, "Explanatory Notes" to *The Tale of Melibee, The Riverside Chaucer,* ed. Larry D. Benson et al., 3d ed. (Boston, 1987), 923. Another example of type no. 1 is John Trevisa's translation of Bartholomaeus Anglicus' *De proprietatibus rerum;* David Greetham has used this text to establish some helpful models for the use of source materials as textual evidence, a topic to be taken up below. See D. C. Greetham, "Models for the Textual Transmission of Translation: The Case of John Trevisa," *Studies in Bibliography* 37 (1984): 131–55.

7. For the alliterative poet's occasional additions to a source he normally "translates with near absolute fidelity," see Hoyt N. Duggan and Thorlac Turville-Petre, *The Wars of Alexander,* EETS, s.s. 10 (Oxford, 1989), xvi. For Chaucer's free adaptation and amplification of Boccaccio's *Filostrato* see Stephen A. Barney's "Explanatory Notes" in *The Riverside Chaucer,* 1021–22. David Greetham remarks that in this work translation "become[s] one of the rhetorical artifices of fiction itself, and the ironic stature and methods of the translator . . . deliberately obscure any models to be found in charting this new construct" ("Models for Textual Transmission," 153).

8. See *The Riverside Chaucer,* 895–901 (Notes to the Franklin's Tale by Joanne Rice).

6. the brief biblical passages or comments from St. Jerome or Innocent III or John of Salisbury or Boethius or popular proverbs that interlard the work of Chaucer and others with passages of only a line or two.

Within this range of source relationships, then, research may have to deal with anything from a single model for the entire contents of the Middle English text to a plurality of sources for discrete and sometimes quite minor elements of the text. The editor's primary responsibility is clearly first of all to identify and examine closely sole or primary sources and only then to worry about minor elements—not all of which may finally be identifiable.

Identification may be a problem for primary sources as well. For the Middle English writer does not always actually name the specific source or sources used, even when the source relationship is that of number 1 above; or the writer may actually *mis*identify the source. Fortunately, the identification of sources for Middle English texts was a major preoccupation of earlier medievalists—a "venerable pastime," in R. E. Kaske's words, "dear to the hearts of scholars a few generations ago."[9] Thus if anything at all has been published on an obscure text, it may often have been an exploration of its sources. A thorough bibliographical search for earlier scholars' work is an obvious first step in the process, then. Aside from any earlier editions of the text itself if available, some places to look are the bibliographies in the various volumes of the revised *Manual of the Writings in Middle English, 1050–1500;* manuscript catalogs, particularly those of the later nineteenth century and after; editions of related or similar works; topical surveys and bibliographies such as Cary's *Medieval Alexander,* Kaske's *Medieval Christian Literary Imagery,* or Edwards's *Medieval Prose;*[10] and of course annual bibliographies both general *(PMLA)* and specific (e.g., the *Bibliographical Bulletin of the International Arthurian Society).* An invaluable new research tool for those questions that are left when

---

9. *Medieval Christian Literary Imagery: A Guide to Interpretation* (Toronto, 1988), xx.

10. These are just examples: George Cary, *The Medieval Alexander,* ed. D. J. A. Ross (Cambridge, 1956); A. S. G. Edwards, ed., *Middle English Prose: A Critical Guide to Major Authors and Genres* (New Brunswick, N.J., 1984); Kaske's *Medieval Christian Literary Imagery* is particularly useful for source type no. 6. Although designed for students of an earlier period, *Sources of Anglo-Saxon Literary Culture: A Trial Version,* ed. Frederick M. Biggs, Thomas D. Hill, and Paul E. Szarmach (Binghamton, NY, 1990), offers useful listings of early manuscripts and other information; see also Thomas Hill's introduction. If your text has a manuscript in the British Library, it is worth looking at not only the catalog for that collection (Royal, Additional, etc.), but also at H. L. D. Ward and J. A. Herbert, *Catalogue of Romances in the Department of Manuscripts in the British Museum,* 3 vols. (London, 1883–1910). *Romance* is broadly interpreted in this work, and there is often useful information. There is less information about sources in Gisela Guddat-Figge, *Catalog of Manuscripts Containing Middle English Romances* (Munich, 1976).

you've worked your way through all the above is the Internet: scholars on the medieval electronic discussion lists such as MedTextL and ChaucerNet are generous in answering intelligent questions.[11]

There are some caveats on the use of early source-scholarship, however: earlier source-seekers often did not have access to the full range of manuscripts now available, or did not have the benefit of more recent scholarly work in classifying manuscripts and versions. It is very seldom, after all, that the modern reader can have access to the actual manuscript the Middle English author himself used, and we are now much more aware that a particular writer's Latin or French source was likely different in many ways from any modern "standard edition" of the text. Thus one must examine the text of a proposed source as critically as that of the work being edited.[12] For example, it has long been recognized that the primary source of both the alliterative *Wars of Alexander* and the prose *Life of Alexander* was the third (I^3) of three late medieval versions of the *Historia de Preliis,* but that the Middle English text in both cases showed some marked differences from the Latin texts of this version that were easily accessible. On this basis, then, G. L. Hamilton proposed in 1927 that both translators had used a fourth, previously unidentified redaction of the Latin work, basing his arguments on only one copy of the I^3 text, an incunable that was available in his university library. Hoyt Duggan has since shown that "there is no basis for this argument," that Hamilton was simply unacquainted with the range of manuscripts for the I^3 version.[13]

Evidently the identification of sources based on others' research should be regarded as tentative and examined critically; and by critical examination I

---

11. The full name of MedTextL is "Medieval texts—Philology Codicology and Technology" (MEDTEXTL@vmd.cso.uiuc.edu); the Chaucer Net also discusses other Middle English literature (CHAUCER%UICVM.BITNET@uga.cc.uga.edu). The Ansax-L discussion list (ANSAX-L@wvnvm.wvnet.edu) focuses on an earlier period in English history and literature, but scholars on this list have a wealth of expertise about Latin sources that they share generously.

12. "The editor has a double responsibility, because he must become an editor of his source text, as well as of its Middle English avatar. . . . To use the source as an adequate tool for determining anteriority of readings, the editor must identify a source manuscript proximate to the translator": Ralph Hanna III, "Editing Middle English Prose Translations: How Prior Is the Source?" *Text* 4 (1988): 211.

13. G. L. Hamilton, "A New Redaction (J^{3a}) of the *Historia de Preliis* and the Date of Redaction J^3," *Speculum* 2 (1927): 113–46; Hoyt N. Duggan, "The Source of the Middle English *Wars of Alexander,*" *Speculum* 51 (1976): 624–36. The quotation is from the Duggan and Turville-Petre edition of *The Wars of Alexander* (note 7 above), xv. I am very much indebted to Duggan's sorting out of the English I^3 manuscripts in my own work on the Thornton *Life of Alexander,* particularly since the modern standard edition of the I^3 *Historia de Preliis* (see next note) collates less than half of the extant manuscripts (Duggan xv–xvi).

mean detailed, line-by-line collation. Let me describe my procedure in work on the *Life of Alexander* (a work whose source relationship seemed to be that of number 1 above) and the results I gained from it. First (with a Latin dictionary and grammar at hand) I collated the English text with the Latin of the standard edition of the I³ *Historia,* that of Karl Steffens, marking passages where the English text varied from the Latin.[14] I then compared these marked variants with microfilms of several of the British manuscripts identified by Duggan as closer to the *Wars* than Steffens's base text.[15] When a number of readings remained unexplained by this procedure, I turned to editions of the other two versions of the *Historia* (I¹ and I²) and repeated the process.[16] By this means I determined that the translator of the *Alexander* had also used a manuscript of the I¹ version, conflating it with his primary I³ source. Moreover, some of the variants were striking enough that I was able to identify a particular manuscript as sharing a number of anomalous features with the English text. I then collated that specific manuscript (British Library ms. Arundel 123) with the text and discovered evidence that the translator had in fact used that very manuscript; for there were a few passages that had been adapted from *other* texts in the manuscript than the *Historia de Preliis,* and the Arundel manuscript has every sign of being a unique and even idiosyncratic compilation of texts.[17]

This textual relationship is uncommon enough that I cannot propose this procedure as a model for anyone else's work; still, some principles seem applicable to other textual situations. First, one should use the standard edition of the source text by all means, but use the textual apparatus as well as the edited text, being alert to variants that may show a closer relationship to the English text. Look for the provenance of the manuscripts: manuscripts in British libraries, manuscripts written in an anglicana hand, manuscripts show-ing evidence of British ownership, are at least marginally likelier to be related to the source of a Middle English text. The edited text in the standard edition may be fully adequate to your needs, particularly if you are dealing with an

---

14. Karl Steffens, ed., *Die Historia de preliis Alexandri Magni Rezension J³,* Beiträge zur klassischen Philologie 73 (Meisenheim am Glan, 1975).

15. I am extremely grateful to Hoyt Duggan for sharing his microfilm printouts with me.

16. A. Hilka and K. Steffens, eds., *Historia Alexandri Magni (Historia de preliis), Rezension J¹,* Beiträge zur klassischen Philologie 107 (Meisenheim am Glan, 1979); A. Hilka, H.-J. Berg-meister, and R. Grossmann, eds., *Historia Alexandri Magni (Historia de preliis), Rezension J²* *(Orosius-Rezension),* 2 vols., Beiträge zur klassischen Philologie 79, 89 (Meisenheim am Glan, 1976–77).

17. Full analysis of these relationships will be published in my edition of the *Life of Alexander,* forthcoming from Garland.

eclectic and creative author of the sort described in numbers 3–6 above, who may well be responsible for any variations himself. For a direct translation like those of numbers 1–2 above, the edited text may not be fully satisfactory; in that case you might select the most relevant of the manuscripts collated in the edition's apparatus and have a direct look at those, on microfilm at the least, remembering that the manuscript as a whole may have information not to be found in the source text itself. Whatever your procedure, close textual comparison is crucial.

What should one be looking for in such textual analyses? A discussion that occurred on the MedTextL net is extremely apropos. James W. Marchand began the discussion by asking, "Since a great deal of our enterprise deals in finding 'sources,' ought we not to have some kind of methodology to appeal to?"[18] To this A. E. Wright responded with some "principles":

1. "verbal echo": the presumed source must offer language identical to that found in the presumed reflex.
2. [A]nd that language must be sufficiently un-commonplace to make it seem unlikely that both source and reflex have come up with it independently. . . .
3. Transmission: you have to be able to imagine how the reflex had access to the source. . . . the ideal situation is a[n] ms. of the source annotated in the hand responsible for the reflex (ideal, and not terribly common).[19]

Charles D. Wright then cited some published discussion of the issue and summarized: "Verbal echo, contextual fit, historical probability, and the intuitive judgment of experienced scholars—all these things inevitably enter into the equation."[20]

---

18. James W. Marchand, "Elephants, Sources," Medieval Texts—Philology Codicology and Technology (MEDTEXTL@vmd.cso.uiuc.edu), May 11, 1994. Quoted by permission.

19. A. E. Wright, "Re: sources," Medieval Texts—Philology Codicology and Technology (MEDTEXTL@vmd.cso.uiuc.edu), May 11, 1994. Quoted by permission.

20. Charles D. Wright, "Sources (was: elephants)," Medieval Texts—Philology Codicology and Technology (MEDTEXTL@vmd.cso.uiuc.edu), May 11, 1994. Quoted by permission. Wright quotes R. E. Kaske, *Medieval Christian Literary Imagery* (note 9 above): "I think the absolutely essential thing is that the allusion being proposed must really 'click' in context—that is, the proposed correspondence must either be precise or complex enough, and must carry an appropriate enough meaning for its context, that to consider it accidental would outrage probability" (xx). He also cites Thomas D. Hill's introduction to *Sources of Anglo-Saxon Culture: A Trial Version* (note 10 above), xv–xxix, on "the problem of defining 'source' and identifying sources." On this problem, see also Kathleen O'Brien O'Keeffe's article (note 5 above), especially 59–60, 70–71.

Sources and the Text

The procedure just described is laborious and time consuming; you may well ask whether it is worth it. A source text once established can be very useful indeed; it can serve as a guide to the solution of textual cruxes or confirmation of questioned readings, both for single-manuscript texts and those with a number of witnesses or versions.[21] But it must be used with care.

The source can be especially valuable when an English text exists only in a single manuscript, where there may be no other resource for checking up on questionable manuscript readings.[22] In my work on the Thornton *Life of Alexander,* for example, I have been able to identify and correct two ghost words in the Westlake edition:[23] on page 64 (l. 34) he records "*per*latanes of golde" as elements of palace decoration (the *MED* offers a definition for this, s.v., as "some kind of lattice-work"); since the Arundel manuscript has at this point *platani aurei,* "golden plane-trees," the correct reading is obviously *platanes*— the *p* has acquired a mistaken *-er* suspension (a crossed descender) in the manuscript. A second example also involves a mistaken suspension: Westlake has on page 67 (l. 18) "he . . . chese owt CL of du*yer*cs"; since the Arundel manuscript has *electis CL ducibus* ("150 guides having been chosen") here, the enigmatic "du*yer*cs" is easily resolved as "duycs" or perhaps "duyks."[24]

These two emendations are simple because they are confirmed, indeed suggested, by a manuscript that I have some confidence the English translator actually used. But, as noted earlier, source texts may be as variable as derived texts, and the English writer's own source manuscript is unlikely to be available. In light of this variability, David Greetham has established some models of possible relationships for source types numbers 1 and 2—translations in which the English writer works on the principle of fidelity to the source. These models suggest different ways of dealing with the evidence when there is disagreement between the source and the translation, but either the source text

---

21. "Using the source reduces immensely the difficulties of coping with a Middle English manuscript tradition. On the assumptions that translators perform consistently and that they routinely try to reproduce their sources with the same rigor at all times, the source allows immediate rejection of a good many variants as merely scribal" (Hanna, "Editing Prose Translations," 209–10). Whether these assumptions hold true in all cases is an issue to be dealt with below.

22. See Jennifer Fellows, "Editing Middle English Romances," in Maldwyn Mills, Jennifer Fellows, and Carol M. Meale, eds., *Romance in Medieval England* (Cambridge, 1991), 13–14.

23. J. S. Westlake, ed., *The Prose Life of Alexander,* EETS 143 (London, 1913; rpt. New York, 1971). This is the only edition of the *Alexander* yet published.

24. Since the mistaken *-er* suspension may echo the ascender-loop of a *k*. For variant spellings including "duyk," see the *MED*, s.v. "duk" n. It is worth noting that this phrase is not to be found in the I[3] or I[2] version of the source, or in any other manuscript of the I[1] version besides Arundel 123.

and the derived text are both self-consistent (that is, all witnesses agree on a particular reading), or one or the other or both are inconsistent (that is, offer different readings).[25] The *Life of Alexander* examples I just used follow Greetham's model A (both consistent); in this case it is only the existence of "some identifiable 'problem' in the translation, noticeable . . . by context but not by collation" (135) that calls forth emendation.[26]

This principle is less clear-cut when the source is used as ground of choice between readings in multi-manuscript texts—that is, Greetham's model B, when the source text is consistent and different versions of the translated text offer different readings. Eugène Vinaver's edition of Sir Thomas Malory's *Morte Darthure,* for example, dealt with two different versions of the work, the Winchester manuscript (*W,* now BL Addit. ms. 59678) and William Caxton's first edition of 1485 (*C*). Using the Winchester manuscript as his base text, Vinaver often chose readings from Caxton on the basis of Malory's French sources:

Among the great prose writers of all time [Malory] is perhaps the one who "invented" least. He may sometimes disagree with the very spirit of his "French books," alter their character and purpose, and introduce an atmosphere and a manner of his own; for all that, the greater part of his narrative is made of the material "drawn briefly out of French." In so far as this material is extant, it can, therefore, provide useful clues; for, barring accident, whatever either of our two texts has in common with the French must have reached it through Malory and can safely be ascribed to him.[27]

As one example of many, where *W* has "toke hys swerde" and *C* has "toke his hors," Vinaver adopts Caxton's reading because the French source has at this point "vient a son cheval et monte" (1:cxv). It is not entirely clear from the context of the phrase that *W*'s "toke hys swerde" is an error; the errand Sir Bors was embarking upon, rescuing a wounded knight from pursuers, would require

---

25. "Models for Textual Transmission," 134–48.

26. Greetham argues that emendation to bring an English text closer to its source is justifiable even when a manuscript reading is plausible, if its difference from the source can be explained in terms of paleographical probability: "it must be easy for the scribal eye in the translating [English] version to create the extant corrupt form from the putative original and virtually impossible for the scribe of the translated [Latin] version to have made a similar error which could have been rendered into English by the translator" ("Models for Textual Transmission," 137). In the case of the *Alexander,* the translator's conflation of two or more sources, not all of which I have yet been able to identify, makes this approach a bit more problematic.

27. *The Works of Sir Thomas Malory,* rev. P. J. C. Field, 3d ed. (Oxford, 1990), 1:cxiv–cxv.

both his sword and his horse (2:1004), and it is possible to conceive of an authorial decision to change the horse to the sword. But Vinaver's experience of working with the French sources persuaded him of Malory's fidelity as a translator, and for that reason his editorial practice makes agreement or disagreement with the source a primary criterion for identification of error and thus for choice of readings. On this basis Vinaver not only chooses occasional Caxton readings over those of the Winchester manuscript, but he sometimes rejects both witnesses and emends his text on the model of the French source, especially for omitted words (cxvi–cxix). The danger in using this procedure as a model is not only that there may be, as Vinaver says, "a reasonable possibility of an *accidental* agreement between *C* and *F* or *W* and *F*" (1:cxvi), but that not all Middle English translators were as reliably faithful to their sources as Malory.[28] Most medieval translators were interpreters, not simply scribes, and many felt free to change some elements of the text for the sake of clarity or style or appeal to a certain audience. Michael Sargent describes how Nicholas Love, for example, omitted some thirty chapters from his source and shortened others, added his own material from time to time, and made other alterations in translating the Latin *Meditationes Vitae Christi* into the English *Mirror of the Blessed Life of Jesus Christ* for "lewde men & women & hem þat bene of symple vndirstondynge."[29] Another kind of writer may add a touch of humor to a solemn Latin narrative, as the author of the *Life of Alexander* calls Alexander's chosen companions in his first armed expedition his "playfers" (playmates), Alexander being only twelve years old at the time: none of the Latin versions uses such a term.[30] If there were another reliable witness to the English text that omitted the "playfers," would that justify relegating the word to the apparatus of the Thornton text?

There are two principles involved here that may be in conflict: the first is that, when two or more versions of a reading in the English translation are extant, the reading that is closest to the source should be chosen, whether or not

---

28. Malory himself was a faithful translator in only a limited (word-for-word, phrase-for-phrase) sense; as Vinaver has demonstrated, "he endeavoured to do two things: to reduce the bulk of the stories and to alter their arrangement" (1:lxviii), by reducing rhetoric, condensing episodes or telescoping them together, and regrouping related episodes. His method was even freer when he had an English source; see pp. 5–6 in my edition of the alliterative *Morte Arthure* (New York, 1984) for a summary of changes, including the reduction of alliterative verse to prose.

29. Michael G. Sargent, ed., *Nicholas Love's "Mirror of the Blessed Life of Jesus Christ,"* Garland Medieval Texts, 18 (New York, 1992), xxx.

30. "Twelue childre þat he chese to be his playfers" translates the I³ version, "XII pueris quos ipse elegerat et iugo suo informaverat" ("twelve boys whom he had chosen and molded to his authority," Steffens, *Historia,* 46, ll. 32–33). This phrase is not in I¹ or I².

other readings are in more reliable witnesses and are contextually plausible. The second principle is that, especially when the fidelity of the English translator cannot be confidently affirmed, one should emend on the basis of the source only when the text being edited is shown by the context to be in error and the source provides a solution to the error. In Vinaver's words,

> We should ask ourselves, in the first place, "What does the extant reading mean?" and if no satisfactory answer is forthcoming, go on to ask: "Can it be shown to be a scribal error?" (1:cvii–cviii)

According to the second principle, only if the answer to the second question is "yes" should the source acquire the authority to confirm alternatives or emend readings.[31] Obviously, it is the task of the editor to weigh these two principles against each other very carefully in light of what he or she knows or can infer about the translational or compositional style of the Middle English writer.

This is particularly true in the case of freer source-relationships such as those of numbers 3–6 above, in which the English writer becomes more of an author than a translator. One's problem as an editor in this case is to determine for particular readings which source or part of a source the author is using, if the author is using a source at all. In working with the alliterative *Morte Arthure,* for example, I had to determine which of the four versions of the Arthurian chronicle story had the poet's attention at a specific point of the text before being able to bring source information to bear on textual questions. An example is the error "deffuse" [of dedez of armes] in line 256; perhaps because the poet's primary source for this part of the work was French, various commentators struggled to explain this form as a version of OF *defois,* "prohibition." In this case, however, the Latin version of the story offered the verbal clue—"usus armorum videtur abesse"—that permitted the emendation *des-*

---

31. Greetham gives priority to the first principle: "If translation is to be considered as a textual paradigm at all, then McKerrow's strict contextual rule [that the editor should depart from 'the originals . . . only where they appear to be certainly corrupt'], at least in reference to the translating language, must be dropped from our editorial discipline in MODEL A" ("Models for Textual Transmission," 136). But it is not clear whether he would apply it so strictly to texts that adapt their sources more freely than Trevisa. Ralph Hanna's somewhat similar position raises the same question, as noted earlier (note 12 above): the assumptions "that translators perform consistently and that they routinely try to reproduce their sources with the same rigor at all times" apply to translators for whom "the source is generally not a model which one aspires to emulate in elegance of rendition, but an authoritative document to be reproduced" (Hanna, "Editing Prose Translations," 209–10)—but not to all medieval writers using sources. For another view on this issue see Rosemarie Potz McGerr, "Editing the Self-Conscious Medieval Translator: Some Issues and Examples," *Text* 4 (1988): 147–61.

suse, "disuse." In contrast, the problematic *chartris* in line 1619, usually (in defiance of French geography) identified as the city Chartres, was explained as "prison" by the French source's verbal clue—"en chartre les fera tenir."[32] In each case a problematic reading led to a search through the possible sources, and once the correct source was found, it acquired authority only because it explained the problematic reading. Such occasions are rare in editing complex works, however; the real usefulness of source research in these is the window it gives into the writer's circumstances, purposes, and techniques.

Sources and Context

I use the rather vague term *context* to suggest other kinds of information the study of sources may offer to the editor about the circumstances, author, and audience of the text. This information is of two kinds: first, the nature of the source or sources; second, the English author's treatment of them.

The first kind of information can tell us something about the background and circumstances of the English writer. For example, the sources may be in English, French, Latin, or Italian: the use of a Latin source suggests a clerical background or at least education for the translator, while a French source suggests a courtly or at least *gentil* upbringing; an Italian source (as in the case of Chaucer or the poet of the alliterative *Morte Arthure*) implies foreign travel; an English source may be localizable by dialect and suggest something (in relation to the writer's own dialect) about the geographical context—or inland travel habits—of the writer. A *combination* of languages, Latin, French, Italian, and English, gives us a highly educated, well-traveled, and intellectually sophisticated author—a Chaucer or a *Morte Arthure* poet.

Sources may be religious or secular, didactic, informational, or entertaining; they may be identified with certain organizations (Franciscans, Carthusians) or other groups. From such aspects as these one may infer (or at least speculate) a certain amount about the circumstances of the English author, especially in combination with the fact of language: a Latin source with Franciscan ties, in the absence of other indications, implies a writer who may be a friar;[33] a French romance with an emphasis on warfare, armor, and heraldry implies a translator who has at least an interest in courtly and chivalric matters and

---

32. See Hamel, *Morte Arthure,* 264, 306.

33. Nicholas Love, who translated the Franciscan *Meditationes Vitae Christi,* was of course a Carthusian: in this case there are plentiful indications (see Sargent, *Nicholas Love's "Mirror,"* xxi–xxx), which should warn us of the limitations of this kind of evidence.

possibly (depending on the accuracy and fullness of the translation) some experience of them.

There may be a wide range and variety of sources for a Middle English text, or a single source. The latter implies a writer in somewhat limited circumstances with perhaps a limited education (since compilation seems to have been a routine technique of clarification and amplification)—or, since Chaucer's *Melibee* falls in this class, simply a writer with a limited purpose. The former offers a window into the English writer's library or freedom of access to someone else's library. Elizabeth Salter pointed years ago to "the households of the great magnates whose estates lay in the west and north of England" as appropriate backgrounds for the poets of the Alliterative Revival, simply because only in such settings were libraries of sufficient size and range to be found to explain the poets' sources.[34] More recently, Peter Field has argued that Sir Thomas Malory must have had "ready access to one of the most remarkable libraries in the country" on the basis of his sources, possibly the library of Caxton's patron Anthony Wydeville, Lord Scales (later the second Earl Rivers).[35] Even the fact that the anonymous translator of the *Life of Alexander* used two different manuscripts of the *Historia de Preliis* implies a somewhat unusual library. And if an actual source manuscript can be identified, there *may* be some information there, in the flyleaves or margins; disappointingly, however, I found no evidence in the Arundel manuscript of its provenance or early ownership, which might have helped me to understand the *Alexander* translator's background and given me clues to his identity.

As for the second kind of information, the English writer's treatment of sources may offer information about purposes and audience. As we have seen in the case of Nicholas Love, the translator may omit significant parts of the source, alter the order of topics or restructure the narrative, and add his own materials or materials from other sources—all for the purpose of making the work more accessible to an unlearned and theologically unsophisticated audience. On the other hand, an English writer may add certain stylistic traits, such as verse, rhetoric, description, dialogue, humor, irony, or other elements of tone, or may develop a narrative persona to vivify a Latin narrative's imper-

---

34. Elizabeth Salter, "The Alliterative Revival," *Modern Philology* 64 (1966–67): 146; I follow Salter's lead in my conclusions about the *Morte Arthure* poet in my edition, pp. 59–61.

35. P. J. C. Field, *The Life and Times of Sir Thomas Malory* (Cambridge, 1993), 144–45, 147. The quotation is from p. 144. Wydeville might even have had a copy of the alliterative *Morte Arthure* in his library: see my "Arthurian Romance in Fifteenth-Century Lindsey: The Books of the Lords Welles," *Modern Language Quarterly* 51 (1992 for 1990): 356–58, for his connections with a family that may well have owned a copy.

sonality. In this case the writer's purposes are surely more literary than didactic, the audience broader and more worldly; and such treatment may imply some ideas about the audience's social class as well. Or an author's compositional technique may suggest some ideas about his or her purposes; for example, the conflation of two or three different versions of the same story in the *Life of Alexander* suggests a desire for historical completeness and fullness of information, whereas the alliterative *Morte Arthure*'s selection from among three or four parallel versions of the Arthurian chronicle suggests a search for the vivid phrase, telling detail, or structural echo: art rather than history.

In my work as an editor of Middle English texts I have found that the study of sources is an essential way into a text. It was not until I began a line-by-line collation of the *Morte Arthure* with its chronicle sources—Geoffrey of Monmouth, Robert Wace, and the rest—that I began to understand what kind of poem it is and what kind of poet wrote it; and this was ten years after I'd begun the task. I wished I had started collating sources earlier.

Annotation

A. S. G. Edwards and Douglas Moffat

Explanatory Notes

Annotation is possibly the aspect of any edition in which the editor is most vulnerable.[1] It requires judgment, conciseness, clarity, tact, and knowledge, particularly knowledge. To pass silently over a crux or to be compelled to acknowledge ignorance is to expose the editor's weaknesses in the starkest way. Anyone who has attempted annotation is conscious of its frustrations, the hours of reading that end up being compressed into a single line in a note. But one is also conscious of its rewards, the illuminating parallel or apposite quotation that serves to clarify the text usefully. Such felicities are not likely to be savored by all scholars. But any editor must be conscious of the urgency of adequate annotation if his or her edition is to be of lasting value. While there can be no hard and fast rules as to what should be annotated or how, in what follows we will try to suggest a few general criteria, with appropriate illustrations.

One must begin by pointing out that the level and degree of annotation will be determined to some extent, and at times to a significant extent, by the nature and format of the projected edition: whether it is to be a school edition primarily for undergraduate use, a full scholarly edition, or a variorum. The first

---

1. For a useful survey of problems of annotation see Ian Small, "The Editor as Annotator as Ideal Reader," in *The Theory and Practice of Text-Editing: Essays in Honour of James T, Boulton,* ed. Ian Small and Marcus Walsh (Cambridge, 1991), 186–209. This essay includes a number of additional references, including Martin Battestin, "A Rationale of Literary Annotation: The Example of Fielding's Novels," *Studies in Bibliography* 34 (1981): 1–22. For some discussion of the issues as they relate specifically to Middle English texts see Anne Middleton, "Life in the Margins; or, What's an Annotator to Do?" *Library Chronicle of the University of Texas* 20 (1990): 167–83; and a number of essays by Ralph Hanna III, including "Annotating *Piers Plowman,*" *Text* 6 (1994): 153–62; "Annotation as Social Practice," in *Annotation and Its Texts,* ed. Stephen A. Barney (New York, 1991), 178–84; and the section on annotation in his *Pursuing History: Middle English Manuscripts and Their Texts* (Stanford, 1996) 247–79.

kind is now often presented with glosses and perhaps notes on the text page (as with the editions of Chaucer by Baugh and Fisher, for instance). Both the nature of the audience and the inevitable space constraints will make annotation extremely concise, probably limited to the most immediate difficulties of lexis, syntax, and allusion. Some editions, like the Riverside Chaucer, attempt to supplement such basic annotation by a more extensive series of notes at the back, thereby seeking to meet the needs of more advanced students. This is a good solution adopted effectively in other recent editions such as Helen Barr's *The Piers Plowman Tradition,*[2] but an editor may not always have control over such questions of format.

More extensive annotation will most often be found in scholarly editions, such as those produced by the Early English Text Society and some university presses. Only rarely do such editions wholly eschew the responsibility of annotation, as in the Athlone Press editions of the A and B texts of *Piers Plowman,* which appear with no explanatory notes at all.[3] Annotation in scholarly editions is likely to be much fuller than in school editions and can sometimes provide detailed support for editorial assumptions. For example, G. V. Smithers's edition of *Havelok*[4] offers extensive historical and metrical annotation that supports particular hypotheses he advances on these matters.

The variorum edition is so specialized in its purposes as to lie outside the purview of most editorial activity. It aims to offer an exhaustive record of all commentary and editorial interventions in the text of a specific work or author. It is seen most elaborately in Middle English literature in the Chaucer Variorum under the general editorship of Paul Ruggiers and Daniel J. Ransom. The result has not been wholly successful.[5] Possibly a more successful solution in executing the aims of a variorum, at least insofar as they relate to annotation, is to abandon editing entirely and produce instead a comprehensive record of critical and scholarly commentary. This has been done recently with great success by Peter Nicholson for Gower's *Confessio Amantis.*[6]

For the present purposes, however, we are concerned with deciding what to

---

2. (London, 1993).

3. An annotation volume for this edition is currently being undertaken by a group of scholars; see articles by Middleton and Hanna cited in note 1 above.

4. (Oxford, 1987).

5. See, for example, the review by Ralph Hanna III of the Nun's Priest's Tale volume of the Variorum, ed. Derek Pearsall, in *Analytical and Enumerative Bibliography* 8 (1984): 184–97, reprinted in Pursuing History, 130–39, and the review by A. S. G. Edwards of the General Prologue volume, ed. Malcolm Andrew and Charles Moorman, *Studies in the Age of Chaucer* 17 (1995): 157–60.

6. *An Annotated Index to the Commentary on Gower's "Confessio Amantis"* (Binghamton, 1989).

annotate and how to do so and not with the comprehensive annotation of the variorum. First of all, certain preliminary matters require consideration.

The presentation of general matters that bear on the understanding of the work being edited, such as literary tradition or history, are often best dealt with comprehensively in the introduction with appropriate cross-references made between it and the notes. This is done helpfully in a number of modern editions. For example, Derek Pearsall's edition of *The Flower and the Leaf* and *The Assembly of Ladies* has a full discussion of the history of the cult of the flower and the leaf in the introduction and the relevant notes simply cite this discussion.[7] The Riverside Chaucer has very helpful headnotes dealing with matters of literary history as well as giving surveys of critical issues in commentary on particular works. For works on scientific or technical subjects, an introductory essay will almost certainly be necessary to enable the reader to gain a broad understanding of the subject matter, since the explanatory notes will probably contain much detailed technical information. A good example of such an essay is that found in John Reidy's edition of Thomas Norton's *Ordinal of Alchemy*.[8]

A rather different issue that usually requires discussion within the introduction and the notes is the treatment of source texts. Barry Windeatt's edition of *Troilus and Criseyde* prints the text of Boccaccio's *Il Filostrato* in parallel, but few other modern editions have sought to present sources in full. Since many Middle English works are translations, adequately presenting the nature of their relationship to the source text from which they derive is a great challenge for editors (see Mary Hamel's essay in this volume). Such general conclusions as can be reached about that relationship should be outlined in the introduction. Ideally, within the notes the editor should try to provide the reader with passages from the source text wherever such passages illuminate an obscurity in the Middle English or assist in establishing the text. The annotation ought, at the very least, to record striking instances of mistranslation or deviation from the original. However, in order to accomplish even this quite modest end, the editor will need a clear understanding of the source text. Among the recent editions that handle the question of treatment of sources with tact and sense in their notes are Duggan and Turville-Petre's *Wars of Alexander,* Rosemarie McGerr's *Pilgrimage of the Soul,* and Frances McSparran's *Octovian* and *Octovian Imperator.*[9]

---

7. *The Flower and the Leaf and The Assembly of Ladies,* ed. D. A. Pearsall (London, 1962), 22–44.

8. EETS 272 (London, 1968).

9. Hoyt N. Duggan and Thorlac Turville-Petre, *The Wars of Alexander,* EETS, s.s. 10 (Oxford, 1989) as well as Turville-Petre's "Editing the *Wars of Alexander,*" in *Manuscript and Text,* ed.

In regard to the annotation itself, two related qualities of the ideal annotator are the capacity to marshal all relevant information already available in the work of other commentators and the perspicacity to discover new possibilities of significance that need to be annotated. For the first point, there can be no simple procedure, only the difficulty of reading as widely as possible and retaining what has been read. For instance, in John Scattergood's excellent edition of Clanvowe's *The Two Ways* there is no note on this passage: "And þat wot þe deuel ful wel. And, þerfore, he dooþ as a foulere þat taaketh first a brid and maakeþ þerof a wacchebrid and setteþ it bisyde his nette for to synge."[10] Yet the tradition of Satan as fowler is a widely attested one that has received a standard study.[11] One assumes that its omission here was inadvertent.

Sound annotation depends not just on a range of knowledge but also a sensitivity to previously unremarked problems in the text. The discovery of some point previously unremarked can illuminate the understanding of a text. For example, no edition of *St Erkenwald* contains a specific note on the opening line: "At London in Englond noȝt full long sythen." However, John Burrow has recently argued that the seemingly redundant "in Englond" offers important insight into the poem's Cheshire origins.[12]

But what in general terms should be annotated? We believe it is possible to categorize some aspects of the text on which all commentators are likely to wish to comment. One approach to this problem would be to adopt and expand upon the schema used by A. V. C. Schmidt in his edition of the B-Text of *Piers Plowman*.[13] Schmidt provides two sets of notes after his text, one to handle textual and lexical matters and the other for historical and literary information. The four categories—textual, lexical, historical, and literary—provide a solid framework for the writing of explanatory notes for most texts, but the form of dividing them is particularly helpful for Middle English ones.

The first of these categories, textual, is dealt with in the second part of this essay, since it is linked to the presentation of the textual apparatus for the edition.

D. Pearsall (Cambridge, 1987), 143–60, esp. 150–51; Rosemarie McGerr, *The Pilgrimage of the Soul,* Garland Medieval Texts, 16 (New York, 1990); Frances McSparran, *Octovian,* EETS 289 (Oxford, 1986) and *Octovian Imperator,* Middle English Texts 11 (Heidelberg, 1979).

10. *The Works of Sir John Clanvowe,* ed. V. J. Scattergood (Cambridge, 1975), 71, lines 550–53.

11. See B. G. Koonce, "Satan the Fowler," *Medieval Studies* 21 (1959): 174–84.

12. J. A. Burrow, *"Saint Erkenwald* Line 1: 'At London in Englond,'" *Notes and Queries,* n.s. 40 (1993): 22–23.

13. *The Vision of Piers Plowman: A Complete Edition of the B-Text,* ed. A. V. C. Schmidt (London, 1978; rev. 1982).

Annotation dealing with lexical matters expands upon the formal apparatus of the glossary (on which see Moffat in this volume). There are often particular words or phrases that require more than a simple gloss. One would wish to note, for instance, usages that antedate or correct those recorded in the *Middle English Dictionary* and/or (as appropriate) *The Dictionary of the Older Scottish Tongue*. Antedatings might, if extensive, be recorded in a separate list in the introduction or signaled in some way in the glossary, such as by an asterisk. But lexical evidence that contradicts or modifies the treatment in a standard work merits discussion. Words that do not appear in standard reference works will clearly require some comment. Peculiarities of syntax should be elucidated, when possible, by reference to Mustanoja or more specialized commentators.[14] Similarly proverbial phrases should be identified according to Whiting.[15]

Related to these questions are problems of language and syntax that require different sorts of annotation. Most obvious among these problems is the need to provide extensive paraphrases of parts of a text that are syntactically and/or lexically obscure. Alliterative poems often pose extended challenges in this respect, and readers of *Sir Gawain and the Green Knight,* for example, must be thankful to such sensitive readers as Burrow and Waldron and Andrew.[16] Apart from its elucidatory value, the act of composing such paraphrases may sometimes help an editor to reconsider his or her established text.

The editor should not shy away from lexical and syntactical ambiguities, especially when the meaning and interpretation of a passage rests on the linguistic analysis. An example involves the phrase "maken it wise" (*Canterbury Tales,* I, 785). "Wise" has usually been interpreted here as the common adjective meaning "prudent," "wise" and the phrase has been translated in the Riverside Chaucer as "deliberate on it [Harry Bailey's proposal]" or "raise difficulties." As a noun, however, "wise" does have a slightly attested Middle English meaning "a contentious matter," therefore, the phrase could be rendered as "to make it a matter for debate or argument." Such lexical evidence, which challenges the traditional definition of the meaning of a word or phrase, deserves to be noted.

The question of historical annotation of specific allusions in the text, whether to persons, events, or institutions, represents a broad range of reference of

---

14. T. F. Mustanoja, *A Middle English Syntax, Part I: Parts of Speech* (Helsinki, 1960).

15. B. J. and Helen W. Whiting, *Proverbs, Sentences, and Proverbial Phrases from English Writings Mainly before 1500* (Cambridge, Mass., 1968).

16. *The Poems of the Pearl Manuscript,* ed. Malcolm Andrew and Ronald Waldron, York Medieval Texts, s.s. (London, 1978); *Sir Gawain and the Green Knight,* ed. John Burrow (Harmondsworth, 1972).

potential difficulty for the annotator. Even the identification of proper names has its difficulties. Take, for example, the lines in *Wynnere and Wastoure:* "Als gude als Arestotle or Austyn the wyse, / That alle schent were those schalkes and Scharshull itwiste" (316–17).[17] In these lines it is clearly necessary to identify "Scharshull" as Sir William Shareshull, the famous fourteenth-century chief justice. But what about "Arestotle" or "Austyn"? Neither of these is discussed in the commentary to the edition we have just quoted, although the modern forms of their names appear in the "List of Names" following the glossary. It may be both pedantic and superfluous to offer such notes as "Aristotle (384–322 B.C.), famous Greek philosopher" or "St Augustine, bishop of Hippo (354–430), widely influential Christian theologian" or some such forms of words. But a decision in such matters may well be determined by the form of edition being undertaken. A scholarly edition of the kind we are citing here is less likely to need shoring up in this way than those intended for undergraduate use.[18]

Problems of a similar kind are posed by allusions to other sorts of figures, particularly classical ones. No note on the mention in Chaucer's *House of Fame,* line 916 of "the kyng, Daun Scipio" is likely to stop with the identification of this figure as "Scipio Africanus Minor (c. 185–129 B.C.), Roman general." It would offer some account of his relationship to the *Somnium Scipionis,* mentioned in the following line, and connect the reference to Chaucer's later *Parliament of Fowls.* It would presumably also mention the fact that Scipio was not a king, noting that Chaucer makes the same error in his *Book of the Duchess,* line 286. Such information fills out the context of the allusion so that the reader can locate it within the larger frame of Chaucer's oeuvre.

Similarly, particular situations will need annotating. It may be that all that is required in the case of "Noes flood" (Miller's Tale, I, 3518) or "Jakke Straw and his meynee" (Nun's Priest's Tale, VII, 3394) is brief reference respectively to Gen. 6–10 and the Peasant's Revolt of 1381 (though the former does not receive a note in the Riverside Chaucer). But the issues are not always so clear-cut. In works dealing with particular events, like Hoccleve's "Remonstrance against Oldcastle"[19] or various of the poems included in Rossell Hope Rob-

---

17. We cite the edition of Stephanie Trigg, EETS 297 (Oxford, 1990).

18. We note, however, that Thorlac Turville-Petre's edition of the same poem in *Alliterative Poetry of the Later Middle Ages* (London, 1989), 56, an edition seemingly intended for undergraduates, does not identify "Arestotle" or "Austyn" either.

19. See the most recent edition in *Selections from Thomas Hoccleve,* ed. M. C. Seymour (Oxford, 1981), 61–74 with commentary on pp. 129–32.

bins's anthology of historical poems,[20] it may be necessary to balance some general account of the event in the headnote or introduction with more specific annotation in the notes.

The range of historical annotation will clearly vary widely from text to text. While the reference to the Peasant's Revolt in the *Nun's Priest's Tale* may require only a brief note, other passages will require much greater contextualization to make their significance clear. Thus the description of the garland at the conclusion of *The Wright's Chaste Wife*—"Of roses whyte þat wyll nott fade, / Which floure all ynglond doth glade" (667–68)[21]—would seem to be a pointed declaration of Yorkist sentiment that may be reflected elsewhere in the poem and needs to be placed in relation to the history of the Wars of the Roses, perhaps in the introduction. In *The Libelle of Englysche Polycye* the densely packed and unmistakable allusions to political affairs and personages as well as geographical locations and matters of trade and naval policy, require extensive annotation.[22] In some contexts, historical annotation may need to be approached more tentatively, as in Kail's edition of what he terms *Twenty-six Political Poems.*[23] To some readers these may not appear to be self-evidently "political" poems, but primarily routine homiletic asseverations, albeit with occasional references to historical events. The editor, however, finds embedded in them many veiled allusions to and commentary upon specific political events of the years 1399–1421. His decision to treat his interpretation of these "allusions" in a preliminary essay, rather than in a series of notes, seems properly tactful, since they are not unequivocally supported by the evidence of his texts.

The area of literary annotation includes allusions to other literary works. The question of "echoes" from other writers is very complex. Discerning them requires an alertness and sensitivity of ear and a sense of general probability. For example, Charlotte D'Evelyn in her edition of Peter Idley notes the parallel between lines 68–70 of the prologue and *Canterbury Tales,* IX, 332–34. She concludes, however: "Considering the nature of the material, that is hardly sufficient evidence for claiming Chaucer as Idley's source. They are probably both making independent use of current verses" (213).[24] Such caution would

---

20. *English Historical Poems of the XIVth and XVth Centuries,* ed. Rossell Hope Robbins (New York, 1959).

21. Ed. F. J. Furnivall, EETS 12 (London, 1865).

22. Generally well provided in the edition of G. F. Warner (Oxford, 1926).

23. Ed. J. Kail, EETS 124 (London, 1904).

24. *Peter Idley's Instructions to His Son* (Boston, 1935).

seem proper were this the extent of the parallel; it seems somewhat less justified in the light of subsequent lines to which she has no note: "Be not autour also of tales new, / ffor callyng to rehersaill lest þou it rewe" (76–77). These lines seem to recall others from the *Manciple's Tale:* "My sone, be war, and be noon auctour newe / Of tidynges, wheither they been false or trewe" (*CT,* IX, 359–60). The balance of probability seems to suggest that we have here another (unrecorded) Chaucer allusion, and an annotator should properly note it. The annotator must have a sensitive ear and an even keener sense of the balance of probabilities. Some years ago, one of us, when reviewing Kinsley's edition of Dunbar, suggested that the line "Tohie, quod scho, and agif ane cawf" was a clear "echo" of a line in the *Miller's Tale:* "Tehee, quod she and clapte the wyndow to" (I, 3740).[25] One's sense of this parallel was strengthened by two factors: that there is clear evidence elsewhere in Dunbar's verse of his reading of Chaucer; and the form "Tehee" is first recorded in the *OED* at these two points. These factors seemed to establish a clear balance of probability favoring what might be at first glance a rather tenuous relationship. But another editor might feel it is too remote a parallel to note. Identifiable borrowings incorporated into the edited work will also be included, preferably, unless they are very extensive, in the form of parallel quotations.[26]

Finally, there are matters to do with the interpretation of the text in literary terms. These can be especially difficult. Take, for example, the "Canticus Troili" in Book V of *Troilus and Criseyde* (V, 638–44). This "canticus" inevitably recalls Troilus's first song in Book I, 400–434, and the general parallel might be noted. But should one go further? Ought one to note that the formal parallel can be linked by parallels in metaphor and symbolic implication. Both passages, for example, employ the metaphor of the lover as boat. In Book I Troilus complains

> Thus possed to and fro,
> Al stereles withinne a bot am I
> Amyd the see, bitwixen wyndes two
> That in contrarye stonden evere mo.

(I, 415–18)

---

25. *The Poems of William Dunbar,* ed. James Kinsley (Oxford, 1979).

26. This may not, of course, always be practicable. Charlotte D'Evelyn in her edition of *Peter Idley's Instructions to His Son* found Idley's borrowings from Mannyng's *Handlyng Synne* and Lydgate's *Fall of Princes* so substantial that she could only indicate the parallel line numbers in footnotes.

In Book V, he is still a boat: "nyght by nyght, / Toward my deth with wynd in stere I sayle" (V, 640–41). But, of course, the fundamental change in the metaphor underscores the larger ironies of the narrative at this point. Whereas before Troilus has no control over the direction of his boat, he now does. But the direction leads only to death. To make this point at such length might be a failure of editorial tact, to try and do the reader's work for him/her and to run the parallel risk of saying too much and hence being too restrictive in the interpretative possibilities the passage may contain. Or is the whole issue so obvious as to not merit commentary? Clearly editors have felt this to be the case.[27] But possibly readers may find such direction helpful.

As we noted at the beginning, the difficulties of annotation are considerable. The suggestions and categorizations we have offered are not intended to be prescriptive. We do hope that they will help to suggest some of the possibilities and responsibilities of fruitful engagement with the edited text.

Sample of Annotation

We offer here a very simple illustration of the practicalities of annotation. It is the opening lines of the hagiographical romance *Robert of Sicily,* as they appear in the Vernon manuscript (Bodleian Library Eng. poet. a. 1), fol. 300[rc]. We provide text and annotation together with a brief rationale for the latter:

Princes proud that beth in pres,
I wol you telle thing not lees.
In Cisyle was a noble kyng,
Fair and strong and sumdel yyng;
He hedde a brother in grete Roome,   5
Pope of al Cristendome;
Another he hedde in Alemayne,
An emperour, that Sarasins wroughte payne.
The kyng was hote kyng Robert;
Never mon ne wuste him fert;   10
He was kyng of gret honour,
For that he was conquedour.

---

27. One obvious solution would be to simply refer to a critical account in print that discussed this point. In general, this would seem the proper course, but in this instance we have not been able to find such a discussion after admittedly cursory searching.

In al the world nas his peer,
Kyng ne prince, fer ne neer,
And for he was of chivalrie flour.   15
His brother was mad emperour;
His other brother, Godes vikere,
Pope of Rome, as I seide ere.

Notes

1. *proud that beth in pres.* That is, "brave in combat;" (cf. *MED* **presse n. 1b**(f) proud in (on) presse).
2. *thing not lees.* That is, "something not false" (i.e., the truth).
3. On the recurrent use of the word "king," used forty-nine times in the poem, and its implications see the Introduction.
7–8. *Alemayne, / An emperour.* Almayne means Germany, but here is probably synonymous with the larger territories under the control of the Holy Roman Emperor.
8. *Sarasins.* The Saracens were Muslim peoples who invaded southern Europe, particularly Italy, Sicily, and Spain in the 9th century. They are the object of the verb phrase *wroughte payne.*
10. That is, "no one ever knew him to be afraid."
13. *his peer.* Robert's sense of his worth, is reiterated (see, for example, lines 25, 28, 311, 339 and introd.) as a way of emphasizing his pride.
15. *for he was of chivalrie flour.* Cf. Robert's own words: "I am flour of chivalrye" (53). The phrase "flower of chivalry" is proverbial (Whiting F 311, not noting these occurrences). The examples in *MED* **flour 5 (a)** make clear that the omission of the definite article from the phrase was common.
17. *Godes vikere.* "God's vicar;" a common locution for "Pope."
18. The main verb *(was)* has to be understood in this sentence.

The general principles here are, we hope, clear and consistent with the precepts outlined above. There are no glosses of individual words since they can be dealt with in the glossary. Certain phrases do appear in the notes; for example, lines 2, 10, and 17; the second of these is a paraphrase of the entire line. Presumably in the glossary there would be cross-references from the forms at these points to these notes. The note on line 18 also seeks to clarify a syntactical point that might present difficulty to some readers. Other notes, for example, those on lines 7, 8, and 17, are simply informational glosses of a noncontroversial kind. The note on line 15 provides information about the larger historical situation of the poem's usage by reference to a standard authority (Whiting). The notes on line 15 and line 1 also draw on the evidence of the standard lexicographical tool, the *Middle English Dictionary (MED)*. More problematic as to inclusion are the notes on lines 3, 13, and the first part of 15. The last draws attention to a verbal parallel within the poem. The first two are of some larger interpretive relevance since they note recurrent words that, it would be argued elsewhere in the edition (in the introduction), have some general significance in the poem through their insistent reiteration. The notes here will therefore appropriately direct the reader to another point in the edition where matters of literary explication rather than explanation are examined.

We choose this passage precisely because none of the points of annotation presents any particular difficulty. Most modern editors are likely to feel that many, if not all, of these matters merit some comment. The notes suggest a basic level of explanatory, historical, and interpretive commentary that addresses the needs of modern readers. Some of these points (for example, those noted for lines 17, 18) may seem elementary to more advanced students and might be eliminated in an edition designed solely for such an audience. But it is not easy to be certain as to how much should be explained and the revelation of the full range of an editor's thinking seems generally helpful, not least, in this instance since the only modern edition of this version of the romance does not provide annotation for any of these points.[28] One may assume that to some degree the previous editors' silence may have been occasioned by economic factors, because the text appears as part of a large collection of romances with generally little commentary. The editor is sometimes required to walk a fine line, not of his/her making, between saying too little and too much. But, in ideal circumstances, it is perhaps generally better to aim for a greater rather than a lesser degree of commentary.

Textual Apparatus and Textual Annotation

The primary goal of the textual apparatus is to provide the reader with the evidence upon which the editor has based editorial decisions concerning the establishment of the text. Therefore it will present information to the reader about the forms in which the edited text appears in authorities other than the one which serves as the base-text for the edition. For Middle English texts such

---

28. *Middle English Metrical Romances,* ed. W. H. French and C. B. Hale, 2 vols. (New York, 1930), 2:933–46.

authorities are usually other manuscripts but may include early printed books if these contain versions of the text that have any claim to authority (i.e., they are not printed from a manuscript that can be identified). There may be some compelling reasons for the editor not to provide variants from all such authorities in the apparatus. Among such reasons may be the type of edition undertaken, for example, a school edition, the decision to edit only a single manuscript tradition of the text, or the decision to provide a critical edition based only on the best manuscripts. These reasons must be thoroughly explained in the introduction and reiterated in the note on the text, the statement of editorial principles and procedures that will normally precede the text itself (see Edwards, "Manuscript and Text," in this volume).

In what follows we will deal with examples that use typical procedures in the editing of Middle English. But the reader should be forewarned that there is considerable variety within the formality of the textual apparatus. The examples we discuss are not to be taken as normative or inclusive in their every detail. More important than the particular formal features of the apparatus is the achievement of complete uniformity in the presentation. Even slight variation can lead to confusion, as will be demonstrated below.

Conventionally, the reading of the base text provides the *lemma*, the norm from which variations are recorded. The lemma is set off by a square bracket from the readings of the other authorities, each of which will be identified by a *sigil*, usually a letter, combination of letters, or combination of a letter and a number. Thus, the following reading from a recent edition of Chaucer's *House of Fame*[29]

96. vilanye] felonye PCxTh

establishes that all the authorities follow the base text in reading "vilanye" (or some spelling variant thereof) except for P (a Magdalene College manuscript, Cambridge ms. Pepys 2006), Cx (Caxton's 1483 edition of *The House of Fame*), and Th (William Thynne's edition of the poem in his 1532 edition of *The workes of Geffray Chaucer*). All these read "felonye" (or some spelling variant thereof). Normally, when authorities agree with the reading of the lemma, in this case "vilanye," they are not cited. Conversely, in the following

77. And (BPCxTh)] That F

---

29. We use the edition of N. R. Havely, Durham Medieval Texts 11 (Durham, 1994).

the form of notation signifies that the authority for the reading of the lemma is provided by the witnesses BPCxTh and that the reading of the base text (F) has, in this instance, been rejected. Such basic conventions—and any others that are employed—are fairly clear, but there may be some value to spelling them out for the user in the note on the text.

These two quite simple examples raise a number of issues of some complexity. Most obviously, and most fundamentally, what variant readings are to be included? Conventionally spelling variants are excluded from the record of variants in the apparatus, because orthographic variation is unlikely to weigh heavily in the establishment of the text. However, such information is of great potential interest to students of language, dialect, or meter, whose work in turn may influence our thoughts about the text itself. Further, other potentially valuable information about features in the authorities such as punctuation is also conventionally excluded from the textual apparatus.[30] To forgo these conventions by including all such evidence of a Middle English work that survives in numerous copies would probably swell the apparatus to enormous and even unmanageable proportions. These conventional limits are almost certainly an inevitable consequence of print technology and the economics of publishing. Computerized technology may, therefore, make it theoretically possible to provide a great deal more textual information about the non–base text witnesses for a work (see Baker in this volume). However, the labor involved in amassing this information may prove to be disproportionate to its ultimate value.

Even if one accepts the convention of not recording orthographic variants, determining what is an orthographic variant can be difficult. For, in a Middle English text the range of orthographic variation (what has traditionally been termed its "accidentals") is considerable and can, at times, become difficult to distinguish from readings that affect actual meaning (often referred to as "substantive" readings).[31] For example, J. M. Manly and Edith Rickert, in *The Text of the Canterbury Tales*,[32] and following them, the Chaucer Variorum, do not record variations involving final -*e*, where that form has potential syllabic value, or, more strikingly, variations between final -*e* and -*en*, which have manifest syllabic value. On the other hand, George Kane and E. Talbot Donald-

---

30. For a good discussion of this matter see Ralph Hanna III, "Producing Manuscripts and Editions," in *Crux and Controversy in Middle English Textual Criticism,* ed. A. J. Minnis and Charlotte Brewer (Cambridge, 1992), 111.

31. The classic formulation of this terminology is in W. W. Greg, "The Rationale of Copy Text," *Studies in Bibliography,* 3 (1950–51): 19–36.

32. J. M. Manly and Edith Rickert, *The Text of the Canterbury Tales,* 8 vols. (Chicago, 1940).

son, in their edition of the B-text of *Piers Plowman,* do include "formal variants about which we can be reasonably certain that they alter the syllabic value of the alliterative line."³³ This seems a properly scrupulous decision, one that regards meter as an aspect of meaning. It is, of course, also a decision that will likely enlarge the apparatus considerably and add to the expense of the edition.

To grasp the full extent of editorial activity, even when editorial changes are clearly indicated in the text itself, the reader must read the text in conjunction with the textual notes and also bear in mind the general comments that have been made in the description of the authorities and in the note on the text. There is no other way to proceed. The editor's job is to make this awkward task as easy as possible. We will examine some of the features of text and apparatus using an example from Kane and Donaldson's *Piers Plowman,* line 2 of the prologue:

I shoop me into [a] shrou[d] as I a sheep weere

The corresponding textual note reads:

2 into] In GYOC²CLMF (to *above line* M). a shroud] a schroude H; shroudes WHmGYOC²CLMF; shroubes Cr. a (2)]*om.* F. sheep] schep H; shepe CrGYCL

In the text itself the convention of indicating editorial interventions in the base text by square brackets is employed. This is the one normally followed in scholarly editions of Middle English. Many editors and readers believe that all such interventions should be indicated in the text, although others prefer an "uncluttered" appearance (see further below). In fact, it is usually not possible to indicate all editorial changes in the text. For example, in most modern editions, punctuation and capitalization are editorial, and the fact that this is so can be noted in the statement of editorial principles that will precede the text. It would be unduly burdensome to indicate all such punctuation within square brackets. Frequently abbreviations within the text are silently expanded and their specific orthographic equivalencies specified in the note on the text; another option sometimes employed is the italicization of expanded abbreviations. There is, however, no clear way of indicating that something from the base text itself has been omitted if it has not been replaced by something else.

---

33. *Piers Plowman: The B Version* (London, 1975 rev. ed. 1988), 218.

A number of aspects of the form and organization of the textual note also merit comment. All editorial interjections in the note are clearly differentiated from the actual manuscript readings, in this example by italics. Each lemma, and each variant of each lemma, is clearly separated, in this case by periods and semicolons respectively. Other formal options are available. Once again, internal consistency is the only point that matters.

The order in which the sigla appear usually reflects editorial judgment about the relationship of the witnesses. This order could be used to represent the editor's impression of the witnesses' relative authority, the more authoritative the witness, the nearer its position to the head of the series. If stemmatic analysis has established filial relationships between various witnesses, the sigla may be ordered to reflect such groupings. Occasionally a second level of sigla might be developed to stand for such groups (see the discussion of Manley and Rickert below). If, on the other hand, the editor does not regard any witness in toto as more or less authoritative than any other, the order of the sigla would be purely arbitrary. It is remarkable that in Kane and Donaldson's *Piers Plowman* the order is not arbitrary, as one might have anticipated, given their rejection of stemmatic analysis. Rather, although not explicitly stated, it reflects the filial relationships that the editors do find between the manuscripts.[34] Whatever order an editor settles on should be adhered to consistently unless a compelling reason arises, for example, if the spelling of a variant in a witness at the head of the series is sufficiently peculiar to cause misunderstanding.

Related, and arguably prior, to the question of sigla order is the issue of variant order. Once again this will reflect editorial policy. One could present variants in order of their apparent closeness to the lemma, regardless of the witnesses that contain them, or one could follow an order reflecting relative authoritativeness among the witnesses, regardless of how distant the variants may be from the lemma. Again, the editor must settle on a procedure and stick with it. Presenting variants in a random order is unwarranted.

The textual apparatus for the *Piers* line above reveals that a single witness H (Harley 3954) retains what the editors feel to be the original reading here, "a shroud" (but its orthographic form is rejected). There is no indication in the note why this emendation has been made. One may also wonder about the necessity for including the final variant: "sheep] schep H; shepe CrGYCL" which seems to be orthographic. Presumably it is included because it is felt to be of some potential metrical value; but the reader is left to puzzle this out for him/herself.

---

34. Ibid., p. 61.

These points raise one of the general problems with the formal textual apparatus. It does not normally allow for anything other than the barest reporting of manuscript evidence. This terseness often requires elucidation, to provide grounds for the emendations that have been made and, at times (as above), for the inclusion of specific variants. Often the interpretation of textual evidence and subsequent decisions affecting the text involve ideas about authorial intention and scribal practice that may not be apparent to the reader. Moreover, consideration of evidence not reflected in the readings themselves, such as the text's source or assumptions about its meter, can come into play. The reader will benefit from a presentation of the editor's reasoning as to whether the reading of the base text should be retained or emended.

If it is to be fully usable then, textual evidence requires two tiers of discussion: the textual apparatus, set out in some way like that of line 2 of *Piers,* and a supporting set of textual notes that provide explanations for salient aspects of the apparatus. Some editions are better at this than others. The Kane and Kane-Donaldson editions of *Piers Plowman* and the Kane-Cowen edition of the *Legend of Good Women,* while all professing to be "open" editions, make it virtually impossible to recover confidently the bases for any particular editorial decision.[35] Other editions in the mode of "direct" editing, such as those of *The Awntyrs off Arthure* by Robert J. Gates and Ralph Hanna III, Rosamund Allen's of *King Horn,* and Bella Millet's of *Hali Meiðhad,* offer scrupulous explanations of the decisions underlying each emendation.[36] Vincent P. McCarren's edition of a fragment of the glossary text *Medulla Grammatice* is exceptional for providing text, apparatus, and notes on a single page, but this format would not be practical for every edition.[37]

It is worth stressing that discussion should not be restricted to emendations in the text. As well, dubious readings retained in the base text, including ones that have previously seemed beyond question, should be considered. Hanneke Wirtjes in her edition of *The Middle English Physiologus* (of which there is a single manuscript) exemplifies an approach that is often very sensitive to the

---

35. These problems have now been partly alleviated in the case of the *Piers Plowman* editions by Peter Barney, "Line-Numbers to the Athlone Press Edition of *Piers Plowman,*" *Yearbook of Langland Studies* 7 (1993): 97–114.

36. Robert J. Gates, ed., *The Awntyrs off Arthure* (Philadelphia, 1969); Ralph Hanna III, ed., *The Awntyrs off Arthure* (Manchester, 1974); Rosamund Allen, ed., *King Horn* (New York, 1984); Bella Millet, ed., *Hali Meiðhad,* EETS 284 (Oxford, 1982).

37. "Bristol Fragment MS D 1, A Fragment of the *Medulla Grammatice:* An Edition," *Traditio* 48 (1993): 173–235.

range of alternative possibilities even when emending.[38] In a truly "open" edition the editor will seek to draw attention to the full range of textual problems in the work, even if emendation is not possible.

The particular problems of any given text may require the editor to develop special methods of presenting information. For texts with large numbers of authorities certain space-saving devices may be employed. Manly and Rickert devised a fairly elaborate system to indicate what they term "constant groups," sequences of manuscripts that are consistent in their readings.[39] This, together with other procedures they employ, tends to create quite complex forms of citation. The following example, for the line "Who shal be slayn or ellis deed for loue," from *The Knight's Tale*,[40] illustrates this complexity:

2038. . . . slayn or ellis deed] s. o. e. dey Hk; s. o. d. *Ne* Ps; s. and who shal be d. He; d. o. e. s. *En²* Ha² *Lc* Ld¹ *Mm* Py *Ry²* Se Sl¹ Tc¹; d. o. s. Ln Pw *Ra²*. *Out* Fi

A great deal of information is conveyed economically here: words in the variant reading(s) that agree with those in the lemma are indicated by their first letters followed by a period, as in the first reading after the lemma where "s. o. e." is the short form for the words "slayn or ellis" in the lemma; such notations as "*En²*" indicate the occurrence of a "constant group"; in this case, that this reading is common to the manuscripts Egerton 2863 and Longleat 257; and finally, the designation "*Out* Fi" indicates that the Fitzwilliam manuscript lacks this line.

The system is logical and succinct. The use of short forms for words is a straightforward, useful space-saving device. However, the idea of constant groups, authorities that generally agree in readings, is not so straightforward. It does save space by eliminating the need to repeat certain sigla, which in the case of a long work could amount to a considerable saving. But the editor, in establishing such groupings, must make it very clear to the reader what the nature of these relationships is, and one is allowed to wonder whether the points where such groupings break down deserve more notice than they receive

---

38. EETS 299 (Oxford, 1991). For example, in line 5 she reads "Draȝeð dust wið his sert ðer he [dun] steppeð" defending the addition of "[dun]" on the basis of rhythm and alliteration. She acknowledges, however, that alliteration on *st* is possible, which would render "[dun]" a questionable emendation, since double alliteration is rare in the poem (see p. 13); see also her discussion of lines 115, 175, 176.

39. Constant groups are discussed in *Text of Canterbury Tales*, 2:49–77.

40. It is taken from 5:196–97.

in the apparatus. This space-saving device adds a further level of complexity to the already onerous task of dealing with such a full and complicated apparatus.

The task of compiling a textual apparatus is complicated for works where the nature of their transmission amounts to virtual rewriting of the text into new forms that cannot be clearly or concisely expressed through conventional forms of notation. This is often the case with romance texts. For some, as Jennifer Fellows argues elsewhere in this volume, the only reasonable course of action may be to edit multiple texts in parallel. In some instances, as in Maldwyn Mills's edition of *Lybeaus Desconus,* this procedure may be partially adopted and other textual evidence indicating patterns of relationship between groups of witnesses relegated to an appendix.[41]

Whatever form of textual apparatus is employed, it is clearly desirable once again that it should be logical and consistent. This may seem self-evident, but not all modern editions, produced under distinguished scholarly auspices, invariably fulfill these requirements. For example, the standard modern edition of William Dunbar contains some curious departures from general editorial procedures as we have articulated them.[42] For example, a prefatory note to number 81 "[May na Man now undemit be]" identifies the base text: "*Text: MS B . . . collated with MS MF (two versions: MFa . . . ; MFb . . .).*"[43] Hence any departures from B would normally be indicated by square brackets. However, when B is emended this is not so: consider, for example, this note on lines 41–45: "War . . . deming be *MFa: not in B* ."[44] The note clearly indicates that lines 41–45 have been supplied from another source *(MFa)* because they do not occur in the base text. We may feel it irresponsible for an editor not to indicate emendation when he has the means to do so. Conversely, in the next poem, number 82 "[How sould I Governe me]" the note on the text reads: "*Text: MS MF . . . collated with MS B.*" This indicates that ms. MF provides the base text. However, lines 16–20 are placed within square brackets, indicating that they are an emendation to MF, presumably on the basis of B. But the textual note reads: "16–20 *not in B.*" Since the reading of the base text is being retained here, to place it in square brackets when no conjecture is involved is bewildering.

Even when editors do give a clear statement of the principles employed in their textual apparatus it still may need to be treated with caution. A case in

---

41. EETS 261 (London, 1969); see especially 272–302.
42. *The Poems of William Dunbar,* ed. Kinsley (see n. 25).
43. *Dunbar,* 211.
44. *Dunbar,* 213.

point is the first volume of the Chaucer Variorum edition of Chaucer's *Minor Poems.*[45] This has a clear statement about the treatment of emendations: "Italics indicate alteration of words by emendation. Letters or words added by emendation are placed within square brackets."[46] This variation from the unambiguous procedure of putting all editorial emendations in square brackets leads to some inconsistency. For example, in line 17 of *Lak of Stedfastnesse,* the text reads "n*o m*an," indicating an "altered" reading, while the textual apparatus gives the rejected reading as "noman"; but in *The Former Age* there is this note for line 39: "(Ii [the base-text] reverses this line and the next)." But these lines are printed in roman type without any indication in the text of the editorial change that has been made. The problems are clear: in the first instance the italicized letters have not actually been changed, so their italicization is misleading; in the second, the order of the lines—which clearly has some substantive effect—has been changed, but the text does not reflect this through italicization. Similar confusions can be found elsewhere. Thus line 35 of *Fortune* reads "no*n*"; but the rejected reading is recorded as "no"; hence, according to the stated editorial principles, since the editorial change involves the addition of a letter, not an alteration, the text should read "no[n]." The reader should note that the confusion here is compounded by the fact that the lemma reads *noon* instead of *non*. These examples, which could be considerably enlarged, indicate the need to keep editorial procedures as clear and as straightforward as possible.

One way to avoid such confusions is to provide a clean text, as in E. V. Gordon's edition of *Pearl,*[47] or Peter J. Lucas's edition of John Capgrave's *Abbreviacioun of Cronicles,*[48] where alterations of the manuscript are not signaled in the edited text by either of the conventions, brackets or italics, that we have been discussing. The great virtue of such a presentation is that it offers the readers no distraction in their perusal of the text, but the reader is obliged to take the responsibility to examine the apparatus to determine what the editor has done. At the other extreme is an elaborate system of presentation designed to convey not simply information about editorial changes but also about the physical state of the manuscript and/or the various levels of revision it may reflect. Examples of editions where the text and apparatus are designed to

---

45. Ed. George B. Pace and Alfred David (Norman, 1982).

46. Pace and David, *Minor Poems,* 11; the statement is quoted from F. Klaeber's 3d edition of *Beowulf* (1950).

47. (Oxford, 1953). Gordon also uses the textual notes to give readings from other editions. This is an option open to editors of texts in unique exemplars.

48. EETS 285 (Oxford, 1983).

reflect such matters are Douglas Moffat's of *The Soul's Address to the Body*[49] and E. J. Dobson's of the Cleopatra manuscript of the *Ancrene Wisse*.[50]

A final issue of fundamental importance touched on earlier is the question of whether the edition actually requires a full textual apparatus. As already mentioned, editions designed for classroom use almost certainly do not need this feature. For lengthy texts surviving in large numbers of copies, it may be practicable only to produce a limited apparatus even for a scholarly edition. Michael Sargent does this with great success in his edition of Nicholas Love's *Mirror of the Blessed Life of Christ,* presented as a best-text edition, corrected against only one other manuscript that can be shown to be closely related to the one chosen as best text.[51] In view of the large number of manuscripts of this work (Sargent lists nearly fifty complete ones) this decision is justifiable. The notes are then limited chiefly to a record of rejected readings.[52]

Any consideration of the form of textual apparatus to be employed will involve a clear articulation on the editor's part of the procedures that are being adopted and the reasons for them. Underlying any presentation should be the principles of clarity, consistency, and conciseness that will enable the user to recover as much significant information as possible about the varying forms of the text that have been available to the editor.

---

49. Medieval Texts and Studies, 1 (East Lansing, Mich., 1987); see especially 59–60.

50. *The English Text of the Ancrene Riwle, edited from B.M. MS. Cleopatra C.VI,* EETS 267 (London, 1972).

51. Garland Medieval Texts, 18 (New York, 1992); see especially cvii.

52. Sargent's preamble to his textual notes states, "The following Textual Notes register all readings in A2 that vary from A1 [his best text], and all readings of A1 and A2 [the other manuscript he collated] where the text has been emended editorially" (243).

Making a Glossary

Douglas Moffat

Is a Glossary Necessary?

Everyone who has used editions of Middle English works can attest to the value of a glossary and to the irritation felt in turning to the back of the volume and not finding one, or finding that it does not contain what you seek. However, it is clear from older editions of Middle English works as well as quite recent ones that a thorough glossary is not regarded by every editor or publisher as a necessity. So, before offering advice on how to compile a glossary for an edition of a Middle English work, I must address two fundamental questions: Is a glossary necessary? Given the fact that all glossaries must be selective to some degree, how does one decide what to include?

I believe the answer to the first question is, unequivocally, "yes," except for very short works in which all the difficulties of vocabulary can be handled in the notes.[1] Even the most experienced readers of Middle English with the clearest of fifteenth-century prose texts before them will be puzzled by the meanings of some words. They will need their guesses and suspicions confirmed or challenged but may not require a full explanatory note. The more unfamiliar the dialect or obscure the subject, the greater the need for a glossary becomes for all readers. It might be argued that sufficient lexicographical tools already exist to help the professional reader who faces lexical difficulties. However, it must be borne in mind that these tools, which will be discussed below, are cumbersome and inconvenient because of the breadth of coverage they seek. Further, they are incomplete in their survey of the extant evidence. While invaluable, they should not be considered the last word, as it were. Readers are much better served by checking a carefully researched and clearly presented glossary keyed to a specific work, even in a separate volume, than they are by combing through vast general dictionaries. The readers will

---

1. There are some other exceptions. One that comes to mind is glossographical texts.

go to the dictionaries when they want to question the glossary's suggestion, or don't find what they are looking for, or, alas, when they find no glossary whatsoever.

The second question, how to decide what material ought to appear in the glossary, is less easy to answer. Ideally every separate lexical item in your text ought to have an entry in the glossary, and every distinct sense or meaning of each item ought to be exemplified within the entry. This is not to say that the glossary should be a record of every occurrence of every lexical item. Even for a short text of a few hundred lines, a complete glossary giving every occurrence is impractical and unnecessary. The longer the text, the more important becomes a plan involving judicious selection. Otherwise the glossary will consume too much research time and become unwieldy; and it will be unattractive, therefore, to the publisher.

There are two ways to approach the selection process: what might be excluded and what must be included. Some opportunities for exclusion are taken by most editors of Middle English. For example, the treatment of very common words (function words, common verbs like *haven* and *ben,* most pronouns) can be significantly curtailed in most glossaries. Also, most editors sharply limit the enumeration of occurrences, giving three or fewer for each meaning. Some researchers, of course, would like more information than this, even complete lists of occurrences for very common words. With the advent of electronic editions these researchers soon ought to be able to generate this evidence for themselves. Some editors (e.g., of volumes in the Middle English Texts Series and of recent volumes of EETS) go further in the process of exclusion. In these glossaries all words judged to be "common" or "Chaucerian" are omitted, unless they exhibit a peculiar meaning. Undoubtedly such glossaries save a great deal of space and reduce costs, but they assume much. One can only hope that the editor's presumption about the general knowledge of common or Chaucerian Middle English is sufficiently capacious to include the varying abilities of the readers that the text might attract, bearing in mind that scholars whose specialities are not Middle English may be interested in the subject matter. One can only hope, as well, that the editor has done a good deal of work toward a fairly complete glossary in order that the selection for what appears in print be truly judicious. It has certainly been my personal experience that doing the glossary for a text, while admittedly tedious, brought things to light that I had not previously noticed or fully understood. However, knowing in advance that the final product would only be very selective, surely one would be tempted to be rather selective in the process as well, passing lightly over what appears to be "common." Unfortunately, the experience of this writer is that these highly selective glossaries too frequently miss lexical peculiarities.

In deciding what must be included in any glossary, an editor should pay particular attention to certain classes of words. If the subject matter of the text causes the writer to use specialized vocabulary, it would be a great benefit to all readers to provide full and clear glossary entries for such words, or references to treatments of them somewhere else in the volume. Specialized vocabulary is an area where general dictionaries do not excel, as a rule. Also, words, meanings, and forms not included in the general dictionaries ought to be treated in the glossary. So the general answer to the second question posed above might be, emphasize what is peculiar in the vocabulary of your text; de-emphasize what is common; avoid repetition.

The glossary is customarily one of the last things that an editor does, but there are advantages to starting in on it fairly early in the editorial process, even though it will likely have to be modified as work progresses. Fortunately, with a computer you can now generate with relative ease the alphabetized word list that will underlie the glossary, and this computer-generated list should not contain the errors of omission that the tediousness of traditional methods made almost inevitable. (Peter Robinson discusses various concording programs in his essay in this volume.) Therefore, once a provisional text has been established and entered into a computer, you can begin work on the glossary. Getting started fairly early in the editing process will help you secure your knowledge of the literal meaning of the text, but it has a more practical advantage as well. Once the structure of the glossary has been established, much of the work on it can be done in very small units that don't require great blocks of time. Glossary work can often be fitted into a busy schedule that would not seem to allow much leeway for research.

Structure of the Glossary

The glossary should be prefaced with a brief statement explaining its structure and the method of selection; a list of abbreviations used should be included. At this stage in the history of Middle English editing both structure and abbreviations have achieved an almost formulaic state, even though there is a variety of particular ways by which to indicate information. In what follows I will comment on structure by discussing the parts of the typical glossary entry. The type of information that should appear in the introduction to the glossary, including abbreviations, will be touched on in passing. The parts of the typical glossary entry are

Headword
Designation of part of speech
Sense and sense division
Other possible features

Headword

Although a computer will provide you with an alphabetized list of words, obviously each of these will not constitute a headword. There are bound to be variant spellings and oblique grammatical forms that will be collapsed into one entry with a single headword. Besides this necessary step of consolidation, you will have to decide whether the headwords should reflect the spelling that appears in the text itself or a more typical Middle English spelling. The convenient solution is to retain the spelling in the text, although in the case of variant spellings of the same word you will have to make a decision about a headword and perhaps supply cross-references in the glossary to direct readers to the correct entry.

While choosing to follow the spelling in the text may be the easy approach in deciding on headwords, you should consider two levels of regularization that will probably make your glossary more useful to a wider range of users. First of all, you should consider taking as your headword a standard, unmarked form of the word, that is, the nominative singular of a noun, the infinitive of a verb, and so on. The advantage of such regularization will not be clear in many cases, but in some, for example, the past-tense forms of strong verbs or mutated plural forms of nouns, it will allow readers who are examining your glossary for specific items to find them more easily. However, if you do this, you should provide the readers with a cross-reference so that they can find the entry in which a particular form is being treated.

The other sort of regularization that will have to be considered by most editors of Middle English texts is that of orthographic variants that appear to be of no phonological significance and may be in free variation in the text. I am thinking here particularly of *i/y, u/v,* and *u/f,* but there are a number of others. My impression is that these variants are treated as alphabetically identical in most, but certainly not all, editions of Middle English. If they occur as variant representations of the same sound, then treating them at one place in the alphabet seems the best policy, that is, vocalic *v* with *u,* consonantal *u* with *v* when it stands for the voiced fricative and with *f* when it stands for the unvoiced. Vocalic *y* would normally be included with *i,* rather than vice versa. It will be apparent that a grasp of basic Middle English phonology will be needed to make these kinds of decisions.

The advantage of this sort of regularization is that readers looking for words will find them spelled in typical ways; the disadvantage is that readers looking for exactly the form in the text may be disappointed not to find it. A statement concerning whatever degree of regularization that has been adopted must appear in the introduction to the glossary, and it is probably a good idea to place cross-references within the glossary at least for words whose initial letter is being treated out of the modern alphabetic sequence.

Part of Speech and Grammatical Designations

The headword will be followed by a designation of the part of speech. The abbreviations used for such designations, while not absolutely fixed, are very well known to most readers who are likely to encounter your edition. Still, a short list in the introduction to the glossary might prove helpful to some. You should be consistent throughout the glossary, and the edition, in using abbreviations. The abbreviations used to designate grammatical functions are similarly well known and should present few readers with insurmountable difficulties. For example, *gs.*, *g.s.*, *gen. sg.*, *gen. sing.* differ from each other only in their brevity; no moderately experienced reader is going to be confused by any of them within the context of the glossary, although in an explanatory note *gs.* may cause a momentary halt. Nevertheless, they too should be included in the list of abbreviations mentioned above.

Abbreviations designating grammatical function will appear before the appropriate forms in the glossary. A very full glossary would include at least one example of the various inflected forms that occur in your text for each word in the glossary, for example, the tenses of the verbs, cases of the nouns and adjectives. In some texts this information can be done within the normal form of the entry. For example, after the gloss "deed, action" for the headword *Werk* you might have "gs. *werkes*" as the exemplification. If your text is long, however, and the amount of lexical data correspondingly large, you might consider the two-part entry used by G. H. V. Bunt in his edition of *William of Palerne*.[2] In this glossary the second part of the entry is devoted to meanings and the first to forms representing both grammatical function and orthographic peculiarity. Bunt's, by the way, is a fine recent example of a full glossary, but he may have been fortunate in having such a generous publisher. The glossary in Hoyt N. Duggan and Thorlac Turville-Petre's edition of *The Wars of Alexander* is much more compact but still very complete.[3] Another good example

---

2. Mediaevalia Groningana 6, (Groningen, 1985).
3. EETS, s.s. 10 (Oxford, 1989).

of a glossary that is widely available is Norman Davis's *A Chaucer Glossary.*[4] If you are doing a very selective glossary, you could certainly dispense with regular inflections, but irregularities ought to be included. It is vital for all glossators, as already mentioned, to include orthographic peculiarities, especially those not covered by the general dictionaries, even if they are treated as well in a note or a discussion of language. Cross-references to such treatments will also be much appreciated.

Sense Division

Most dictionaries divide entries of more than one meaning into numbered senses and lettered subsenses. Even this simple system will likely prove over-elaborate for most glossaries of editions. Dividing senses with semicolons will often be adequate. However, you should bear in mind that readers will be tempted to find significance in any variance in procedure, so make a brief explanatory statement in the glossary's introduction about your method, and be consistent. In regard to order of senses, one might follow the arrangement in one of the general dictionaries. Alternatively, the most common usage in your text could come first, least common last.

Finding Meanings: There are a number of reference works you may have cause to consult when looking for the meaning of Middle English words; the most important ones are listed in appendix C of this volume. The obvious starting place is *The Middle English Dictionary.* This dictionary, like so many other dictionaries of medieval vernaculars, is very hard to use because of the heterogeneous, one is tempted to say chaotic, orthography of the evidence. No amount of cross-referencing can fully overcome this problem, and it is to be hoped therefore, if the dictionary is ever completed, that an electronically accessible version of it can be made in order to ease this difficulty.

The *MED* far outstrips any other lexicographical resource for Middle English, but you should bear certain realities in mind when using it. While the Middle English data used by the *MED* dwarfs what was available for any previous dictionary, it is still limited; the *MED* is the most complete Middle English dictionary, but it is by no means complete. Also important to remember is that the compilers of the *MED,* or any other general dictionary, cannot be specialists in every field, let alone every text. By taking a strict, lexicographical tack the *MED* editor can arrive at a defensible meaning of a particular word in a

---

4. Compiled by Norman Davis, Douglas Gray, Patricia Ingham, and Anne Wallace-Hadrill (Oxford, 1979).

particular, limited context. But a specialist in a field or a text, which is what you are or will be when you edit, ought to be in a better position than is the lexicographer to provide an assured meaning of many words.

If you don't find a word, or a meaning of a word, in the *MED*, then you must examine *The Oxford English Dictionary*. Even if you do find a somewhat satisfactory meaning for a particular word in the *MED*, it is a good practice to consult the *OED* as well. You ought not to discover Middle English words or Middle English meanings of words in the *OED* that do not appear in the *MED*: if you do, either you are not looking in the right place in the *MED*, or the *MED* has made a mistake. However, you could well find Early Modern English evidence for words or meanings that the *MED* has omitted for lack of the Middle English evidence that you will now be able to supply from your text. Also, it is important to bear in mind that where the *MED* and *OED* share evidence, the *OED* provides what amounts to a very learned second opinion. It may corroborate, clarify, or contradict what the *MED* says, but you will be in a stronger position to write your own gloss by considering both interpretations. The *OED* is electronically accessible, and a third edition is in preparation. It will be useful to future lexicographers and lexicologists, by the way, to have somewhere in your edition a list of words in your text that antedate *MED* and *OED* attestations.

Examining the Old English lexicographical resources might also prove necessary, especially if you are working on an earlier text. Just as a word or sense not treated by the *MED* may occur in Early Modern English and appear therefore in the *OED* but not the *MED*, so too might a word or meaning be found in one of the Old English dictionaries but not in the *MED*. The *OED* does provide a little Old English evidence, and the *MED* treats a number of Middle English translations of Old English works, but neither will give you an adequate picture of Old English. If *The Dictionary of Old English* has reached the word you are examining, then that is the first place to go. However, for some time to come the most complete Old English dictionary will continue to be *Bosworth-Toller*. You will have to check both volumes as well as the supplement at the end of volume 2. For peculiar spellings the *Microfiche Concordance of Old English* can be very helpful.

There are many dictionaries that you could well end up looking into in order to track down a particularly inscrutable word. A brief list of the most commonly used dictionaries for Middle English scholars appears in appendix C of this volume. It is worth mentioning here that the firmer your grasp of paleography and of English (and non-English) phonology, the more likely you will be to discover what the word really is that you are staring at.

How to Gloss: Defining a word is an act of interpretation fraught with practical and philosophical difficulties of almost paralyzing complexity. If you dwell on these difficulties, you will never complete your glossary or your edition. To help you get along with the process of defining you might bear in mind one of the "dicts" of lexicography: "gloss the word, not the context." We might want to leave the defining of *word* to the semanticists, but in fact it may become a practical consideration for you. While Middle English scribes more often approximate Modern English word division than their Anglo-Saxon predecessors, there are likely to be places in the text where you will have to make decisions on this question. You should be particularly alert for prepositions and adverbs that can also function as prefixes, for example, *out, to, up,* and so on. The *MED* tends to treat such forms as prefixes when they occur before the simplex, that is, where a prefix would appear; otherwise, they are taken as separate words. G.V. Smithers, on the other hand, in his edition of *Havelok,* treats some of these forms as separable prefixes, and therefore he has in his glossary some regularized headwords that appear neither in his text nor elsewhere in Middle English, as near as one can judge.[5] If you decide to follow his lead, you must provide clear cross-references for the reader.

Putting aside the question of what is a "word," one might still fairly ask of the lexicographer, what constitutes "context?" The candid answer might be "enough of the surrounding text to substantiate a literal definition." Obviously the pragmatism of this approach imposes limitations. There is no question but that the broader understanding of the context of a particular word that you will have as an editor—hundreds of words in either direction, the whole work in which it occurs, the whole genre that the work exemplifies, a particular source in English or some other language—ought to sharpen your understanding of its meaning.

It will likely prove valuable, nonetheless, to keep the dictum "gloss the word, not the context" in mind when defining words for your glossary. Thinking in this traditional way will allow you to avoid one of the common pitfalls of glossators: using the glossary surreptitiously to justify an interpretation of the text. This practice is not confined to literary interpretation but can equally occur in the glossing of words in a mundane piece on a mundane topic, like horse diseases or weaving. What I am referring to is the decision of an editor to choose an unusual gloss for a word that encourages the reader to accept the editor's interpretation of the passage in question, which might be discussed elsewhere in the edition. If you find that a definition you would prefer is not

---

5. (Oxford, 1987). For examples, see the *up*-entries in his glossary.

exemplified in the general dictionaries, or is very rare, then you should ask yourself whether you are genuinely trying to gloss the literal meaning of the word or are providing an interpretive gloss not really justified at the literal level. If you still believe you are correct, you ought to defend your decision against the general dictionaries and other scholars in a note. The reader should be alerted to this note in the glossary entry.

It will be useful to readers and future researchers if you will include in your glossary phrases and syntactical usages that strike you as peculiar. As you know, words frequently acquire differences of meaning when they fall into collocation with certain other words, and a glossary that calls attention to these special phrases will be of great value. The conventional way to render phrases is to use a tilde as a substitute for the headword, for example, ~ *and side,* in the entry for *wide.*

Other Possible Features

1. The *MED* and *OED* (and the various English etymological dictionaries for surviving words) provide etymological information about Middle English words, so the argument could be made that providing this information in your glossary is superfluous. It is certainly true for most words that you would be doing nothing more than replicating a perfectly obvious and accessible etymon, and swelling the size of the glossary unnecessarily. If you provide an *MED* headword for each glossary entry (see below), you will direct the reader to the etymological information there, which will usually be sufficient.

Nevertheless, you should still consider the value of researching the etymologies of each entry, whether you intend to include this information or not. You may benefit by discovering something about a word that you had not suspected. Moreover, you may come up with information that causes you to disagree with the prevailing opinion about a word's etymology. And if you have a word not treated in the *MED,* you will want to provide an etymon for it, if you can.

The list in appendix C of this volume contains the most useful dictionaries for researching etymologies.

2. Inclusion of the corresponding *MED* headword for each entry is not a feature one finds in glossaries of Middle English works, but it could be a useful addition, especially if your own headword is different. What this inclusion will do is allow the readers to find the *MED* entry with ease so that they can check other Middle English evidence for themselves. If you have a word that is not in

the *MED,* this fact could be indicated in the glossary where the *MED* headword would usually appear. A separate list of such words could also be included in the edition to provide easy access for those particularly seeking this information.

3. Various forms of cross-reference are necessary for a glossary. Some have been mentioned already. Within the glossary itself cross-references should be made between

words that occur in remarkable collocation
different words with identical spellings
prefixed and unprefixed forms.

Cross-reference should also be made to words whose peculiar meaning, spelling, or etymology is treated elsewhere in the edition, i.e., in the discussion of language or some other part of the introduction or in an explanatory note.

4. Clear indication should be given in the glossary of emended forms, and the unemended form ought to be given along with it.

5. Although not often done, you should consider including in the glossary at least noteworthy forms that for one reason or another do not appear in the edited version of the text. In most cases these will be variants in some non-preferred version of the text. It is not uncommon for unusual words and usages to appear in such versions, and it will be of great value to future researchers if you would provide them with some help in finding such words and in understanding what they might mean.

Editing and the Computer

The Computer and the Making of Editions

Peter M. W. Robinson

It is a commonplace now for articles touching on any aspect of scholarly publishing and computing to observe that the impact of computing on scholarship in the late twentieth century is at least as great as was the impact of printing in the fifteenth century.[1] Indeed, there is reason to think that the effect of computing on textual scholarship may be even greater than that of printing. Not only do computer methods offer cheaper means of distribution (as did printing, compared to hand copying) but they offer, as printing did not, new possibilities in the making of editions. The advent of printing did not much alter the way in which scholars made editions, though greatly changing the dissemination of what the scholars made. In contrast, computer methods may change what scholars do.

Peter Baker's companion essay on computing and editing in this volume will deal with the first aspect, of how computer methods will change the presentation and dissemination of texts and their scholarly use. In this essay I concentrate on this second aspect, of how computer methods are altering what scholars do as they edit. Computer methods may touch every aspect of what scholars do: they may change how we acquire and view images of manuscripts and what we look for in them; how we transcribe the manuscripts; how we collate the transcriptions; how we analyze the collations in search of a rationale for the history of the text; how we compile glossaries and research word use and spelling in the text. We are still years away from the full realization of these methods, with many of them still under development or dependent on changes

---

1. For example: "We believe that the most fundamental change in textual culture since Gutenberg is now under way," in George P. Landow and Paul Delaney, *The Digital Word: Text-Based Computing in the Humanities* (Cambridge, Mass., 1993), 5. For the impact of printing on textual scholarship, see the accounts in L. D. Reynolds and N. G. Wilson, *Scribes and Scholars,* 3d ed. (Oxford, 1991), 154–58; and, in more detail, in D. C. Greetham, *Textual Scholarship: An Introduction* (New York, 1992), 77–112.

in the computing environment in which we work. For example, fundamental advances are still necessary in computer storage and network technology before high-resolution manuscript images can become widely available. But enough has been done for us to see what we can do now and what will be possible soon. The *Canterbury Tales* Project, for which I am executive officer, is using many of these methods, and most of the examples I give below are drawn from that project.[2]

For an editor of a Middle English text, editing begins (with a few exceptions, such as editors of Caxton) with a manuscript. Unless you are lucky enough to be editing a text in just one manuscript, with that manuscript available to you in a local library, you will have to work from a reproduction of the manuscript, and not the manuscript itself. Indeed, it is likely that even where the manuscript itself is available, librarians will not be happy to allow the lengthy access to the manuscript itself that editing might require. Almost invariably, the manuscript reproduction will be based on microfilm: either the library will provide a copy of the microfilm itself, or it will provide (as do the Bodleian and British Libraries) paper prints from the microfilm. Machines are now available that can convert entire microfilms into computer images, so that one can view a manuscript page not on a microfilm viewer, or on a printed page, but on a computer screen. This process is very cheap, very convenient where microfilm copies already exist, and the resulting computer files can be made sufficiently small as to be easily distributed.[3] Libraries and microfilm companies have already shown considerable interest in this technology, and most of the manuscript page images on the first *Canterbury Tales* Project CD-ROM, containing eleven hundred page images for all of the surviving fifty-four manuscripts and four pre-1500 printed editions of the Wife of Bath's Prologue, are so derived from microfilm.[4]

---

2. The *Canterbury Tales* Project is directed by Professor Norman Blake of the University of Sheffield, with Elizabeth Solopova as principal transcriber. The project has received support from the Universities of Sheffield and Oxford, the British Academy, and the Leverhulme Trust. Cambridge University Press has published the Wife of Bath's Prologue on CD-ROM (1996), which contains manuscript images, transcriptions, collations and analyses. The project also publishes a newsletter and the Occasional Papers volumes, two of which have appeared: N. F. Blake and P. M. W. Robinson, eds. *The Canterbury Tales Project: Occasional Papers,* no. 1 (Oxford, 1993) and no. 2 (Oxford, 1997).

3. There is an account of the possibilities for the making of computer images of manuscript and other primary sources in my report on digitization of primary textual sources: P. M. W. Robinson, *The Digitization of Primary Textual Sources* (Oxford, 1993).

4. During 1993, the British Library carried out tests with a Mekel microfilm scanner and achieved typical digitization rates of twenty frames a minute with satisfactory resolution. In discussions with the author, the principals of several microfilm companies stated their intention to

One can expect that in the near future libraries may offer microfilm images in scanned computer-readable form as well as in film or page forms. At present, acquisition of manuscript reproductions is a lengthy process. Typically, one must write to the library to enquire about availability and cost; await a reply; then pay for the reproductions; finally wait for them to be sent. Even under ideal conditions this may take several weeks, and several months is more usual. Distribution of computer images by network will allow this to be telescoped into a few minutes, or even seconds. Indeed, the manuscript images might not be distributed at all: a scholar might dial into the library, or archive, from his or her computer and view the image within the archive, with obvious advantage to the library as it keeps control of the image.

The convenience alone of this distribution of microfilm-based computer images may be a considerable boon. But computer methods may offer much more than this. Microfilm is actually a very poor method of reproducing a manuscript. Modern high-contrast microfilm is very well suited to archiving of printed materials, with plain black text on white paper, but is very poor for reproduction of manuscript materials. Manuscripts may have fading brown ink on darkening parchment, with different hands writing in different inks, with different pen-pressure for punctuation and calligraphic flourishes, with scribal rubrication and ornamentation in various colors. Scholars are increasingly aware of the importance in a manuscript of not only the letterforms made by the scribe but their disposition upon the page: the use of color, as emphatic or structural or decorative device; the layout of scribal signs upon the page; a hierarchy of scripts within the inscribed text; indications of correction, annotation, or deletion; the physical characteristics of the manuscript itself.[5] All this is lost in high-contrast microfilm; only color reproduction can capture it. However, color photography and reproduction are extremely expensive, so much so that there is not a single color facsimile of any complete Middle English manuscript of Langland or Chaucer. The advent of digital photography, with devices such as the Kontron ProgRes camera demonstrating that images of

---

digitize some (at least) of their microfilms in the near future.

    5. Many scholars, working in widely separated fields, have recently stressed the importance of the physical expression of primary texts. For medieval texts, see the discussion of the changes in manuscript presentation in the context of the development of research tools in the twelfth and thirteenth centuries in M. A. Rouse and R. H. Rouse, *Authentic Witnesses: Approaches to Medieval Texts and Manuscripts* (Notre Dame, 1991), 191–258; for modern texts see the work of Jerome McGann on "bibliographic codes" (e.g., his 1991 article "What Is Critical Editing" *Text* 5 [1991]: 15–30); D. F. McKenzie's *Bibliography and the Sociology of Texts,* The Panizzi Lectures (London, 1986); and the summary discussion in Greetham, 291–94.

astonishing clarity may be made rapidly and cheaply, may change all this.[6] The images made by this and similar cameras are at least as good as those available from large-format transparencies (60 mm, or 10 by 8, etc.), and to the viewer are equivalent to seeing the manuscript under full daylight. The first *Canterbury Tales* Project CD-ROM will include a few such images, and later CD-ROMs should include many more such. It is conceivable that a single CD-ROM, costing around ten pounds to produce, could contain a complete color record of the whole Ellesmere manuscript.[7]

Color images of this quality will give scholars detail about the manuscripts hitherto available only to those fortunate enough to live close to the great research libraries. In itself, this may revolutionize textual scholarship.[8] The intense study of manuscript detail for Chaucer and Langland found in the last decades in the work of Malcolm Parkes and Ian Doyle will become accessible to a much wider scholarly community.[9]

Valuable though dissemination of such images might be in itself, an editor who does no more than accumulate and distribute them will not deserve the name of editor. To begin to unlock the information in them, one must transcribe

---

6. An example of modern color printing of a high-quality facsimile is the process found necessary by Alecto Historical Editions for their photographic facsimile of the Domesday Book. Every page had to be photographed five times, with film of differing grains and sensitivity, each photograph developed and plates made, and then the facsimile made by overlay printing of the five plates with different colors onto specially chosen paper (personal communication, J. G. Studholme of Alecto Historical Editions). Compare the account of Griggs's printing of the color pages of the 1911 Ellesmere facsimile in Ralph Hanna, ed., *The Ellesmere Manuscript of "The Canterbury Tales": A Working Facsimile* (Cambridge, 1989), 4–9. With (for example) the Kontron camera, one simply places the manuscript under the camera; the computer image appears on the screen within thirty seconds. Three color plates in my *Digitization of Primary Textual Sources* are printed from manuscript photographs taken with the Kontron camera.

7. At the time of writing, the Huntington Library was considering the possibility of the making of an electronic facsimile of the Ellesmere Chaucer.

8. There has been considerable excitement at the prospect of image enhancement techniques on digital photographs of manuscripts yielding new readings, and confirming or denying old ones. In fact, experiments so far have not confirmed this promise. Image enhancement appears a useful way of making a poor photograph better and is simply not needed (beyond basic magnification) when working with a high-quality image such as those provided by the Kontron or similar devices. See Kevin Kiernan, "Digital Image Processing and the Beowulf Manuscript," *Literary and Linguistic Computing* 6 (1991): 20–27; and Robinson, *Digitization*, 55–59.

9. For example, the seminal "The Production of Copies of the *Canterbury Tales*," in Malcolm Parkes, *Scribes, Scripts, and Readers: Studies in the Communication, Presentation, and Dissemination of Medieval Texts* (London, 1991), 210–48, originally published in *Medieval Scribes, Manuscripts, and Libraries: Essays Presented to N. R. Ker*, eds. M. B. Parkes and A. G. Watson (London, 1978), 163–210, and their essay on the Hengwrt manuscript in P. Ruggiers, *The Canterbury Tales. Geoffrey Chaucer. A Facsimile and Transcription of the Hengwrt Manuscript, with Variants from the Ellesmere Manuscript* (Norman, Okla., 1979).

the manuscripts from these images. The computer provides new possibilities—and difficulties—in the process of transcription. Possibilities, for the low cost of computer distribution means that one can "publish" the computer transcriptions themselves, with the transcriptions linked by hypertext software to the images. Difficulties, for there is a fundamental difference between transcription for the computer and transcription for a traditional scholarly edition. When one is transcribing for a traditional edition, the choices are bounded by the characters available in the printer's fount; further, the end of the transcription is its printing, and not its distribution in electronic form. But one can expect a computer-readable transcription to be searched, analyzed, and edited in ways not possible with a printed transcription. Thus, when making a computer transcription one must consider the possible uses of this transcription by other scholars and let this weight decisions about what to include, what not to include.

This suggests that manuscript transcription for the computer is a complex business, with many subtle choices having to be made. It is far from the mechanical affair that it is sometimes thought to be, as instanced by the recurrent discussion on scholarly electronic discussion groups about possible machine systems for "reading" manuscripts. Computer transcription, with its special requirements of consistency across a possibly huge body of material, highlights what manuscript scholars have always known: that reading manuscripts might draw on all of a scholar's training and knowledge. In essence, transcription is a series of acts of translation, from one semiotic system (that of the manuscript) to another semiotic system (that of the computer). Like all acts of translation, it must be seen as fundamentally incomplete and fundamentally interpretive.

After three years of work on the manuscripts of the Wife of Bath's Prologue, we are still uncertain about exactly what marks we should record, and how we should record them. In our "Guidelines for Transcription" we identified four possible levels of transcription: *regularized,* with all manuscript spellings leveled to a particular standard; *graphemic,* with all manuscript spellings preserved without distinction of particular letterforms; *graphetic,* with discrimination of all distinct letterforms; *graphic,* with every mark in the manuscript represented in the transcription.[10] The choice among these levels is not simple, and we have found that it is not possible to achieve a stringent conformancy to any one level in the course of a long transcription of many manuscripts. Thus,

---

10. P. M. W. Robinson and E. Solopova, "Guidelines for the Transcription of Manuscripts of The Wife of Bath's Prologue," in *Occasional Papers* 1:19–52 (see n. 2).

while we aim at a graphemic transcription such as will be useful to students of the language of the manuscripts, the uncertain graphemic status of many marks in the manuscripts (particularly, tails and flourishes) means that our transcription includes some graphic and graphetic elements. Exact documentation of what we have done is therefore vital if others are to use our transcripts. We have attempted to provide that in our "Guidelines for Transcription" and recommend strongly that other scholars engaged in manuscript transcription for the computer also document their practice.[11]

One must also decide exactly how one does the transcription: what word processor, what computer, does one use? It is tempting to use one's favorite word processor and to make up an ad hoc markup system deploying the facilities most systems now provide for italics, underlining, special characters, and different fonts, and so forth, to register various manuscript features.[12] This is convenient and satisfying for the transcribing scholar. But it can lead to problems when the transcript files are shifted to another system (or even, when the word processor software is upgraded), or when one attempts to use the files alongside transcripts made by other scholars using different systems, or to use them with different software. These problems can be minimized by use of a widely supported standard system of computer markup. This will make it far easier for the transcript files (representing a considerable investment of scholarly time and effort) to survive changes in computer systems and will make them available to a wider scholarly community and amenable to different software packages. One such standard system of markup is that specified for the computer collation package Collate:[13] this is the system used by the *Canterbury Tales* Project, and by several other major editing projects. Files using

---

11. Instances of similar statements of practice for machine-readable transcription of manuscript materials are: A. Van Arkel-De Leeuw Van Weenen, *Möðruvallabók,* AM 132 Fol. 2 vols. (Leiden, 1987); H. Fix, "Production and Usage of a Machine-Readable Manuscript: A Report on the Saarbrücken Version of Grágás Konungsbók," in *Computer Applications to Medieval Studies,* ed. A. Gilmour-Bryson, Studies in Medieval Culture, 17 (Kalamazoo, Mich., 1984); R. D. Stevick, *Beowulf: An Edition with Manuscript Spacing Notation and Graphotactic Analyses* (New York, 1975).

12. Several such "home-grown" systems of transcription are surveyed in my report on transcription for the computer, P. M. W. Robinson, *The Transcription of Primary Textual Sources Using SGML* (Oxford, 1993).

13. P. M. W. Robinson, "Collate: A Program for Interactive Collation of Large Textual Traditions," in S. Hockey and N. Ide, eds., *Research in Humanities Computing* (Oxford, 1995), and *Collate: A Program for Interactive Collation of Large Textual Traditions. Version 1.1.* Computer Program distributed by the Computers and Manuscripts Project, Oxford University Computing Services, Oxford, 1992.

this markup can be collated by Collate and also searched, indexed, and con-corded by the Oxford Concordance Program.

Though adequate for its immediate purposes, the Collate markup scheme (like all such specialized markup schemes) has severe limitations. In the long term, it is likely that editors will use the dialect of Standard Generalized Markup Language (SGML; itself a widely supported International Standard, ISO 8879) currently under development for encoding of scholarly texts by the Text Encoding Initiative (TEI). The TEI is a major international collaboration aimed at developing guidelines for the encoding and interchange of machine-readable scholarly texts. A first draft of its recommendations was published in 1990. A much revised and enlarged version appeared in 1994.[14] The TEI system has yet to be tested in extensive use, and software will have to be developed to make it accessible to manuscript scholars. However, its promise is such that for the present no scholarly transcription should proceed without some thought as to future translation of its files into SGML form. The *Canterbury Tales* Project will be publishing its transcription files in both Collate and SGML/TEI format.

Where one is editing a text in many manuscripts, the next step, presuming one has transcribed all the manuscripts, is collation of the transcripts.[15] Once the transcripts are in electronic form, collation by computer is logical. The scholar has a choice of many collation programs, including the widely used programs developed by Ott and Shillingsburg.[16] There are considerable advan-tages in computer collation where one desires the most complete, word-by-word record of manuscript agreements and disagreements. One may experi-

---

14. C. M. Sperberg-McQueen and L. Burnard, *Guidelines for Electronic Text Encoding and Interchange* 3d ed. ("P3"), 2 vols. (Chicago, 1994).

15. Obviously, not all manuscripts of all texts are of such interest as to merit the full transcrip-tion here outlined, and proposed by the *Canterbury Tales* Project. One might carry out a full transcription only of samples of the text in all the manuscripts, or transcribe all the text only in some manuscripts, etc. Whatever fractions of text are transcribed, the techniques here described hold good.

16. For Ott's TUSTEP, a set of routines (including a collation facility) for editing and for processing of scholarly information, see the summaries in I. Lancashire, *Humanities Computing Yearbook* (1991): 407–8 and in *Literary and Linguistic Computing* 4 (1989): 235–37. TUSTEP is available from the Zentrum für Datenverarbeitung, University of Tübingen, Brunnenstrasse 27, D-7400 Tübingen, Germany. For Shillingsburg's CASE, available on many different computer platforms and used (for example) in editions of Thackeray, Dreiser, Conrad, Hardy, and Carlyle see P. L. Shillingsburg, *Scholarly Editing in the Computer Age: Theory and Practice* (Athens, Ga., 1986). The program is available from the Department of English, Mississippi State University, Miss. 39762.

ment with collations with different levels of regularization, or with different master texts. For example, collation of the unregularized transcripts of the earliest manuscripts of the Wife of Bath's Prologue has shown remarkable agreements in spelling (as against substantive variation) between each of two pairs of manuscripts thought by many scholars to have been written by the one scribe.[17] Also, it is likely that computer collation will give a far more accurate and complete record of variation than is possible from manual collation. If the transcripts are accurate, then the collation will be accurate, and it is easier to check a transcript against a manuscript than to check a manual collation. In the first case, you are comparing just two things (the transcript and the manuscript); in the second you have to compare three things (the manuscript, the master, and the collation).

The *Canterbury Tales* Project is using Collate, developed by the author specifically for the collation of medieval vernacular texts.[18] Accordingly, it contains powerful regularization facilities. It is able (for example) to declare that a particular word (e.g. *god*) should be read one way in some places in some witnesses (e.g. to "gode") and other ways in other places in the same or other witnesses (e.g. to "God"). As part of the regularization process, Collate creates a complete record of every regularization it does of every word (or group of words, in the case of word division). The regularization records created by the various collations, of all or some of the witnesses, can be output to "spelling databases." Though these are referred to as spelling databases, they will also include information about punctuation and morphological variation, for example, different verb forms. The spelling databases will permit all the variant forms in them to be sorted, counted, and viewed side by side. One may correlate the distribution of different forms with known facts about the provenance of individual manuscripts or of the geographical and historical distribution of particular forms and use the results to advance knowledge both about the manuscripts themselves and about the linguistic and dialectical variation

---

17. P. M. W. Robinson, "An Approach to the Manuscripts of the Wife of Bath's Prologue," in I. Lancashire, ed., *Computer-Based Chaucer Studies: CCH Working Papers* 3 (Toronto, 1993), 17–47. The two pairs of manuscripts are Hengwrt and Ellesmere; Corpus Christi Oxford and Harleian 7334, characterized by Parkes and Doyle, "Production of Copies," as written by "hand b" and "hand d" respectively. For a different view, see R. Vance Ramsey, "The Hengwrt and Ellesmere Manuscripts of the *Canterbury Tales:* Different Scribes," *Studies in Bibliography* 35 (1982): 133–54, and "Paleography and Scribes of Shared Training," *Studies in the Age of Chaucer* 8 (1986): 107–44.

18. See note 13.

they contain. This information will greatly facilitate studies such as those of Smith and Samuels into the "orthographic layering" of manuscripts.[19]

The principal reason for collation of many manuscripts of a text is, of course, to try to discover what the author actually wrote. An essential step in this process is recovery of the history of the development of the tradition. A reasoned discrimination of what the author wrote (whether as fair copy, cancellation or revision, etc.) from what scribes have interpolated, omitted, or rewritten must be based on a secure and full determination of just how the manuscripts are related to one another. Only then will it be possible to decide exactly at what point a particular reading entered the tradition and to use this knowledge as part of the evidence for or against the originality of a particular reading. In a complex and large manuscript tradition the scale of variation, with around sixteen thousand substantive variants in the witnesses to the Wife of Bath's Prologue alone, defeats manual analysis. The recent application of methods of computer analysis to the reconstruction of the history of textual traditions suggests that computer-aided techniques may succeed where traditional manual methods may not.

Notable among these computer techniques is cladistic analysis. This is a technique developed in evolutionary biology to reconstruct the "family tree" of related species by study of the characteristics they share and do not share. The success of cladistic analysis, working from manuscripts' agreements and disagreements on particular word as generated by Collate, has been demonstrated on a variety of texts, particularly the forty-six manuscripts of the Old Norse narrative sequence *Svipdagsmál*.[20]

The success of cladistic analysis needs some explanation. Fundamental to cladistic analysis is the identification of ancestral readings and their elimination from analysis at every point. Thus: cladistic analysis hypothesizes a tree of descent for the manuscripts. It then "measures" the tree by spreading all the data about manuscript agreements across the tree: the shortest possible tree will be the one involving the fewest variant changes. When thus measuring each hypothetical tree, cladistics identifies just what variants are "inherited" at each node and then rules those out of consideration as it evaluates the tree. This

---

19. See, for example, the essays collected in J. J. Smith's *The English of Chaucer and His Contemporaries* (Aberdeen, 1988).

20. P. M. W. Robinson and R. J. O'Hara "Report on the Textual Criticism Challenge, 1991," *Bryn Mawr Classical Review* 3 (1992): 331–37, and "Cladistic Analysis of an Old Norse Manuscript Tradition," in S. Hockey and N. Ide, eds., *Research in Humanities Computing* 4 (Oxford, 1996).

elimination of "ancestral variants" brings cladistics very close to traditional stemmatic practice of insisting that only "errors," or readings introduced below the archetype, may define subgroups of manuscripts. In fact, cladistics actually elaborates this elimination of ancestral readings further than does traditional stemmatics. Whereas stemmatics only concerns itself with distinguishing readings in the presumed single archetype from all other introduced readings (usually defined as errors), cladistics seeks to identify not just the readings ancestral at the "top" of the tree but those ancestral at every node within the tree. This has a remarkable and most powerful consequence. Because inherited variants are eliminated at every node, wherever it lies in the tree, one does not need to specify beforehand just what variants are ancestral to the whole tree. The tree is unrooted: whichever way it is oriented, the ancestral variants are discounted. Therefore, cladistic analysis offers a way around the paradox of recension identified by Talbot Donaldson: that one cannot create a stemma until one knows what readings are archetypal, but one cannot determine what readings are archetypal until one has a stemma.[21] One can use cladistic analysis to create an unrooted tree, deferring judgment on just what readings are ancestral to the whole tree until one has this unrooted tree. Then, one can decide which of the branches of the tree lies closest to the archetype and root the whole tree at this branch. This was the technique used by Dr. O'Hara with the *Svipdagsmál* material.[22]

A further reason for the success of cladistics is that it works explicitly on the tree model. It assumes that a varied group of objects (whether of manuscripts or of species) is the result of a sequence of branching descents over time. Cladistics simply finds the shortest (or most "parsimonious") tree of descent that explains the agreements and disagreements within this group. The overall similarity or dissimilarity of the objects under study, so important in statistical clustering, is unimportant in cladistics. Like species, manuscripts may appear alike but be genetically quite distinct because of their disagreement on just a few key readings: cladistics recognizes this explicitly. There are many types of manuscript analysis (particularly, studies of dialectal, paleographic or other scribal phenomena) for which measures of similarity are appropriate. It may also be appropriate in those cases where contamination between manuscripts has so obscured relationship by descent as to make it impossible to determine

---

21. E. Talbot Donaldson, "The Psychology of Editors," in *Speaking of Chaucer* (London, 1970), 107.

22. Robert O'Hara and I have used the cladistic program PAUP ("Phylogenetic Analysis Using Parsimony"; Swofford 1991) on NEXUS files generated by Collate direct from the collation output. Later releases of Collate will refine the interface between it and cladistic programs.

genetic affiliation. But such cases apart we have every reason to think that manuscripts descend from one another just as do species. Therefore, a tool that seeks to reconstruct the stages of descent is appropriate: cladistic analysis is such a tool.

I have discussed cladistic analysis at some length because it is that rarest of phenomena: a completely new tool that offers fundamental advances far beyond what might be achieved simply by the refinement of existing methods. The availability of cladistic analysis was decisive in persuading us that it was possible to go beyond Manly and Rickert's analyses of the relationships among the manuscripts of the *Canterbury Tales*, and hence that the Project might be worthwhile. Preliminary work suggests that this confidence is reasonably based.[23]

For all its power, cladistic analysis cannot, of itself, explain exactly how each and every witness is related. It can suggest, by way of a "first guess," that there might be a relationship between certain witnesses, but cannot determine just what the relationship is: whether descent from a common exemplar, or one from another. Cladistic analysis may also be misled by contamination into thinking that manuscripts are much more closely related than they are. In order to determine exactly how manuscripts are related, one needs ready access to the variants themselves that evidence a relationship. For example, in pursuing the relationship between Ellesmere (El), Hengwrt (Hg), and Harleian 7334 (Ha4) among the manuscripts of the *Canterbury Tales* one needs answers to questions like "what variants are found in El and in Ha4, and in no more than three other manuscripts, but not in Hg." This is precisely the sort of task at which well-designed databases can excel, providing in seconds what might take hours or days to discover manually. The *Canterbury Tales* Project uses a variant database facility built into Collate for just this purpose. This database facility will also be available to work on other traditions.

One should not expect that the reconstructions of manuscript traditions hypothesized with these tools will provide conclusive evidence of the originality of any one reading. Rather, we conceive this information as an additional tool in the hands of scholars. For example, if it can be shown that a particular reading first appeared in Ha4, and was thence introduced into El, that information might dispose a scholar to doubt the authenticity of that reading since Ha4 appears to contain widespread evidence of scribal, nonauthorial, intervention in its text.

---

23. Robinson, "Approach to Manuscripts."

I have concentrated here on the rather special case of an important work in many manuscripts. Most Middle English texts exist in only a few manuscripts, or in only one. For these texts, the heavy artillery of collation and cladistic analysis described earlier is unnecessary. However, computers can still provide powerful help for editors of these texts. Once one has a machine-readable version of the text (whether of one manuscript or many, or of the editor's own reconstructed text), a concordance or index of every occurrence of every word in the text may be made very easily. The information from these can be used to compile glossaries, or to forward stylistic and authorship studies. A variety of text analysis packages, many of them free, are available on many different machines for these purposes. The oldest, and still in some ways the most flexible of these, is the Oxford Concordance Program.[24] This began life as a mainframe package and is now also available in a microcomputer form, as Micro-OCP, distributed by the Electronic Publishing division of Oxford University Press.[25] OCP is a "command-driven" program and runs in a batch mode: one asks the program to index or concord a particular text, and then waits (perhaps, for quite a long time) while the program runs the job. The freeware Macintosh concordance program Conc works in a similar fashion.[26] The command language built into OCP permits framing of the most sophisticated queries, with searches on collocations, "wild-card" searches, and all manner of output sorting possible. However, the delay between query and result inherent in OCP's architecture can be frustrating. Other text analysis programs avoid this delay by having the program operate on an indexed file: only a much smaller index, and not the whole text file, need be searched in response to queries. Both the commercial search-engine WordCruncher and the freeware text analysis package TACT work in this manner.[27] All of these tools have their own virtues, well suited to the different needs of different scholars.

---

24. S. Hockey and J. Martin, "The OCP Program Version 2," *Literary and Linguistic Computing* 2 (1987): 125–31.

25. The mainframe version of OCP is available from Oxford University Computing Services, 13 Banbury Road, Oxford OX2 6NN, UK. The personal-computer version, Micro-OCP, is distributed by Oxford University Press, Electronic Publishing, Walton Street, Oxford OX2 6DP.

26. Conc is available as "freeware" from the International Academic Bookstore, Summer Institute of Linguistics, 7500 Camp Wisdom Road, Dallas, TX 75236, USA.

27. WordCruncher is distributed by Johnston and Company, Electronic Publishers and Consultants, PO Box 446, American Fork, UT 84003, USA. TACT is available from the Centre for Computing in the Humanities, Robarts Library, Room 14297A, University of Toronto, Toronto, Ontario M5S 1A5, Canada. There are several other text-retrieval packages available beside those here mentioned: e.g. askSam and GOfer. For details of these and further discussion of the packages here outlined see C. Davis, M. Deegan, and S. Lee, *Resources Guide, March 1992* (Oxford, 1992), 13–19.

In addition to these, scholars working with text marked up in SGML may find the search, analysis, and presentation capacities of DynaText attractive.[28] Scholars with access to considerable computing power who want the most rapid searches of large corpora of richly marked-up texts (of the size of the complete Migne *Patrologia,* or even larger) are well served by Open Text Corporation's PAT application: it is this that underlies the remarkable performance of the *OED* second edition on CD-ROM.[29]

I remarked at the beginning of this essay that computer methods would change the way editions were made, as well as how they are presented. But the same computer tools available to the scholar who makes the edition can also be made available to the reader who uses the edition. Not only this, but the same base materials (manuscript reproductions, transcriptions, collations) upon which the scholar employs these tools and bases the edition can also be provided to the reader in the context of the electronic edition. We will be providing exactly these facilities in the *Canterbury Tales* Project CD-ROMs. The reader will be able to test and redo every aspect of the scholar's work: to transcribe, to collate, to index, to reconstruct, to hypothesize. In the last sentence of the introduction to their edition of the B version of *Piers Plowman,* Kane and Donaldson forbid assessment of their work by stating it could only be judged by redoing it: "Whether we have carried out our task efficiently must be assessed by reenacting it."[30] That is exactly what editions of the future will permit. Electronic editions may be much less of the authoritarian editor handing down the definitive text, and much more of a partnership between editor and reader. This creates new possibilities, new responsibilities—and new dangers. Our response to these challenges will determine the utility of the new texts we make by these new means.

---

28. DynaText is available from Electronic Book Technologies, One Richmond Square, Providence, RI 02906, USA.

29. Open Text Corporation is at Suite 550, 180 King St., S. Waterloo, Ontario, Canada N2J 1P8.

30. George Kane and E. Talbot Donaldson, *Piers Plowman: The B Version* (London, 1975), 202.

The Reader, the Editor, and the Electronic Critical Edition

Peter S. Baker

Some years ago I wrote to ANSAXNET, the on-line forum for Anglo-Saxonists, "The day is not yet in sight when we will be curling up with a good computer program or relaxing under a tree with our favorite laptop [computer]" (14 Oct. 1991). At the time, the notion that one might someday lounge beneath a tree with an electronic text as one now does with a book seemed barely thinkable: then, as now, electronic texts were used for almost anything *but* reading. Yet I have for some time been fascinated by the possibility—I think, the certainty—that the computer will one day be a medium for readers; that day is still not here, but one can no longer say that it is not in sight. Let's look at the features we will need in computers to make them as easy to read as books:

Better displays. The printed page is very good ergonomically; the closer the computer screen comes to replicating its look, the more comfortable it will be to read from. Screen resolution must be high enough that characters are well formed and spaced, screens must use reflected rather than artificial light, and contrast must be high between characters and background.

Smaller, sturdier machines. The computer must be small and light enough to carry like a book, and sturdy enough that we do not feel we must carry it like a carton of eggs. It should be easy to hold in the hand while operating, and we should be able to hold it in a variety of positions.

Alternative input devices. In a machine used for reading, the keyboard will be in the way; it should be detachable, and we should be able to control the computer with pointing devices such as pens.

I wish to thank Hoyt N. Duggan, John Price-Wilkin, and A. C. Spearing for reading and commenting on a draft of this essay.

263

Longer-life batteries. It is essential that the computer be untethered from the wall socket; we should be able to use it all day without recharging the batteries.

More storage. Already portable computers often come equipped with large hard disks; a typical portable can easily store Chaucer's works. With the advent of CD-ROM drives, a reader can carry the *Oxford English Dictionary* or the *Patrologia Latina* in a purse or jacket pocket.

Cordless modems. We must be able to tap into the vast textual and bibliographical databases now available, whether or not we are near a telephone jack.

All of these goals either have been achieved already or soon will be. I am persuaded that within five years our hypothetical scholar beneath a tree will find the computer as comfortable to read as a book and far more versatile, for a well-equipped computer can, in effect, give the reader access to an entire library of books.

But I am also persuaded that neither improvements in computer technology nor increased availability of electronic texts will be enough to enable the computer to compete with the book as a medium for readers. Until the electronic text offers a reading experience that the book does not, it will remain a specialty item—good for automated analysis, searching, comparison and collation, but not at all for reading. Perhaps the most significant new feature the computer can offer to readers is hypertextuality: the ability to link the text into a web of information that includes related texts, commentaries, dictionaries and other reference works, manuscript facsimiles, artwork, music, and videos. In a hypertext system, the electronic text becomes one element in an electronically replicated cultural context that, in theory at least, may be as open-ended as the real-world context on which it is modeled. The reader will navigate this web of information by following hypertextual links that connect the text to various kinds of related information.[1]

---

1. For hypertext projects now underway, see Caroline Davis et al., *CTI Centre for Textual Studies Resources Guide, March 1992* (Oxford, 1992). Among the significant projects for medievalists are The *Beowulf* Workstation by Patrick W. Conner (see his "Beowulf Workstation: One Model of a Computer-Assisted Literary Pedagogy," *Literary and Linguistic Computing* 6 [1991]: 50–58) and the Seafarer project directed by Allen J. Frantzen, both for the Apple Macintosh. A model for literary scholars in all fields is provided by Jerome McGann's archive of the literary and artistic works of Dante Gabriel Rossetti. This archive is being prepared on the IBM RS/6000 running a version of the Unix operating system, but as it is being marked up in SGML (discussed below), it should be portable to any system equipped with appropriate software and capable of processing the large volume of data the archive contains. For further information, see the World Wide Web site http://jefferson.village.virginia.edu/rossetti/rossetti.html.

If the notion of the hypertextual link seems a little esoteric, try imagining it as an animated footnote. For example, in *The Riverside Chaucer* a note "links" lines 127–40 of *The Parliament of Fowls,* "Thorgh me men gon into that blysful place," to Dante's *Inferno* iii. 1–9, which interested readers must obtain for themselves if they wish to read it.[2] In a hypertext of *The Parliament of Fowls,* the reader could, by pointing at these lines, cause a text or translation of the relevant passage of *Inferno* to appear in a window on the screen. In the ideal hypertext system, the link would be not to a fragment of *Inferno,* but to the relevant passage in a full text of *Divina Commedia,* itself completely outfitted with its own hypertextual links (one of which might, incidentally, lead the reader straight back to this passage of Chaucer). This ideal system, of course, amounts to a complete library of electronic editions, dictionaries, art, and so on, all "annotated" with hypertextual links. It will be a long time before such a library is a reality, but I believe we are headed in that direction more rapidly than many of us realize.

Here I would like to discuss what kind of electronic text will be needed in the ideal system I spoke of, how that text is likely to look to the reader, and how editors of today can prepare their editions in such a way that they will be ready to be integrated into the electronic library of tomorrow.

The major electronic editing projects now under way for Middle English, the *Piers Plowman* project headed by Hoyt N. Duggan and the *Canterbury Tales* Project headed by Norman Blake and Peter Robinson, aim to produce texts of two kinds.[3] One is a diplomatic transcript of a single manuscript. The *Piers Plowman* project, for example, plans to issue in stages transcripts of all witnesses to the text, with annotations and selected facsimiles. The *Canterbury Tales* Project plans to issue transcripts of all manuscripts, tale by tale. These projects will produce archives of unprecedented inclusiveness, which will be useful to medieval scholars in ways that even their creators have not envi-

---

2. Larry D. Benson, ed., *The Riverside Chaucer,* 3d ed. (Boston, 1987), 387, 997.

3. For descriptions of these projects, see Duggan, "The Electronic *Piers Plowman* B: A New Diplomatic-Critical Edition," *Aestel* 1 (1993): 55–75; the World Wide Web site http://jefferson. village.virginia.edu/piers/archive.goals.html; the article by Peter M. W. Robinson in this volume; and the World Wide Web site http://www.cup.cam.ac.uk/Chaucer/ctptop.html. I leave out of this account such projects as the Chadwyck-Healey database of English poetry, which offers digitized versions of editions that are out of copyright. Such projects are at best a stopgap; at worst, they can set back the field of textual criticism by inducing readers to prefer obsolete over current editions and encouraging the belief that such features as a textual apparatus can be dispensed with. Digitized versions of recent printed editions would be better, but still far from ideal since printed editions will be difficult to adapt to the electronic medium.

sioned; however, readers as opposed to researchers may have some difficulty knowing what to make of a disk full of variant versions of a single text: confronted with fifty-one texts of the Wife of Bath's Tale, which one should readers read? Fortunately, the second kind of text both of these projects plan to issue is the critical edition; that is still the most useful kind of edition for readers.

Rather than describe the critical editions envisioned by these projects, I would like to consider the matter from the reader's point of view by looking at a working model of a program for readers of electronic editions that I have been preparing for about five years. By way of disclaimer, I do emphasize the words "working model": the program is not now a useful tool, and I have no plans to create such a tool. Further, it is designed specifically to work with Old English poetry, and so my illustrations are from *The Battle of Brunanburh* and *Beowulf;* but as the issues for Old and Middle English editors are quite similar, nearly identical software would perform equally well for *Piers Plowman* or *Sir Gawain and the Green Knight.*

The program's screen, shown in figure 1, is designed to look familiar to readers of printed editions and users of word processors.[4] Imagine the text as if it consisted of a diplomatic transcript of a base text printed on white paper. On top of that text are several transparent overlays: modern punctuation is printed on one of them; lift the overlay up and the medieval punctuation shows instead. Other overlays contain modern capitalization, word division, and diacritics. There are still more overlays, one for each witness to the text. On each of these are printed just the readings that differ from those of the base text, and each of these variant readings can be switched "on," making it visible, or "off," making it invisible. A reading that is switched "on" covers the reading of the base text. That is how this kind of electronic edition is organized: it consists of a diplomatic transcript of a base text optionally accompanied by instructions for modernizing punctuation, capitalization, word division, and diacritics, and a collection of variant readings, each marked with its source and linked to its proper place in the text.

The editor is responsible for transcribing the base text and collecting and organizing the variants; the editor also decides which variants are significant enough to be reported in the apparatus at the bottom of the screen and which

---

4. The program is written in the C++ programming language for Microsoft Windows. As the general layout of the screen will be familiar to users of Windows, the Macintosh, and many DOS programs (such as WordPerfect 6.0), I will not describe certain standard features of the screen, such as the menu bar, the scroll bar, and the dialog box. I invite the reader to obtain a free copy of this program at the following web site: http://www.engl.virginia.edu/OE/.

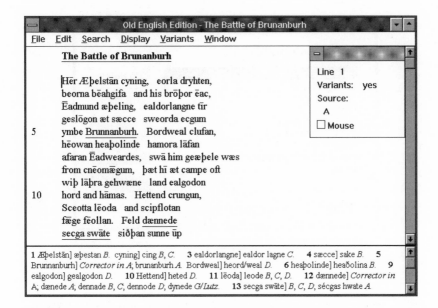

Figure 1

should be displayed in place of the readings of the base text. In figure 1, readings not in the base text are underlined (on a color screen, highlighted in light blue). The apparatus reports that in lines 5 and 12 *Brunnanburh* and *dænnede* are the work of a corrector in the base text, A, not the original scribe; in line 13 *secga swate* is actually from B, though C and D contain the same reading.[5]

But if the editor supplies the text and variants and makes the initial decisions concerning the selection of readings, the reader can also function as an editor, creating a personalized or specialized text. For example, the apparatus for line 1 reports that B reads *æþestan* where the other manuscripts read *Æþelstan*. The reader who preferred the reading of B would first make sure the upright cursor was in line 1 and then bring up the dialog box shown in figure 2

---

5. The manuscripts of *The Battle of Brunanburh* are these: A = Corpus Christi College, Cambridge, ms. 173 (base text); B = British Library, ms. Cotton Tiberius A. vi; C = British Library, ms. Cotton Tiberius B. i; D = British Library, ms. Cotton Tiberius B. iv; G = British Library, ms. Cotton Otho B. xi, as reconstructed by Angelika Lutz, *Die Version G der angelsächsischen Chronik* (Munich, 1981). The manuscript sources are transcribed from Fred C. Robinson and E. G. Stanley, eds., *Old English Verse Texts from Many Sources: A Comprehensive Collection,* Early English Manuscripts in Facsimile, 22 (Copenhagen, 1991).

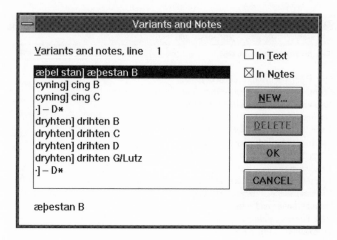

Figure 2

(which, unlike the apparatus at the bottom of the screen, shows a complete list of variants in the line).[6] A variant can be marked for display in the apparatus by highlighting it and checking the "In Notes" box at the top right (the *æþestan* variant is already so marked). Similarly, the reader can mark a variant to be displayed in the text by highlighting it and checking the "In Text" box. After doing so and clicking "OK" or pressing the Return key to dismiss the dialog box, the screen looks as in figure 3. Now the reading *Æþestan* appears in the text instead of *Æþelstan*. Notice several things: First, although the variant reading selected from the list in the dialog box was not capitalized, it is capitalized once it appears in the text; that is because the program is still being instructed to modernize capitalization. Second, I have placed the cursor on the variant reading to illustrate the workings of the box in the upper-right corner of the screen, which reports the number of the line containing the cursor (or the mouse pointer), whether that line contains variants, and the source of the character immediately to the right of the cursor. Finally, the textual note at the bottom of the screen has been rewritten to reflect the change: neither the editor nor the reader writes these textual notes, but they are always generated by the program.

---

6. Because the collection of variants in the *Brunanburh* edition is exhaustive, some of them can be difficult to interpret. Two of the variants in figure 2 concern punctuation only: the dashes signal that the points are not in D, and the asterisks signal that the program will not write textual notes for those variants unless explicitly made to do so.

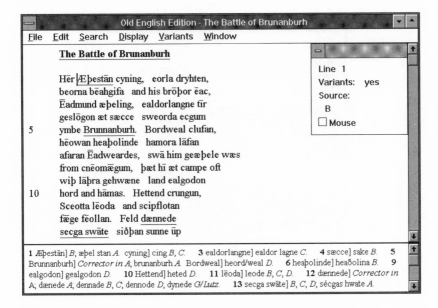

Figure 3

The reader can manage the text not only variant by variant, but also witness by witness, by turning on or off *all* of the variants in any particular overlay. Because the *Brunanburh* edition contains a complete set of variants, for example, it implicitly contains scribal versions of all the manuscripts. To produce such a scribal version, one can bring up the dialog box in figure 4, which lists the overlays, or sources of variant readings. In addition to manuscripts (or scribes like "Corrector in A"), one overlay is reserved for notes on the base text (e.g. "a letter erased between *a* and *b*"), one for the reader who wishes to emend the text (more on this presently), and one for the editor's own emendations. By highlighting an overlay and checking "Suppress," the reader can exclude all variants in that overlay both from the text and from the apparatus. Clicking the "Suppress all" button places a checkmark in the "Suppress" boxes for all overlays, thus instantly producing an unemended version of the base text. By highlighting an overlay and checking "All in text," the reader can cause the program to treat all variants from the overlay as if marked for inclusion in the text. In the dialog box pictured in figure 4, I have suppressed all overlays except the one for manuscript C, which I have marked "All in text." The result is a scribal version of C, which for comparison I here place next to the edited text. To illustrate the program's ability to select medieval or modern acciden-

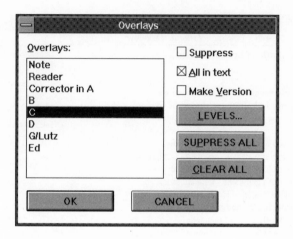

Figure 4

tals, I have turned off the overlays containing modern punctuation, capitalization, and diacritics (the operation took about five seconds):

Edited text		C	
Her Æþelstan cyning,	eorla dryhten,	Her æþelstan cing·	eorla drihten·
beorna beahgifa	and his broþor eac,	beorna beahgyfa	7 his broðor eac
Eadmund æþeling,	ealdorlangne tir	eadmund æþeling·	ealdorlagne tír·
geslogon æt sæcce	sweorda ecgum	geslogon æt sæcce·	swurda ecgum·
ymbe Brunnanburh.	Bordweal clufan,	embe brunnanburh·	bordweall clufon·
heowan heaþolinde	hamora lafan	heowon heaþolinda·	hamora lafum·
afaran Eadweardes,	swa him geæþele	aforan eadweardes·	swa him geæþele
wæs		wæs·	
from cneomægum,	þæt hi æt campe	fram cneomægum	þæt hi æt campe
oft		oft·	
wiþ laþra gehwæne	land ealgodon	wið laþra gehwæne	and ealgodon·
hord and hamas.	Hettend crungun,	hord 7 hamas	hettend crungon·
Sceotta leoda	and scipflotan	scotta leode·	7 scypflotan·
fæge feollan.		fæge feollan	

The program looks a little like a word processor, but works very differently. While users of a word processor have complete freedom to edit the text as they like, this program gives readers no access either to the base text or to the variant

readings, but rather only the ability to decide whether to display variant readings in the text and notes. Thus the reader can override the editor's decisions
concerning the selection of readings, but cannot alter the textual evidence
itself. Further, the reader's actions are nothing more than overlays upon the
editor's work, which is neither discarded nor altered, but can be recovered at
any time. This system in which all editorial activity, whether by editor or
reader, takes place in overlays that leave information at lower levels un-
disturbed, encourages the editor to respect the textual evidence, and the reader
to respect both the textual evidence and the editor's labor and expertise.

Though readers cannot alter the base text or those variants supplied by the
editor, the program does give them a way to add variants to the "Reader"
overlay reserved for their use. For an illustration of the utility of this overlay,
consider the edited text of line 40 of *Brunanburh,* which reads,

mecea gemanan; he wæs his mæga sceard

The apparatus for this line reads,

40 mecea] *B;* mæcan *A;* meca *C;* in ecga *D.*

The reading *mecea* is from B; A reads *mæcan.* Alistair Campbell thought that
D read not *in ecga,* as here, but *mecga,* and he adopted that reading in his text.[7]
The reader who prefers Campbell's reading can bring up the "Variants and
Notes" dialog box for this line, highlight any variant of A's *mæcan,* click the
"New" button, and enter the new reading in a dialog box, shown in figure 5.
When the dialog boxes are dismissed, the new reading is added to the collec-
tion of variants and displayed in the text.[8] The reader can also bypass the
"Variants and Notes" dialog box, entering a new reading where there were no
variants before.

I pass over a number of details and incidental features of the program (e.g.,
searching text, color-coding variants according to source, communication with
other programs). Rather, I will turn to *Beowulf* to illustrate further the utility of
overlays. *Beowulf,* of course, is preserved in a single manuscript, and so overlays are not needed for recording variant readings. They are, however, useful

---

7. *The Battle of Brunanburh* (London, 1938), 88, 94, 110–11.

8. Two features of the "Reader's Emendation" dialog box are not fully explained here: the
"Layer" field allows one to identify layers of revision within a single source, and the "Auto note"
box allows one to decide whether, under certain circumstances, the program will automatically
generate a textual note for the reading.

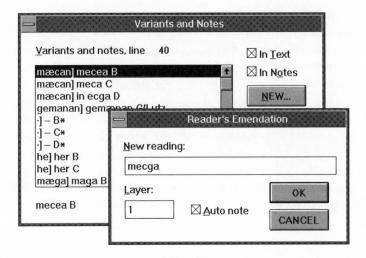

Figure 5

for recording the readings of the Thorkelin transcripts in those places where the manuscript is defective, and they can distinguish different kinds of editorial emendation. Consider, for example, the screen shown in figure 6, where readings from a number of different overlays are displayed in the text:

Corrector in manuscript: 158 *beorhtre*

Transcript A: 160 *deaþscua, duguþe;* 162 *cunnon*

Transcript B: 161 *sinnihte*

Editor's restoration of manuscript (where transcripts cannot supply a damaged passage): 159 *ac se æglæca ehtende wæs*

Editor's emendation (where scribal error is suspected): 149 *secgum*

Normalization (where unusual spellings might cause problems for some readers): 156 *feo;* 158 *banan*

Because different kinds of editorial intervention are isolated in their individual overlays, various groups of readers can easily adapt the text to their requirements. Students, for example, will want to keep the normalizations turned on, while Old English scholars will probably turn them off. Readers who disapprove of emendation on principle can turn the emendations off *en bloc*. Readers who wish to study damaged passages can turn off restorations. And readers who wish to see exactly what remains in the manuscript can turn off the two transcripts. The ways in which electronic texts like this one can be manipu-

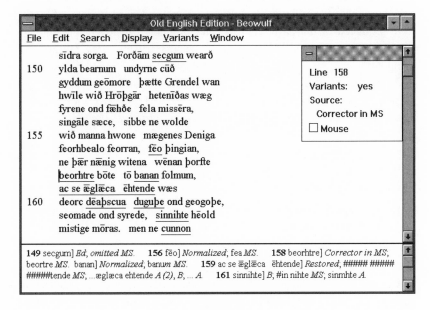

Figure 6

lated would seem to be limited only by the ingenuity of editors and readers. For example, an editor of *Beowulf* could report in separate overlays the opinions of scholars on what is visible in damaged portions of the manuscript; an editor of any text that has been edited before could report emendations proposed by earlier editors.

Even if it does not look exactly like the model I have presented here, the electronic critical edition of the future will be animated and interactive, allowing and even encouraging readers to adapt the text to meet their needs or reflect their theoretical orientations. The methods by which editors produce such editions will differ little in kind from those now in use: editors will still transcribe a base text, collate it with some or all of the witnesses to the text, analyze the relations among those witnesses, select readings for the final, critical text, and, if they wish, modernize accidentals.[9] But editors will produce

---

9. Some of these steps can now be partially automated. To help with collation, editors may use Peter M.W. Robinson's Collate program for the Apple Macintosh (see Robinson, "Collate: A Program for Interactive Collation of Manuscripts," *Old English Newsletter* 24 [1990]: 27–31). Whether this program saves time will depend on whether the editor's method calls for producing complete transcripts of all witnesses to the text—a procedure that will remain unnecessary for

a final product very different from the typescripts and word processor files they have produced in the past. Those earlier products had to be intelligible to human readers; the electronic edition, on the contrary, must be intelligible to a computer.

To illustrate why an edition designed for a human reader may be incomprehensible to a computer, let us consider just two lines (i. 85–86), with apparatus, from R. K. Root's classic edition of *Troilus and Criseyde:*[10]

The noise up ros whan it was first aspied   85
Thorugh al the town, and generaly was spoken,

85. αTh Grete rumour gan (W Grete noyse began; Ph was, Th rose *for* gan). 86. H3RCxTh openly.

Once the organization of this apparatus is understood, it is clarity itself, even though its style is compressed. Greek letters refer to reconstructed archetypes;[11] a Roman capital (optionally followed by a lowercase letter or a number) refers to an existing manuscript or early edition. Since there can be no ambiguity about where these sigils begin and end, there is no need to separate them with punctuation or even spaces. In a note that reports the reading of an archetype, where witnesses descended from that archetype have different readings these are given in parentheses. For example, in line 85 the α archetype (with Thynne's edition) reads *Grete rumour gan* for *The noise up ros,* but W reads *Grete noyse began,* Ph reads *Grete rumour was,* and Th reads *Grete rumour rose.*[12] Notes that do not refer to an archetype generally record either

---

many. Editors who have produced complete transcripts of all witnesses may gain insights into their relations by using a cladistic-analysis program, bearing in mind that, since cladistic analysis takes no account of contamination and assumes that the simplest stemma is the correct one (an assumption that will often be invalid in the messy world of manuscripts), it will rarely provide definitive answers (see further Robinson, "Redefining Critical Editions," in George P. Landow and Paul Delaney, eds., *The Digital Word: Text-Based Computing in the Humanities* [Cambridge, Mass., 1993], 282–83, and his essay in this volume).

10. Robert Kilburn Root, ed., *The Book of Troilus and Criseyde* (Princeton, 1945), 7. The abbreviations for the witnesses are listed on p. xc.

11. Root's classification of manuscripts and reconstruction of archetypes has been challenged by B. A. Windeatt and is not now widely accepted: for a summary of scholarship and references, see Stephen A. Barney's introduction to the textual notes on *Troilus and Criseyde* in *The Riverside Chaucer,* 1161–62. I here use Root's edition because his apparatus presents interesting problems in electronic markup, not because I agree with his views.

12. Because Root's apparatus does not report all spelling variants, these phrases represent only the wording, not the spelling, of the witnesses.

isolated variants or variants in witnesses descended from the β archetype, which is the basis of Root's text. This, then, is a two-level apparatus, containing both variants from the edited text and, quite often, variants from the variants.

If fed the text and apparatus exactly as printed, a properly programmed computer could "understand" much of it, because the apparatus is organized logically and contains clear typographical signals (spaces, capitals, parentheses) marking the functions of various elements in the notes. It would, however, be difficult, and sometimes impossible, for the computer to connect individual notes from Root's apparatus to their proper places in the lines. The reason is that the apparatus rarely refers explicitly to the word or words varied by the witnesses cited in the notes. For example, in line 86 four witnesses have *openly* instead of some unspecified word in the text. It is easy for a reader to decide that the varied word is *generaly,* the only adverb in the line, but to make that decision requires some linguistic expertise, and computers are not yet able to interpret natural languages reliably. More recent editions than Root's typically supply lemmata in the apparatus; in this style the note to line 86 might read, "generaly] openly *H3, R, Cx, Th.*" The computer could connect such a note to its proper place in the text, but only by searching line 86 for the lemma, much as a word processor searches a document. If the computer were required to process a large number of textual notes, these searches would be inefficient; they could also be complicated by lemmata that occur more than once in a line or that contain codes such as word processors insert to switch on italics, underlining, and bold.

Indeed the problems involved in making a computer read the apparatus from any printed edition range from difficult to insuperable. We must abandon the notion that the critical apparatus in any form now familiar to us can be processed by the computer. With that notion we must abandon the common conception of the electronic text as a thing to be read on the screen of WordPerfect or Nota Bene, for if we want truly interactive critical editions, we will find that no word processor can supply the capabilities we need, and no file format devised by a commercial software company can support the kind of instructions that must be coded into the text. Finally, editors preparing electronic editions should resist the temptation to work up ad hoc file formats, as many have done in the past and some continue to do. We need to agree on a file format in which to issue electronic editions. Fortunately, a very good standard is now available.

The Standard Generalized Markup Language (SGML) is a set of rules for devising codes, or "tags," to be embedded in a text to mark its structural features.[13] It is concerned with the *content* of a document, not with the way it might be printed. For example, to mark a title, the user of a word processor inserts tags meaning "begin italic" and "end italic"; in SGML one would instead insert tags meaning "begin title" and "end title," thus distinguishing the title from all other elements that might be italicized.[14] The implication of the SGML philosophy for the processing of electronic texts is clear: while it is very easy for the human reader to infer the information conveyed by the format of a printed page (for example, that the italicized word *for* in Root's note to line 85 marks a lemma and is not a title, not emphatic, not part of the Middle English text), that same task is very difficult for the computer, which possesses nothing remotely resembling human intelligence. It is far better to tell the computer explicitly, "this is a lemma," "this is a line number," "this is a sigil," thus excusing it from tasks it does poorly and allowing it to get on with tasks it does well. Further advantages of SGML are that it is an international standard, not a commercial product, so its continued viability is not tied to the financial health (or the whimsy) of any company, and that one can write an SGML document using just those characters that are recognized by virtually every computer, so it is independent of particular machines and operating systems.

Since 1988, a project called the Text Encoding Initiative (TEI), organized and conducted by scholars in the humanities, has been working up guidelines for encoding various kinds of texts in SGML. The first edition of the TEI *Guidelines* appeared in 1990; a revised and greatly expanded edition is now available both in print and on-line.[15] The goal of TEI is to make its guidelines flexible enough to facilitate the production of many kinds of document, not to impose any ideology or method. Whether this goal is achievable remains to be seen; but SGML itself is flexible enough that the editor who does not find a needed feature in the TEI *Guidelines* should be able to devise a way of encoding that feature while still writing correct SGML. TEI-compliant SGML (TEI/

13. Many descriptions of SGML are available: see Peter Robinson's essay in this volume, and for a more thorough introduction, C. M. Sperberg-McQueen and Lou Burnard, *Guidelines for Electronic Text Encoding and Interchange* 3d ed. ("P3"), 2 vols. (Chicago, 1994), section 1.2 ("A Gentle Introduction to SGML").

14. Some word processors are beginning to incorporate features like those of SGML. In this essay, which I am writing with Microsoft Word, various stretches of text that show as italic on my screen are marked not "italic," but rather "title," "emphasis," "foreign text," and "SGML attribute." As I write, I am trying to decide whether twelve citations of SGML attributes that come later in the essay should be bold rather than italic. If I change my mind, I have only to change the style "SGML attribute," and the twelve citations will be changed automatically.

15. See n. 13 above. The latest revision (P3) is also available in both SGML and PostScript format at an anonymous ftp site (sgml1.ex.ac.uk) and from several other sources. A very convenient on-line version is available at http://etext.virginia.edu/TEI.html.

SGML) is now being used by a number of text archives, including the Oxford Text Archive and the University of Virginia's Electronic Text Center. It will also be used by the Society for Early English and Norse Electronic Texts (SEENET), recently founded by Hoyt N. Duggan and Thorlac Turville-Petre, which, in association with the University of Michigan Press, will issue at least one scholarly edition per year.[16] In short, TEI/SGML appears already to be established as the standard for the electronic encoding of literary texts and to lack serious competition; at present it makes little sense either to adopt any other encoding scheme or devise a new one.

Let us look again at our two lines of *Troilus and Criseyde,* this time marked up in TEI/SGML. There are in fact several ways to encode the passage; I have chosen one that I think both flexible and conceptually elegant.[17]

⟨lg type=stanza⟩⟨s⟩
⟨l n=85⟩⟨anchor id=b85.1⟩ The noise up ros ⟨anchor id=e85.1⟩ whan it was first
          aspied
⟨app from=b85.1 to=e85.1⟩
     ⟨rdg wit='α Th'⟩⟨anchor id=b85.2⟩ Grete rumour ⟨anchor
          id=b85.3⟩ gan
          ⟨anchor id=e85.3⟩⟨anchor id=e85.2⟩ ⟨/rdg⟩
     ⟨app from=b85.2 to=e85.2⟩
         ⟨rdg wit='W'⟩ Grete noyse began ⟨/rdg⟩
     ⟨/app⟩
     ⟨app from=b85.3 to=e85.3⟩
         ⟨rdg wit='Ph'⟩ was ⟨/rdg⟩
         ⟨rdg wit='Th'⟩ rose ⟨/rdg⟩
     ⟨/app⟩
⟨/app⟩
⟨l n=86⟩ Thorugh al the town, and ⟨anchor id=b86.1⟩ generaly ⟨anchor id=e86.1⟩
          was spoken,

---

16. For further information on SEENET, see the World Wide Web site http://jefferson.village. virginia.edu/seenet/home.html.

17. The markup for this passage is fuller than it needs to be, in part to promote legibility. However, the very explicit marking of "from" and "to" points in the text and apparatus, while not necessary when the apparatus is embedded in the text, as here, is recommended, for it allows the apparatus to be moved out of the text and gathered at the end of the file, or in another file. Among the various methods of encoding variants proposed in the TEI *Guidelines,* I consider this "double end-point attachment" method to be most generally serviceable.

I wish to thank Peter Robinson for letting me look at advance versions of two chapters of the TEI Guidelines, "Transcription of Primary Sources" and "Additional Tag Set for Critical Apparatus" (part IV, sections 18 and 19).

⟨app from=b86.1 to=e86.1⟩
    ⟨rdg wit='H3 R Cx Th'⟩ openly ⟨/rdg⟩
⟨/app⟩

The reader's first reaction will, of course, be horror, for the text looks incomprehensible. Bear in mind, however, that it is intended to be read by a computer, not a human being; just as a text designed for a human reader is difficult for a computer to read, so it should come as no surprise that the reverse is true. The important point is that a computer can be programmed to present a text like this one in a readable style—even reproduce the format of Root's edition, if desired—either on screen or on paper. The SGML markup, which makes this passage so ugly, should always be invisible to the reader.

A tag used in SGML to mark a structural feature of a text consists of a word or abbreviation enclosed in angle brackets; other items of information ("attributes") can also be placed between the brackets. A single tag may mark a place in a text: here the ⟨anchor⟩ tag does nothing more than attach an identifier ("id") to a place in the text so that the computer can refer to that place by its identifier.[18] A more common kind of tag marks a stretch of text (an "element") with some structural significance: here the ⟨lg⟩ tag marks the beginning of a line group (specifically a stanza), the ⟨s⟩ tag the beginning of a sentence, and the ⟨l⟩ tag (which also contains a line number) the beginning of a line. Since any sentence, stanza, or line must end before another begins, I need not bother to mark the ends of these structures; rather, I can specify elsewhere that the beginning of one of them implies that the one before it has ended.[19] Often, however, a tag that marks the beginning of an element (e.g., a title or proper name) must be matched by a tag that marks its end. In such cases, the ending tag simply repeats the name of the beginning tag, but with a slash before it. In the sample text, the ⟨app⟩ ("apparatus") tag marks the beginning of a textual note, and the ⟨/app⟩ tag marks its end.

---

18. In my sample text I have chosen identifiers that mean something: "b85.1" means "the beginning of the first variant in line 85," and "e85.1" means "the end of the first variant in line 85." While this style of reference makes no difference at all in terms of computer processing, it is clearer to the human editor than the style used in the TEI guidelines, which appears to advocate numbering anchors sequentially throughout the text.

19. Such information is given in the "Document Type Declaration," or DTD. The DTD is highly technical and difficult to write; fortunately, most editors will be able simply to copy the relevant portions of the DTDs supplied by the TEI, or even ignore the problem altogether: SEENET, for example, will issue standard DTDs and work with editors to adapt them to the needs of individual editions.

The apparatus for line 86 is simpler than that for line 85, so let us begin there. The ⟨app⟩ tag that begins the textual note contains two attributes, *from* and *to,* signaling that the stretch of text referred to starts at the tag ⟨anchor id=b86.1⟩ and ends at the tag ⟨anchor id=e86.1⟩. These place references serve the same function as the lemma in a conventional apparatus, but are much easier for the computer to handle: it would be easy, for example, for the computer to delete the text between the two anchors and replace it with a variant reading, or to copy out the same text and print it as the lemma in a textual note. Inside the ⟨app⟩ tags is another element, tagged ⟨rdg⟩ ("reading"). The opening tag contains a *wit* ("witness") attribute, identifying those witnesses that contain the variant reading, and between the opening and closing tags is the variant reading itself. Had there been another variant for this place in the text, I could simply have reported it immediately after the first one, and in the same style, thus:

⟨app from=b86.1 to=e86.1⟩
    ⟨rdg wit='H3 R Cx Th'⟩ openly ⟨/rdg⟩
    ⟨rdg wit='Yy'⟩ prively ⟨/rdg⟩
⟨/app⟩

Had any witness omitted the word altogether, I could have reported nothing between the ⟨rdg⟩ tags:

⟨app from=b86.1 to=e86.1⟩
    ⟨rdg wit='H3 R Cx Th'⟩ openly ⟨/rdg⟩
    ⟨rdg wit='Yy'⟩ prively ⟨/rdg⟩
    ⟨rdg wit='Zz'⟩ ⟨/rdg⟩
⟨/app⟩

The apparatus for line 85 works just like that for line 86, with this difference: there are variants among the descendants of the α archetype (for which the sigil has been replaced with a special code called an "entity reference").[20] These variants are recorded by marking the text inside the ⟨rdg⟩ tags with

---

20. An entity reference is nothing more than a string of characters that stands for one or more characters (an "entity"): the ampersand marks the beginning of the entity reference and the semicolon marks its end. Here I use an entity reference instead of α because many computers do not have α in their character sets, and those that do often store it internally in quite different ways. The entity reference, on the other hand, contains only characters that virtually all computers recognize. A program written for a computer capable of displaying Greek characters could substitute α for the entity reference.

⟨anchor⟩ tags, just as in the main text,[21] and supplying textual notes nested within the ⟨app⟩ tags of the larger textual note, thus:

⟨app⟩

    . . .

    ⟨app⟩

       . . .

    ⟨/app⟩

⟨/app⟩

The α variant appears as a tiny edition, complete with its own apparatus. The computer can handle such nested elements very well; the indentation of the inner note, while not really necessary, makes it easier for the human reader to follow.

Suppose that the scholar preparing the electronic edition decided that the variant *openly* belonged in the text of line 86 instead of *generaly.* In the tradition of the printed edition, the ordinary procedure would be to insert the variant in the text and report the reading of the base text in the notes. In TEI/ SGML the result might be encoded as follows:

⟨l n=86⟩ Thorugh al the town, and ⟨anchor id=b86.1⟩ openly ⟨anchor id=e86.1⟩
                  was spoken,
⟨app from=b86.1 to=e86.1⟩
    ⟨lem wit='H3 R Cx Th'⟩ openly ⟨/lem⟩
    ⟨rdg wit='α β γ'⟩ generaly ⟨/rdg⟩
⟨/app⟩

Here one must insert a ⟨lem⟩ ("lemma") element to report explicitly which witnesses contain the reading *openly;* the format of this element is like that of ⟨rdg⟩. The reading of the base text (β or β) must be reported in the ⟨rdg⟩ element along with the readings of those witnesses that agree with it. Given this much information, the computer could reconstruct the β text with perfect reliability.[22]

---

21. Strictly speaking, the last two ⟨anchor⟩ tags in the variant reading could have been one, since only one place is being marked. However, to simplify various kinds of text processing, I prefer to mark the beginning and end of every lemma explicitly with its own tags, even if the beginning or end of two lemmata coincide.

22. A method similar to this one would be most suitable for editions (like many classical editions) in which the text is not represented as a transcript of a single witness. In such an edition, however, the ⟨lem⟩ element is not necessary, as it can be assumed that any witnesses whose readings are not reported in the apparatus are in agreement with the edited text.

However, earlier in this paper I suggested that, in an electronic edition, the body of textual evidence might be separated from the work of the editor by leaving the base text unaltered and letting the computer perform the work of constructing the critical text. To produce this kind of edition, we need some way of telling the computer to display variants in the text. The current draft of the TEI *Guidelines* suggests the following method:

⟨l n=86⟩ Thorugh al the town, and ⟨anchor id=b86.1⟩ generaly ⟨anchor id=e86.1⟩
                was spoken,
⟨app from=b86.1 to=e86.1⟩
        ⟨rdg resp=PSB wit='H3 R Cx Th'⟩ ⟨corr⟩ openly ⟨/corr⟩ ⟨/rdg⟩
⟨/app⟩

Here the reading *openly* is marked with a ⟨corr⟩ ("correction") tag to indicate that it is proposed as a correction to the base text; the *resp* ("responsibility") attribute in the ⟨rdg⟩ tag indicates that the editor "PSB" is responsible for proposing the correction. Given the information that "PSB" is the current editor, the computer could automatically insert the reading *openly* in the text. A possible problem with the example above is that placing the *resp* attribute in the ⟨rdg⟩ tag suggests that "PSB" is somehow responsible for the readings of the four witnesses H3, R, Cx and Th. It would be better to move the *resp* attribute to the ⟨corr⟩ tag, thus:

        ⟨rdg wit='H3 R Cx Th'⟩ ⟨corr resp=PSB⟩ openly ⟨/corr⟩ ⟨/rdg⟩

Now the tags state correctly that "PSB" is responsible for suggesting *openly* as the "correct" reading of the text. The *resp* attribute would more logically be placed in the ⟨rdg⟩ tag when an emendation was proposed without manuscript authority:

        ⟨rdg resp=PSB⟩ ⟨corr⟩ prively ⟨/corr⟩ ⟨/rdg⟩

The ⟨corr⟩ tag, being embedded in the ⟨rdg⟩ element, would "inherit" the *resp* attribute from it.

But matters are beginning to look needlessly complicated. The problem of where to place a *resp* attribute, while important from a programmer's point of view, may well seem annoyingly trivial to the scholarly editor: should we really have to worry about such stuff? Further, the kinds of computer processing likely to be set in motion by ⟨rdg⟩ and ⟨corr⟩ seem pretty much the same:

since both tags enclose matter that may be displayed in place of the reading of the base text, do we really need both of them?[23] An alternative is to stretch the meaning of the *wit* attribute a bit, declare the current editor and, indeed, all previous editors to be "witnesses" to the text, and report manuscript readings and editorial choices in exactly the same way. There can be no difficulty with this method, as long as the sigils for manuscripts are distinguished from those for editions in the electronic "front matter" of the edition;[24] the method conforms fully to the TEI/SGML specification. And it certainly cuts back the number of tags the editor must learn to work with.

Let's mark up line 86 of *Troilus and Criseyde* again, this time introducing two imaginary editors Smith and Jones, an imaginary manuscript Zz, and a new attribute for the ⟨rdg⟩ tag:

⟨l n=86⟩ Thorugh al the town, and ⟨anchor id=b86.1⟩ generaly ⟨anchor id=e86.1⟩
             was spoken,
⟨app from=b86.1 to=e86.1⟩
    ⟨rdg wit='Zz' type=orthographic⟩ generally ⟨/rdg⟩
    ⟨rdg wit='H3 R Cx Th PSB' type=substantive⟩ openly ⟨/rdg⟩
    ⟨rdg wit='Smith' type=substantive⟩ prively ⟨/rdg⟩
    ⟨rdg wit='Jones' type=substantive⟩ ⟨/rdg⟩
⟨/app⟩

The apparatus tells us that one manuscript reads *generally* for *generaly,* that four manuscripts have *openly* for *generaly* (a reading adopted by editor

---

23. The ⟨corr⟩ tag and the related ⟨sic⟩ tag are likely to be most useful in editions of texts in single manuscripts. For example, in J. R. R. Tolkien and E. V. Gordon, eds., *Sir Gawain and the Green Knight,* 2d ed., rev. N. Davis (Oxford, 1967), line 58 reads "Hit werere now gret nye to neuen" in the manuscript, and the editors emend *werere* to *were.* The change could be encoded in the text itself, without ⟨anchor⟩ tags or an ⟨app⟩ element, in either of two ways:

Hit ⟨corr sic="werere")were(/corr⟩ now gret nye to neuen
Hit ⟨sic corr="were")werere(/sic⟩ now gret nye to neuen

The first example inserts the emendation in the text and reports the manuscript reading in the tag; the second leaves the text unaltered but recommends an emendation. A computer could produce either an emended or an unemended text from either of these examples. I suspect that ⟨corr⟩ and ⟨sic⟩ will rarely be suitable for scholarly editions: an editor of *Sir Gawain* who wished to report the conjectures of earlier editors would have to use the ⟨app⟩ method to do so.

24. The current version of the TEI/SGML *Guidelines* suggests placing a list of witnesses (tagged ⟨witList⟩) at the beginning of the edition. Within the list the full name of each witness (tagged ⟨wit⟩) would be associated with its sigil. The specification for the ⟨wit⟩ element could usefully be expanded by the inclusion of a *type* attribute allowing the editor to specify whether the witness is a manuscript or a printed edition, and whether it is to be regarded as a primary or secondary source.

"PSB"), that editor "Smith" emends *generaly* to *prively,* and that editor "Jones" emends by dropping the word *generaly.* The *type* attribute classifies each variant: the current draft of the TEI *Guidelines* suggests "orthographic" and "substantive" as useful types, and others might include "punctuation," "dia-critic," or "normalized." A further type, "emendation," is implicitly expressed here by the lack of manuscript authority for the readings of Smith and Jones. This apparatus presents a great deal of information that even a relatively simple program like mine could process in a variety of useful ways. For example: If the program were informed that "PSB" was the current editor, it could initially display in the text all variants marked "PSB." It could be instructed to display only substantive variants in the apparatus at the bottom of the screen. It could be instructed to exclude all emendations from the apparatus or the text. It could reconstruct any witness, or the edited text of "Smith," "Jones," Tyrwhitt, Skeat, or Robinson. Since all of these tasks can be performed by processing just the two tags ⟨app⟩ and ⟨rdg⟩, any software that handles them, whether a hypertext "reader" or a publisher's page layout program, can be kept relatively simple. And since the ⟨app⟩ and ⟨rdg⟩ tags are inherently flexible, the number of uses to which they can be put is limited primarily by the ingenuity of the editor, and the software need not anticipate those uses.

In this quick introduction to the production of electronic critical editions I have omitted a great deal. Those who intend to produce such editions should refer to the current edition of the TEI *Guidelines* (P3 or later) for fuller information. Writing in TEI/SGML will not be easy at first, even with the help of word processors that use SGML as their native language;[25] specialized software designed to ease the task of scholarly editors will be a long time in coming. But the reward for preparing editions in this new way will be very great indeed: it will be nothing less than to participate in the reconceptualization of the text, the library, and the act of reading itself.

---

25. One such word processor is Author/Editor by SoftQuad, available for Microsoft Windows, the Macintosh, and Unix. WordPerfect (versions 7 and higher) also enables users to edit and validate SGML documents.

Postduction

"Glosynge Is a Glorious Thyng, Certayn"

David Greetham

Invoking such an unseemly character as Chaucer's Summoner may not look very auspicious for my "postduction": lecherous, drunken, disfigured, flatulent, corrupt, hypocritical, ventriloquistic, and bearing a "stif burdoun" to his sexually ambivalent and equally rapacious "compeer," the Pardoner, he is hardly a positive role model. But unattractive as the Summoner, his tale, and his companion may be, the qualities of disfigurement, corruption, ventriloquism, and so on are appropriate emblems for my position and task in this volume. Like the Summoner in the General Prologue, I come near the end of this procession, a "theoretical" hanger-on among these "practical" textual folk, an ancillary member of a professional discourse that, while it may recognize that it needs the services of an interlocutor to connect with the postlapsarian world of poststructuralism and other dispensations inimical to the dissemination of revealed truth, may still find the forced relationship with "theory" an uncomfortable marriage of convenience, a sign of these latterday corrupting times. In the language of Lyotard's *Postmodern Condition,* both Western Christendom and the positivist philology inherited from the Enlightenment have become symptoms of those master narratives that have lost their coherence and power to "comprehend" the totality of discourse that they formerly commanded.[1] With the breakup of such narratives in a postmodernist entelechy and epistemology, characters like the Summoner and David Greetham will serve either as a means of accommodation to the new realities or as suspect and perhaps fraudulent testimony to the decline of moral and scholarly rigor.

Gerald Graff, for example, has seen the attempt by scholarly editing to align itself with "theory" as a symptom of the loss of prestige and power of the

---

1. Jean-François Lyotard, *The Postmodern Condition: A Report on Knowledge,* trans. Geoff Bennington and Brian Massumi (Minneapolis, 1984), esp. xiii, 37. See my *Theories of the Text* (Oxford, 1997), esp. "Textual Theory and the Territorial Metaphor," for an account of the textual significance of Lyotard's thesis.

philological discipline within the academy. He argues that if textual study can appear "relevant" in the current configuration of our profession only through this uncomfortable alliance with theory, then the glory days of editing as the sine qua non, the ne plus ultra, the rite de passage for entry to the profession are clearly over and that editing is merely fighting a rearguard battle by temporarily aligning itself in a compact that would in better days have been seen as a union with the forces of darkness.[2] Conscious of the widely held suspicion of theory in such apparently empiricist redoubts as scholarly editing, I have consistently turned Graff's figure of alignment on its head: rather than theory being a corrupting latecomer to the philological feast, I have held that theory has always been present at the symposium of editing, but that, like Banquo's ghost, it can be seen only by those who, like Macbeth, have some guilty secret about their role in the festivities. Like Ralph Hanna (who has maintained that annotation, by dispersing its residual authority throughout an edition, symptomatises a "guilty knowledge" that editors possess but cannot admit to)[3] I have argued that the power of editing is not in its apparently positivist empiricism, which becomes an embarrassment in these poststructuralist days, but in its hermeneutics, its conceptual construction of an active, interpretative, phenomenology of text, answering more to a Heideggerian historicized *Dasein* than to a transcendental phenomenology in the manner of Husserl and Hirsch.[4] This persuasion, that philology is not "prehermeneutic" but is the hermeneutic circle writ large, has led me to reject both Paul de Man's argument that "the turn to theory occurred as a return to philology, to an examination of the structure of language prior to the meaning it produces"[5] and to question

---

2. See the account of these fraught relations in my "Resistance to Philology" (*Margins of the Text* [Ann Arbor, 1997]) and in the introduction to *Theories of the Text.* My basic position is that what we now call theory has always been a part of editorial and text-critical operations, but that an acquired institutional blindness, confirmed by nineteenth-century positivist empiricism, has led to our inability to "see" theory. I therefore question Gerald Graff's assertion (*Professing Literature: An Institutional History* [Chicago, 1987], esp. 354) that textual theory and literary theory occupy two different parts of the intellectual map and that the fortunes of textuists depend on their making an alliance with literary theorists.

3. Ralph Hanna III, "Annotation as Social Practice," in *Annotation and Its Texts,* ed. Stephen Barney (Oxford, 1991).

4. See the "Phenomenology" and "Intention" chapters of my *Theories of the Text* for a full account of this important distinction between transcendental and historicized phenomenology and the ramifications on textual practice. For a summary account see my review-essay, "Practise! Practise!" (*Text* 7 [1994], esp. 467–69). The problem of local, historicized, and mutable meaning on the Heideggerian model surfaces in this current collection in Helen Cooper's essay on "miswriting" and in Douglas Moffat's account of the concept of meaning in a glossary.

5. Paul de Man, "Return to Philology," in *The Resistance to Theory* (Minneapolis, 1986), 24. See my "Resistance to Philology" for the argument against de Man's contention that philology is

the validity of Jonathan Culler's call for an "anti-foundationalist philology."[6] Put bluntly, if theory and conceptual hermeneutics have always been "in" textual editing, they cannot now be "added" to it, and thus Graff misperceives the figure of alliance, de Man celebrates a quality that is merely an illusion, and Culler foresees a condition that is already present. According to this reformulation of the relationship between the master narrative and its postmodern avatars, the Summoner and I, through the very act of "corrupting," suborning, and ventriloquizing the positivist discourse and showing its breaks and fissures, become the proper exemplars of the "hermeneutics of suspicion" that, I have argued, is the founding metaphor for textual study.[7]

But the Summoner and I have more in common than just this role of belated interrogators of a failed or incomplete narrative: just as, under the aegis of

---

"pre-hermeneutic." The issue of whether the sort of linguistic analysis that de Man promotes can pre-exist a hermeneutic response is taken up in this collection in the essays by Lucas and Mills.

6. Jonathan Culler, "Anti-Foundational Philology," in *On Philology*, ed. Jan Ziolkowski (University Park, Pa., 1990). Using a long-outdated model, Culler argues that philology needs to free itself from its "foundationalist" (i.e., positivist and empiricist) pretensions and instead should promote an "anti-foundational" epistemology to show how "philological projects rely uncritically on literary and cultural conceptions that come from the domains of thought that are supposedly secondary" (50). In "Resistance to Philology" and elsewhere, I claim that Culler has overlooked the critical, interventionist, hermeneutic, philological procedures of many textual critics and editors, from Bentley to Housman to Tanselle and McGann. This question of the proper and usual bounds of "philology" is explored in the present volume in, for example, Norman Blake's account of the inherent conservatism of what he calls "philological editions."

7. See, for example, my "Suspicion of Texts" (*Thesis* 2 [1987]: 18–25), "[Textual] Criticism and Deconstruction" (*Studies in Bibliography* 44 [1991]: 1–30, rpt. in *Textual Transgressions: Essays toward a Biobibliography* [New York, 1997]). My figure of "suspicion" derives from Eugène Vinaver's claim that the phrase "textual criticism" implies a "mistrust of texts" ("Principles of Textual Emendation," in *Studies in French Language and Literature Presented to Professor M. K. Pope* [Manchester, 1930], 351–69, esp. 352). There is some irony that this motto derives from a textual scholar who, in the same essay, declared that the "scientific" editing of medieval texts had now been successfully achieved by implementation of Bédier's "best-text" theory (see "La Tradition manuscrite du *Lai de l'Ombre:* Réflexions sur l'art d'éditer les anciens textes," *Romania* 54 [1928]: 161–96, 321–56; rpt. as pamphlet, 1970). For a recent account of the theoretical and practical implications of Bédier's "scientific" claim, see Mary B. Speer, "Old French," in *Scholarly Editing: A Guide to Research,* ed. D. C. Greetham (New York, 1995). The theme of "mistrust" and the relations between the "hermeneutic" and "scientific" affiliations of textual criticism and editing occur at various points in this current collection, for example, in Mary Hamel's account of sources, Norman Blake's depiction of a medieval reader "making the best of a text," in A. S. G. Edwards on manuscript and text, in McCarren and Moffat's coverage of recension and "deep editing," in McCarren on manuscripts and scribes, in Lucas and Mills on *LALME,* Moffat on dictionaries, Mooney on catalogs and microfilms, Keiser on hypercorrection, and so on. The issue of mistrust versus fidelity will obviously continue to be a major procedural, technical, and moral question for textuists. See my "Textual Forensics" (*PMLA* 111 [1996]: 32–51) for a survey of this problem under the auspices of a postmodernist interrogation of the value and interpretation of textual evidence.

postmodernism, no edition can, with an epistemological straight face, refer to itself as "definitive" (in the sense of having fixed the text for all time), so this *Guide* will not arrest or finally determine the textual critique of Middle English texts. All Chaucerians will doubtless have already spotted that my attribution of the "glosynge" epigraph of my postduction to the Summoner is a co-optive misrepresentation: the speaking voice within those quotation marks is in fact the Friar, the target of the Summoner's scabrous, sacrilegious,[8] and scatological tale of the "gift" of the divisible fart—a problem in "arsmetrike." The Summoner is *imputing* to his enemy the Friar, through the act of ventriloquism that is the storyteller's function and prerogative, a Scholastic opinion that acquires a further level of "glossing" by being put into the mouth of a professional rival, for whom "glosing" is the technical skill ("the best beggere in his hous") that will reveal the hidden meaning, money—or fart. That is, the conflict between the Friar and Summoner for control of the narrative of story-telling (with each ventriloquistically placing the other inside his own tale) is emblematic of the "real-life" struggle between friars and summoners as rival "glossers" (interpreters) and "glosers" (flatterers): if a friar can offer "plesaunt . . . absolucioun" (for a price—"a good pitaunce") he undercuts a summoner's authority to "curs" for moral crimes; and if a summoner can "excuse" a "good felawe to have his concubyn" (for a price—a "quart of wyn"), he undercuts a friar's "power of confessioun." Each thus presents a misprision of the other's narrative, deliberately presenting as "hard" a "reading" of the rival text in order to advance his own role as glosser.[9]

All of the pilgrim-narrators and "glossators" are, of course, practitioners of this ventriloquism (and thus suppression of one set of quotation marks), and the

---

8. For example, when the Summoner relates the story of the friars in Hell living inside Satan's arse, he is very likely offering a misprision of the famous mural in Pisa (probably seen by Chaucer) in which the Friars in Heaven are given special favor by sheltering under the Virgin's cloak. This misquotation and misglossing of a cultural icon is, of course, one of the main rhetorical methods of the Wife of Bath, whose biblical "gentil text" ("Go forth and multiply") is buttressed by her selective misquoting and misglossing of, for example, Saints Paul and Jerome (see III (D) 142–43; 158–59). In this volume, Douglas Moffat attends to the problem of the "construction" of gloss as a separate and (mis)representative discourse. See the "Supplément" chapter of my *Theories of the Text* for an account of the text/gloss question in current textual speculation.

9. The conflation (and confusion) of "glossing" and "glosing," with the ironic implications I have suggested, occurs at various places in Chaucer; for example, "I kan nat glose, I am a rude man" (Merch. 2351); LGW G "For in pleyn text, it nedeth nat to glose"; "And therewithal so wel koude he me glose" (Wife 509); "Ye shal ek sen, youre fader shal yow glose / To ben a wif" (*Troilus* 4.1471–72); "Glose who wole, and seye bothe up and doun / That they were maked for purgacioun / Of uryne" (Wife 120–22). The nature and function of the cumulative glossing that is the glossographical text is, of course, central to Vincent McCarren's account in this volume.

ventriloquist par excellence is the "repertour" of the tales at large, the Geoffrey Chaucer who writes himself out of the glossing contest by constructing a text *(Sir Thopas)* so comically inept that the Host's interrupting gloss ("drasty rymyng") is at the same time both an appropriate commentary and a (typical) failure to observe the embedded levels of voice within the narrative.[10]

But the Summoner is a particularly apt figure for my epigraph on glossing since it is ventriloquism, speaking in another's voice through a co-opted precedent text, that is his characteristic mode of discourse. The "fewe termes" of Latin that he "lerned out of som decree" provide him with the rhetorical formulas ("Ay 'Questio quid iuris' wolde he crie") that set him up as glossator of precedent texts of which he has no direct knowledge. Combined with his vernacular mottos ("'Purs is the ercedekenes helle,' seyde he"), these belated tags, occasioned and reinforced by wine, become a pervasive part of his professional armory and serve to advance his standing as glossator and ventriloquist. His manner is the epitome of the gloss as free play (Derridean *jeu*), unsecured by the substance of the text it supposedly comments upon. So dangerous is this successful glosing/glossing that he is the only pilgrim whom the narrator Chaucer the pilgrim actually accuses of misprision: "But wel I woot he lyed right in dede."

Why then would I want to align myself and my role in this volume with such a dangerous and deceitful character? If corruption and misrepresentation are indeed the singular features of the Summoner as professional and as tale teller, why should my postduction be sullied by such a cohabitation? I have in part provided answers to this general epistemological question (what is the nature of commentary and what is the function of the multilayered speaking voice in scholarly editing?) in some of my recent work.[11] I have argued that the Summoner-like misprisions of commentary and editing through the assumed

---

10. The concept of authorial/editorial ventriloquism as figure for the "composition" of a text out of multiple voices has recently become one of the most-debated issues in textual criticism. See my summary account in "'What Does It Matter Who Is Speaking,' Someone Said, 'What Does It Matter Who Is Speaking,'" in *The Editorial Gaze,* ed. Paul Eggert and Margaret Sanger (New York: 1997). Adopting the "voice" of another (author, scribe) as an aspect of this "ventriloquism" is inferentially confronted in the essays in the current volume by Jacobs, and McCarren and Moffat. Edwards sets himself an even more complex metaventriloquistic task by dealing with the pedagogical problem of acting as yet another interpretant and speaker, in his essay on the teaching of alliterative verse.

11. In addition to "What Does It Matter" (n. 10), see also the chapter on "Intention" in *Theories of the Text.* I have examined the function of rhetoric and its relation to evidence and textual "fact" in "Textual Forensics" and in "Naming of Parts; or, Bibliographical-Textual-Comical-Historical-Pastoral" *(Bulletin of the Bibliographical Society of Australia and New Zealand* 19 [1995]: 167–93, esp. 172–73).

voice(s) of the textuist are as endemic to bibliography, paleography, annotation, and textual criticism as they are to any other historicized hermeneutic. I have, for example, used Peter Davison's argument that, even in "strict and pure" bibliography, "we *find* differences in running titles, in spellings, types; from this we *create* evidence about compositorial practice; upon this we *base* our conjectures" (105).[12] And I have co-opted G. Thomas Tanselle's thesis that Simon Schama's apologetics for the mixing of fact and fiction in *Dead Certainties/Unwarranted Speculations* is too concessive, for in declaring that "historical knowledge must always be fatally circumscribed by the character and prejudices of its narrator,"[13] Schama adopts as a liability that very quality that Paul Needham, with Tanselle's approval, embraces as the paradigm for bibliographical speculation: that historical awareness and belated commentary on the artifacts of the past depend on "creative thinking"[14] and not on "a specific knowledge [of incunables]."[15]

I am obviously cautious in associating the pragmatic historicism of our leading bibliographical commentator with the misprisions of the Summoner and his conflation of "glosing" and "glossing." But the Summoner's ventriloquistic foisting of the language of my epigraph on his enemy the Friar and his free-floating glosses on unknown and unknowable texts are just particularly egregious examples of the dangers of a glossing that operates without any normative protocol beyond that of self-advancement. That the Summoner's glossing is successful in this postlapsarian world testifies to the failures of rhetoric and demonstration in that world. As Tanselle notes, the "truth" of an hypothesis "depends on whether it can stand up to criticism" (284), for "the limit that human perception places on verification is simply a given in everything we do, and we proceed from there" (286). If all editing and textual criticism, as forms of historical and hermeneutic enquiry, are inevitably glosses on a precedent text, then the function of glosses on glosses (like Chaucer's

---

12. Peter Davison, "The Selection and Presentation of Bibliographical Evidence," *Analytical and Enumerative Bibliography* 1 (1977): 101 (qtd. in "Textual Forensics," 34).

13. Simon Schama, *Dead Certainties/Unwarranted Speculations* (New York, 1991), 322; qtd. G. Thomas Tanselle, "Printing History and Other History," *Studies in Bibliography* 48 (1995): 286; qtd. D. C. Greetham, "Naming of Parts," 171.

14. Tanselle, "Printing History," 284. The concept of editorial "creative thinking" is particularly challenging in those genres that were originally identified as "difficult" in the proposal for this volume: see especially Keiser on scientific texts, Mooney on astrological texts, Hieatt on culinary texts.

15. Paul Needham, "Slipped Lines in the Mainz Catholicon: A Second Opinion," *Gutenberg Jahrbuch* (1993): 25, qtd. Tanselle "Printing History" 284, qtd. Greetham "Naming of Parts," 171.

upbraiding of the "lie" in the Summoner's motto) is to interrogate the substance of the gloss (which now becomes a precedent text) and its position in the ongoing epistemological history of the discipline.[16]

What appeared to Charlotte Brewer as the "lie" of Kane-Donaldson's B-Text *Piers* (i.e., its glossarial or belated misrepresentation of the textual conditions and the authorial dispersal of *Piers*) was demonstrated not just in the series of critical glosses on that edition but by the rival hypothesis that the Z-Text manuscript provided more direct access to the "text" that was Langland's original intention.[17] To George Kane, however, this Z-Text was evidence not for authorial intention but for that scribal misprision that he had already recorded as the garbled misconstruction of intention.[18] Like the Friar and Summoner, Kane and Brewer offer a series of glosses on one another's text, seeking to give textual precedence to their own construal of meaning and to make the other's a glossarial misprision. In this ongoing march of precedent texts and glosses, each gloss reconstrues the previous hypothesis as itself a misrepresentative gloss. It can be no other way, for the dialectic that is textual criticism feeds on shifting binaries whereby the roles of text and gloss are continually reversed and reinterrogated. The Summoner glosses the blank and absent text and makes his own gloss (on the Friar) into a text. It is indeed a glorious thing.

---

16. Perhaps the best-known bibliographical "lie" (after Valla's unmasking of the *Donation of Constantine* as a papal fraud) was the "lie" in T. J. Wise's "forgeries" of nineteenth-century "first editions": a gloss misrepresenting itself as a precedent text (i.e., precedent to those texts that had formerly been acknowledged as "first editions"). When Carter and Pollard, in glossing Wise, argued that the kernless type used by Wise did not actually appear until after 1883—although the Wise "first editions" dated from the 1840s—they reversed the precedence of text and gloss. See John Carter and Graham Pollard, *An Enquiry into the Nature of Certain Nineteenth-Century Pamphlets* (London, 1934) 2d ed.; ed. Nicholas Barker and John Collins, *A Sequel to "An Enquiry into the Nature of Certain Nineteenth-Century Pamphlets"; The Forgeries of H. Buxton Forman and T. J. Wise Re-Examined* (London, 1983).

17. See, for example, "Authorial vs. Scribal Writing in *Piers Plowman*," in *Medieval Literature: Texts and Interpretation,* ed. Tim William Machan (Binghamton, 1991), 59–89; "The Textual Principles of Kane's A-Text," *Yearbook of Langland Studies* 3 (1989): 67–90; *Piers Plowman: The Z Version,* ed. Charlotte Brewer and A. G. Rigg (Toronto, 1983). The problem of intentionality as valid editorial rationale is taken up in this volume by, for example, Blake, Jacobs, and Fellows.

18. George Kane, "The 'Z' Version of *Piers Plowman*," *Speculum* 60 (1985): 910–30. See my summary account of the implications of this debate in "Reading in and around *Piers Plowman*," in *Texts and Textuality,* ed. Philip Cohen (New York, 1996); and see A. S. G. Edwards's setting of the contention over the *Piers* text within the wider issues of Middle English editing in his "Middle English," in *Scholarly Editing,* ed. D. C. Greetham (New York, 1995), an essay that offers the most perceptive analysis of Middle English textual editing to date.

Maybe. For now I must appear to shift into the assigned rhetoric and genre of this postduction: "a paper assessing the foregoing statements from the perspective of current theoretical debate within and beyond the field of textual criticism" was once the brief given to me and my postduction in the contents for this volume. This is an uneasy genre to occupy—somewhere between the review-essay and the publisher's blurb, or between the "gloss" and the "glose." I'll admit that I brought it on myself, for when Douglas Moffat and Vincent McCarren first approached me about a contribution to their collection (to question "assumptions about what 'text' is" [correspondence, 6 October 1992]), I turned their abstract formulation toward the practical: what if my precedent texts for this questioning were to be those very essays assembled in the volume? More work, of course, but perhaps an apt demonstration of the text/gloss relationship that I found most challenging. In this way, I might further "problematize" the genre of the response, both resident within and yet partly outside the collection, by placing it in this ambiguous ground between "gloss" and "glose."

This is a ground I have become familiar with, for a good deal of my recent work has been of the scholiastic, marginal commentary, post- and preductive type.[19] Indeed, the figure of the alien, transgressive observer, a free-floating and ungrounded commentator practicing what contemporary cultural anthro-

---

19. See, for example, "Textual Scholarship," in *Introduction to Scholarship in Modern Languages and Literatures,* ed. Joseph Gibaldi (New York, 1992); my prefaces to Jerome McGann's *A Critique of Modern Textual Criticism* (Charlottesville, 1992) and Peter L. Shillingsburg's *Scholarly Editing in the Computer Age* (Ann Arbor, 1996, 3d ed.); my response "If That Was Then, Is This Now?" to Alexander Pettit's special (largely eighteenth-century) issue of *Studies in the Novel* on editing the novel (fall, 1995): 427–50; my review-essays from "outside" or "in the margins" of a period or discipline, e.g., on the *Cornell Yeats* ("'Changed, Changed Utterly / A Terrible Beauty Is Born'" *Yeats: An Annual of Critical and Textual Studies,* 1995); on the *Cornell Wordsworth* (forthcoming in *Analytical and Enumerative Bibliography*); my reviews of, say, Jack Stillinger's *Coleridge and Textual Instability* (Oxford, 1993), in *JEGP,* forthcoming, George Bornstein's *Representing Modernist Texts: Editing as Interpretation* (Ann Arbor, 1991), ("Total Utterance and the Modernist Voice," in *Yeats: An Annual of Critical and Textual Studies* 1992), W. Speed Hill's *New Ways of Editing Old Texts: Papers from the Renaissance Society of America* (Binghamton, 1993) in *Modern Philology* 93 (1995): 249–53, Harold Love's *Scribal Publication in Seventeenth-Century England* (Oxford, 1993) in *Papers of the Bibliographical Society of America* (1995): 101–4, and of Bornstein, Hans Walter Gabler, and Gillian Borlan Pierce's *Contemporary German Editorial Theory* (Ann Arbor, 1995) for *Modern Philology,* forthcoming. My general point is that the lack of a "medieval" or any other center to my work has perhaps made me a useful figure for looking at a discipline from outside and offering speculative comments that would be more difficult for professionals working *within* a discipline or specialty to articulate. Ironically, it may have been my relatively thin medieval credentials (compared with the other contributors to this volume) that led the editors to co-opt me.

pologists have designated as the "poetics of dispersion," has gradually become the operative and enabling metaphor for my critical method. So it was quite fitting that Professors Moffat and McCarren should assign me the postduction, and that I should push this genre further toward the scholiastic and glossatorial by suggesting a response to the precedent texts of their book.

The complicating problem was that, as the book began to be formulated, it changed its contours, its contents, maybe even its purposes, so that the relation between response and precedent text became ever more contingent, temporary, and free-floating, with the attendant dangers that Chaucer noted about the unsecured and free-floating glosses of the Summoner. The book became a shimmering, unstable series of intertextual relations, as each shift in contents, balance, organization, and emphasis produced a different compendium with a different meaning. Topics came and went, contributors fell in and out, sections of the book were renamed, and parts of the text were moved from one section to another. The greatest problem for me was that, as the book's shape changed, so the themes under which I had proposed to conduct my theoretical response were gradually cut free from the text I was responding to, or changed in their relationship to it. Thus, the original concerns of my "theoretical" essay were to have been sources, annotation, and difficulty—all of which have become critical issues in a poststructuralist climate. But one of the three topics ("Editing in Difficult Genres" in the original table of contents for the book) disappeared completely, its contents subsumed under other taxemes; another ("Annotation") lost its author and then changed its coverage; and the third ("Sources") went through a series of intertextual shifts. It was almost as if the editors were trying to emulate bibliographically the unstable and contingent ephemeralities of the medieval book itself, so different from the relative consistency and integrity of the modern book. Or perhaps that they were out to demonstrate to this glossator the validity of Hans Zeller's argument that every variant in a text produces a new work, for each recalibration of the text sets off ripples that construct new relations in the composite of text that is "tissue" and "network."[20] Tanselle's practical demurral against Zeller's prescription (that by his concept of text and work the multiple variants in Emily Dickinson's "Those fair-fictitious People" would produce 7,680 "works")[21] was brought forcefully

20. Hans Zeller, "A New Approach to the Critical Constitution of Literary Texts," *Studies in Bibliography* 28 (1975): 231–64. See also Donald H. Reiman, "'Versioning': The Presentation of Multiple Texts," in *Romantic Texts and Contexts* (Columbia, 1987) and the essay on versioning by Fellows in the current volume.

21. G. Thomas Tanselle, "Editorial Problem of Final Authorial Intention," *Studies in Bibliography* 29 (1976), esp. 208.

home to me when I saw entire sections of the book I was to comment on dismantled before my eyes, when "versioning" became the preferred mode of textual production by many of the contributors, and when my own essay (still unwritten) continued to be assigned different titles[22] and find different bedfellows, from a group on "The Edition in the World," whose members changed with each new reformulation[23] to a solitary position just before the appendices (am I in the "text" proper or not?).

This history of book production is not a "Compleynt" or *Planctus.* On the contrary, the *mouvance* that I encountered and documented in the ongoing construction of *A Guide to Editing Middle English* was not only a nice reflection of my interest in glossing the variant but also demonstrated that the editors and the contributors were sensitive to textual relations and to the variable hermeneutic that these relations embodied.[24] The variance even gave me a chance to play editor myself, for I could construct variorum editions of the changing texts and could speculate on the potential complexity of interauthorial intentions and expectations as drafts passed across my desk, sometimes to be superseded by revised texts that I did see, sometimes not. Thus variance was both pertinent to the assignment and made it fun.

But my play in the text could not entirely remove that unease about the Summoner's free-floating or unsecured gloss. Like the editor/readers of *Piers* or *The Canterbury Tales* or any other multiple-witness, versionist text, I have read *A Guide to Editing Middle English* several times in its several documentary states, but I am (again, like many, perhaps most Middle English editors) not yet certain that I "comprehend" the final shape, content, and intention of the

---

22. From "Editing Practice and Theory" (as per the editors' original invitation) to "The Impact of Current Theoretical Issues on Editing" to "Postduction"—my favorite.

23. The original members were Helen Cooper, Nicolas Jacobs, and Tony Edwards, to which I was added. Then Jacobs (first assigned to write on "The Status and Utility of the Authorial Text") was transferred out of the "World" to the "Author, Scribe, and Editor," where his brief became "Kindly Light or Foxfire? The Authorial Text Reconsidered", Cooper (at one time writing under the rubric "A Comparison of Editions of Chaucer") and Edwards were shifted to "Perspectives" and the "World" vanished. Throughout this round of musical titles, only Edwards held on to his "Editing and [the] Teaching [of] Alliterative Texts," though the contextual significance of his essay kept shifting.

24. On the new philology and *mouvance* see, Bernard Cerquiglini, *Éloge de la variante: Histoire critique de la philologie* (Paris, 1989) and commentary by, for example, Stephen G. Nichols, "Introduction: Philology in a Manuscript Culture," *Speculum* 65 (1990): 1–10; Suzanne Fleischmann, "Philology, Linguistics, and the Discourse of the Medieval Text," *Speculum* 65 (1990): 19–37; Sherry Reames, "*Mouvance* and Interpretation in Late Medieval Latin: The Legend of St. Cecilia," *Medieval Literature: Texts and Interpretation* (see n. 17): 159–89; Derek Pearsall, "Theory and Practice in Middle English Editing," *Text* 7 (1994): 107–26, esp. 123–25; and Mary B. Speer, "Old French" (see n. 7).

book. Like the Hengwrt scribe who left a blank page rather than the unresolved link at the end of the Man of Law's Tale (who is speaking about his/her "joly body"—the Shipman, the Squire, the Summoner, the Wife of Bath?); who was unaware at the time of the inscription that there was a latecomer (the Canon's Yeoman) still to be added to the roster; and who waited patiently for the completion of the Cook's Tale and eventually had to admit defeat in the "gap" of the text ("Of this Cokes tale maked Chaucer na moore"), I felt the text of my *text,* on which my *gloss* was to be constructed, slipping through my hands and forever unreachable. In other words, I was reading a medieval text. The slippage made me nervous as well as excited, for I kept thinking about a particularly embarrassing moment when the shifting relations between text and response had caused me public chastisement and pain.

"I hear you have double-crossed me, David." The Bowers smile, part-ironic, part-avuncular, flashed on and off, and I was left bewildered as the dean of American bibliography walked into the auditorium to deliver his first address to the Society for Textual Scholarship in 1981. What could he mean? Fredson Bowers was a respondent at that meeting of STS, delivering one of his famous "*X:* Another View" essays, a rhetorical genre that allowed him to take up the issues raised in a precedent text and then to bring the weight of his scholarship and range of reference to show these issues in a light undreamed of by the precedent author. This match of discourses worked only if the two texts (text and commentary if you like) remained relatively stable in their relationship: "Another View" could be just that only if the target text under such view did not continually reform itself. And the re-formation of the precedent text would be particularly problematic if it was undertaken *in response to* "Another View": the "*supplément*" would then have become another precedent text for further visions and revisions. This, I learned later, was what had happened to Bowers: the draft of his response to Claire Badaracco's "The Editor and the Question of VALUE" had been sent to Badaracco as a courtesy, but she had then revised her original "Proposal" in the light of Bowers's criticisms without informing either him or me. As he walked into the conference session, he had just learned that the text of which he thought he was presenting "another view" had disassembled itself and that he was about to talk into a deconstructive *mise en abyme,* with one text continually embedded in another. No wonder he felt he had been "double-crossed."

This cautionary tale has obvious lessons for all "supplementary" authors, especially those who are engaged to construct a postduction for a multiform and variant range of texts: make sure your target "text(s)" remain stable or you will find yourself staring down into that *mise en abyme* that Bowers faced; try to preserve the distinction between text and commentary or intertextual chaos will invalidate any sense of sequential linearity. But as most postmodernist textuists now recognize, and as most medievalists have known for centuries, the lessons, while sound in principle, are untenable in the realities of text production. Texts, perhaps particularly premodern texts, do not meekly obey generic or discourse requirements; they do not stand still while belated commentators try to fix their sights on them; texts are composites of the two main strands of their etymology—the *textus* as "authority" and the *textile* as weave or pattern—and, like Penelope continually weaving and unweaving a tapestry, textual critics, editors, and composers of postductions or "other views" participate willy-nilly in the reforming and reinvention of the figures in the carpet.

This collusion of the postmodern and the medieval meant that it was thus no cultural accident that in the *Supplément* chapter of my *Theories of the Text,* which confronts this textual *mise en abyme,* the greater part of the illustrative citations embedded in the six levels of commentary and supplementary annotation are drawn from recent writings by medievalists (especially on the concept of the postduction or supplement) and by theorists and practitioners of hypertext and hypermedia.[25] Hypertext has made visible what toilers in the fields of medieval textuality have generally accepted but been unable to chart effectively within the constraints of the print medium: that intertextual penetration and consubstantiation is the norm, not the aberration, in medieval textuality, and that postmedieval (especially modernist) essentialist theories of genre and form[26] cannot adequately represent the documentary pluralism, fragmental-

---

25. See the essays by Baker and Robinson in the present volume and my further account in "Phylum-Tree-Rhizome," *Huntington Library Quarterly* 58 (1996): 99–126.

26. See my "Editorial and Critical Theory: From Modernism to Postmodernism" (*Palimpsest: Editorial Theory in the Humanities,* ed. George Bornstein and Ralph Williams [Ann Arbor, 1993]) for a general account of editorial modernism and postmodernism. Note that Lee Patterson ("The Logic of Textual Criticism and the Way of Genius," in *Textual Criticism and Literary Interpretation,* ed. Jerome J. McGann [Chicago, 1985]) sees the Kane-Donaldson edition of *Piers Plowman* as an emblematically New Critical, "modernist" work of scholarship, but that Anne Middleton ("Life in the Margins; or, What's an Annotator to Do?" in *New Directions in Textual Studies,* ed. Dave Oliphant and Robin Bradford [Austin, 1990] and Robert Adams ("Editing *Piers Plowman B:* The Imperative of an Intermittently Critical Edition," *Studies in Bibliography* 45 [1992]: 31–68) both interrogate the propriety of this formulation and editorial method for a complex text like *Piers.* I see a nice cultural irony in the fact that medieval textual studies may be more in tune with contemporary post-Platonist views of text than, say, the great "formalist" editions of the canon of Anglo-American nineteenth- and twentieth-century literature produced under the auspices of the MLA's Center for Editions of American Authors and Center for (later Committee on) Scholarly Editions. See the "Formalism" chapter of my *Theories of the Text* for a further account of how textual scholarship, especially in its medieval manifestation, is an exemplar of the postmodernist

ism, and antidisciplinary cross-fertilizations of the postmodern and the pre-modern.[27] In a wonderful cultural and historical hermeneutic circle, it has taken the destabilizing electronic configurations of hypertext to embody the medieval condition of *mouvance,* and it is therefore no surprise that hypertext has been seized on by medievalists as a particularly fruitful medium for the productive display of the "web" we have felt to be the presiding figure of medieval textuality.[28]

The emblem of the *tree (Stammbaum)* dominated nineteenth- to late-twentieth-century textual editing because this was the period (roughly from the late Enlightenment to analytical philosophy) when a form of philological positivism attested to the evidentiary value of a sequential, linear, and hier-archical arrangement of data. The stemma of classical Lachmannian historical philology was simply an iconic adumbration of this underlying thesis: given enough data, the textual universe will be seen to cohere as a totalizing struc-ture, just as the physical universe would eventually yield its form in a unified field theory. Whether or no quantum mechanics and postmodernist deferral combined will render the thesis itself untenable, there can be little doubt that the tree organization of textuality has begun to lose its efficacy as a presiding figure, to be replaced by the rhizome structure (or grass) of Deleuze and Guattari.[29] That is, the conflational and indeterminate web manifest in the navigation of hypertext is rhizomelike, in that there is no fixed head or Aristo-telian beginning, middle, and end; the tree of Lachmannian stemmatics ab-horred contamination (indeed, as Maas acknowledged, contamination could not be adequately plotted in the two-dimensional space of the *Stammbaum),*[30] whereas the hypertext demands it.

I can testify to this iconic slippage in my own work. As a neophyte textual

---

interstitial breakdown of modernist great narratives, including that of a singular, coherent textuality.

27. See, for example, Peter M. W. Robinson's electronic *Canterbury Tales* project (e.g., Robinson, "Collation, Textual Criticism, Publication, and the Computer" *Text* 7 [1994]: 77–94), Hoyt N. Duggan's *Piers Plowman Archive* (Ann Arbor, 1995–). Note that, following the lead of Jerome J. McGann's *Complete Writings and Pictures of Dante Gabriel Rossetti: A Hypermedia Research Archive* (see McGann's rationale and description, *Text* 7 [1994] 95–105), the term *archive* rather than *edition* is the preferred generic marker for hypertext/hypermedia textual projects, and that the *Piers* archive had to struggle to free itself from modernist, hierarchical formulations inherited from the print medium (see my "Reading in and around *Piers Plowman,*" n. 18).

28. I explore the epistemological and procedural implications of this shift from tree to rhizome in my essay "Phylum-Tree-Rhizome" (see n. 25).

29. See Gilles Deleuze and Félix Guattari, *A Thousand Plateaus: Capitalism and Schizo-phrenia,* trans. Brian Massumi (Minneapolis, 1987).

30. Paul Maas, *Textual Criticism,* trans. Barbara Flower (Oxford, 1958).

editor, I did not question the hierarchical tree figure employed in the collaborative editing of Trevisa's *Properties of Things* and continued to use the icon in
yet more complex trajectories (as for example in my treatment of stemmatic
relations across language and/or influence boundaries, cited in Mary Hamel's
treatment of "sources" in this volume). And while the hierarchical model
began to slip a little in the mapping of the editing protocols of Hoccleve's
Regement of Princes (with a potentially circular flow-chart of operations re-
placing a purely linear configuration), the force of the underpinning stemma
still compromised the move away from the hierarchical. In one of my current
projects, a hypermedia archive of citation, the tree is almost entirely subsumed
within the rhizome, even though citation may, of course, be epistemologically
constructed as the relations between a precedent and postductive text: source
and derivative.

And it is this double bind of the source and derivative, text and gloss, that
underwrites the problematic rhetoric of my postduction. If we accept James C.
Nohrnberg's argument that "every isolatable unit in a given discourse functions
as a comment on, supplement of, or gloss upon some prior instance of that
discourse, right back to the clearing of the throat in advance of the externaliz-
ing of articulation,"[31] then only the "silence" that preceded the editorial articulation of this present collection can possibly be regarded as not part of the
glossarial, postductive rhetoric that I have now implausibly taken as my peculiar responsibility. Is this book itself a gloss and a postduction? Well, yes, of
course. It is a collection of belated commentaries on texts that have long since
been historicized by our culture as betraying "l'éloignement du moyen âge, la
distance irrécupérable qui nous en séparé" (Zumthor, *Essai de poétique médi-
évale*). But if, as Nohrnberg contends, any one of these early texts is itself "a
tissue of glosses, that render the unreadable as readable" (12), is not the main
task of the belated glossers in this book and their even more belated glosser in
this postduction to confer legibility, or at least visibility, on the text-cum-
gloss?[32] How then, have the contributors to this collection responded to this
task? And if, as Nohrnberg also maintains, that these precedent texts "are not

---

31. James C. Nohrnberg, "Justifying Narrative: Commentary within Biblical Storytelling,"
(Annotation and Its Texts, ed. Barney, see n. 3), 3.

32. See Anne Middleton ("Life" see n. 26, esp. 179) on the function of glossator to confer
"legibility" on a text. See also Ralph Hanna III ("Annotating" see n. 3, esp. 154–58) versus Derek
Pearsall (*Piers Plowman: An Edition of the C-Text* [London, 1978]) on the concept of plenitude in
legibility, where Hanna argues that Pearsall makes the text of *Piers* too legible by providing more
annotation and a "deeper or denser or richer text" than the author "had in mind" (155). See my
analysis of this and other problems in citation and allusion in my forthcoming *Copy/Right.*

perceived as glosses, because they have already fallen into a prior pattern of coherence that establishes their unity as discourse and therefore marginalizes attempts to supplement that unity—or that coalescence of discourse—as glosses" (12), then what prior pattern of coherence might the contributors have discovered in Middle English texts, and what pattern in their discoveries would I have discerned if I had written a postduction that was *only* a response? In so doing, conferring a formal, proprietary shape onto these essays assembled here, would I have therefore been guilty of compounding the dissimulation already practiced by the authors? For if I were to look for patterns in the "coalescence of discourse" called *A Guide to Editing Middle English,* would I not have obscured the rhizomelike structure of these glosses under the pretence that they were really trees? The bind is, as Nohrnberg recognizes, that "one has to speak as if we can distinguish the text from the glosses, which are typically identified as instances of inconstant specification, parenthetical or interpolated comment, internal but nonetheless extracontextual reference, overdetermined prose discourse, editorial cross-referencing, and the like" (13).

In my role as postductor I have been speaking so, conscious of the impropriety of that speech and of its duplicitous nature, but unable to proceed without admitting a contingent structuralist bar between text and gloss as a convenient protocol for my occasional piece. As I have already suggested, I am therefore seeming to admit to the "guilty knowledge" that Ralph Hanna argues is the empowering metaphor for annotation (after all, you as reader would never have known about the generic shifts, structural revisions, and individual textual variants in the history of this book if I had not admitted to them, would you?). By placing the discourse of my essay as somehow *outside* or *after* the discourses of the essays *in* the book proper, I may appear to be recognizing the supplementary and now-coherent knowledge that Hanna claims is usually dispersed throughout an annotated edition. If all of this had been so, here would have been some guilt-free, but nonetheless corrupt, glosses. But it is not so, and as quasi-commentator on this *Guide* I embrace not my singularity and separateness but my involvement in the *graft*[33] that is this and all other "volumes." When, on a conference roster heavily populated by medievalists, Derrida announced *(orally,* at a meeting of which the proceedings were to be *published),* "This Is Not an Oral Footnote,"[34] he was playing on the two occasions and two media in which that statement would be transmitted, as well as on the supple-

---

33. See my analysis of the "graft" as "very figure of textuality" and its relations to medieval textuality and editing in the "Supplément" chapter of *Theories of the Text.*
34. Derrida, "This Is Not an Oral Footnote," in Barney (see n. 3).

mentary nature of the footnote to the "superior" text. When I admit that I will only hint at the "guilty knowledge" I might have had as scholiast, and when I play with the possibility of this essay serving as a "footnote" of explication to the real text above it, I have doubtless failed to fill my contractual obligations to produce a gloss on this book, but in so doing I have produced a glos[e]. *Explicit.*

Appendices

A Practical Guide to Working with Middle English Manuscripts

The following guide is aimed at the novice editor or student of manuscripts. It will acquaint the beginner with the scholarly works that must be consulted in order to describe a Middle English manuscript accurately, and it is intended to offer suggestions that should allow common errors or oversights to be avoided. Each of the many topics introduced in the following pages could be the subject of a book, and most have been.[1]

Locating Manuscripts

Usually one begins the task of editing by trying to locate the manuscript copies of the work to be edited. Even if this work has been settled upon in the course of looking at a particular manuscript, the search for other manuscript copies will start from the work itself. Therefore, one must be familiar with the various bibliographical resources used by all Middle English scholars, since these bibliographies usually indicate the manuscripts in which a particular work occurs. If the work to be edited is in verse, then the primary bibliographical source will usually be Carleton Brown and Rossell Hope Robbins, eds., *The Index of Middle English Verse* (The Index Society: New York, 1943) and its *Supplement,* ed. Rossell Hope Robbins and J. L. Cutler (Lexington, 1965).

This appendix is a collaboration. The lion's share of the bibliographical work and the early drafts were done by Roy Michael Liuzza. He felt, however, that he could not take credit for the final form of the work, but we would like to thank him for allowing us to use his material. The general editors take responsibility for this version but acknowledge the advice of A. S. G. Edwards and George R. Keiser.

1. A more comprehensive treatment of most of the topics to be discussed in this appendix can be found in D. C. Greetham, *Textual Scholarship: An Introduction* (New York and London, 1994).

For prose works the situation in Middle English is less satisfactory in regard to bibliography, although it is steadily improving. For works that have already appeared in print, one can consult Robert E. Lewis, N. F. Blake, and A. S. G. Edwards, eds., *The Index of Printed Middle English Prose* (New York, 1985). This bibliography does not cover documents, records, and so forth, nor does it treat dissertation editions of Middle English prose, but these have been covered by B. S. Donaghey and G. A. Lester, "A Checklist of Middle English Prose in Theses," *Leeds Studies in English,* n.s., 19 (1988), 167–202. An *Index of Middle English Prose* is being planned, to be based on a series of *Handlists* of particular collections that have been appearing since 1984. Obviously, until this *Index* appears an efficient and comprehensive search for manuscripts containing a particular Middle English prose text will not be possible. However, the sophistication of the indices in the *Handlists,* arranged according to *incipit, explicit,* and subject matter, increases the cast of one's bibliographical net.[2]

Another important source of bibliographical information that connects Middle English works with their manuscript locations is *The Manual of Writings in Middle English,* the ongoing expansion of the J. E. Wells's *Manual.* Each bibliographical entry in the *Manual* begins with a list of the surviving manuscripts of a work. The *Manual* is organized according to subject and therefore treats both verse and prose, and it aims to provide its users with a wide range of bibliographical information. It must be borne in mind that it is not primarily an index attempting to present the user with a comprehensive list of texts and all the known versions of them; the lists of manuscripts it gives, therefore, are not necessarily complete.[3]

If further searching beyond the range of the Middle English bibliographies is required, one must turn to the catalogs of libraries. For manuscripts located in Great Britain, the Middle English editor will go in the first instance to N. R. Ker, *Medieval Manuscripts in British Libraries,* 4 vols. (Oxford), vol. 1: *London,* 1969; vol. 2: *Abbotsford-Keele,* 1977; vol. 3: *Lampeter-Oxford,* 1983; vol. 4: (with A. J. Piper) *Paisley-York,* 1992. For North American locations, see Seymour De Ricci and W. J. Wilson, *Census of Medieval and Renaissance Manuscripts in the United States and Canada,* 3 vols. (New York, 1935, 1940;

---

2. Reference to some specialized bibliographies can be found in the essays by Keiser, Hieatt, and Mooney in this volume. Another such work is Veronica M. O'Mara, "A Checklist of Unedited Middle English Sermons that Occur Singly or in Small Groups," *Leeds Studies in English,* n.s., 19 (1988): 141–66.

3. If you are confused by an off-hand reference to a manuscript for which no precise ascription is given, like the Thornton Manuscript or the Vernon Manuscript, you might find the information you seek in Wilma Fitzgerald, *Ocelli Nominum: Names and Shelf Marks of Famous/ Familiar Manuscripts,* Subsidia Mediaevalia, 19 (Toronto, 1992).

rpt. 1961). This last should be used in conjunction with Christopher Faye and William H. Bond, eds., *Supplement to the Census of Medieval and Renaissance Manuscripts in the United States and Canada* (New York, 1962), and Jeanne E. Krochalis and Jean F. Preston, *Teachers' Guide to Finding Western Medieval Manuscripts in North American Collections* (Kalamazoo, Mich., 1988).

Ker's catalog does not describe muniments, and more importantly he had to omit the massive collections of medieval manuscripts in the British Library, the Bodleian Library at Oxford, Cambridge University Library, and the National Libraries of Scotland or Wales (1:v–vi). The first three in this list in particular contain vast numbers of Middle English manuscripts. However, Ker does provide, at the appropriate heading in his catalog, references to printed and unprinted catalogs of these important collections. Useful in finding other catalogs of medieval manuscripts is Leonard O. Boyle, *Medieval Latin Palaeography: A Bibliographical Introduction,* Toronto Medieval Bibliographies, 8 (Toronto, 1984), nos. 1442–1510. Also of continuing importance for the location of published and unpublished catalogs is Paul O. Kristeller, *Latin Manuscript Books before 1600: A List of the Printed Catalogues and Unpublished Inventories of Extant Collections,* 3d ed. (New York, 1965). See also G. Dogaer, "Quelques additions au répertoire de Kristeller," *Scriptorium* 22 (1968): 84–86, and C. H. Lohr, "Further Additions to Kristeller's *Repertorium,*" *Scriptorium* 26 (1972): 343–48.

In searching for descriptions of a particular manuscript, one should not overlook the introductions to editions of other works that appear in that manuscript. For more recent studies, periodicals like *Manuscripta, Scriptorium,* and *English Manuscript Studies: 1100–1700* should be perused.

Obtaining and Using Copies

Once you have located the manuscript you want to study you must obtain a copy of it. Unless a facsimile edition exists (see appendix B), this almost always means a roll of 35 mm microfilm. L. N. Braswell, *Western Manuscripts from Classical Antiquity to the Renaissance: A Handbook* (New York, 1981), nos. 511–51, lists sources and collections of microform manuscript materials in North America and elsewhere. Of particular note for students of Middle English is the British Manuscripts Project, a collection of 2,652 reels of microfilm devoted to manuscript collections in England and Wales. A large number of Middle English manuscripts are included. A few North American research libraries have complete sets of this collection, and the Library of Congress sells copies of individual films at a relatively low cost. See Lester K. Born, *British Manuscripts Project: A Checklist of Microfilms Prepared in England and Wales for the American Council of Learned Societies, 1941–45* (New York, 1955, 1968). Normally, however, one must write directly to a library to request a microfilm copy of any manuscript; addresses for European libraries can be found in R. C. Lewanski, *European Library Directory: A Geographical and Bibliographical Guide* (Florence, 1968), and the annual *World of Learning* (42d ed., London, 1992). First write a letter explaining your interest and requesting a price; most libraries expect payment in advance, in their native currency. In most cases, libraries also require a signed agreement that one will not publish any reproductions of the manuscript without permission. If you plan to include a facsimile of a particular page in your finished edition, write later, explaining your intentions, and request a larger and better-quality photograph.

There are many opinions on the use of microfilms for manuscript study. Microfilms save time, and even the costliest ones are less expensive than an airfare. However, microfilms are often blurry, dishonest, dim, and immensely frustrating. They are almost never in color, so distinctions of capitals or different shades of ink, which might distinguish a scribe from a later corrector, are nearly impossible to detect. (Some libraries supply negative copies, whose only advantage is that different shades of ink often appear with stark clarity.) A hole in a manuscript that lets a letter from the page below peek through can look like a bizarre reading that you may spend hours trying to interpret; a speck on the film can look like a mark of punctuation. The size and shape of a page are often disguised by the magnitude of reproduction. A tightly bound book will distort or lose the first or last few letters of each line in a shady gutter down the middle of each exposure, and folds and creases can prevent accurate reading; marginalia are sometimes not photographed. Furthermore, of course, microfilms are useless for understanding the composition of a book, its collation, and the details of parchment or binding that might tell you something crucially important about the text.

In short, studying a microfilm, or even a fine facsimile, of a manuscript is never a substitute for looking at the manuscript itself. Nevertheless, despite its limitations, examining the photographic copy of the manuscript is always important preparation for dealing with the manuscript itself. It allows you to become familiar with the handwriting, the location and order of the texts, and the scattering of difficult or obscure readings in a text. Time spent with the microfilm increases the efficiency of time spent with the manuscript.

To see the manuscript you will need permission. Always write first, long before you make any irrevocable reservations for your travel. University and cathedral libraries, and other repositories and collections, frequently do not keep regular business hours, or do so seasonally; often a lack of staff or space means that access to medieval manuscripts is necessarily restricted. Send a letter to the keeper of manuscripts with some indication of what you want to see, and why, and when you will be in the neighborhood. A letter of introduction from a dean, department chairperson, or professor might prove necessary for less well established scholars. In addition to your work with the microfilm, be sure you have read the library's catalog description of the manuscript you are examining. If possible, keep a transcript or photocopy of it with you, but don't be surprised if your own findings differ in some details from the catalog.[4]

If you have not had a great deal of experience in working with medieval manuscripts, it would be wise to try to prepare yourself as much as possible for this important (and for the first-timer usually memorable) experience. Three highly recommended works to consult are G. S. Ivy, "The Bibliography of the Manuscript-Book," in *The English Library before 1700,* ed. Francis Wormald and C. E. Wright (London, 1958), 32–65; Barbara Shailor, *The Medieval Book,* Medieval Academy Reprints for Teaching, 28 (Toronto, 1991); and Albert Derolez, *Codicologie des manuscrits en écriture humanistic sur parchemin* (Brepols, 1984).

Transcription

The best way to get to know a scribe is to do the scribe's job—to transcribe the manuscript, or that portion you are editing, line for line, letter for letter, mark for mark. This will give you familiarity with the scribe's letterforms and train you to read his or her hand with some fluency. There are different degrees of fidelity in transcription; as the first stage in editing, and as a way of coming to know a scribe's practice, you should produce the most precise and thorough transcription possible, indicating corrections, insertions, loss, damage, and page layout. Do not expand abbreviations or provide emendations of even the most obvious errors. If you are not transcribing line by line, you may record the ends of lines in prose texts by a vertical stroke; scribes are more likely to make mistakes at the ends of lines. Certain conventional marks are used in transcribing; see M. B. Parkes, *English Cursive Book Hands, 1250–1500* (Oxford, 1969; rpt. Berkeley, 1979), xxviii–xxx. A copy of these pages should be available for consultation when you are transcribing. Transcriptions can be

---

4. See Edwards, "Manuscript and Text," in this volume.

done from microfilm, but the results should always be checked against the manuscript.

One learns how to read old scripts by reading them, abundantly and at great length, in a variety of formats and styles.[5] L. C. Hector comments, "the reading of manuscripts is not so much the application of theoretical knowledge as the exercise of a skill, analogous to swimming or bicycle-riding, in the acquisition of which the decisive effort is made by the learner himself."[6] For Middle English paleography, Parkes's *English Cursive Book Hands* has become the standard. There are several other good introductions as well; most contain plates with full transcriptions, on which one might like to practice before tackling a microfilm or manuscript.[7]

You will find transcription difficult for various reasons, not all of them related to the inscrutability of the scribe's handwriting. Again L. C. Hector: "There is some truth in the paradox that legibility in a manuscript document consists chiefly in the reader's prior knowledge of what it contains. Certainly the most difficult documents to read are by no means necessarily those in the most outlandish hands: they are far more likely to be those which are cast in a form outside the reader's experience."[8] If you have some sense of what the scribe *should* be writing, you will often find it easier to read what he or she *is* writing (the danger lurking in this truth, of course, is that at times you will see what ought to be there rather than what is there).

Writing is both an art and an act of communication; when you are confused by the tangled aesthetic obscurity of a scribe's work, remember that he or she was, in the vast majority of cases, honestly trying to produce something that a reader could understand. Most difficult scripts become less mysterious when you understand their construction. There are three parts of a letter: the *body,*

---

5. A good start toward recognizing letterforms is in Eileen A. Gooder, *Latin for Local Historians,* 2d ed. (London, 1978), 110–17. In fact this book in general is a good practical guide to the Latin of medieval documents, which are sometimes attached to the endleaves or binding of literary texts and are sometimes reliable clues to the origin or early provenance of a work. Tables of easily confused letters are set out in L. C. Hector, *The Handwriting of English Documents,* 2d ed. (London, 1966),131–32.

6. Hector, 26.

7. N. Denholm-Young, *Handwriting in England and Wales* (Cardiff, 1954); L. C. Hector (above, n. 5); Jean Preston and Laetitia Yeandle, *English Handwriting, 1400–1650,* Medieval and Renaissance Texts Series (Binghampton, 1992); C. E. Wright, *English Vernacular Hands from the Twelfth to the Fifteenth Centuries* (Oxford, 1960).

8. Hector, *The Handwriting of English Documents,* 14. Although not focused on English, Arrigo Castellani's "Transcription Errors," in *Medieval Manuscripts and Textual Criticism,* ed. Christopher Kleinhenz (Chapel Hill, 1976), 167–73, is a short, sobering examination of the hazards of transcription.

which all letters have; the *ascender*, as in the letters *b, d, f, l;* and the *descender*, as in *g, p, y.* A short vertical stroke from the *baseline* (the horizontal line on which the writing sits) to the top of the body, as in the letter *i,* is a *minim.* Resolving a series of hastily written minims is a common frustration for the transcriber; for example, should a series of six undifferentiated minim-sized marks preceding the letters *or* be read as *minor* or *iunior?*

Beyond the letterforms themselves, certain medieval writing practices cause problems in a transcription. The most common source of ambiguity is abbreviation, although, outside of documents, it is far less frequent in vernacular writing than in Latin. The standard work on abbreviation in medieval manuscripts is Adriano Cappelli, *Lexicon abbreviaturarum: Dizionario di abbreviature latine ed italiane usate nelle carte e codici specialmente de medio evo,* 6th ed. (Milan, 1961). Auguste Pelzer, *Abbréviations latines médiévales,* 2d ed. (Louvain, 1966), is a supplement to Cappelli; Adriano Cappelli, *The Elements of Abbreviation in Medieval Latin Palaeography,* trans. David Heimann and Richard Kay (Lawrence, Kan., 1982) is a translation of Cappelli's introduction. Useful references for abbreviation in English works include the introductions to Hector (pp. 29–35), and Wright (p. xvii), mentioned in footnotes 5 and 7 respectively.

English abbreviations are based on Latin practice, but the English language was hardly stable in its spelling at any point in the Middle Ages; there will generally be some question as to how to expand an abbreviation like w^t: should it be *with, wyt, wyth,* or some other variant? Is a curlicue at the end of a word meant to represent *-is, -es,* or *-us?* In the edited text, generally speaking, you will be forced to decide how to expand these, but don't try to do this before you've transcribed the whole text.

Another area of difficulty is numerals; help with these can be found in Hector (pp. 41–45), Cappelli (pp. 413–28), and G. F. Hill, *The Development of Arabic Numerals in Europe Exhibited in Sixty-four Tables* (Oxford, 1915).

On the technique of manuscript collation, see John Whittaker, "The Practice of Manuscript Collation," *Text* 5 (1991): 121–30.

Writing the Description

Editors will not usually provide full descriptions of manuscripts such as one finds in facsimiles. However, looking at such descriptions is useful for familiarizing oneself with the language and techniques of this practice, because at least for many features you can turn to the photographic representation of the manuscript to see exactly what is being described. A good example is P. R. Robinson's description of Cambridge University Library ms. F.f.2.38. (See appendix B for references to this and other facsimile editions.) More typical for the editor is a terse description of the manuscripts relied on, sometimes with particular attention being given to the base manuscript, and sometimes to particular features therein.[9] For a recent example, see Hoyt N. Duggan and Thorlac Turville-Petre, *The Wars of Alexander,* EETS, s.s. 10 (Oxford, 1989), ix–xii.

A thorough description will contain information about most of the following points: shelfmark, date, contents, material, number of leaves and foliation, size, pricking and ruling, quiring, script, punctuation, decoration, binding.[10]

Shelfmark. Where the manuscript is now. This takes a simple form: city, library, collection (if necessary), and number, e.g., London, BL Cotton Nero A.x; Cambridge, Corpus Christi College 286; New Haven, Beinecke Library 587.

Date, with full evidence.[11] Dates assigned to an undated manuscript are expressed in roman numerals, e.g., *s. xiv in.,* which means the beginning of the fourteenth century (the end of a century is signified by *ex.*); "second quarter of s. xii" or "second half of s.xii" (*s. xii²* is ambiguous, referring in some catalogs to the second quarter of the century and in others to second half); *s. xiii/xiv* (1275–1325, or the turn of the thirteenth century). Using this relatively imprecise system ensures that everyone recognizes the date as an opinion rather than a fact. If you are more specific than a fifty-year guess (e.g., "written 1285–

---

9. See Edwards, "Manuscript and Text," in this volume, on the difference between editorial and codicological description.

10. Ker in *Medieval Manuscripts,* vii–xiii, divides his catalog descriptions into sixteen parts, almost all of which are included in the twelve categories here. The only exception is his sixteenth category, the opening words of the second leaf, which he claims can provide useful evidence about the provenance of the manuscript. Obviously, an editor would be unwise to ignore altogether a potential source of information that Ker thought valuable, but, as Edwards points out in his "Manuscript and Text," an editor, unlike a cataloger, is not obliged to deal with all of these categories.

11. For a discussion of dating, see Edwards, "Manuscript and Text," in this volume. The following volumes are valuable for providing photographs of datable manuscripts: Pamela Robinson, *Catalogue of Dated and Datable Manuscripts c. 737–1600 in Cambridge Libraries* (Cambridge, 1988); A. G. Watson, *Catalogue of Dated and Datable Manuscripts c. 700–1600 in the Department of Manuscripts, the British Library,* vol. 1 (text), vol. 2 (plates) (London, 1979) (see especially 1:165–68 on reasons for rejecting manuscripts); A. G. Watson, *Catalogue of Dated and Datable Manuscripts c. 435–1600 in Oxford Libraries,* vol. 1 (text), vol. 2 (plates) (Oxford, 1984); C. Samaran and R. Marichal et al. *Catalogue des mss en écriture latine portant des indications de date, de lieu, ou de copiste* (Paris, 1959–).

1300"), you must have overwhelming evidence for your opinion, thoroughly detailed in your description.

Contents. Manuscripts containing a single text are easy to describe, but these are surprisingly uncommon. Usually a manuscript contains a number of items, some related, some not, some original, some added later. For such manuscripts, providing a full list of the contents should be considered, even if the other texts seem to be unrelated to the text you are editing. In the general absence of titles, medieval works are identified by their first line or *incipit.* Books containing lists of *incipits* of Latin works are listed in Boyle (nos. 1930–1953). For English works see the Brown-Robbins *Index of Middle English Verse* and *Supplement,* the various *Handlists* for the *Index of Middle English Prose,* both mentioned above.

Material. Manuscripts are written either on paper or skin, which is commonly called *parchment* or *vellum.* Technically the word *vellum* refers to calfskin only; *parchment* is the preferred generic term. In examining a manuscript, one should pay attention to the distribution of hair and flesh sides of each folio. The two sides of a piece of parchment look different; one is relatively smoother and whiter (the original flesh-side), the other relatively rougher and darker (the hair side), often with clearly visible pinpoint holes where the animal's pelt used to be. Useful is R. Reed, *Ancient Skins, Parchments, and Leathers* (London and New York, 1972).

Paper manuscripts of literary works are rare before the end of s. xiv, and after that date are often found as part of some combination of paper and parchment—paper with inner and outer wrappers of parchment, or strips of parchment (usually from discarded manuscripts, often with some legible words still on them) on the outer and inner folds of paper quires. These strips are then part of the binding, not the manuscript. With paper manuscripts, pay attention to the watermark—a faint design left on the paper during the manufacturing process—and relate it to the catalog found in C. M. Briquet, *Les Filigranes: Dictionnaire historique des marques du papier dès leur apparition vers 1282 jusqu'en 1600,* 2d ed. (Paris, 1923; rpt. New York, 1966, Amsterdam, 1968, with helpful introduction and index by A. Stevenson). Also important are A. Stevenson, "Paper as Bibliographical Evidence," *Library,* 5th ser., 17 (1962): 197–212, and, by the same author, "New Uses of Watermarks as Bibliographical Evidence," *Studies in Bibliography* 1 (1948–49): 149–82, and "Water Marks Are Twins," *Studies in Bibliography* 4 (1951–52): 57–91.

Number of leaves and foliation. A text in a manuscript is usually referred to by the number of its *folio* rather than page. A folio is a leaf, front and back; a reference to "fol. 2v" or "2b" means the back or *verso* (as opposed to the *recto* or front) of the second folio—what would be p. 4 in a printed book. Most manuscripts have some indication of their folio numbers, a foliation, penciled in by a librarian; sometimes there are competing foliations; a good many manuscripts have pagination either in addition to or instead of foliation. In order to locate your text precisely in a manuscript, you should consider constructing your own description of foliation and related matters, particularly if the existing foliation seems faulty.

Endleaves are usually easy to tell apart from the folios of the main text. You should distinguish the endleaves from the text of the book, even if the endleaves contain some writing on them; though the endleaves often contain clues to the book's early history, they are properly speaking part of the binding, not the book. Record the number and the nature of leaves, that is, whether they are text or endleaves, and how they are marked (foliated or paginated). Express these findings in this form: "xii + 103 + vi, foliated in pencil i–xii, 1–109": this means there are twelve leaves at the beginning (probably some combination of endleaves and added leaves), then 103 leaves of text, then six endleaves in the back, foliated by an earlier librarian as detailed. The foliation is usually different from the nature of the leaves. There are sometimes mistakes in foliation—folio 16a may follow fol. 16, which will throw off the count—so one cannot always depend on an earlier foliation. The description should note where the foliation is marked (top right of recto, top center of verso, etc.), its probable date, and whether it is in ink or pencil.

Size. If you wish to describe the size of the leaves, record the dimensions of the leaf from edge to edge, in millimeters, height first, then width. Record also the dimensions of the written space, which is agreed to be the height from the top of the body of a letter on the first line to the bottom of the body of a letter on the last line, followed by the width of the widest line (if there are columns, record the width of each column, or of one column only if these are the same). Your record will look like this: "page 206 × 165 mm, written space 165 × 90 mm." In well-made manuscripts, the width of a leaf and the height of the written space are often identical, but since leaves have usually been cropped by postmedieval binders, this feature may be obscured. On this subject, see G. Pollard, "Notes on the Size of the Sheet," *Library,* 4th ser., 22 (1941–42): 105–37.

Pricking and ruling. When a pile of parchment was prepared for writing, lines had to be made on the sheets; the lines were guided by tiny holes made at close intervals down the margins. The holes, called "prickings," were made with an awl, knife, pair of compasses, or perhaps a small wheel with spikes on it that could be rolled down the margins of the folio. Pricking can be done in two ways: the sheets can be folded first into a quire (see under "Quiring" below), then pricked, then ruled, or they can be laid flat and pricked, then ruled, then folded. Prick marks in the inner margins are a good indication that the double sheets were folded and then pricked on the top sheet. This is the early Insular practice; it is also the practice in s. xii and xiii. If there are no prick marks in the inner margins, then the double sheets were probably laid flat and pricked, then ruled and folded.

Until s. xii ruling was done in drypoint with a sharp stylus that was pushed firmly against the top of the first sheet, creating tiny furrows and ridges on all the sheets. The number of leaves ruled at one time may vary, and a scribe might rerule a sheet if the ruling did not go through the first time (in the process he or she might misrule, get the number of lines wrong, and so on, so the ruling will be less uniform than it should be). After s. xii ruling is done with a lead plummet or crayon. Still later (in s. xiv), ruling can be done in black or colored ink. Ruling methods differ from place to place and time to time, and may be significant for dating or localizing a manuscript. But local or ad hoc variations in practice may have occurred at any time, so ruling alone is not sufficient to date or place a manuscript.

If you have cause to describe the ruling, concentrate on the system of ruling rather than the actual lines. Record where and how much ruling is on the page. Does the ruling accommodate all the features of the text (initials, capitals, glosses), or is there an apparent discrepancy between the text and the page design? Are there rulings for initials? Columns? What happens between the columns? How many lines go right across the page from one edge to another, and how many are contained within the frame of the margins? Is the writing on the top of the first line of the ruling? See T. S. Pattie, "The Ruling as a Clue to the Make-up of a Medieval Manuscript," *British Library Journal* 1 (1975), 15–21.

Quiring. Manuscript books are made up of self-contained units of leaves, each of which is called a *quire*. A quire is made up of several sheets of parchment or paper, each folded down the middle to give two leaves. This folded sheet is called a *bifolium*. Four sheets stacked on top of one another and folded into bifolia gives a quire of eight folios or sixteen pages, sometimes referred to by the medieval name *quaternion* (five sheets gives a quire of ten folios, six of twelve, and so on, though more than this is uncommon). Groups of quires are placed one atop the other to make a book. A description of the quires—their composition, order, additions and losses—is called a *collation*.

Knowing a manuscript's collation can be vital if you suspect that your text has missing or misarranged material. Collation can be determined by a number of methods. Look for identifying marks, usually inconspicuously written, on each quire—check to see if every eighth (or tenth, or twelfth) page has something unusual on it. Look for catchwords (see below). Check the arrangement of hair and flesh, if possible, which will help determine *conjugate* leaves (the two halves of a bifolium). Check the pattern of pricking and ruling, which may vary slightly from one quire to another. But the most common and effective way to start a collation is gently to open the book flat, flip through the pages, look in the gutters and notice where the threads are. Quires are sewn down the middle bifolium; from the middle of each quire work backward and forward through pairs of conjugate leaves to determine the quire boundaries. Write out everything, very explicitly, as you go; later you will be able to edit your description into a standard notation of almost algebraic brevity.

The number of leaves in a quire may vary; in the earlier period (up to about 1200) the usual number is eight, then until the fifteenth century ten or (more commonly) twelve, then back to eight. Smaller books and paper books show considerable variation. The most important fact to remember is that leaves are folded into a book in pairs—a normal quire must contain an even number of leaves. Single leaves (called *singletons*) may be sewn into a quire but they will require a stub, sticking out where their phantom conjugate would have been, to keep them from falling out.[12] If you find a quire with an odd number of folios, then either something has been added in, or something has fallen out; a quire of seven leaves must be explained as either $8 - 1$ or $6 + 1$. A simple notation is used as follows: "1^8 wants 1 before fol. 1." This means that the first quire consists of eight leaves, of which the first leaf is lost. "$1^6 + 1$ (fol. 5) after 4" means that the quire originally had six leaves and one has been added in the middle. If you can't tell the original position of a missing leaf, spell out the number, e.g., "1^4 wants one." It is always a good idea to include the folio number for any irregularity in the quiring structure; this helps the comparison between the collation and the contents.

Usually several quires in a row will have the same number of leaves; this can be briefly noted as follows: "$1-5^8$," which tells the reader that the first five quires all consist of eight leaves each with no additions or losses. Any anomalies of missing or added leaves must be recorded: "$1-3^8$, 4^8 wants 7 after fol. 30, 5^8." Some earlier books (and occasionally later ones) contain quires composed of single sheets between two double sheets—the inner and outer sheets

---

12. In rare cases single leaves may be pasted or pinned in.

of a quire are a bifolium to protect the single leaves. This is described as "1⁶ leaves 2 and 5 (fols. 2 and 5) are singletons in place of a bifolium." Finally, if a quire can't be collated or explained (as is sometimes the case with badly damaged manuscripts), it must be spelled out: a preliminary group of three leaves, all separate, without any evidence for their connection, should be described simply as "1 three leaves (fols. i–iii)."

To be bound properly into a book, the separate quires, once written, had to be kept in order. One practice was to write the first word of the next quire at the bottom of the last page of the previous quire. Such a notation is called a *catchword;* these are often chopped off in the binding process. While collating, record the traces of catchwords, if any; note these in your description in brief words such as "center of bottom margin last verso." Two other methods for maintaining the order of the quires were the use of quire or leaf signatures. These should be noted. The former is usually a sequence of numbers at the bottom of the last verso or first recto of the quire, running i, ij, iij, iiij, etc. The latter, which are more common after s. xiv, occur on each leaf in the first half of the quire and usually take the form ai, aij, aiij; bi, bij, biij; etc. Such numeration, where it exists, begins on the second quire, not the first; remember too that the medieval alphabet did not include the letters *j, v,* or *w.*[13]

Script. The script should be described using the system put forward in Parkes, *English Cursive Book Hands* (see above).[14]

Punctuation. As an editor you must consider how the texts are marked for punctuation because you might want to indicate the system and the sorts of marks used. Note the height of the *punctus* in relation to the height of the letter, and in relation to other points in the text. Punctuation is often corrected. If you find this to be the case, try to work out why alterations may have occurred; changes in the punctuation can tell you how and where the text was read. A good general guide to the development of medieval systems of punctuation is M. B. Parkes, *Pause and Effect: An Introduction to the History of Punctuation in the West* (Berkeley, 1992). Punctuation includes musical notation. This is a complex field; a good initial guide is Andrew Hughes, *Style and Symbol: Medieval Music, 800–1453,* Wissenschaftliche Abhandlungen, 51; Musicological Studies, 51 (Ottawa, 1989).

Decoration. Decoration must be considered in describing a manuscript.[15] Two works by J. J. G. Alexander provide good introductory information: "Scribes as Artists," in *Medieval Scribes, Manuscripts, and Libraries: Essays*

---

13. Ker, *Medieval Manuscripts,* ix–x.
14. See Edwards, "Manuscript and Text," in this volume.
15. See Edwards, "Manuscript and Text," in this volume.

Presented to N. R. Ker, ed. M. B. Parkes and Andrew G. Watson (London, 1978), 87–116, and *The Decorated Letter* (New York, 1978).

Binding. Descriptions of bindings start from the inside and work their way out. Note the pattern of sewing in each quire; look (very gently!) under the thread for holes, which are evidence of resewing. Notice the number of cords by which a quire is sewn. Books that survive in their medieval bindings deserve more consideration than those that were rebound by later owners. See G. Pollard, "Describing Medieval Bookbindings," in *Medieval Learning and Literature: Essays Presented to Richard William Hunt,* ed. J. J. G. Alexander and M. T. Gibson.

Facsimiles of Middle English Manuscripts

Richard Beadle

As the list that follows shows, the reproduction by photographic means of Middle English manuscripts in their entirety (or in large part) only became common in the latter half of the twentieth century. Facsimile reproduction of smaller parts of them by one means or another has a much longer history, which it would be interesting to trace in detail. Medieval scribes themselves could, and did, imitate one another's handwriting, out of a variety of motives. The execution of forged documents called forth the skill to produce convincing imitations of obsolete scripts. "Archaizing" hands were ready to provide supply leaves for older manuscripts that had been damaged, and whole manuscripts might be copied upon commission in a style modeled more or less accurately on scripts that had been in use generations or even centuries earlier.[1] Early manuscripts of the writings of John Gower provide examples of scribes who entered revisions of the texts in hands assimilated to the styles of their contemporaries,[2] but the urge to produce a facsimile of another's hand did not necessarily require specific motivation. For example, the main scribe of Cambridge, Magdalene College, Pepys 2125 seems to have been so taken by the idiosyncrasy of a hand in the exemplar from which he was copying (now, apparently, London, British Library, Harley 2398), that he amused himself by abandoning his usual style and imitating it for half a page.[3]

---

1. See M. B. Parkes, "Archaizing Hands in English Manuscripts," in J. P. Carley and C. G. C. Tite, eds., *Books and Collectors, 1200–1700* (London, 1997) 101–44.

2. See M. B. Parkes, "Patterns of Scribal Activity and Revisions of the Text in Early Copies of Works by John Gower," in R. Beadle and A. J. Piper, eds., *New Science out of Old Books: Studies in Manuscripts and Early Printed Books in Honour of A. I. Doyle* (Aldershot, 1995), 81–121 and plates 12–19.

3. *Catalogue of the Pepys Library at Magdalene College, Cambridge,* vol. 5, Manuscripts, part 1, Medieval, compiled by R. McKitterick and R. Beadle (Cambridge, 1992), xxv, 59.

The making of facsimiles by manual means did not cease with the end of the Middle English period, and it has been continued by calligraphers down to modern times.[4] In the sixteenth and seventeenth centuries, collectors and antiquaries sometimes became interested in imitating the hands found in the manuscript books that had descended to them, with the more eminent, such as Matthew Parker and William Cecil, Lord Burghley, even directing members of their household to produce manuscripts "counterfeited in antiquity," as Parker put it in a letter to Burghley.[5] An example of a seventeenth-century collector who tried his hand at copying Middle English texts in the original script was Richard Smith, whose enormous library, including a significant number of Middle English manuscripts, was put up for auction in 1682.[6] Systematic interest in script as a historically developing phenomenon came later, in the wake of Mabillon's *De re diplomatica* (1681). One of its first English manifestations was the calligraphical albums assembled by Samuel Pepys in about 1700, though he was in the fortunate position of being able to use fragments of real manuscripts rather than imitations for the purpose of illustrating changes in styles of handwriting.[7] Script also interested John Bagford in much the same way at the time, and his collections of "fragmenta manuscripta" have survived.[8] Not so, apparently, and alas, Humfrey Wanley's notable "Book of Hands," which seems to have been the earliest attempt to assemble the kind of

---

4. The modern calligraphic movement was begun by Edward Johnston's oft-reprinted *Writing & Illuminating & Lettering* (London, 1906); for a recent example see M. Drogin, *Medieval Calligraphy: Its History and Technique* (Montclair, N.J., 1980).

5. See the letter from Parker to Burghley dated 24 January 1566, as cited by W. W. Greg, "Books and Bookmen in the Correspondence of Archbishop Parker," *Library,* 4th ser., 16 (1935): 243–79 (273–74). Stephen Batman, well known as an agent of Parker's in obtaining manuscripts, sometimes imitated the old hands he found in them; see for example Cambridge, Magdalene College, MS Pepys 2498, as described in *Catalogue of the Pepys Library* (see n. 3 above), p. 87.

6. See E. Gordon Duff, "The Library of Richard Smith," *Library,* 2d ser., 8 (1907): 113–33, and London, British Library, Harley 1212 for one of Smith's attempts at copying a Middle English text in facsimile.

7. *Catalogue of the Pepys Library at Magdalene College, Cambridge,* vol. 4, Music, Maps, and Calligraphy, compiled by J. Stevens et al., MS 2981. Interest in script as a historically evolving phenomenon is also evinced in John Evelyn's little-known essay "Of Manuscripts," composed toward the end of the seventeenth century, but unpublished in his lifetime; see *Memoirs illustrative of the life and writings of John Evelyn . . .* , ed. W. Bray, vol. 2, part 1 (London, 1819), 321–36.

8. M. McC. Gatch, "John Bagford as a Collector and Disseminator of Manuscript Fragments," *Library,* 6th ser., 7 (1985): 95–114, and idem. *"Fragmenta manuscripta* and *varia* at Missouri and Cambridge," *Transactions of the Cambridge Bibliographical Society* 9 (1986–90): 434–75. Bagford supplied both Pepys and Wanley (see next note) with samples for their paleographical albums.

conspectus of dated and datable manuscripts, with facsimile alphabets derived from them, that makes systematic paleographical investigation possible.[9] Wanley's skill in making facsimiles of manuscripts (including Old and early Middle English items) was outstanding, and it is amply displayed in the second volume of Hickes's *Linguarum Veterum Septentrionalium Thesaurus* (1703– 5), containing Wanley's catalog of the Anglo-Saxon manuscripts. It may have been Wanley, or it must have been someone equally skilled, who, sometime not long after 1693, provided a series of almost incredibly accurate facsimile supply leaves to restore a defective Wycliffite Octateuch owned by Pepys.[10] Cambridge, University Library ms. Additional 6578 (Nicholas Love's *Mirror of the Blessed Life of Jesus Christ*), on the other hand, provides on fol. 3 a rather less skilled attempt by a postmedieval hand to copy the script of the original, supplying the text of a lost or damaged first leaf.

Eighteenth- and early-nineteenth-century catalogs and editions that either touch on or concern Middle English materials sometimes contain engraved plates showing the handwriting of the time, though usually no more than a few lines at most; David Casley's catalog of the manuscripts in the Royal Library and Sir John Fenn's edition of the Paston Letters are examples.[11] Reproductions of the scripts of the time also appear in the early paleographical handbooks of Thomas Astle and Andrew Wright.[12] From the mid-nineteenth century, plates, frontispieces and the like, produced by various technically advancing means of the time (of which Traube eventually gave an account),[13] become relatively common in the publications of series such as the Early English Text Society, the Chaucer Society, and the Rolls Series. Examples from a number of Middle English manuscripts appear in the hefty albums

---

9. *Letters of Humfrey Wanley,* ed. P. L. Heyworth (Oxford, 1989), 67 n. 1, and also appendix 1, for Wanley's draft proposal for a "Palaeographical Survey of English Hands from the Earliest Times."

10. *Catalogue of the Pepys Library,* as cited in n. 3 above, pp. xxiii, 24. A plate showing the original side-by-side with the facsimile is included in Parkes, "Archaizing Hands," 127.

11. D. Casley, *A Catalogue of the manuscripts in the King's Library . . . one hundred and fifty specimens of the manner of writing in different ages, from the third to the fifteenth century . . .* (London, 1734); J. Fenn ed., *Original Letters, written during the reigns of Henry VI. Edward IV. and Richard III . . .* (London, 1787–89).

12. T. Astle, *The Origin and progress of writing . . . illustrated by engravings taken from marbles, manuscripts, and charters, ancient and modern . . .* (London, 1784); A. Wright, *Courthand restored* (London, 1773).

13. L. Traube, "Das Zeitalter der Photographie," in *Zur Paläeographie und Handschriftenkunde, Vorlesungen und Abhandlungen,* 1 (Munich, 1909), 57–80. See also H. Zotter, *Bibliographie faksimilierter handschriften* (Graz, 1976).

issued by the New Palaeographical Society, and F. J. Furnivall plainly discerned the potential importance to scholarship of facsimiles, in promoting reproductions of pages from some of the principal manuscripts of the *Canterbury Tales,* and R. K. Root's *Manuscripts of Chaucer's Troilus,* the latter a model that ought long ago to have been followed for a number of late-medieval English authors whose writings survive in a multiplicity of manuscript copies.[14] The Early English Text Society's first complete facsimile, that of London, British Library, Cotton Nero A. x (see below), was to have been the first of a series of similar publications that it intended to bring forth as its official memorial to Furnivall. The first paleographical guide or handbook devoted to early vernacular manuscripts was W. W. Skeat's *Twelve Facsimiles of Old English Manuscripts* (Oxford, 1892), which despite its title was devoted predominantly to Middle English items.[15]

Looked at as publishing ventures, the facsimiles listed below are a very mixed bag, their variety reflecting the often widely differing motives of those who have been concerned in putting them out—a spectrum of interests where it can be difficult to distentangle antiquarianism from high scholarship from commercial opportunism from connoisseurship, and so on. The choice of manuscripts of which facsimiles happen to have been made has been very much a matter of policy (especially library conservation policy) where the originals are in institutional hands. Fidelity to those originals in point of size, quality of photographic work, the number of tones used in the printing, and the quality of the printing itself ranges from that which leaves a very great deal to be desired, to examples of almost miraculous verisimilitude offered at prices that even the most major libraries wonder if they can afford. The introductory or descriptive apparatus can vary no less widely, some facsimiles being accompanied by what are effectively important scholarly monographs, others by anything from a few cursory or amateurish remarks, or virtually nothing at all.

Depending of course to some extent on their quality, facsimiles can be used for many, but not all purposes in place of the original. In some circumstances they have acquired an independent authority of their own as witnesses to the

---

14. F. J. Furnivall, ed., *Autotype specimens of the chief Chaucer manuscripts,* part 1, Chaucer Society, 1st ser., 48 (1876), part 2, 56 (1878), part 3, 62 (1880), part 4, 74 (1885); R. K. Root, ed., *The Manuscripts of Chaucer's Troilus, with Collotype Facsimiles of the Various Handwritings,* Chaucer Society, 1st ser., 98 (1914).

15. Also of note in this respect is W. W. Greg's *Facsimiles of Twelve Early English Manuscripts in the Library of Trinity College, Cambridge* (Oxford, 1913).

texts that they reproduce. In at least one case on the list below, the facsimile preserves readings that are no longer visible to the naked eye in the manuscript itself. In others, a facsimile is, in one instance, a vital record of a manuscript that has long been mislaid or lost, and in another, remains as the precious image of a manuscript that has certainly been destroyed.

The list that follows is restricted to facsimiles of Middle English manuscripts (i.e., of the period from ca. 1150 to ca. 1500), published in printed form, and is for the most part confined to manuscripts that have been reproduced as a whole, or in large part. Except in special circumstances, shorter extracts reproduced in facsimile from longer manuscripts have been excluded. The publication details are those given on the title pages of the facsimiles, occasionally supplemented (usually by the date or place of publication) from information printed elsewhere in the book.[16]

ABERYSTWYTH, NATIONAL LIBRARY OF WALES

MS Peniarth 392D (Hengwrt).
The Canterbury Tales. Geoffrey Chaucer. A Facsimile of the Hengwrt Manuscript, with Variants from the Ellesmere Manuscript.
Edited by Paul G. Ruggiers.
Introductions by Donald C. Baker and by A. I. Doyle and M. B. Parkes.
Norman, Okla.: University of Oklahoma Press, and Folkestone: Wm. Dawson and Sons, Ltd., 1979.

MS Porkington 8 (on deposit from Lord Harlech).
Brogyntyn Manuscript No. 8 [fragment of the Middle English prose *Brut*].
Translated and transcribed by Rosalynn Voaden, with an introduction by Felicity Riddy.
Moreton-in-Marsh: Porkington Press Limited, 1991.

---

16. I am grateful to A. I. Doyle for information about several of the more out-of-the-way items listed below. Users of the list should also be aware of a very large body of Middle English manuscripts effectively available in facsimile, in the shape of rotographs of all the manuscripts of the *Canterbury Tales* used by Manly and Rickert in their work on the text, copies of which are available for consultation in the Department of Manuscripts in the British Library (classmark "MSS Facs."), and at the University of Chicago Library; see J. M. Manly and E. Rickert, *The Text of the Canterbury Tales* (Chicago, 1940), 1:6. No attempt has been made here to trace the existence of reproductions of Middle English manuscripts contained in unpublished theses or dissertations, or to document the current commercial availability of such material in the form of microfilm or microfiche, or as digitized images on CD-ROM.

Brussels, Bibliothèque Royale

MS 4869.
P. Pintelon, *Chaucer's Treatise on the Astrolable. MS. 4862–4869 of the Royal Library in Brussels.*
Antwerp: De Sikkel, and 's-Gravenhage: Martinus Nijhoff, 1940.

Cambridge, Corpus Christi College

MS 61.
Troilus and Criseyde. Geoffrey Chaucer. A Facsimile of Corpus Christi College Cambridge College MS 61
With introductions by M. B. Parkes and Elizabeth Salter.
Cambridge: D. S. Brewer Ltd., 1978.

Cambridge, Magdalene College

Old Library MS F. 4. 34 + Pepys Library, MS Pepys 2124.
The Metamorphoses of Ovid translated by William Caxton 1480.
New York: George Braziller, in association with Magdalene College, Cambridge, 1968. 2 vols.

Pepys Library, MS Pepys 1047.
Stere Htt Wele: A Book of Medieval Refinements, Recipes and Remedies, from a Manuscript in Samuel Pepys's Library.
With foreword and modern English version by G. A. J. Hodgett and an introduction by Della Smith.
London: Cornmarket Press, 1972; also Adelaide: Mary Martin Books, n.d.

Pepys Library, MS Pepys 2006.
Manuscript Pepys 2006. A Facsimile. Magdalene College, Cambridge.
Introduction by A. S. G. Edwards.
Norman, Okla.: Pilgrim Books, and [Woodbridge:] Boydell and Brewer Ltd., for A Variorum Edition of the Works of Geoffrey Chaucer, 1985.

Cambridge, Peterhouse

MS 75.I, fols 71v–78v.
Reduced facsimile of Geoffrey Chaucer(?), *The Equatorie of the Planetis,* in *The Equatorie of the Planetis,* edited from Peterhouse MS. 75.I by Derek J. Price, with a linguistic analysis by R. M. Wilson.
Cambridge: Cambridge University Press, 1955.
See also in Kari Anne Rand Schmidt, *The Authorship of the Equatorie of the Plan-etis,* Cambridge: D. S. Brewer, 1993 (facsimile further reduced).

CAMBRIDGE, ST. JOHN'S COLLEGE

MS L. 1.
St John's College, Cambridge Manuscript L. 1. A Facsimile. [Geoffrey Chaucer,
  Troilus and Criseyde]
Introduction by Richard Beadle and Jeremy Griffiths.
Norman, Okla.: Pilgrim Books, and [Woodbridge:] Boydell and Brewer Ltd., for A
  Variorum Edition of the Works of Geoffrey Chaucer, 1983.

CAMBRIDGE, TRINITY COLLEGE

MS R. 3. 19.
Manuscript Trinity R.3.19. A Facsimile. Trinity College, Cambridge University.
  [Poems by Geoffrey Chaucer, John Lydgate etc.]
Introduction by Bradford Y. Fletcher.
Norman, Okla.: Pilgrim Books, for A Variorum Edition of the Works of Geoffrey
  Chaucer, 1987.

CAMBRIDGE, UNIVERSITY LIBRARY

MS Additional 5943.
*A Fifteenth-Century Song Book: Cambridge University Library Additional MS 5943
  made in facsimile.*
With an introduction by Richard Rastall.
Leeds: Boethius Press, 1973.

MS Ff. 1. 6.
The Findern Manuscript. Cambridge University Library MS. Ff. 1. 6. [Courtly and
  moral verse; romances]
Introduction by Richard Beadle and A. E. B. Owen.
London: The Scolar Press, 1977. Rpt. with amendments, 1978.

MS Ff. 2. 38.
Cambridge University Library MS Ff.2.38. [Romances and religious poems]
With an introduction by Frances McSparran and P. R. Robinson.
London: Scolar Press, 1979.

MS Gg. 4. 27.
*Poetical Works. Geoffrey Chaucer. A Facsimile of Cambridge University Library MS
  GG. 4 27.*
With introductions by M. B. Parkes and Richard Beadle. 3 vols.
Cambridge: D. S. Brewer, 1979 (vol. 1), 1980 (vols 2–3).

DUBLIN, PUBLIC RECORD OFFICE

*MS of *The Pride of Life,* destroyed 1922.
See below, Davis, *Non-Cycle Plays.*

DUBLIN, TRINITY COLLEGE

*MS D. 4. 18 (432), fols. 74v–81r.
The Northampton play of *Abraham and Isaac.*
See below, Davis, *Non-Cycle Plays.*

*MS F. 4. 20 (652), fols. 338r–356r.
The Play of the Sacrament.
See below, Davis, *Non-Cycle Plays.*

EDINBURGH, NATIONAL LIBRARY OF SCOTLAND

MS Advocates' 19. 2. 1.
The Auchinleck Manuscript. National Library of Scotland Advocates' MS. 19. 2. 1.
    [Romances, religious verse, etc.]
With an introduction by Derek Pearsall and I. C. Cunningham.
London: The Scolar Press, in association with the National Library of Scotland,
    1977.

GUERNSEY, ST. PETER PORT

Privately owned MS: Mr J. Stevens-Cox.
*St Anselm's Treatise on Free Will. A facsimile of the complete text of a recently
    discovered fifteenth century manuscript.*
Edited by G. Stevens-Cox.
St. Peter Port: Toucan Press, 1977.

LINCOLN, CATHEDRAL LIBRARY

MS 91.
The Thornton Manuscript (Lincoln Cathedral MS. 91). [Miscellaneous verse and
    prose]
Introductions by D. S. Brewer and A. E. B. Owen.
London: The Scolar Press, 1975. Rpt. with amendments, 1977.

LONDON, BRITISH LIBRARY

*MS Additional 23986.
Interludium de Clerico et Puella.
See below, Davis, *Non-Cycle Plays.*

MS Additional 35290.
The York Play. A Facsimile of British Library MS Additional 35290 together with a Facsimile of Ordo Paginarum section of the A/Y Memorandum Book [York City Archives].
With an introduction by Richard Beadle and Peter Meredith and a note on the music by Richard Rastall.
Leeds: The University of Leeds, School of English, 1983.

MS Additional 59678.
The Winchester Malory. A Facsimile.
With an introduction by N. R. Ker.
Early English Text Society, Supplementary Series No. 4.
Oxford: Oxford University Press, for the Early English Text Society, 1976.

MS Additional 60577.
The Winchester Anthology. A Facsimile of British Library Additional Manuscript 60577. [Miscellaneous verse and prose; music].
With an introduction and list of contents by Edward Wilson and an account of the music by Iain Fenlon.
Cambridge: D. S. Brewer, 1981.

MS Cotton Caligula A. ix, fols. 233r–246r.
The Owl and the Nightingale.
See below, Oxford, Jesus College, MS 29.

MS Cotton Nero A. x.
Pearl, Cleanness, Patience and Sir Gawain reproduced in facsimile from the unique MS. Cotton Nero A. x in the British Museum.
With an introduction by I. Gollancz.
Early English Text Society, Original Series, No. 162.
Oxford: Oxford University Press, for the Early English Text Society, 1922.

MS Cotton Vespasian D. viii.
The N-Town Plays. A Facsimile of British Library MS Cotton Vespasian D. VIII.
With an introduction by Peter Meredith and Stanley J. Kahrl.
Leeds: The University of Leeds, School of English, 1977.

MS Harley 2253.
Facsimile of British Museum MS. Harley 2253. [Lyrics, religious poems, etc.]
With an introduction by N. R. Ker.
Early English Text Society, No. 255.
Oxford: Oxford University Press, for the Early English Text Society, 1965.

NAPLES, BIBLIOTECA NAZIONALE

MS XIII. B. 29.
*Un Ignoto Ricettario Medico Inglese del XIV Secolo trovato nella Biblioteca
Nazionale di Napoli. Compreso nel codice XIII. B. 29.* Testo originale, tran-
scrizione a fronte, introduzione, note e glossario a cura di T. Vallese.
Naples: n. p., 1940.

NARA (JAPAN)

Privately owned MS: Mr S. Asahata.
*Manuscript of Geoffrey Chaucer's Astrolabe and other Middle English Documents
(c. 1460–1487).*
Reproduced in photogravure from the copy of Asahata Collection, with an introduction by Shozo Asahata.
Nara: Asahata Barmen Lace Co., 1995.
[Note: this is a section of a dismembered manuscript formerly in the collection of
the Marquess of Bute; see Sotheby's *Catalogue of the Bute Collection of forty-
two Illuminated Manuscripts and Miniatures,* 13 June 1983, lot 32.]

NEW HAVEN, YALE UNIVERSITY LIBRARY,
BEINECKE RARE BOOK AND MANUSCRIPT LIBRARY

*MS 365, fols. 15r–22r.
The Brome *Abraham and Isaac* play.
See below, Davis, *Non-Cycle Plays.*

NEW YORK, PIERPONT MORGAN LIBRARY

MS M. 817.
The Pierpont Morgan Library Manuscript M. 817. [Geoffrey Chaucer, *Troilus and
Criseyde*]
Introduction by Jeanne Krochalis.
Norman, Okla.: Pilgrim Books, for A Variorum Edition of the Works of Geoffrey
Chaucer, 1986.

OXFORD, BODLEIAN LIBRARY

MS Arch. Selden B. 24.
The Works of Geoffrey Chaucer and "The King's Quair." A Facsimile of Bodleian Library MS Arch Selden B.24.
Edited by Julia Boffey and A. S. G. Edwards.
Cambridge: D. S. Brewer, 1997.

MS Bodley 34.
Facsimile of MS. Bodley 34. [*Katherine* Group]
With an introduction by N. R. Ker.
Early English Text Society No. 247.
London: Oxford University Press, for the Early English Text Society, 1960.

MS Bodley 638.
Manuscript Bodley 638. A Facsimile. Bodleian Library, Oxford University. [Geoffrey Chaucer, minor poems, etc.]
Introduction by Pamela Robinson.
Norman, Okla.: Pilgrim Books, and [Woodbridge:] Boydell and Brewer Ltd., for A Variorum Edition of the Works of Geoffrey Chaucer, 1982.

MS Bodley 851, fols. 124r–140v.
Piers Plowman. A Facsimile of the Z-Text in Bodleian, Oxford, MS Bodley 851.
Introduced by Charlotte Brewer and A. G. Rigg.
Cambridge: D. S. Brewer, 1994.

MS Digby 86.
Facsimile of Oxford, Bodleian Library, MS Digby 86.
With an introduction by Judith Tschann and M. B. Parkes.
Early English Texts Society, s.s. 16.
Oxford: Oxford University Press, for the Early English Texts Society, 1996.

MSS Digby 133, fols. 37r–50v, 95r–169v, and e Museo160, fols. 140r–172r.
The Digby Plays. Facsimiles of the Plays in Bodley MSS Digby 133 and e Museo 160.
With an introduction by Donald C. Baker and J. L. Murphy.
Leeds: The University of Leeds, School of English, 1976.

MS Douce 104.
Piers Plowman. A Facsimile of Bodleian Library, Oxford, MS Douce 104.
With an introduction by Derek Pearsall and a catalog of the illustrations by Kathleen Scott.
Cambridge: D. S. Brewer, 1992.

MS Eng. poet. a. 1.
The Vernon Manuscript. A Facsimile of Bodleian Library, Oxford, MS Eng. poet. a. 1.
With an introduction by A. I. Doyle.
Cambridge: D. S. Brewer, 1987.

*MS Eng. poet. f. 2(R).
Dux Moraud.*
See below, Davis, *Non-Cycle Plays.*

MS Fairfax 16.
Bodleian Library MS Fairfax 16. [Chaucer, Hoccleve, Lydgate etc.]
With an introduction by John Norton-Smith.
London: Scolar Press, 1979.

MS Rawlinson C. 259.
The New Testament in English. Translated by John Wycliffe 1382, revised by John
    Purvey 1388. First Facsimile of the First English Bible from Bodleian Rawlinson
    MS 259.
Introduction by D. L. Brake.
Portland, Ore.: International Bible Publications, 1986.

MS Tanner 346.
Manuscript Tanner 346. A Facsimile. Bodleian Library, Oxford University. [Geoffrey
    Chaucer, minor poems, etc.]
Introduction by Pamela Robinson.
Norman, Okla.: Pilgrim Books, and [Woodbridge:] Boydell and Brewer Ltd., for A
    Variorum Edition of the Works of Geoffrey Chaucer, 1980.

OXFORD, JESUS COLLEGE

MS 29, fols. 156r–168v.
The Owl and the Nightingale. Reproduced in facsimile from the surviving manu-
    scripts, Jesus College Oxford 29 and British Museum Cotton Caligula A: ix.
With an introduction by N. R. Ker.
Early English Text Society No. 251.
London: Oxford University Press, for the Early English Text Society, 1963.

SAN MARINO, CALIFORNIA, HENRY E.
HUNTINGTON LIBRARY

MS EL 26 C 9 (Ellesmere).
(i) *The Ellesmere Chaucer Reproduced in Facsimile.*
Preface by Alix Egerton. 2 vols.
Manchester: Sherratt and Hughes, Publishers to the Victoria University of Manches-
    ter, and Manchester University Press, 1911.

Reprinted in one volume at 75 percent of original size as *The Ellesmere Manuscript of Chaucer's Canterbury Tales: a working facsimile.*
Introduction by Ralph Hanna III.

Cambridge: D. S. Brewer, 1989.
(ii) *The New Ellesmere Chaucer Facsimile (Huntington MS EL 26 C 9).*
Edited by Daniel Woodward and Martin Stevens.
Tokyo: Yushodo Co. Ltd., and San Marino, Calif.: Huntington Library, 1995.

MS HM 1.
The Towneley Cycle. A Facsimile of Huntington MS HM 1.
With an introduction by A. C. Cawley and Martin Stevens.
Leeds: The University of Leeds, School of English, 1976.

MS HM 143.
Piers Plowman: The Huntington Library MS (HM 143).
Introduction by R. W. Chambers, technical examination by R. B. Haselden and H. C. Schultz.
San Marino, Calif.: Henry E. Huntington Library, 1936.

WASHINGTON, D.C., FOLGER SHAKESPEARE LIBRARY

MS V. a. 354.
The Macro Plays. A facsimile edition with facing transcriptions.
Edited by David Bevington.
New York: Johnson Reprint Corporation, and Washington, D.C.: The Folger Shakespeare Library, 1972.

WINCHESTER, WINCHESTER COLLEGE

*MS 33, fols. 54v–73v.
The Winchester Dialogues.
See below, Davis, *Non-Cycle Plays.*

DAVIS, *NON-CYCLE PLAYS*

*The items marked with an asterisk will be found in *Non-Cycle Plays and Fragments and the Winchester Dialogues. Facsimiles of plays and fragments in various manuscripts and the Dialogues in Winchester College MS 33.*
With introductions and a transcript of the Dialogues by Norman Davis.
Leeds: University of Leeds, School of English, 1979.

Dictionaries of Use to an Editor of Middle English

"The dictionary is an editor's primary instrument."

—George Kane

ENGLISH

An Anglo-Saxon Dictionary Based on the Manuscript Collections of the Late Joseph Bosworth, ed. T. Northcote Toller (London, 1898). Supplement by Alistair Campbell, 1921; addenda, 1972. Bosworth-Toller will eventually be superseded by *DOE.*

Dictionary of Old English, ed. Angus Cameron et al. (Toronto, 1986–) (*DOE*).

Middle English Dictionary, ed. Hans Kurath et al. (Ann Arbor, 1952–) (*MED*). An electronic version of *MED* is in the planning stages.

Oxford English Dictionary, ed. James Murray et al. (London, 1884–1928). Supplement, 1933. A second edition of *OED* that merged the 1933 and 1972–86 supplements appeared in 1989. A third edition is currently being prepared. Electronic versions are available.

The Barnhart Dictionary of Etymology, ed. Robert K. Barnhart (New York, 1988).

The Concise Oxford Dictionary of Etymology, ed. Terry Hoad (Oxford, 1986). Based on the *ODEE* below but with numerous changes.

The English Dialect Dictionary, ed. Joseph Wright (London, 1898–1905) (*EDD*).

The Microfiche Concordance of Old English, compiled by Antonette diPaolo Healey and Richard L. Venezky (Toronto, 1980) (*MFCOE*).

The Oxford Dictionary of English Etymology, ed. C. T. Onions et al. (Oxford, 1966; corrected 1969) (*ODEE*).

SCOTS

A Dictionary of the Older Scottish Tongue, ed. William A. Craigie et al. (Chicago and Aberdeen, 1937). An electronic version of DOST is in the planning stages.

SCANDINAVIAN

Altnordisches Etymologisches Wörterbuch, ed. Jan De Vries (Leiden, 1962).

Concise Dictionary of Old Icelandic, ed. G. T. Zöega (Oxford, 1910). Zöega is based on the following but lacks illustrative quotations.
Icelandic-English Dictionary, ed R. Cleasby and G. Vigfusson (Oxford, 1874; 2d ed. 1957). Cleasby-Vigfusson will eventually be replaced by *Ordbok,* below.
Ordbok over det norrøne prosaprog (Copenhagen, forthcoming).

Middle Dutch

Middelnederlandisch Woordenboek, ed. E. Verwijs and J. Verdam (The Hague, 1885–1941).

Classical and Medieval Latin

For a more complete list of Latin and Greek dictionaries, see list in McCarren in this volume.
A Glossary of Later Latin to 600 AD, A. Souter (Oxford, 1949).
A New Latin Dictionary, ed. Charlton T. Lewis and Charles Short (New York, 1879). Lewis and Short is primarily devoted to classical Latin but does deal with language up to the 8th century.
Dictionary of Medieval Latin from British Sources, ed. R. E. Latham et al. (London, 1975–). DMLBS covers the 6th to 17th centuries and will eventually replace Latham.
Glossarium mediae et infimae latinitatis, ed. C D. DuCange (Paris, 1840–50). (5th to 15th centuries)
Lexicon latinitatis medii aevi, ed. A. Blaise (Turnholt, 1975). (7th to 18th centuries)
Mediae latinitatis lexicon minus, ed. J. F. Niermeyer (Leiden, 1954–). (550 to 1150)
Oxford Latin Dictionary, ed. P. G. W. Glare (Oxford, 1968–82). OLD is the standard dictionary of classical Latin extending to the 3d century.
Revised Medieval Latin Word-List from British and Irish Sources, ed. R. E. Latham (London, 1965). Latham covers 8th to 16th century and will eventually be replaced by DMLBS.

French

Altfranzösisches Wörterbuch, ed. A. Tobler and E. Lommatzsch (Berlin, 1925–). Tobler-Lommatzsch covers from 1000 to 1400.
Anglo-Norman Dictionary, ed. L. W. Stone and W. Rothwell (London, 1977–1993). AND covers from 1066 to 1500; a revision is underway.
Dictionnaire de l'ancienne langue française, ed. F. E. Godefroy (Paris, 1880–1902). Godefroy will be superseded by Tobler-Lommatzsch but does contain 15th-century vocabulary.
Französisches Etymologisches Wörterbuch, ed. W. von Wartburg (Bonn, 1948).

Contributors

Peter S. Baker is Professor of English at the University of Virginia.

Richard Beadle is a University Lecturer in the Faculty of English at the University of Cambridge and a Fellow of St. John's College.

N. F. Blake is Director of the Humanities Research Institute at the University of Sheffield and also the Director of the *Canterbury Tales* Project.

Helen Cooper is a Tutorial Fellow of University College, Oxford, and Professor of English Language and Literature.

A. S. G. Edwards is Professor of English at University of Victoria, British Columbia, Canada.

Jennifer Fellows, a graduate of Cambridge University, is a freelance editor in academic publishing and is Assistant Editor of *Medium Aevum.*

David Greetham is Distinguished Professor of English and Medieval Studies at the City University of New York Graduate School.

Mary Hamel is Professor of English at Mount St. Mary's College.

Constance B. Hieatt is Emeritus Professor of English at the University of Western Ontario.

Nicolas Jacobs is Fellow and Tutor in English at Jesus College, Oxford University.

George R. Keiser is Professor of English at Kansas State University.

Peter J. Lucas is the Statutory Lecturer in Old and Middle English at University College, Dublin.

Vincent P. McCarren, Primary Research faculty member, is retired from the Middle English Dictionary at the University of Michigan.

Maldwyn Mills is Emeritus Professor of English in the University of Wales, Aberystwyth.

Douglas Moffat is a former editor at the Middle English Dictionary, University of Michigan.

Linne Mooney is Associate Professor of English at the University of Maine.

Peter M. W. Robinson is Senior Research Fellow at the Institute for Electronic Library Research, De Montfort University, Milton Keynes, and also Deputy Director of the *Canterbury Tales* Project.

Index